CCSP Flash Cards and Exam Practice Pack

Behzad Behtash
Grant Moerschel

Cisco Press

800 East 96th Street
Indianapolis, IN 46240 USA

CCSP Flash Cards and Exam Practice Pack

Grant Moerschel and Behzad Behtash

Copyright© 2006 Cisco Systems, Inc.

Cisco Press logo is a trademark of Cisco Systems, Inc.

Published by:
Cisco Press
800 East 96th Street
Indianapolis, IN 46240 USA

Printed in the United States of America 1 2 3 4 5 6 7 8 9 0

First Printing   December   2005

Library of Congress Cataloging-in-Publication Number 2004108818

ISBN: 1-58720-133-X

Warning and Disclaimer

This book is designed to provide information about the CCSP certification exams. Every effort has been made to make this book as complete and as accurate as possible, but no warranty or fitness is implied.

The information is provided on an "as is" basis. The authors, Cisco Press, and Cisco Systems, Inc. shall have neither liability nor responsibility to any person or entity with respect to any loss or damages arising from the information contained in this book or from the use of the discs or programs that may accompany it.

The opinions expressed in this book belong to the author and are not necessarily those of Cisco Systems, Inc.

Trademark Acknowledgments

All terms mentioned in this book that are known to be trademarks or service marks have been appropriately capitalized. Cisco Press or Cisco Systems, Inc. cannot attest to the accuracy of this information. Use of a term in this book should not be regarded as affecting the validity of any trademark or service mark.

Feedback Information

At Cisco Press, our goal is to create in-depth technical books of the highest quality and value. Each book is crafted with care and precision, undergoing rigorous development that involves the unique expertise of members from the professional technical community.

Readers' feedback is a natural continuation of this process. If you have any comments about how we could improve the quality of this book, or otherwise alter it to better suit your needs, you can contact us through email at feedback@ciscopress.com. Please make sure to include the book title and ISBN in your message.

We greatly appreciate your assistance.

Publisher	John Wait
Editor-in-Chief	John Kane
Executive Editor	Brett Bartow
Cisco Representative	Anthony Wolfenden
Cisco Press Program Manager	Jeff Brady
Production Manager	Patrick Kanouse
Senior Development Editor	Christopher Cleveland
Production	Deadline Driven Publishing
Technical Editors	Greg Abelar, Yusuf Bhaiji, Brian Done, Bob Eckhoff, Randy Ivener, Jag Kang, Paul Qiu
Editorial Assistant	Raina Han
Cover Designer	Louisa Adair
Book Designer and Composition	Mark Shirar

Cisco Systems

Corporate Headquarters
Cisco Systems, Inc.
170 West Tasman Drive
San Jose, CA 95134-1706
USA
www.cisco.com
Tel: 408 526-4000
800 553-NETS (6387)
Fax: 408 526-4100

European Headquarters
Cisco Systems International BV
Haarlerbergpark
Haarlerbergweg 13-19
1101 CH Amsterdam
The Netherlands
www-europe.cisco.com
Tel: 31 0 20 357 1000
Fax: 31 0 20 357 1100

Americas Headquarters
Cisco Systems, Inc.
170 West Tasman Drive
San Jose, CA 95134-1706
USA
www.cisco.com
Tel: 408 526-7660
Fax: 408 527-0883

Asia Pacific Headquarters
Cisco Systems, Inc.
Capital Tower
168 Robinson Road
#22-01 to #29-01
Singapore 068912
www.cisco.com
Tel: +65 6317 7777
Fax: +65 6317 7799

Cisco Systems has more than 200 offices in the following countries and regions. Addresses, phone numbers, and fax numbers are listed on the **Cisco.com Web site at www.cisco.com/go/offices**.

Argentina • Australia • Austria • Belgium • Brazil • Bulgaria • Canada • Chile • China PRC • Colombia • Costa Rica • Croatia • Czech Republic • Denmark • Dubai, UAE • Finland • France • Germany • Greece • Hong Kong SAR • Hungary • India • Indonesia • Ireland • Israel • Italy • Japan • Korea • Luxembourg • Malaysia • Mexico • The Netherlands • New Zealand • Norway • Peru • Philippines • Poland • Portugal • Puerto Rico • Romania • Russia • Saudi Arabia • Scotland • Singapore • Slovakia • Slovenia • South Africa • Spain • Sweden • Switzerland • Taiwan • Thailand • Turkey • Ukraine • United Kingdom • United States • Venezuela • Vietnam • Zimbabwe

About the Authors

Behzad Behtash is an IT consultant with more than 12 years of experience in Cisco networking and security. He holds a bachelor of science degree in chemical engineering from the University of Wisconsin at Madison and resides in Oakland, California. Behzad is the author of the Cisco Press title, *CCSP Self-Study: Cisco Secure PIX Firewall Advanced (CSPFA)*, Second Edition, and holds the CCSP, CISSP, CCNP, CCDP, and MCSE certifications.

Grant Moerschel is cofounder of WaveGard, Inc. (www.wavegard.com), an information protection consultancy that specializes in wireless and wired security, wireless technology training, standards-based risk analysis, risk mitigation, and network design. He has 16 years of IT experience and holds the CCSP, CISSP, CWNA, and CWSP certifications. Grant holds a bachelor of science degree from the University of Delaware and resides in the Washington, D.C., metropolitan region.

About the Technical Reviewers

Greg Abelar has been an employee of Cisco Systems, Inc., since December of 1996. He was an original member of the Cisco Technical Assistance Security Team, and helped hire and train many of the engineers. He has held various positions with both the Security Architecture and Security Technical Marketing Engineering Teams at Cisco. Greg is the primary founder and project manager of the written Cisco CCIE Security exam. He is the author of *Securing Your Business with ASA and PIX Firewalls* published by Cisco Press.

Yusuf Bhaiji, CCIE No. 9305 (R&S and Security), has been with Cisco Systems, Inc. for 5 years and is currently the content manager for the CCIE Security certification and proctor in the Cisco Systems Sydney, Australia lab. Before this, he was technical lead for the Sydney TAC Security and VPN Team.

Yusuf's passion for security-and VPN-related technologies has played a dominant role in his 15 years of industry experience, from as far back as his initial master's degree in computer sience, and since reflected in his numerous certifications.

Yusuf prides himself in his knowledge-sharing abilities. He has mentored many successful candidates and designed and delivered several security- and VPN-related solutions around the globe. He is a well known speaker and presented in several conferences and seminars worldwide.

Yusuf is the author of the Cisco Press publication *CCIE Security Practice Labs*. He is presently working on his second Cisco Press publication titled *Network Security Technologies and Solutions*, which will be available in 2006.

He has also been a technical reviewer for several Cisco Press publications and written numerous articles for various publications/magazines. His recent article, "Cracking the Code," was published in *Cisco Packet Magazine*, Vol. 16, No.3.

Brian Done, CCNP, CCDP, CCSP, NSA IAM, CHSP, CISM, ISSAP, ISSMP, and CISSP is a technical director for ManTech International Corporation. He attained an MBA with a major in InfoSec. In addition to his corporate duties, he is a principal InfoSec advisor and provides support on diverse enterprise topics to the U.S. government. More information can be obtained at BrianDone.com or Leadership1st.org (the foundation he founded).

Bob Eckhoff, CCNA, CCSP, is an educational specialist at Cisco Systems, Inc., where he designs and develops courseware on Cisco network security products to include CSVPN, CSPFA, an SNPA. Bob has been at Cisco for over 5 years and has more than 20 years of experience in the education field. He has been a technical instructor and a course developer for Codex, Motorola, Altiga, and Cisco. He graduated from New York State University at Buffalo with a bachelor's and master's degree in education.

Randy Ivener, CCIE No. 10722, is a security specialist with Cisco Systems Product Security Incident Response Team. He is a CISSP and ASQ CSQE. Randy has spent many years as a Network Security Consultant to help companies understand and secure their networks. Before becoming immersed in information security, he spent time in software development and as a training instructor. Randy graduated from the U.S. Naval Academy and holds a master's degree in business administration.

Jagdeep S. Kang, CCSP, CCNP, CCNA, and MCSE, is a consulting education specialist at Cisco Systems, Inc. He designs and develops training on the Cisco network security products. Jagdeep has over 7 years experience in the technology field, specializing in LAN, WAN, and security technologies. Previously, Jagdeep held the position of network security engineer at Lockheed Martin. He has a master's of science degree from Ohio State University at Columbus and his has a master's in business administration in marketing from India.

Paul Qiu, CCIE in routing and switching and CCIE No. 9974 (Security), is technical lead for the Security and VPN Team in the Cisco Asian Pacific Technical Assistance Center. He is responsible for diagnostic and troubleshooting customer's security and VPN networks, acting as local escalation engineer for high complexity security and VPN technical issues. He also has published many CCO sample configurations and technical tips for Cisco security and VPN products including IDS, PIX, IOS firewall, AAA, VPN 3000, VMS, IPSEC VPN, and so on. Paul has been at Cisco for 4 years and has worked as a network engineer for 10 years.

Dedications

Grant Moerschel:

I dedicate this book to my wonderful wife and best friend, Sarah, who inspires me. It is also dedicated to my smart and beautiful children, Will and Hannah, who make me happy and proud. You guys are great.

To my mom and dad for the basic tools necessary for success.

Behzad Behtash:

I dedicate this book to my beautiful wife, Anita, and my wonderful children, Tiana and Daryan.

I further dedicate this book to my parents and brothers for their love and support throughout my life.

Oh, and, On Wisconsin!

Acknowledgments

Grant Moerschel:

I'd like to thank my friend Behzad Behtash for inviting me to share in this project. I truly respect his knowledge and problem-solving skills and enjoy working with him. Behzad, I just want to know, "When are you moving to D.C.?" Your presence is requested.

I'd also like to thank my friend and WaveGard business partner, Rick Dreger, for his support and encouragement throughout this project, even at times when I probably should have been working on something else.

Behzad Behtash:

I would like to thank Grant Moerschel for accepting my invitation to coauthor this book. Grant's friendship and insight have been invaluable to me over the years.

I would also like to thank Michelle Grandin, who introduced me to this project before she left Cisco Press for school. I appreciate Michelle's guidance with this and other projects, and I wish her success in her new endeavors.

I am also grateful for the support and encouragement I received from my colleagues at Tetra Tech EM Inc.; in particular Anthony Garcia, Chris Marquez, and Andrew Perry.

From both authors:

Special thanks goes to the Cisco Press team including those we worked with directly—Brett Bartow, Chris Cleveland, Ginny Munroe, and Tammi Barnett—as well as the behind-the-scenes folks who make it all come together.

We also thank our technical editors: Greg Abelar, Brian Done, Bob Eckhoff, Randy Ivener, Jag Kang, Paul Qiu, and Fahim Hussain Yusuf. They improved the quality of this book with their hard work and dedication to this project.

Contents

Icons Used in This Book

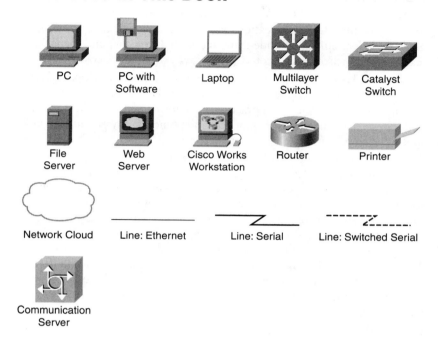

PC   PC with Software   Laptop   Multilayer Switch   Catalyst Switch

File Server   Web Server   Cisco Works Workstation   Router   Printer

Network Cloud   Line: Ethernet   Line: Serial   Line: Switched Serial

Communication Server

Command Syntax Conventions

The conventions used to present command syntax in this book are the same conventions used in the IOS Command Reference. The Command Reference describes these conventions as follows:

- **Boldface** indicates commands and keywords that are entered literally as shown. In actual configuration examples and output (not general command syntax), boldface indicates commands that are manually input by the user (such as a **show** command).

- *Italics* indicate arguments for which you supply actual values.

- Vertical bars (|) separate alternative, mutually exclusive elements.

- Square brackets [ ] indicate optional elements.

- Braces { } indicate a required choice.

- Braces within brackets [{ }] indicate a required choice within an optional element.

Foreword

CCSP Flash Cards and Exam Practice Pack is an excellent self-study resource for the CCSP certification exams. A CCSP certification validates the knowledge, skills, and understanding needed to secure and manage network infrastructures to protect productivity and reduce costs.

Cisco Press Flash Card titles are designed to help educate, develop, and grow the community of Cisco networking professionals. The guides arm readers with a series of effective exam practice tools, formats, and environments to build their confidence, provide practice, and point out any potential trouble spots. Developed with the Cisco certifications team, Cisco Press books are the only self-study books that Cisco Systems authorizes.

Most networking professionals use a variety of learning methods to gain necessary skills. Cisco Press self-study titles are a prime source of content for some individuals, and can also serve as an excellent supplement to other forms of learning. Training classes, whether delivered in a classroom or on the Internet, are a great way to quickly acquire new understanding. Hands-on practice is essential for anyone seeking to build or hone new skills. Authorized Cisco training classes, labs, and simulations are available exclusively from Cisco Learning Solutions Partners worldwide. Please visit http://www.cisco.com/go/training to learn more about Cisco Learning Solutions Partners.

I hope and expect you find this guide to be an essential part of your exam preparation and a valuable addition to your personal library.

Don Field
Director, Certifications
Cisco Systems, Inc.
July 2005

Introduction

Since the Cisco Systems, Inc., career certification programs were announced in 1998, they have been the most sought-after and prestigious certifications in the networking industry. For many people, achieving the CCSP certification is a crucial step to build a rewarding career in networking or obtain career advancement.

Notorious as being some of the most difficult certifications in the networking industry, Cisco exams can cause stress to the ill-prepared. Unlike other certification exams, the Cisco exams require that students truly understand the material, instead of just memorizing answers. This pack has been designed to help you assess whether you are prepared to pass all five of the CCSP exams. This pack contains flash cards that assist in memorization, quick reference sheets that provide condensed exam information, and a powerful exam engine to help you determine if you are prepared for the actual exam.

The Purpose of Flash Cards

Flash cards have been recognized as a quick and effective study aid. They have been used to complement classroom training and significantly boost memory retention.

The flash cards in this pack serve as a final preparation tool for the CCSP exams. They work best if you use them with official study aids for the CCSP exam. Table I-1 presents the required exams and recommended study for CCSP certification. Note that these cards and quick reference sheets can be used with any other CCSP exam preparation book or course of study. They might also be useful to you as a quick desk or field reference guide.

Table I-1   *Exams and Courses Required to Achieve CCSP Certification*

Exam	Exam Number	Course(s) Most Closely Matching Exam Requirements
SND	642-551 SND	Securing Cisco Network Devices (**SND**)
SNRS	642-502 SNRS	Securing Cisco Networks with Routers and Switches (**SNRS**)
SNPA	642-522 SNPA	Securing Networks with PIX and ASA (**SNPA**)
IPS	642-532 IPS	Implementing Cisco Intrusion Prevention Systems (**IPS**)
CSVPN	642-511 CSVPN	Cisco Secure Virtual Private Networks (**CSVPN**)

You must have your CCNA certification as a prerequisite to earn your CCSP certification. CCSP certifications are valid for 3 years. Be sure to check Cisco.com for any changes.

Who Should Use These Flash Cards

These flash cards are designed for network administrators, network engineers, Cisco Networking Academy Program students, and any professional or student looking to advance his or her career with a Cisco CCSP certification.

How To Use These Flash Cards

Review one section at a time, and read each flash card until you can answer it correctly on your own. When you can correctly answer every card in a given section, move on to the next.

These flash cards are a condensed form of study and review. Don't rush to move through each section. The amount of time you spend reviewing the cards directly affects how long you can retain the information needed to pass the test. Review each section as a final refresher a few days before your exam.

Although these flash cards are designed to be used as a final-stage study aid (30 days before the exam), they can also be used in the following situations:

- **Pre-study evaluation**—Before charting out your course of study, read one or two questions at the beginning and end of every section to gauge your competence in the specific areas.

- **Reinforcement of key topics**—After you complete your study in each area, read through the answer cards (on the left side of the pages) to identify key topics and reinforce concepts.

- **Identify areas for last-minute review**—In the days before an exam, review the study cards and carefully note your areas of weakness. Concentrate your remaining study time on these areas.

- **Post-study quiz**—If you flip through this book at random and view the questions on the right side of the pages, you can randomize your self-quiz to be sure you're prepared in all areas.

- **Desk reference or field guide to core concepts (quick reference sheets section only)**—Networking professionals, sales representatives, and help-desk technicians alike can benefit from a handy, simple-to-navigate book that outlines the major topics aligned with network security principles and CCSP certification.

Quick Reference Sheets

At the end of each part of the book after the flash cards, you find some quick reference sheets, which serve as both a study guide for the CCSP exam and as a companion reference to the text. For readers who seek CCSP certification, these quick reference sheets are well-suited to reinforce the concepts learned in the text—they are not just source of information. For readers who have either already obtained CCSP certification or simply need a basic overview, these sheets can serve as a standalone reference. A complete set of the notes can also be printed from the enclosed CD-ROM.

Please note that there is some overlap of content in the Cisco CCSP certification courses and corresponding exams. We chose to make each section of this book stand on its own, and we covered the material for each exam independently, so that you can focus on each exam without the need to reference a common topic from a different exam's section. Because of this, you might notice redundant coverage of topics in certain sections of the book.

What Is Included on the CD-ROM

The CD-ROM includes copies of the flash cards and quick reference sheets presented in the physical set. Also included is an electronic version of the flash cards that runs on Windows, Packet PC, and Palm platforms. The CD-ROM allows you to shuffle the flash cards, so that you can randomize your study. The CD-ROM also includes a powerful practice test engine designed to simulate each of the CCSP exams. The practice test engine help you become familiar with the format of the exams and reinforce the knowledge needed to pass them.

Special Features

You might notice that some flash cards on the CD-ROM provide pointers to the quick reference sheets included on PDF, to provide you with an additional mode of reviewing. Additional CD-ROM features include the following:

- Palm and Pocket PC formats, so that you can study for the CCSP tests on your handheld device.

- The ability to shuffle the flash cards and the option to review custom sets that focus your study on difficult terms, basic concepts, or a "final exam."

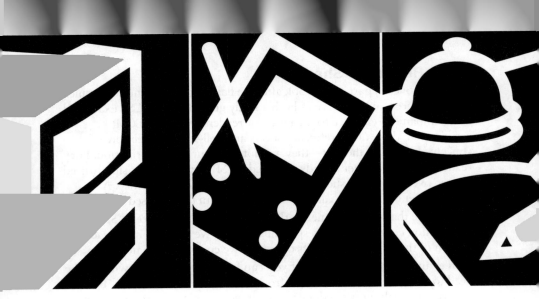

Part I

Securing Cisco Network Devices (SND) Flash Cards

The flash cards in this part of the book prepare you for the Securing Cisco Network Devices (SND) exam (642-551) to achieve your CCSP certification. Over 300 more questions for this section of the book can be found on the CD-ROM accompanying this book. The flash cards address specific topic areas for this exam and are organized as follows:

- **Section 1: Network Security Overview**—Evaluates your familiarity with general network security concepts including policies, attacks, and threats. This section also tests your general familiarity with Cisco Self-Defending Network initiative and its various components.

- **Section 2: Securing the Perimeter**—The flash cards in this section test your knowledge of security for router and switches, AAA advance authentication, Cisco Secure ACS, device hardening, ACLs, secure management and reporting, and mitigation of Layer 2 attacks.

- **Section 3: Cisco Security Appliances**—The flash cards in this section quiz your knowledge of Cisco security appliance models, features, and general configuration procedures.

- **Section 4: Securing Networks with Host- and Network-Based IPS**—The flash cards in this section quiz your knowledge of host and network intrusion detection and prevention technologies and the concepts behind their setup, operation, and management.

- **Section 5: IPsec VPNs**—The flash cards in this section cover general VPN technology topics including IKE, IPSec, and authentication and encryption algorithms. Your knowledge of Cisco VPN portfolio is also tested.

Section 1
Network Security Overview

Question 1

What type of a threat does a disgruntled employee pose to an organization?

Question 2

What type of an attack involves an intruder attempting to discover and map the systems, services, and vulnerabilities in your network?

Question 3

List three of the solutions that can be used to secure a network and protect information.

Question 1 Answer

A disgruntled current or former employee presents an internal threat to the network.

Question 2 Answer

Reconnaissance attacks

Question 3 Answer

- Encryption
- Firewalls
- Authentication
- Vulnerability patching
- Intrusion prevention

Question 4

Describe a closed network.

Question 5

A password brute-force crack is what kind of an attack?

Question 6

Describe a man-in-the-middle attack.

Question 4 Answer

A closed network is one that is not connected to other networks, such as the Internet or a business partner's network.

Question 5 Answer

A password brute-force crack is an example of an access attack.

Question 6 Answer

A man-in-the-middle attack occurs when an attacker sits in between two-way client and server communications to intercept them.

Question 7

What is privilege escalation?

Question 8

Which RFC describes network filtering that lets you source packets to be sent to your ISP with network ranges you control and that lets receive packets from your ISP with destination network ranges you control?

Question 9

Which is more secure and why, FTP or SCP?

Question 7 Answer

Privilege escalation occurs when legitimate users with lower levels of access privileges, or intruders who have gained lower privileged access, get information or run procedures that are not authorized at their current level of access.

Question 8 Answer

RFC 2827

Question 9 Answer

SCP is a far more secure file transfer method compared to FTP. SCP is secure copy and transmits and receives data securely, encrypted within an SSH tunnel, whereas FTP sends all information (including usernames and passwords) in clear text.

Question 10

What are the four steps required to mitigate worm attacks?

Question 11

What is a FWSM?

Question 12

What are the primary components of Cisco Security Agent (CSA)?

Question 10 Answer

Step 1—Contain

Step 2— Inoculate

Step 3— Quarantine

Step 4— Treat

Question 11 Answer

A firewall services module (FWSM) is a specialized firewall blade for Catalyst 6500 Series switches and Cisco 7600 Series routers.

Question 12 Answer

The primary components of CSA are:

- Management Center for Cisco Security Agent
- CSA agent software
- Administrative Workstation

Question 13

Which Cisco product provides AAA services?

Question 14

What is the Cisco HIPS product?

Question 15

What system layers are protected by CSA's defense-in-depth approach?

Question 13 Answer

Cisco Secure Access Control Server (ACS) provides authentication, authorization, and accounting services via RADIUS or TACACS+ standards.

Question 14 Answer

CSA is the Cisco host-based IPS (HIPS) solution.

Question 15 Answer

The protected layers are:

- Network
- File system
- Configuration
- Execution space

Question 16

What is a benefit of IPS compared to IDS?

Question 17

What phase of self-defending networks relies on firewalls, intrusion prevention, and secured connectivity?

Question 18

Why is the distribution of security technologies throughout the network critical in self-defending networks?

Question 16 Answer

IPS systems work inline and can stop attacks before they can enter the network.

Question 17 Answer

Firewalls, intrusion prevention, and secured connectivity are the products and technologies used in Phase 1, Integrated Security, of self-defending network development.

Question 18 Answer

Distribution of security technologies throughout the network is critical to achieve the goal to enable every network element as a point of defense and stop attacks as far away from their intended destination and the core of the network as possible in self-defending networks.

Question 19

Which Cisco endpoint security product is designed for use with the WebVPN feature of the Cisco VPN 3000 Concentrator?

Question 20

What security feature of Cisco IOS allows single command lock-down of IOS devices according to NSA standards?

Question 21

What function is served by CoPP?

Question 19 Answer

Cisco Secure Desktop software is an integrated endpoint security client used with the WebVPN feature on the Cisco VPN 3000 Series Concentrator.

Question 20 Answer

The "autosecure" feature, available with IOS Software Version 12.3 or 12.3T or greater, provides a single command lock-down of IOS devices and are compliant with security settings recommended by the NSA.

Question 21 Answer

Control-Plane Policing (CoPP) throttles the amount of traffic forwarded to the route processor of a router to limit CPU use and prevent network performance degradation or loss of connectivity.

Section 2
Securing the Perimeter

Question 1

Which enable password is cryptographically most secure?

Question 2

Which router vty line configuration commands must be run to enable successful Telnet sessions to the router?

Question 3

What does AAA stand for?

Question 1 Answer

Enable secret passwords are stored as an MD5 hash, which is more secure than the legacy enable password. The legacy enable password should be disabled when not needed.

Question 2 Answer

The commands **login** and **password** must run at the **router(config-line)#** prompt for a remote Telnet connection to work. Note that Telnet is insecure and that SSH is the recommended command-line interface access protocol because of its inherent security.

Question 3 Answer

Authentication, Authorization, and Accounting

Question 4

Which part of AAA determines what activities are allowed for the user?

Question 5

Name two two-factor authentication technologies.

Question 6

What is packet mode access?

Question 4 Answer

Authorization

Question 5 Answer

Token card and soft tokens

Question 6 Answer

Packet mode access is remote network access by users, such as a PPP dial-in connection to an ISP's system.

Question 7

Name the two types of AAA server protocols.

Question 8

List three user accounts database types CSACS can interact with.

Question 9

How does an administrator log into and control a CSACS?

Question 7 Answer

RADIUS and TACACS+

Question 8 Answer

Windows SAM (Windows NT), Windows Active Directory (Windows 2000 and newer), ODBC, LDAP, and Novell NDS

Question 9 Answer

CSACS is managed through a web browser interface either directly on the local CSACS host or over a network.

Question 10

Which global command disables source routing, an IP feature allowing packets with a predefined route to override local routes?

Question 11

Which command disables a router's SNMP process?

Question 12

Which interface command disables ICMP notifications of unreachable networks?

Question 10 Answer

The **router(config)#no ip source-route** command

Question 11 Answer

The **router(config)#no snmp-server** command

Question 12 Answer

router(config)#no ip unreachable

Question 13

What are the valid numbering ranges of extended ACLs?

Question 14

What type of ACL creates openings during specified time slots?

Question 15

After an ACL is created, what is the next step to place it into production?

Question 13 Answer

100 to 199 and 2000 to 2699

Question 14 Answer

Time-based

Question 15 Answer

Apply it to an interface with the **ip access-group** interface configuration command or the **access-class** line configuration command.

Question 16

Which type of management network separates management traffic from general user and system traffic?

Question 17

Which command-line access application is discouraged?

Question 18

Which IOS command generates a crypto keypair for use with SSH?

Question 16 Answer

Out-of-band (OOB)

Question 17 Answer

Telnet. Use SSH whenever possible.

Question 18 Answer

The **crypto key generate {options}** command

Question 19

What are the three SNMP security model versions?

Question 20

What are the three SNMP security levels?

Question 21

What does Cisco recommend for securing trunks?

Question 19 Answer

SNMP version 1, version 2c, and version 3

Question 20 Answer

noauth, auth, priv

Question 21 Answer

Allow only the VLANs that must traverse the trunk to be configured on the trunk. Prune all other VLANs. Assign dedicated VLAN numbers as the native VLAN number.

Question 22

Which IOS switch command controls the number of allowable MAC addresses on a port?

Question 23

What are the three switchport violation modes?

Question 24

Which IOS command prevents a port from sending or receiving bridge protocol data units (BPDUs) to mitigate spanning tree protocol attacks?

Question 22 Answer

The **switchport port-security maximum** {*number*} command

Question 23 Answer

Protect, restrict, and shut down.

Question 24 Answer

The **spanning-tree bpdufilter enable** command

Question 25

Private VLAN introduces what function within a VLAN?

Question 26

What is the main objective of a VLAN proxy attack?

Question 25 Answer

Promiscuous, Isolated, and Community ports that control intra-segment communication.

Question 26 Answer

A VLAN proxy attack is an attempt to circumvent private VLAN controls.

Section 3
Cisco Security Appliances

Question 1

Which layers of the OSI model are used by proxy firewalls?

Question 2

What are the drawbacks of proxy firewalls?

Question 3

What tool provides a web-based GUI management interface for Cisco security appliances?

Question 1 Answer

Proxy firewalls are application-aware and operate on layers 3 through 7 of the OSI model.

Question 2 Answer

Single point of failure

Difficult to add support for new applications and protocols

High processing overhead

Question 3 Answer

Cisco Adaptive Security Device Manager (ADSM) provides a GUI management interface for Cisco security appliances.

Question 4

What license options are available for the ASA 5500 Series security appliances?

Question 5

For traffic flow from a more secure interface to a less secure interface, what is the security appliance's default behavior?

Question 6

What is the default security level of the outside interface?

Question 4 Answer

ASA 5510: Base, Security+

ASA 5520: Base, VPN+

ASA 5540: Base, VPN+, VPN Premium

In addition, GTP/GPRS inspection and additional security contexts can be licensed.

Question 5 Answer

Traffic from a more secure interface to a less secure interface is allowed by default (FWSM behavior is different, and no traffic flow is allowed by default).

Question 6 Answer

The outside interface is set at security level 0 by default. The user can change its value.

Question 7

What is the security appliance's default behavior for traffic flow between two interfaces with equal security level values?

Question 8

What is the tftp-server command used for?

Question 9

Why is TCP easier to inspect than UDP?

Question 7 Answer

Traffic between two interfaces with the same security value is not allowed by default. With Security Appliance software version 7.0 or later, communication between interfaces with the same security level can be allowed if you use the following command:

```
fw(config)# same-security-traffic permit inter-interface
```

Question 8 Answer

The **tftp-server** command can be used to simplify the syntax of **write net** and **configure net** commands by predefining the TFTP server IP address, filename, and the path used with these commands.

Question 9 Answer

TCP is a connection-oriented protocol, and therefore easier to inspect, as conversations between internal and external hosts are more easily tracked in the session table of the security appliance.

Question 10

Which protocol is easier to inspect, TCP or UDP?

Question 11

What is a TCP three-way handshake?

Question 12

At what layer of the TCP/IP protocol stack do translations occur?

Question 10 Answer

TCP is connection-oriented and easier to inspect.

Question 11 Answer

TCP connections are established when you use a three-way handshake, which includes a three-step exchange of SYN, SYN/ACK, and ACK packets between two hosts.

Question 12 Answer

Translations occur at the IP layer of the TCP/IP stack.

Question 13

Which command is used to display the current translations on a security appliance?

Question 14

What is port address translation?

Question 15

What command is used to configure PAT with the IP address of the external interface?

Question 13 Answer

The **show xlate** command displays the current translations.

Question 14 Answer

PAT can use a single mapped IP address to translate thousands of local (real) IP addresses. To properly distinguish conversations between internal and external hosts, PAT uses unique source port numbers for each translation.

Question 15 Answer

You must use a **nat** command with the following **global** command:

```
fw(config)# global (outside) 1 interface
fw(config)# nat (inside) 1 0.0.0.0 0.0.0.0
```

Question 16

What is ASDM?

Question 17

What version of the Microsoft JVM is supported with ASDM 5.0?

Question 16 Answer

Cisco Adaptive Security Device Manager (ASDM) is a browser-based configuration and monitoring tool designed for management of PIX and ASA security devices. ASDM offers a simple graphical interface and does not require extensive command-line interface (CLI) experience from the administrator.

Question 17 Answer

Microsoft JVM is not supported with ASDM 5.0. Java plug-in 1.4.2 or 1.5.0 are required.

Section 4
Securing Networks with Host- and Network-Based IPS

Question 1

What is IPS?

Question 2

What is the Cisco host IPS product?

Question 3

Define false positive.

Question 1 Answer

Intrusion prevention system

Question 2 Answer

The CSA

Question 3 Answer

A condition when nonmalicious traffic causes an alarm.

Question 4

Define a signature.

Question 5

Describe the function of a sensor engine.

Question 6

Define a custom signature.

Question 4 Answer

A set of conditions that describes an intrusive event

Question 5 Answer

Sensor signature engines are the internal software processes designed to examine the many types of flows that can occur on a network to spot unauthorized activity. Each engine is optimized to examine a particular type of communication.

Question 6 Answer

A custom signature is a new signature that is built from scratch or based upon a copy of a built-in signature.

Question 7

List the signature alert severity categories.

Question 8

What protocol is used to pull sensor events from a sensor?

Question 9

What Cisco software products are used for sensor management?

Question 7 Answer

Informational, low, medium, and high

Question 8 Answer

Security Device Event Exchange (SDEE)

Question 9 Answer

IPS Device Manager (IDM) and the CiscoWorks VMS Management Center for Intrusion Detection Prevention System Sensors (IPS MC)

Question 10

Before you use a sensor's GUI or an SSH connection, what is the required first step in the setup process?

Question 11

A sensor initialization is the process of defining sensor operational parameters. Which CLI command starts this process?

Question 12

Describe CSA.

Question 10 Answer

Initial CLI configuration of a sensor via a console cable or directly connected keyboard (if supported on that sensor) is necessary (and required) before you use SSH or a GUI interface for more advance, detailed configuration.

Question 11 Answer

The **setup** command

Question 12 Answer

CSA is a distributed (centrally controlled) personal firewall and HIPS.

Question 13

Describe CSA's reliance on signatures.

Question 14

What are the two components of a CSA deployment?

Question 15

What is CSA's INCORE technology?

Question 13 Answer

CSA does not rely on signatures and does not inspect content; it analyzes system behavior for abnormal activity.

Question 14 Answer

CSA host software and the CSA Management Center (CSA MC), which is part of the CiscoWorks VMS security management platform

Question 15 Answer

Intercept Correlate Rules Engine. INCORE examines all system calls to the host's file system, network interfaces, Windows Component Object Model (COM), and Windows registry.

Question 16

What is a permissive security policy?

Question 17

What is the role of a CSA agent kit?

Question 16 Answer

Permissive policies deny malicious behavior and allow all other actions.

Question 17 Answer

Agent kits are designed around common group needs and are deployed to the hosts within the groups.

Section 5
IPSec VPNs

Question 1

What are the three primary types of VPNs?

Question 2

What is the IP protocol number for ESP (Encapsulating Security Payload)?

Question 3

What port does IKE (Internet Key Exchange) use?

Question 1 Answer

- Remote-access VPNs
- Site-to-site VPNs
- Firewall-based VPNs

Question 2 Answer

ESP's IP protocol number is 50.

Question 3 Answer

IKE operates on UDP port 500.

Question 4

Name the two modes of IPSec operation.

Question 5

Which IPSec mode of operation does not require the host to perform any encryption?

Question 6

What length digest is produced with HMAC-SHA1?

Question 4 Answer

IPSec can operate in Tunnel mode or Transport mode.

Question 5 Answer

Tunnel mode is typically implemented between two VPN devices that perform encryption and decryption tasks, eliminating the need for the host to perform such operations.

Question 6 Answer

HMAC-SHA1 hash function produces a 160-bit digest for authentication.

Question 7

What is a transform set?

Question 8

List the three commonly used key lengths with AES encryption.

Question 9

What is the protocol IKE uses that allows two peers to establish a secret key over an insecure communications channel?

Question 7 Answer

A transform set is a specific combination of message authentication and encryption algorithms that IPSec peers use.

Question 8 Answer

AES encryption uses 128-bit, 192-bit, or 256-bit encryption keys.

Question 9 Answer

The Diffie-Hellman protocol

Question 10

What key length does DH Group 5 use?

Question 11

What protocol uses bidirectional SAs?

Question 12

Which IKE Phase 1 mode involves three two-way exchanges between peers?

Question 10 Answer

DH group 5 uses a 1536-bit key.

Question 11 Answer

IKE SAs are bidirectional.

Question 12 Answer

IKE Main mode involves three two-ways exchanges between peers.

Question 13

How does IKE Aggressive mode differ from IKE Main mode?

Question 14

Which Cisco VPN product is considered the most appropriate choice for building remote access VPNs?

Question 15

Which mode of Hardware Client operation uses PAT?

Question 13 Answer

IKE Aggressive mode uses a single exchange between peers. It generates the DH pair on the first exchange, but it does not provide identity protection. IKE Main mode involves three two-way exchanges between peers to generate the DH pair; however, it also authenticates the identity of the peer.

Question 14 Answer

Although remote access VPNs can be implemented using several different Cisco products, the Cisco VPN 3000 Concentrator is considered the most appropriate choice.

Question 15 Answer

Client mode. In this mode, the clients behind the Hardware Client are not directly accessible from the central site. Instead, the Hardware Client uses port address translation (PAT), and the addresses of the individual hosts behind it remain hidden.

Question 16

What type of pre-shared key is typically used for remote access VPNs?

Question 17

Which screen on the web-based management interface is used to configure group settings?

Question 18

Which tunneling policy allows clear text access to Internet sites while encrypting traffic to intranet sites?

Question 16 Answer

A "group" pre-shared key is used for remote access VPNs and is associated with a specific group name. The group can be the base group or any other group defined by the administrator.

Question 17 Answer

Group settings are configured via **User Management > Groups** from the web-based interface.

Question 18 Answer

The split-tunneling option provides encrypted acces to the remote site and unencrypted access to to all other Internet sites as well as local LAN traffic.

Question 19

On which tab of the software client do you configure IPSec over TCP settings?

Question 20

What settings are specified in files ending with .pcf?

Question 21

What IKE proposals are best to use with 3.x and 4.x software clients?

Question 19 Answer

Transparent tunneling options are accessed via the Transport tab on the software client.

Question 20 Answer

Profile (.pcf) files define authentication, transport, backup servers, and dialup settings for each profile.

Question 21 Answer

IKE proposal with names that begin with CiscoVPNClient are appropriate for use with 3.x and 4.x software clients.

CCSP: Securing Cisco Network Devices (SND) Quick Reference Sheets

Network Security Overview

This section presents an overview of network security concepts, including common threats, attack types, and mitigation techniques. It also includes an overview of the Cisco security portfolio.

Please note that there is some overlap of content in the Cisco CCSP certification courses and corresponding exams. We chose to make each section of this book stand on its own, and we covered the material for each exam independently, so that you can focus on each exam without the need to reference a common topic from a different exam's section. Becuase of this, you might notice redundant coverage of topics in certain sections of this book.

The Need for Network Security

Networked systems must be designed and implemented with security in mind because most contemporary systems are interlinked or "open" in contrast to a previous time when systems were "closed" islands. This interlinking, often demanded by business processes and information exchange, increases a system's vulnerability, risk of attack, and exploitation by threats. Comprehensive network security safeguards are needed because attacking systems has become easier for two reasons:

- Software development tools and easy-to-use operating systems provide attackers with a basis to develop attack tools.

- The Internet allows attackers to not only distribute attack tools and related attack techniques but also gain the necessary connectivity required for the attack.

In addition, the following three major dynamics have converged to further increase the need for network security in any successful organization:

- New or pending regulations in the United States, European Union, and elsewhere mandating better protection of company-sensitive and personal information
- Increasing terrorist and criminal activity directed at communication infrastructures and private and government networks and computer systems
- Increasing number of perpetrators conducting cyber attacks and hacking with greater ease as worldwide use of Internet technology and connectivity increases.

Network Security Challenges

The primary challenge of implementing network security is to strike the right balance between providing convenient access to systems and information as required to conduct business and the need to protect those same systems and information from attacks and inappropriate access. The emergence of the Internet and e-business has made this challenge more difficult. E-business demands stronger relationships with suppliers, partners, and customers, and often requires companies to provide access to their systems and critical information over the Internet.

Security within the system is important for the following reasons:

- Digital data exchange among organizations is crucial to an economy. These processes must be protected.
- Private data often travels via insecure networks, and precautions must be taken to prevent it from being corrupted or changed.
- Government regulations often dictate standards for information assurance compliance, especially in publicly held organizations.

Network Security Policy

To be effective, network security must be a continuous process and must be built around a security policy. The policy, which is an overall strategic vision, is defined first and the tactical processes and procedures to support that policy are designed around it. The RFC 2196, *Site Security Handbook*, describes a security policy as, "…a formal statement of the rules by which people who are given access to an organization's technology and information assets must abide."

A security policy is necessary because it:

- Creates a baseline of current security posture and implementation
- Clearly defines what behaviors are allowed and what behaviors are not
- Helps determine necessary tools and procedures
- Helps define roles and responsibilities
- Informs users of their roles and responsibilities
- States the consequences of misuse
- Enables global security implementation and enforcement
- Defines how to handle security incidents
- Defines assets and how to use them
- Provides a process for continuing review

Security policies can be as simple as one document or they might consist of many documents that describe every aspect of security. The organization's needs, in addition to any regulations to which the organization must adhere, drive the level of detail. A comprehensive security policy should describe some of the following concepts in writing:

- Statement of authority and scope
- Acceptable-use policy
- Identification and authentication policy
- Internet use policy
- Campus-access policy
- Remote-access policy
- Incident handling procedure

Network Security Process

A continuous security process is most effective because it promotes the retesting and reapplying of updated security measures on a continuous basis as illustrated in the following figure.

Cisco Security Wheel

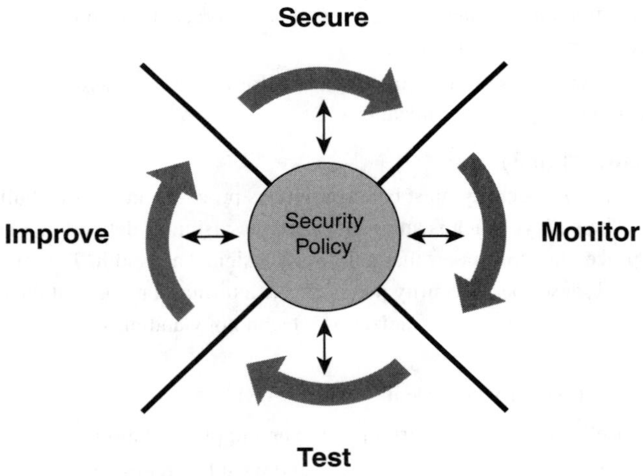

Secure

Improve   **Security Policy**   **Monitor**

Test

The Cisco Security Wheel provides a four-step process to promote and maintain network security:

Step 1   **Secure**—Implement security safeguards, such as firewalls, identification and authentication systems, and encryption with the intent to prevent unauthorized access to network systems.

Step 2   **Monitor**—Continuously monitor the network for security policy violations.

Step 3   Test—Evaluate the effectiveness of the in-place security safeguards by performing tests, such as periodic system vulnerability analysis and application and operating system hardening review.

Step 4   Improve—Improve overall security by collecting and analyzing information from the monitoring and testing phases to make judgments on ways to make security more effective.

Primary Types of Threats

There are four ways to categorize threats to network security:

- **Unstructured threats**—Threats primarily from inexperienced individuals using hacking tools available on the Internet (script kiddies).

- **Structured threats**—Threats from hackers who are more motivated and technically competent. They usually understand network system designs and vulnerabilities, and they can create hacking scripts to penetrate network systems.

- **External threats**—Threats from individuals or organizations working outside your company who do not have authorized access to your computer systems or network. They work their way into a network mainly from the Internet or dialup access servers.

- **Internal threats**—Threats from individuals with authorized access to the network with an account on a server or physical access to the wire (typically disgruntled current or former employees or contractors).

Mitigating Network Attacks

The following sections discuss expected attacks to networks and related mitigation techniques.

Physical and Environmental Threats

A common threat to network security is improper installation of network security devices or software applications. Default installation of many hardware devices or software applications can result in substandard security with such shortcomings as easily guessed or even blank default passwords, unnecessary running services, or disabled desirable services.

Devices are generally categorized into the following two groups:

- **Low-risk devices**—Typically low-end or small office/home office (SOHO) devices implemented in remote locations or branch offices with minimal impact on the corporate network.

- **High-risk (mission critical) devices**—Devices used in larger offices, hub locations, or corporate headquarter locations with the potential to impact a large portion of the network and user base.

Consider the following common threats when installing physical devices:

- **Hardware threats**—Threat of intentional or unintentional physical damage to devices, such as routers, firewalls, and switches.

- **Environmental threats**—Include threats of temperature and humidity conditions that can damage hardware devices.
- **Electrical threats**—Include threats, such as voltage spikes, insufficient voltage (brown outs), power loss (black outs), or unconditioned power.
- **Maintenance threats**—Improper practices that can result in outages. For example, mislabeled devices or improper handling or static electricity.

Use the following techniques to mitigate hardware threats:

- Limit physical access to authorized personnel only.
- Maintain an audit trail for access to the equipment, preferably using electronic access control.
- Implement a surveillance system such as cameras or CCTV.

Use the following techniques to mitigate environmental threats:

- Include temperature and humidity control measures.
- Maintain positive air flow.
- Implement remote temperature and humidity monitoring and alarm systems.
- Limit electrostatic and magnetic interferences.

Use the following techniques to mitigate electrical threats:

- Install Uninterrupted Power Supplies (UPS).
- Install generators for the mission-critical systems.
- Implement routine UPS and generator testing and maintenance.
- Use redundant power supplies on critical devices.
- Use filtered power when possible.
- Monitor power supply conditions.

Finally, to mitigate maintenance-related threats, use the following techniques:

- Clearly label devices and cabling.
- Use cable runs or raceways for rack-to-ceiling or rack-to-rack connections.
- Use proper electrostatic discharge procedures.
- Log out of administrative interfaces when it is no longer necessary.
- Do not rely on physical security alone (no room is completely secure). If a breach of physical security occurs and other security measures are not in place, an intruder can simply connect a terminal to the console port of a Cisco router or switch.

Reconnaissance Attacks

Reconnaissance is an attempt to discover and map systems, services, vulnerabilities, and publicly available information about target systems often as a prelude to more sophisticated attacks.

Reconnaissance methods include:

- **Internet Information queries**—Data collection about the organization from public sources, such as newspapers, business registries, public web servers, tools such as WHOIS, DNS records, and ARIN and RIPE records.

- **Port scans and ping sweeps**—Used to identify online hosts, their services, their operating systems, and some of their vulnerabilities. Mitigation includes controlling the visibility of hosts and services from untrusted networks by measures, such as filtering Internet Control Message Protocol (ICMP) echo and echo-reply traffic at the network edge and deploying network-based or host-based intrusion prevention systems.

- **Packet sniffers**—After hosts are compromised, rogue software can force their network cards to promiscuous mode and the hosts can become packet sniffers for further reconnaissance. The sniffing host can potentially collect network data-like passwords and data on the wire, and an attacker can retrieve this information for use in other attacks. Mitigation techniques include:

  — Use of strong authentication and One Time Passwords (OTP)
  — Switched infrastructures to prevent sniffing
  — Use of Host Intrusion Prevention Systems (HIPS) to detect disallowed host activities
  — Cryptography for data privacy

Access Attacks

Access attacks attempt to exploit weaknesses in applications, so that an intruder can gain unauthorized access. They include:

- **Password attacks**—An attempt to gain account access by obtaining its password using the following techniques:

  — Online and offline brute force repeated logon attempts. Mitigated with strong passwords, OTP systems, automatic account disabling after "X" number of failed attempts, limit password reuse, and periodic password testing to ensure policy compliance.
  — Packet sniffing collection of passwords off the medium. Mitigated with encryption, switching, and HIPS.
  — Internet Protocol (IP) and Media Access Control (MAC) spoofing to appear as a trusted system, so that users unknowingly send their passwords to attackers. Mitigated by device authentication.
  — Trojan horse software that collects password information then, and sends this information to attackers. Mitigated by use of host and network Intrusion Prevention Systems (IPS).

- **Trust exploitation**—An attacker takes advantage of the fact that other hosts will trust one host that has been compromised, potentially allowing unauthorized access. To mitigate trust exploitation attacks, create tight constraints on trust levels within a network and disallow Internet hosts complete access to internal hosts through the firewall. Limit trusts for systems outside of the firewall to specific protocols and grant them based on something other than an IP address when possible.

- **Port redirection**—A trust exploitation attack whereby an attacker that does not have direct access to an end target uses an intermediate host (that the end target trusts) as a launching point. The attacker compromises the intermediate host and from this point attacks the end target. Mitigation techniques include:
  - Use of HIPS to detect suspicious events
  - Implementation of a network-specific trust model with more granular firewall filtering
- **Man-in-the-middle**—An attacker sits in between two-way client and server communication to intercept it. Use of effective encryption protocols (IPSec and SSL, for example) mitigates this exposure. The following are man-in-the-middle attack examples:
  - Stealing or analyzing the information contained in packet payloads
  - Altering or introducing new packet data as it flows between the legitimate hosts
  - Hijacking the client's session, so that the attacker can pose as the client and gain trusted access
  - Creating Denial of Service (DoS) conditions by interrupting packet flow
- **Unauthorized access**—Internal or external attacks by people attempting access to systems or applications to which they do not have access. The following are examples of these attacks:
  - **Unauthorized system access**—Intruders gain access to a host to which they do not have access. Mitigate by use of OTP systems, advance authentication, and reduction of attack vectors by using stringent firewall filters to reduce attack opportunity. Warning banners alert unauthorized persons that their activities are prohibited and might be logged.
  - **Unauthorized data manipulation by an authorized user**—Users read, write, copy, or move files that are not intended to be accessible to them. Mitigate by use of stringent OS trust model controls to monitor privilege escalation and HIPS.
  - **Unauthorized privilege escalation**—Legitimate users with a lower level of access privileges, or intruders who gain lower privileged access, get information or process procedures without authorization at their current level of access. Mitigate by use of stringent OS trust model controls to control privilege escalation and HIPS.

IP Spoofing Attacks

IP spoofing occurs when an attacker attempts to impersonate a trusted IP address, so that the target accepts communications from the attacker.

IP spoofing mitigation techniques include:

- **Use of RFC 2827 filtering on routers and firewalls as follows**:
  - Traffic entering your network should be destined only for IP addresses you control.
  - Traffic leaving your network should be sourced only with IP addresses you control.

— Traffic leaving your Internet Service Provider's (ISP) network intended for your network should be destined only for IP addresses you control. Your ISP must implement these filters because they own this equipment.

- **Access control configuration**— Prevents traffic entering your network with source addresses that should reside on the internal network. Block all IP addresses reserved for private or other special uses, such as RFC 1918 private addresses and other "bogon" addresses.

- **Encryption**—Prevents compromising of source and destination hosts.

- **Additional authentication**—IP spoofing attacks rely on IP address-based identification and authentication of host. By deploying another authentication method (other than IP address), IP spoofing attacks become irrelevant.

DoS Attacks

DoS is the act of barraging a network or host with more connection requests or data than usually handled for the purpose of permanently or temporarily denying access to systems, services, or applications. DoS and Distributed DoS (DDoS) focus on disabling or drastically slowing IT services by overwhelming them with requests from one or many distributed attackers. DoS attacks most often target services already allowed by the firewall, such as HTTP, SMTP, and FTP. DoS can shut down a network by consuming all available bandwidth.

DoS mitigation techniques include:

- Use of RFC 1918 and RFC 2827 filtering

- Use of Quality of Service (QoS) rate limiting to control data flow

- Use of anti-DoS features on firewalls and routers to limit half open Transmission Control Protocol (TCP) connections

- Use of advanced authentication to prevent invalid host-to-host trusts

Worms, Viruses, Trojan Horses, Phishing, and Spam Attacks

Malicious code usually targets workstations and servers to subvert their operation. Malicious code types include:

- **Worms**—Malicious code that installs a payload onto a host using an available exploit vector and attempts to replicate to other hosts through some propagation mechanism. After installation of the payload, privilege escalation often occurs.

- **Viruses**—Malicious code attached to another program (such as email) that attempts some undesirable function on the host (such as reformatting the hard drive) after the user runs the rogue program.

- **Trojans**—Malicious code that appears to be legitimate and benigns but is a vector for an internal or external attack.

- **Phishing**—An attempt to deceive users into revealing private information to an attacker.

- **Spam**—Multiple unwanted emailed offers that flood inboxes.

Virus and Trojan horse mitigation techniques include:

- Using HIPS software.

- Acquiring effective and up-to-date host antivirus software.

- Performing effective maintenance of operating system and application patches.

- Staying up-to-date with the latest developments in attacks of this type and new mitigation methodologies.

Mitigate the affect of worms through the following steps:

Step 1   Contain with defense in depth techniques at major network junctions.

Step 2   Inoculate systems with antivirus updates.

Step 3   Quarantine infected machines.

Step 4   Treat infected machines with appropriate fixes.

Incident response methodologies are subdivided into the following six major categories based on the Network Service Provider Security (NSP-SEC) incident response methodology:

- **Preparation**—Acquire the resources to respond.

- **Identification**—Identify the worm.

- **Classification**—Classify the type of worm.

- **Traceback**—Trace the worm back to its origin.

- **Reaction**—Isolate and repair the affected systems.

- **Postmortem**—Document and analyze the process used for the future.

Application Layer Attacks

Application-layer attacks have the following general characteristics:

- They are designed to exploit intrinsic security flaws and known weaknesses in protocols, such as sendmail, HTTP, and FTP.

- They use standard ports that are commonly allowed through a firewall, such as TCP port 80 or TCP port 25.

- They are difficult to eliminate because new vulnerabilities are often discovered.

Stateful firewalls generally do not stop these attacks because these devices are not designed to perform deep packet inspection. Proxy firewall functions, such as PIX application inspection (formerly "fixups"), Cisco IPS, and Cisco Adaptive Security Appliances (ASA), are designed for deeper application inspection and control.

Mitigation techniques include:

- Implementing application inspection within the firewall device.

- Implementing HIPS to monitor OS and specific applications for illegal or suspicious calls.

- Implementing network IPS to monitor network communications for known attacks and activity outside of normal baseline.

- Keeping the host OS and applications patched.

- Logging events, parsing events, and performing analysis.

- Subscribing to mailing lists that alert you to new vulnerabilities in a timely manner.

Management Protocols and Vulnerabilities

Management protocols such as Simple Network Management Protocol (SNMP), syslog, Trivial File Transfer Protocol (TFTP), and Network Time Protocol (NTP) have been around for a number of years and were originally designed with little or no security considerations. Most of these protocols have been upgraded to newer versions that provide improved security measures. For example, SNMP Version 3 provides authentication and encryption of communications.

Mitigation techniques include:

- Using secure protocols, such as Secure Shell (SSH) or Secure Sockets Layer (SSL), when connecting to devices over the network and avoiding clear-text protocols, such as telnet or HTTP.

- Using Access Control Lists (ACLs) to limit administrative access to network devices.

- Using RFC 3704 filtering at the perimeter to prevent outside attackers from accessing devices by spoofing the address of (legitimate) management hosts.

- SNMP recommendations:

    — Configure SNMP with read-only (ro) community strings.

    — Limit access to management hosts on the managed devices.

    — Use SNMP version 3 or higher (authentication and encryption).

- Syslog recommendations:

    — Encrypt syslog traffic using IPSec.

    — Implement RFC 2827 filtering.

    — Set up ACLs on the firewall to limit access to the servers.

- TFTP recommendations:

    — Encrypt TFTP traffic using IPSec.

- NTP recommendations:

    — Implement an internal master clock when possible.

    — Use NTP version 3 or higher (authentication).

    — Use ACLs to control access to specific NTP servers.

Determining Network Vulnerabilities

An important aspect of securing any network is proper assessment to determine existing vulnerabilities. Use the following tools and techniques to evaluate the network and discover security vulnerabilities:

- **Netcat**—A networking utility that reads and writes data across network connections using the TCP/IP protocol. Netcat is a network debugging and exploration tool that creates many connections useful for evaluation of network security.

- **Blue's Port Scan**—A port-scanning tool (can scan 300 ports per second).

- **Ethereal**—An open-source, packet-capturing application that runs on most popular computing platforms, such as UNIX, Linux, and Windows. Ethereal is a full-featured protocol analyzer and includes remote capturing capabilities.

- **Microsoft Baseline Security Analyzer (MBSA)**—MBSA is a free Microsoft-supplied security assessment tool for Windows clients. This tool scans Windows systems and discovers missing patches. It also functions as a best-practices vulnerability assessment tool by highlighting any setting on the scanned system that is not in compliance with best security practices as recommended by Microsoft.

Introducing the Cisco Security Portfolio

Cisco provides an extensive portfolio of security appliances, management platforms, and software applications designed for securing small and large networks alike.

The following sections describe Cisco security products based on different security-need categories.

Perimeter Security Products

Cisco perimeter security products include:

- **Cisco PIX 500 Series Security Appliance Series**—Security appliances designed for small and large networks (SOHO to ISP).

- **Cisco ASA 5500 Series Security Appliance Series**—Expandable security devices combining the functionality of PIX 500 Series security appliances, Cisco Virtual Private Network (VPN) 3000 Concentrators, and Cisco 4200 Series IPS devices.

- **Cisco Firewall Service Module (FSWM)**—Firewall module designed for the Catalyst 6500 Series switch and Cisco 7600 Series router.

- **VPN Acceleration Card Plus (VAC+)**—High performance, hardware-based encryption with support for AES and 3DES encryptions standards.

- **Cisco IOS Firewall**—Integrated firewall and intrusion detection functionality on a wide range of Cisco IOS software-based routers. Specific highlights include:
  - Stateful Cisco IOS Firewall Inspection
  - Intrusion detection
  - Firewall voice traversal

— ICMP inspection

— Authentication proxy

— Destination URL policy management

— Per-user firewalls

— Cisco IOS router and firewall provisioning

— DoS detection and prevention

— Dynamic port mapping

— Java applet blocking

— VPNs, IPSec encryption, and QoS Support

— Real-time alerts

— Audit trail

— Integration with Cisco IOS software

— Basic and advanced traffic filtering

— Policy-based multi-interface support

— Network address translation

— Time-based access lists

— Peer router authentication

Virtual Private Network Solutions

VPNs provide secure, reliable, encrypted connectivity over a shared public network infrastructure such as the Internet. This shared infrastructure allows connectivity at a lower cost than that provided by existing dedicated private networks.

There are three basic VPN scenarios:

- **Intranet VPN**—Used to link corporate headquarters to remote offices, offering a lower-cost alternative to traditional WANs.

- **Extranet VPN**—Used to securely link network resources with third-party vendors and business partners over the public network.

- **Remote-access VPN**—Used to securely connect telecommuters and mobile users to corporate networks over the public network.

Cisco provides VPN functionality on the following products:

- Cisco VPN 3000 Series Concentrators:

  — Have models available for small businesses (100 connections) up to large enterprises (10,000 connections).

  — Are scalable and resilient.

  — Provide unlimited Cisco VPN Client licensing.

  — Support several access methods including WebVPN (SSL VPN), Cisco VPN Client (IPSec VPN), Microsoft-embedded clients (PPTP and L2TP), and Nokia Symbian Client for wireless phones and PDAs.

— Include integrated Web-based management for configuration and monitoring.

— Support Cisco Network Admission Control (NAC).

- Cisco PIX 500 Series and ASA 5500 Series Security Appliances:

  — Provide combined firewall and VPN functionality.

  — Support several access methods, including WebVPN (SSL VPN, available on ASA 5500 Series only), Cisco VPN Client (IPSec VPN), Microsoft-embedded clients (L2TP only), and Nokia Symbian Client for wireless phones and PDAs.

- Cisco VPN-enabled IOS routers:

  — Operate at site-to-site VPNs.

  — Offer scalability, network resiliency, bandwidth optimization and QoS, and deployment flexibility.

  — Include the Cisco 800 Series, 900 Series, 1700 Series, 2600 Series, 2700 Series, 3600 Series, 3700 Series, and 7000 Series routers.

  — Use the VPN Accelerator Module 2 (VAM2) to enhance VPN performance in the Cisco 7000 series routers.

  — Include built-in hardware-based VPN acceleration with the Cisco 1800 Series, 2800 Series, and 3800 Series Integrated Services Routers (ISR).

- Cisco VPN Hardware and Software Clients:

  — Include Cisco VPN Software Client version 4.x, Cisco VPN 3002 Hardware Client, several models of Cisco IOS routers, and Cisco PIX 501 and 506 security appliances.

  — Incorporate a centralized push policy technology foundation.

  — Work with all Cisco VPN concentrators, Cisco IOS routers, and PIX security appliances.

  — Work with non-Windows operating systems (Linux, Mac, and Solaris).

The following table provides an overview of Cisco VPN product positioning.

Network Size	Intended Use		
	Remote Access	Site-to-Site	Firewall-Based
Large Enterprise and Service Provider	Cisco VPN 3060 and VPN 3080 Concentrators	Cisco 7200 Series router, Cisco 3800 Series ISRs and higher	Cisco PIX 525, PIX 535, and ASA 5540 security appliances
Medium Enterprise	Cisco VPN 3030 Concentrator	Cisco 3600 Series and 7100 Series router, Cisco 2800 Series and 3800 Series ISRs	Cisco PIX 515 and ASA 5520 security appliances
Small Business or Branch Office	Cisco VPN 3005, VPN 3015, and VPN 3020 Concentrators	Cisco 3600 Series, 2600 Series, and 1700 Series routers, Cisco 1800 Series ISRs	Cisco PIX 506, PIX 515, and ASA 5520 security appliances
SOHO Market	Cisco VPN Software Client and VPN 3002 Hardware Client	Cisco 800 Series and 900 Series routers	Cisco PIX 501 and PIX 506 security appliances

IPS Solutions

The Cisco IPS is a network-based intrusion protection system that detects unauthorized activity. For example, if hackers attack, it can analyze traffic in real time. Cisco IPS sensors can tap into data from outside the forwarding path andfunction as traditional Intrusion Detection System (IDS) devices, sending alarms to a management console and controlling other systems, such as routers, to terminate the unauthorized sessions. With IPS software version 5.0 or higher, Cisco IPS devices can also operate "inline," terminating unauthorized sessions by dropping the attack packets in contrast to relying on other blocking devices, such as firewalls or routers.

The Cisco IPS sensor portfolio consists of the following:

- Cisco IDS/IPS 4200 Series appliances
- Cisco Catalyst 6500 Intrusion Detection System Module (IDSM2)
- Network Module-Cisco IDS (NM-CIDS) modules designed for Cisco 2600XM Series, Cisco 2691, Cisco 3660, and Cisco 3700 Series IOS routers
- Advanced Intrusion and Prevention Security Services Module (AIP-SSM) for Cisco ASA 5500 Series security appliances

In addition to the listed sensors, Cisco IOS routers, PIX 500 Series, and ASA 5500 Series security appliances include basic IPS capabilities. These capabilities were significantly improved in Security Appliance Software version 7.0 and Cisco IOS Software Release 12.3(8)T; however, compared to the Cisco full-featured IPS sensors, these platforms still detect a more limited subset of attacks.

Cisco IOS IPS is an inline, deep-packet inspection-based solution and offers the following features and benefits:

- New enhancements that provide broadly deployed worm and threat mitigation services
- A design that loads and enables IPS signatures in the same manner as Cisco IDS sensor appliances
- Support for 700+ of the same signatures supported by Cisco IPS sensor platforms
- Custom signatures to mitigate new threats
- An ideal solution for remote branch office applications
- Support for Trend Micro antivirus signatures

HIPS Solutions

In addition to network-based IPS solutions, Cisco provides HIPS solutions for threat mitigation throughout the network.

- HIPS audits host log files, host file systems, and resources.
- An advantage of HIPS is that it can monitor operating system processes and protect critical system resources and files.
- Cisco HIPS combines behavioral analysis and signature filters.

- HIPS combines the features of antivirus, network firewalls, and host-based application firewalls.

- HIPS can be implemented on critical systems anywhere on the network (not just the perimeter).

Cisco provides the Cisco Security Agent (CSA) as its HIPS solution. CSA includes the following components:

- **Management Center for Cisco Security Agent (CSA MC)**—CSA MC provides centralized management of CSA agents. The CSA MC can maintain a log of security violations and send alerts through e-mail or via a pager.

- **CSA Agents**—CSA agents are installed on the host systems to continually monitor local system activity and analyze the operations of that system. When necessary, CSA agents block attempted malicious activity. They also poll the CSA MC at configured intervals and download policy updates as appropriate.

- **Administrative workstation**—An administrative workstation connects securely to the CSA MC using an SSL-enabled web interface and is used to configure CSA settings on CSA MC.

Identity Solutions: Cisco Secure ACS

Cisco Secure Access Control Server (ACS) provides Authentication, Authorization, and Accounting (AAA) services.

Some of the services provided by Cisco ACS include:

- RADIUS services
- TACACS+ services
- Web-based Graphical User Interface (GUI) administration interface
- Scalable data replication for redundant ACS implementations
- Full accounting and user reporting
- Support for Active Directory, Windows NT Domains, LDAP, Novel NDS, and ODBC external databases

Network Admission Control

The Cisco NAC is a multivendor framework designed to prevent noncompliant endpoint devices from accessing the network.

NAC currently provides support for endpoints running Windows NT, 2000, and XP operating systems. Compliance level of endpoints are accessed based on OS patch levels and antivirus status. Noncompliant endpoints can be:

- Permitted access
- Denied access
- Restricted
- Quarantined

NAC architecture consists of the following components:

- **Endpoint Security Software**—Antivirus client, CSA, Personal Firewall, and the Cisco Trust Agent

- **Network Access Devices**—Network devices (routers, switches, wireless access points, and security appliances) that enforce admission control policy

- **Policy Server**—Cisco ACS and third-party policy servers, such as an antivirus policy server responsible for evaluating the endpoint security information

- **Management System**—CiscoWorks VMS and CiscoWorks Security Information Manager Solution (CiscoWorks SIMS) or appropriate third-party management systems used to configure Cisco NAC elements and provide monitoring and reporting operational tools

Security Management Solutions: Security Management Center

The CiscoWorks VMS management platform provides centralized configuration, management, and monitoring capabilities to simplify implementation of various components of the Cisco security portfolio. The platform's web-based tools provide the following simplified solutions for configuring, monitoring, and troubleshooting:

- VPNs

- Firewalls

- Network-based IPS devices

- HIPS

- Routers

CiscoWorks VMS includes the following applications:

- **Firewall Management Center**—Enables the large-scale deployment of Cisco firewalls.

- **Network-based IPS (IPS) and router-based IPS Management Center**—Allows large-scale deployment and management of sensors and router-based IPS using group profiles.

- **Host IPS Management Center**—Scalable to thousands of endpoints per manager, supports large-scale deployments.

- **VPN Router Management Center**—Facilitates setup and maintenance of large-scale deployment of VPN-enabled routers, Cisco IOS firewalls, and Cisco Catalyst 6000 IPSec VPN Service Modules.

- **Security Monitor**—Provides comprehensive view of security-related logging, and provides event correlation for improved detection of threats.

- **Performance Monitor**—Provides monitoring and troubleshooting services.

- **VPN Monitor**—Allows management of remote-access or site-to-site VPNs.

- **Operational Management**—Provides network inventory, reports on hardware and software changes, and manages software updates on multiple devices.

Building Cisco Self-Defending Networks

The Cisco Self-Defending Network strategy consists of three main components aimed at reducing exposure to security risks inherent in many networks by deploying three categories of overlapping and complementary security solutions:

- **Secure connectivity**—This pillar provides secure and scalable network connectivity, incorporating multiple types of traffic.

- **Threat defense**—This pillar prevents and responds to network attacks and threats using network services.

- **Trust and identity**—This pillar intelligently protects endpoints using technologies, such as NAC, identity services, and 802.1X.

The following three phases explain the development of self-defending networks:

- **Phase 1: Integrated Security**—This phase aims to distribute security technologies throughout every segment of the network to enable every network element as a point of defense. Products and technologies used in Phase 1 include firewall, intrusion prevention, and secured connectivity.

- **Phase 2: Collaborative Security Systems**—Phase 2 introduces the NAC industry initiative and aims to enable the security technologies throughout the network to operate as a coordinated system to defeat attacks. Products and technologies used in Phase 2 include NAC, Network Foundation Protection (NFP), Voice Over IP (VoIP), wireless, and service virtualization.

- **Phase 3: Adaptive Threat Defense**—This phase aims at deploying innovative and threat defense technologies throughout the "integrated security" fabric of the network. Products and technologies used in Phase 3 include application inspection and control, real-time worm, virus, spyware prevention, and Peer-to-Peer (P2P) and Instant Messaging (IM) controls.

Adaptive Threat Defense

Adaptive Threat Defense (ATD) is the primary goal of self-defending networks. ATD building blocks include the following:

- **Firewall services**—These services provide access control and traffic inspection.

- **IPS and network antivirus (AV) services**—These services provide application intelligence with deep packet inspection.

- **Network intelligence**—This service includes network security services, such as segmentation through Virtual LANs (VLANs), identity for user knowledge, QoS for controlling use of bandwidth, routing for topological awareness, switch root, and NetFlow for global traffic visibility. "Virtualization," or "virtualized fabric" is the virtualization of services for cost-effective deployment.

ATD enables the following services on the network:

- **Application security**—This service provides granular application inspection in firewalls and IDS and IPS appliances and allows enforcement of application-use policies, such as those controlling IM usage. Application security services allow control of web traffic and guard against applications that abuse port 80 (for example, IM and P2P), and provide protection for web services (for example, XML applications).

- **Anti-X defenses**—A new class of servicees that provide broad attack mitigation capabilities, such as malware protection, AV, message security (antispam, antiphishing), antiDoS, and antiworm. Deployment of anti-X defenses can occur throughout the network to effectively stop attacks as far from their intended destination and the core of the network as possible.

- **Network containment and control**—These services provide network intelligence and virtualization of security technologies to layer auditing, control, and correlation capabilities to control and protect any networked element.

The following table provides a summary of recently announced Cisco products and technologies that support ADT (please check Cisco.com for an up-to-date listing):

Products	Application Security	Anti-X	Containment and Control
Security Appliance 7.0 Software	Application inspection and control for firewalls and VoIP security		Virtual firewall, QoS, transparent firewall, and IPv6 support
IPS 5.0	Multivector threat identification	Malware, virus, and worm mitigation	Accurate prevention technologies for inline IPS
VPN 3000 Concentrator 4.7	SSL VPN Tunnel Client and fully clientless Citrix	Cisco Secure Desktop	Cisco NAC
Cisco IOS Software Release 12.3.(14)T	Application inspection and control for Cisco IOS firewalls	Enhanced in-line IPS	NPF, virtual firewall, and IPSec virtual interface
Cisco Security Agent 4.5		Spyware mitigation and system inventory auditing	Context-based policies
Catalyst DDoS Modules		Guard and Traffic Anomaly Detector	
Cisco Secure MARS			Event correlation for proactive response
Cisco Security Auditor		Cisco 800 Series and 900 Series routers	Network-wide security policy auditing

The following sections discuss several of the products and technologies listed in the previous table.

Cisco PIX Security Appliance Software Version 7.0

Cisco PIX Security Appliance Software Version 7.0 provides advanced firewall and deep inspection services to improve overall security. Highlights of the new features include:

- Web security:
  - Prevents web-based attacks and port 80 misuse with advanced HTTP firewall services.
  - Controls P2P actions to protect network capacity.
  - Polices IM usage to ensure compliance with company policies and prevent covert transmissions of sensitive information.
- Voice security:
  - Secures next-generation converged networks.
  - Controls VoIP security with improved H.323, Session Initiation Protocol (SIP), Media Gateway Control Protocol (MGCP), Real-Time Streaming Protocol (RTSP), and fragmentation/segmentation support.
  - Supports global system for mobile communication (GSM) wireless networks with General Packet Radio Service (GPRS) inspection engine and GPRS tunneling protocol (GTP).
- Advanced application and protocol security provides protocol conformance, state tracking, and security checks for over 30 protocols.
- Flexible policy control provides a policy framework for granular control of user-to-user and user-to-application network communications.
- Scalable security services (security contexts).
- Easy-to-deploy firewall services (transparent firewall capabilities).
- Improved network and device resiliency:
  - Active/active and active/passive failover for enhanced high-availability.
  - Zero-downtime software upgrades.
- Intelligent network integration:
  - QoS traffic prioritization.
  - IPv6 support for hybrid IPv4 and IPv6 network environments.
  - PIM sparse mode multicast support.

Cisco DDoS Modules

Cisco DDoS modules are available for the Catalyst 6500 Series switch and 7600 Series router and are designed to provide detection and automatic defense against DDoS attacks. Feature highlights include:

- **Anomaly Guard**— This feature performs attack analysis and mitigation services. The anomaly guard, or "Guard," uses a special traffic diversion technique that scrubs identified DDoS traffic while allowing legitimate traffic to continue unaffected. The Guard provides multiple layers of defense including dynamic filters and active antispoofing.

- **Traffic Anomaly Detector**— This feature passively monitors traffic and can generate alarms or activate the anomaly guard feature for automated threat mitigation.

Cisco Secure Monitoring, Analysis and Response System

Cisco Secure Monitoring, Analysis and Response System (CS-MARS) is an appliance-based solution designed to allow organizations to better identify, manage, and counter security threats. CS-MARS aims to address specific security issues and challenges such as:

- Security and network information overload
- Poor attack and fault identification, prioritization, and response
- Increased attack sophistication, velocity, and remediation costs
- Compliance and audit requirements
- Security staff and budget constraints

CS-MARS helps businesses meet these challenges by:

- Integrating network intelligence to modernize correlation of network anomalies and security events
- Visualizing validated incidents and automating investigation
- Mitigating attacks by fully leveraging network and security infrastructure
- Monitoring systems, network, and security operations to aid in regulatory compliance
- Delivering a scalable appliance to simplify use and deployment scenarios and lower Total Cost of Ownership (TCO)

CS-MARS features and benefits include:

- Capability to accurately identify, correlate, visualize, prioritize, investigate, and report incidents and mitigate attacks in progress
- Appliance-based architecture, offering turn-key installation and an easy-to-use interface covering a wide spectrum of security devices
- Capability to collect events from firewalls, VPN concentrators, network- and host-based intrusion prevention systems, and system logs, and to correlate event information with vulnerability assessment and NetFlow data to detect anomalies
- Capability to extend the Cisco Self-Defending Network initiative by identifying and mitigating threats in the network

Cisco Security Auditor

Cisco Security Auditor provides crucial network and security compliance auditing services. Cisco security auditor operational highlights include:

- Examining multiple router, switch, security appliance, and VPN Concentrator configurations against available best-practices checklists, such as the NSA-, CIS-, SAFE-, and TAC-approved configurations

- Benchmarking and scoring lists of policies against published best practices

- Generating audit reports linking to security vulnerabilities found

- Providing recommendations to fix discovered vulnerabilities and deviation from best-practices

Securing the Network Infrastructure with Cisco IOS Software Security Features

Cisco IOS software provides features designed to increase the security of Cisco routers and switches, and consequently, the networks where they deploy. Cisco SAFE axioms, Routers Are Targets and Switches Are Targets, highlight the importance of router and switch security to the overall security and heath of any network.

Cisco IOS software provides the following services and features to better protect routers and switches:

- **AutoSecure**—Provides a single command lock-down of IOS devices according to published NSA standards. Disables nonessential system processes and services to eliminate potential security threats.

- **Control-Plane Policing (CoPP)**—Some DoS attacks target a router's control and management plane, resulting in excessive CPU utilization and degradation or interruption of network connectivity. CoPP throttles the amount of traffic forwarded to the route processor of a router to prevent excessive CPU utilization on the router and avert the network connectivity issues that can result. CoPP uses the Modular Quality of Service Command-Line Interface (MQC).

- **Silent mode**—This feature reduces a hacker's ability to scan and attack an IOS device by stopping the router from generating certain informational packets such as ICMP messages and SNMP traps that the router usually generates. Because hackers rely on system messages to conduct reconnaissance, use of the silent mode feature reduces the ability of hackers to perform effective reconnaissance.

- **Scavenger-Class QoS**—Scavenger-class traffic is based on an Internet2 draft outlining a Less Than Best Effort (LBE) service. IOS routers can permit Scavenger traffic (for example, traffic generated by applications such as KaZaA, Napster, and other nonbusiness or gaming applications) as long as the service of more important traffic classes is adequate. If congestion occurs, the scavenger class is the first dropped. This feature ensures that management traffic gets through to the router and allows administrators to implement appropriate ACLs or other mitigation measures to effectively deal with in-progress network attacks.

Self-Defending Network Endpoint Security Solutions

An important aspect of the Self-Defending Network initiative is distribution of security technologies throughout the network to enable every network element as a point of defense. Cisco endpoint security solutions provide distributed threat mitigation and include the following products:

- **Cisco Secure Desktop**—The Cisco Secure Desktop software is an integrated endpoint security client used with the WebVPN feature on the Cisco VPN 3000 Concentrator Series.

- **Cisco Clean Access (CCA)**— CCA provides similar functionality to the more robust and scalable NAC, but its design is for the small-medium business market where a turnkey solution is preferred. Similar to NAC, it enforces endpoint policy compliance and enables organizations to provide access to endpoints that have been judged as "clean." CCA can direct noncompliant endpoints to a quarantine role with access only to resources required to achieve policy compliance, such as AV upgrades and OS patches.

Securing the Perimeter

This section provides a review of the concepts, features, and procedures for securing Cisco layer 2 and layer 3 equipment.

Securing Administrative Access to Cisco Routers

Access to routers can occur through serial console and aux ports or via a network interface using Telnet, SSH, a web browser (HTTP or the more secure HTTPS), SNMP, and the Cisco Security Device Manager (SDM).

Command-line modes for IOS-based routers and switches are:

- **ROM Monitor**—The reduced functionality IOS mode to which a device boots if the system IOS image is missing or corrupt.

- **User EXEC mode**—The default IOS shell with limited command access.

- **Privileged EXEC mode**—Commonly referred to as enable mode, this shell can allow access to all IOS commands.

- **Configuration modes**:

    - **Global configuration**—Allows global configuration settings
    - **Interface configuration**—Allows configuration settings for individual interfaces
    - **Line configuration**—Allows configuration settings for virtual terminal line (vty), console, and aux ports

Locally stored passwords, and in some cases usernames and passwords, are the first lines of defense in protecting a router from unauthorized access via these access methods. In more sophisticated setups, AAA authentication servers centrally store the credentials of users in lieu of local username and password storage.

Password complexity should meet or exceed an organization's quality standard. Cisco suggests nondictionary passwords of at least 10 characters. Cisco routers have the following password-creation bounds:

- 1–25 characters comprised of any or all alphanumeric, upper and lower case, symbols, and spaces.
- Any character can be the first character except a space.

Cisco router password types include:

- **Enable Secret**—The privileged mode (enable mode) access password. Stored as an MD5 hash. Cryptographically more difficult to break.
- **Enable**—The privileged mode (enable mode) access password used exclusively by older versions of IOS. Still present today for backwards compatibility. Stored insecurely in the configuration. Disable it if not required.
- **Password**—The line-level password used to protect vty, console, and aux ports.

The following table shows examples of Cisco password and logon-related commands.

Password and Logon-Related Commands	Command Explanation
`rtr8#config terminal`	Enter global configuration mode.
`rtr8(config)#security passwords min-length 10`	Enforces a minimum length for passwords. At least 10 characters are suggested.
`rtr8(config)#enable secret g0bU115#23`	Sets the enable secret password to g0bU115#23.
`rtr8(config)#no enable password`	Disables the use of an enable password.
`rtr8(config)#access-list 5 permit 10.5.5.5`	Defines access list 5. Permits this host to access the vty lines (applied later).
`rtr8(config)#access-list 5 deny any`	Defines access list 5. Denies all other access to the vty lines.
`rtr8(config)#line console 0`	Enters console line configuration mode.
`rtr8(config-line)#login`	Allows login to the console port. Also requires a password to be set.
`rtr8(config-line)#password %%st5St635`	Sets the password for logging onto the console port to %%st5St635.
`rtr8(config-line)#line vty 0 4`	Enters vty line configuration mode for vty lines 0 through 4.
`rtr8(config-line)#login`	Allows login to the vty lines. Also requires a password to be set.
`rtr8(config-line)#password dR3gerM31ster`	Sets the password for logging onto the vty lines to dR3gerM31ster.
`rtr8(config-line)#access-class 5 in`	Applies access list 5 for inbound vty connections.
`rtr8(config-line)#transport input ssh`	Limits inbound vty line connections to SSH. Telnet is now disabled because it is not specified.

Password and Logon-Related Commands	Command Explanation
`rtr8(config-line)#exec-timeout 4 30`	Terminates idle vty sessions after 4 minutes and 30 seconds.
`rtr8(config-line)#line aux 0`	Enter aux line configuration.
`rtr8(config-line)#login`	Allows login to the aux line. Also requires a password to be set.
`rtr8(config-line)#password al!T3ab3rRy!`	Sets the password for logging onto the aux port to al!T3ab3rRy!.
`rtr8(config-line)#no exec`	Prevents authenticated users from getting a user EXEC shell after logging on.
`rtr8(config-line)#exit`	Exits line configuration mode.
`rtr8(config)#no service password-recovery`	Disables the capability to enter ROM monitor mode. Typically done for password recovery operations.
`rtr8(config)#service password-encryption`	Encrypts passwords within the configuration. **password 7** refers to Vigenere cipher encrypted passwords and are considered cryptographically weak. **password 5** refers to MD5 encrypted passwords and are considered to be stronger than Vigenere.
`rtr8(config)#username hqadmin secret 0 This1sThePa55word`	Adds an entry to the local security database. Defines the username **hqadmin** and a secret password that is encrypted in the configuration with MD5.
`rtr8(config)#username hqadmin privilege 15`	Assigns privilege level 15 to **hqadmin** user. There are 16 levels of access (0–15, defining most to least restrictive respectively) that grant users system privileges. Custom privilege levels that define permitted commands can be customized and tied to a logon account. Default levels are 1 (EXEC) and 15 (privileged EXEC).
`rtr8(config)#security authentication failure rate 12 log`	Configures the number of allowable unsuccessful login attempts before a 15-second delay is introduced. Logs the authentication failure to syslog.
`rtr8(config)#banner motd %`	Defines a system banner and a delimiting character (%). Other banner types: exec, incoming, login, slip-ppp. Craft banners to meet an organization's legal requirements. Always use banners to warn those about to log on that they must have authorization and that unauthorized use is prohibited.
Notice: Unauthorized access to this system is prohibited!! %	Sample banner text with second delimiting character (%) to denote the banner end.
`rtr8(config)#`	Return to configuration mode command line.

Configuring AAA for Cisco Routers

AAA ("triple A") is a set of security services used by administrators requiring remote admin-istrative access to network devices (TTY, vty, AUX, and console ports and HTTP-based access) and user verification to network resources (802.1X wired and wireless network access, dialup, VPN access). AAA defines who can access the system, the authorization users have after the system has approved their logon, and an auditable accounting trail of their activities while they were connected.

The AAA acronym stands for:

- **Authentication**—Who are you? Prove your identity.

- **Authorization**—With what resources are you allowed to interact?

- **Accounting**—When logged in, what did you do?

AAA implementation on networking devices occurs in three ways:

- A self-contained AAA local security database containing usernames and passwords directly on the device (see the following figure). Targeted for networks with a small num-ber of users.

Router with Local
AAA Database

- A Cisco Secure Access Control Server (ACS) server. An external AAA server installed onto a Windows server system that scales well.

- Cisco Secure ACS Solutions Engine. A dedicated external AAA server platform that scales as illustrated in the following figure.

AAA is configured on Cisco "clients" that are network devices, such as routers, switches, wireless access points, PIX security appliances, and VPN 3000 concentrators. Clients can reference their own security database or communicate with a central AAA server. Using either the TACACS+ or RADIUS protocol, the client sends authentication requests to its AAA server. The AAA server verifies the username and password against its databases and replies to the device client with a success or failure response. When the user authenticates successfully, the AAA server indicates this with one or more authorization attributes to the client. Additionally, the AAA server can send session attributes to the client to provide additional security and control of privileges such as an ACL or IP addressing information. Device clients can be configured to direct all end-user activities to its AAA server.

Authentication methods in order of ascending complexity are:

Step 1 No username or password.

Step 2 Username and static password.

Step 3 Username and aging password. Password must be reset periodically.

Step 4 One Time Password (OTP)—A password can be used only one time. By the time an attacker intercepts it, it has expired. S/KEY is an OTP technology that uses MD4 and MD5 hashed passwords.

Step 5 Token cards and soft tokens. Based on something you have (token card or soft token) and something you know, such as a personal identification number (PIN). Token authentication is two-factor authentication that relies on a token server that communicates with the CSACS. Token solutions are time-based or challenge response-based.

Remote administrative access to vty, AUX, and console ports is known as character mode access. Remote network access by users is known as packet mode access.

The following table is a set of example AAA authentication commands.

AAA Authentication Commands	Command Explanation
`rtr4#config terminal`	Enters global configuration mode.
`rtr4(config)#aaa new-model`	Enables the AAA access control model for the device.
`rtr4(config)#username thelma secret 0 djj$&&S1wQ privilege 15`	Creates a local user with the highest privilege level.
`rtr4(config)#aaa authentication login default group tacacs local enable`	Defines the default authentication method used by all interfaces and the user database used for login checking. For all interfaces, use the TACACS+ server by default. If this fails, use the local user database. If this fails, use the enable secret password.
`rtr4(config)#aaa authentication enable default group radius enable none`	Specifies a method for checking privileged command line access. This example checks radius; then uses the enable secret if radius is not available; then grants access without authentication if enable is not set.
`rtr4(config)#aaa authentication login console-auth local`	Defines an authentication method called **console-auth** that uses the local security database.
`rtr4(config)#line con 0`	Switches to line console 0 configuration.
`rtr4(config-line)#login authentication console-auth`	Defines console authentication as using the **console-auth** method previously defined. Overrides the **default** authentication method.
`rtr4(config-line)#exit`	Leaves the line configuration mode.
`rtr4(config)#aaa authentication ppp t1-in local none`	Defines the **t1-in** authentication method for ppp connections as using the local security database. Other methods include group radius, group tacacs+, none, and so on.
`rtr4(config)#interface serial0`	Enters interface configuration mode.
`rtr4(config-if)#ppp authentication chap t1-in`	Uses the **t1-in** list for PPP CHAP authentication.

The following table is a set of example AAA authorization and accounting commands.

AAA Authorization & Accounting Commands	Command Explanation
`rtr7(config)#aaa authorization exec default group radius if-authenticated`	If properly authenticated by Radius, authorizes the user a privileged EXEC shell.
`rtr7(config)#aaa authorization commands 15 default group radius`	Authorizes users at this privilege level access to all commands by default.
`rtr7(config)#aaa accounting exec start-stop group radius`	Records both start and stop times for privileged EXEC shell sessions.
`rtr7(config)#aaa accounting commands 15 default stop-only group radius`	Records the commands processed in the privilege EXEC shell by users at the specified privilege level. Sends a **stop** accounting notice at the end of the requested user process.

debug commands assist in troubleshooting AAA configuration problems. Turn on **debug** for a subset of router processes and the associate messages will log to the destination of choice as long as the destination specifies the event level **debug**.

AAA Authorization and Accounting Commands	Command Explanation
router#**debug aaa authentication**	Authentication troubleshooting.
router#**debug aaa authorization**	Authorization troubleshooting.
router#**debug aaa accounting**	Accounting troubleshooting.
router#**undebug all**	All possible debugging turns off.

Cisco Secure ACS for Windows Server

Cisco Secure ACS (CSACS) AAA servers are centralized systems that run on the Windows platform. CSACS enables centralized control of credential information, access policies, and activity logging information, so that each device does not require its own security database. The following are uses for CSACS:

- Network administrator access authentication to network devices
- User access authentication to network devices:
  - User access to the wired network (802.1X authentication to switches)
  - User access to the wireless network (802.1X authentication to wireless access points)
  - Firewall
  - Dialup
  - VPN
  - VoIP
- Authorization privilege enforcement
- Accounting logging

CSACS-enabled systems have three components:

- **Client**—The device that sends requests to the CSACS. For example, a router or switch.
- **Server**—The CSACS server itself.
- **User Accounts Database**—The list of users, passwords, and permissions contained within the CSACS or on an external server to which the CSACS makes queries (ODBC, LDAP, NDS, Windows SAM, Windows AD, and others).

The following table compares CSACSs use of TACACS+ and RADIUS AAA protocols:

Point of Comparison	TACACS+	RADIUS
Intended Purpose	Device management (router, switch, WAP). Cisco proprietary.	User access control (802.1x authentication, IOS firewall authentication proxy). Industry standard.
Transport Protocol	TCP—Connection-oriented.	UDP—Connectionless.

continues

Point of Comparison	TACACS+	RADIUS
Encryption	Full packet encryption between the client device and AAA server.	Encrypts the shared secret password between the client device and AAA server.
AAA Architecture	Separate control of each service: authentication, authorization, and accounting.	Authentication and authorization combined as one service.

CSACS-supported authentication mechanisms include:

- ASCII
- Password Authentication Protocol (PAP)
- Challenge Handshake Authentication Protocol (CHAP)
- Microsoft Challenge-Handshake Authentication Protocol (MS-CHAP)
- Appletalk Remote Access Protocol (ARAP)
- Cisco Lightweight Extensible Authentication Protocol (LEAP)
- Advanced authentication with Extensible Authentication Protocol (EAP)—PEAP, EAP-TLS, EAP-FAST, and others

CSACS authorization features consist of the following:

- Authorization by user or group
- Access profiles built upon security level, time, and service
- Failed access-attempt account suspension
- Maximum concurrent sessions by user or group
- Usage quotas

CSACS accounting features consist of the following:

- CSV or ODBC log recording
- Session start and stop times
- Client messages by username, caller ID, and duration

When used in conjunction with router (or other network device) administration, CSACS provides these features:

- Authentication by user, group, or network device group
- Command authorization by user, group, or network device group
- Commands entered by accounting history

Configuring Basic Services on a CSACS

A web browser interface manages CSACS either directly on the local host or over a network. The basic steps to configure a CSACS are:

Step 1   Connect to the CSACS via a supported web browser.

Step 2   For security reasons, create an administrator username and assign a password.

Step 3   Configure the CSACS link to external user databases if the internal CSACS user database will not be used.

Step 4   Configure the CSACS user interface to display the desired components.

Step 5   Configure CSACS system parameters (logging, certificates, IP pools, database backup, and other components).

NOTE   The previous steps are a condensed list of CSACS configuration activities.

Disabling Unused Cisco Router Network Services and Interfaces

By default, Cisco routers enable certain insecure services and settings often for the purpose of supporting legacy environments. If the mode of these settings has no bearing on the environment, they should be hardened accordingly. Note that some versions of IOS have these various settings in a default secure mode.

From **config terminal**, consider the global security commands described in the table that follows if they are not critical to operations.

Feature	Description	Recommended Action	IOS Command
Bootp service	Bootp allows the router to act as an IOS image server for other routers booting up.	Disable.	**no ip bootp server**
Cisco Discovery Protocol (CDP)	Proprietary layer 2 device discovery protocol global toggle.	If CDP is not needed, disable it globally.	**no cdp run**
Finger service	A *nix user lookup service allowing the remote listing of users.	Unauthorized persons do not need to know this, disable it.	**no ip finger** **no service finger**
HTTP service	Web-based administrative router access.	Disable if not used. If required, use via out-of-band channels and secure access with ACLs. Use secure HTTP if offered by IOS.	**no ip http server** **ip http authentication local** **ip http authentication aaa**
Nagle service	A traffic congestion control algorithm for Telnet to reduce number of packets sent during sessions.	Enable Nagle.	**service nagle**

continues

Feature	Description	Recommended Action	IOS Command
PAD service	X.25 packet assembly/ disassembly (PAD) service.	Disable.	**no service pad**
TCP and UDP small services	Standard TCP network services: echo, daytime, chargen. Standard UDP network services: echo, discard.	A legacy feature that attackers exploit.	**no service tcp-small-servers no service udp-small-servers**
TCP Keepalive service	Router tests for orphaned Telnet and SSH sessions.	Enable.	**service tcp-keepalives-in service tcp-keepalives-out**
Configuration automatic load	Upon boot up, router will attempt loading IOS from a network bootp server.	Disable.	**no service config no boot network**
Domain Name Service	Routers can perform DNS name resolution for host names in the configuration.	Generally disable a router's capability to be a DNS client.	**no ip domain-lookup no ip name-server**
TFTP server	Router acts as a TFTP server.	Disable to prevent unauthorized reading and writing.	**no tftp-server flash:**
FTP server	Router acts as an FTP server.	Disable to prevent unauthorized reading and writing.	**no ftp-server enable no ftp-server write-enable**
Identification (auth) protocol	Allows any host to ask the router who it is. Used in reconnaissance.	Disable.	**no ip identd**
IP source routing	An IP feature allowing packets with a predefined route that overrides local routes.	Disable.	**no ip source-route**
Gratuitous Address Resolution Protocols (ARPs)	Ensures that the router will not generate gratuitous ARP messages.	Disable.	**no ip gratuitous-arps**
SNMP	SNMP enables remote set and query of configuration information.	Disable if not used. Otherwise use complex community strings and restrict access with ACLs.	**no snmp-server snmp-server community c0MplExPasSword ro {acl#}** no snmp-server community public rw no snmp-server enable traps**

Consider the security related interface configuration commands in the following table:

Feature	Description	Recommended Action	IOS Command
Shutdown unused interfaces	Shutdown unused interfaces to prevent unwanted use.	Apply to all unused interfaces.	**shutdown**
Cisco Discovery Protocol (CDP)	Proprietary Layer 2 device discovery protocol per interface CDP toggle.	Disable CDP on interfaces that connect to untrusted networks.	**no cdp enable**
IP-directed broadcast	Potential DoS activity that sends broadcasts to all hosts on a network.	Disable.	**no ip directed-broadcast**
IP mask reply	ICMP mask replies can echo the network mask in reconnaissance activities.	Disable on all interfaces.	**no ip mask-reply**
IP redirects	An attacker can use an ICMP redirect to modify a local routing table.	Disable on all interfaces.	**no ip redirect**
IP unreachable notifications	ICMP unreachables can notify senders of incorrect IP addresses in reconnaissance activities.	Disable on all interfaces.	**no ip unreachable**
NTP	A router can act as a time server or client. Use to synchronize log time entries with other devices.	Disable on all interfaces except the ones that communicate with authorized NTP systems. When using NTP, use authentication and ACLs that specify trusted hosts.	**ntp disable**
Proxy ARP interface command	Proxy ARP is the technique in which one host, usually a router, answers ARP requests intended for another machine. By "faking" its identity, the router accepts responsibility for routing packets to the "real" destination. Proxy ARP can help machines on a subnet reach remote subnets without configuring routing or a default gateway. This might not be desirable.	Disable on all interfaces.	**no ip proxy-arp**
Digital Equipment Corporation Maintenance Operation Protocol (DEC MOP) service	Digital Equipment Corporation Maintenance Operation Protocol	Disable.	**no mop enable**

Mitigating Threats and Attacks with ACLs

Use IP access lists to limit which hosts can interact with a device and the services it offers. ACLs are applied inbound or outbound on interfaces and vty lines and sequentially evaluate traffic as it leaves or enters the interface. Types of ACLs include:

- Standard ACL—Numbered from 1–99 and 1300–1999, these ACLs permit or deny based on the source address only. Example:

```
access-list 2 permit host 209.165.200.225
access-list 2 deny any
access-list 3 deny any
```

- Extended Numbered ACL—Numbered from 100–199 and 2000–2699, these IP ACLs permit or deny based on source and destination IP addresses, layer 4 protocols (ICMP, TCP, UDP, EIGRP, ESP, and others), and ports. For example:

```
access-list 150 permit tcp host 209.165.200.225 10.5.5.0 0.0.0.255 eq 22
access-list 150 permit udp host 209.165.200.226 10.5.5.0 0.0.0.255 eq 500
access-list 150 permit esp host 209.165.200.226 10.5.5.0 0.0.0.255
access-list 150 permit icmp host 209.165.200.225 10.5.5.0 0.0.0.255 echo-
reply
access-list 150 deny ip any any
```

- Extended Named ACL—Similar to numbered ACLs, but use names as identifiers. Note that the named ACL below is identical to the previous bullet's numbered ACL but that the syntax is slightly different. For example:

```
ip access-list extended production-inbound-acl
 permit tcp host 209.165.200.225 10.5.5.0 0.0.0.255 eq 22
 permit udp host 209.165.200.226 10.5.5.0 0.0.0.255 eq 500
 permit esp host 209.165.200.226 10.5.5.0 0.0.0.255
 permit icmp host 209.165.200.225 10.5.5.0 0.0.0.255 echo-reply
 deny ip any any
```

Enhanced ACLs include:

- **Dynamic**—"Lock-and-key" ACLs creating temporary openings in response to valid user authentication

- **Time-based**—Openings created during specified time slots

- **Reflexive**—ACLs that create dynamic entries for IP traffic on one interface of the router based upon sessions originating from a different interface of the router

- **Context-based access control (CBAC)**—Stateful ACL processes that improve upon reflexive ACL technology by examining upper layer IP information

Apply defined ACLs to an interface for filtered evaluation to occur. Each router interface can have one inbound ACL and one outbound ACL. Inbound ACLs evaluate traffic coming into an interface sequentially line by line. Outbound ACLs evaluate traffic leaving an interface sequentially line by line. Outbound ACLs do not evaluate traffic originating from the router but instead evaluate traffic that comes from some other segment through the router and out.

If the router IOS revision supports it, the **access-list compiled** command (Turbo ACL) can decrease sequential ACL lookup time by compiling them into more efficient lookup tables.

Command	Explanation
`rtr2(config)#interface s0`	Switch to Serial 0 interface configuration mode.
`rtr2(config-if)#ip access-group 150 in`	Apply access list 150 to filter inbound traffic.
`rtr2(config-if)#ip access-group 162 out`	Apply access list 162 to filter outbound traffic.

To secure these access portals, apply ACLs to vtys.

Command	Explanation
`rtr2(config)#line vty 0 4`	Enter line configuration mode for vty lines 0–4 (routers can have more than these five). Lines are most often used for SSH and Telnet access to routers.
`rtr2(config-line)#access-class 2 in`	Apply access list 2 for inbound traffic.
`rtr2(config-line)#access-class 3 out`	Apply access list 3 for outbound traffic. In this example, a user with an SSH or Telnet session to the device cannot establish another outbound SSH or Telnet to another host.

Other administrative services, such as SNMP and HTTP, should use access lists to permit a limited set of hosts access to the device.

Command	Explanation
`rtr2(config)#access-list 5 permit host 10.1.230.4`	Creates the ACL defining a central management host as permitted. All others hosts are implicitly denied.
`rtr2(config)#snmp-server community C0mplexpas5word ro 5`	Defines the read-only (ro) SNMP string and specify that ACL 5 should be used to limit access to the router's SNMP processes.
`rtr2(config)#ip http access-class 5`	Specifies that ACL 5 hosts can interact with the router's HTTP process.
`rtr2(config)#access-list 60 permit 10.2.2.0 0.0.0.255`	Defines ACL 60 for inbound RIP updates. Only routes that match a 10.2.2.xxx format are put in the routing table.
`rtr2(config)#router rip 1`	Enters the RIP routing process # 1.
`rtr2(config-router)# distribute-list 60 in`	Connects ACL 60 to the RIP process.

Good security practices that use ACLs include the following:

- Using RFC 1918 filtering to prevent non-Internet-routable reserved addresses within egress or ingress Internet traffic:
  - 10.0.0.0 /8 (10.0.0.0 through 10.255.255.255)
  - 172.16.0.0 /12 (172.16.0.0 through 172.31.255.255)
  - 192.168.0.0 /16 (192.168.0.0 through 192.168.255.255)

- Using RFC 2827 antispoofing features:
  - Prevents ingress traffic from the ISP destined for networks you do not control.
  - Prevents ingress traffic from the ISP sourced with IP addresses of your internal network.
  - Prevents egress traffic to your ISP sourced with addresses of networks you do not control internally.
- Filtering other network ranges (bogon networks) that you should not route across network boundaries, such as localhost, multicast, and test network ranges.
- Filtering ports and protocols (especially insecure ones) that need never cross a network boundary. For example:
  - TFTP
  - SNMP
  - Telnet
- Filtering ingress ICMP messages used against your network, such as echo, redirect, and mask-request. To keep the network running properly, never filter certain types of egress ICMP message types including destination unreachable, time-exceeded, parameter-problem, and packet-too-big, Maximum Transmission Unit (MTU) path discovery.
- Blocking UDP-based traceroute communication across untrusted network boundaries.
- Avoiding DDoS attacks by filtering and logging hits on these well known attacks including Trin00, Stacheldraht, Trinityv3, SubSeven, and others.

Implementing Secure Management and Reporting

The following are two types of networks that manage routers and other network devices:

- In-Band
  - Management traffic flows with regular user traffic.
  - Management traffic should be encrypted with IPSec, SSH, or HTTPS when possible.
- Out-of-Band (OOB)
  - Management traffic flows on a dedicated, protected network different from the user network.
  - Should be firewalled from the in-band network and routing onto and off of should be tightly controlled.
  - Should use different network address space from the in-band network.
  - Communication leaving the OOB should use Network Address Translation (NAT).
  - OOB layer 2 networks should use private VLANs to protect hosts on the same segment from each other.
  - Hosts should use OTP or other advanced authentication.
  - Use SNMP version 3 where possible.

The following table describes the major protocols, both secure and insecure, commonly used to manage network-connected devices. Regardless of the management protocols in use, network-accessible devices should use access control lists (ACLs) whenever possible to selectively specify the permitted remote device source addresses. Note that not all options are available for all IOS revisions.

Protocol Name	Secure?	Used For	Standard Port and Protocol	Description	Notes
SSH	Yes	Command-line configuration management.	22/tcp	Authenticated and encrypted remote access to devices.	Used as a secure substitute to Telnet.
Telnet	No	Command-line configuration management.	23/tcp	Cleartext remote access to devices.	Passwords and data can be intercepted with a network sniffer.
HTTPS (SSL)	Yes	GUI-based configuration management via the SDM.	443/tcp	Authenticated and encrypted remote access to devices.	Used as a secure substitute to HTTP.
HTTP	No	GUI-based configuration management via the SDM.	80/tcp	Cleartext web protocol.	Passwords and data can be intercepted with a network sniffer.
SCP (Secure Copy)	Yes	Data transfer.	22/tcp	Tunneled in SSH.	Used as a secure substitute to TFTP.
TFTP	No	Data transfer.	69/udp and >1023/udp	Cleartext data transfer.	Common way to upload or download images and configurations.
SNMP version 1 and 2c	No	Device management.	161/udp, 162/udp	Read-only and read-write device access and management.	Use complex, nondefault community strings.
SNMP version 3	Yes	Device management.	161/udp, 162/udp	Read-only and read-write device access and management with added security.	Helps prevent exposure to interception by using encryption.

SSH is a security protocol that has many uses including tunneling insecure protocols within SSH sessions. As a command-line application, SSH is a secure alternative to Telnet. To enable SSH on a router, the IOS revision must have the cryptographic components to support it (look for "k8" or "k9" in the IOS filename). The table that follows lists SSH-related commands.

SSH-related Command	Command Explanation
rtr7(config)#ip domain-name mydomain.com	Define your domain name.
rtr7(config)#crypto key generate rsa general-keys modulus 1024	Generate a crypto keypair. Note that several options exist for generating keys. This is one example.
rtr7(config)#ip ssh authentication-retries 4	Number of allowable failed logon attempts.
rtr7(config)#ip ssh time-out 120	Time in seconds the router will wait for communications from an SSH client before disconnecting.
rtr7(config)#line vty 0 4 rtr7(config-line)#transport input ssh	Turns on the capability to use SSH for vty access and implicitly disables Telnet because it is not specified within the command.

Use event logging to record device events as they occur. Routers can send logging output to one or more configured destinations including:

- Serial console port
- Terminal line (vty) sessions
- Memory buffer
- SNMP management host
- Syslog server

Logging events are tagged with a number denoting their level of seriousness. Whereas level 6 is an "informational" message, level 1 "alerts" are highly severe and require immediate attention. The graphic that follows is a review of logging levels and logging destination commands. Disable any logging destination by preceding the command with **no**.

Regardless of the level at which you log, the messages to be logged will include those at the specified level plus all levels more severe (see the following figure). For example, when logging at level 6 (informational), levels 6–0 are logged.

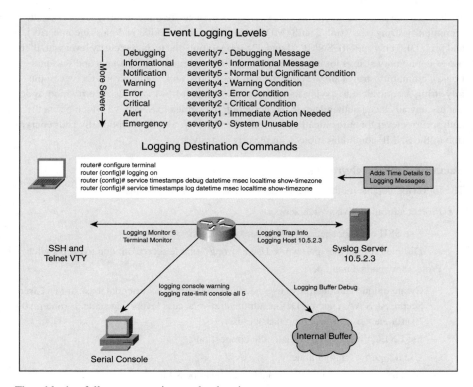

The table that follows summarizes syslog logging setup:

Syslog Commands	Command Explanation
r2(config)#**logging on**	Turns logging on.
r2(config)#**logging 10.5.2.3**	Defines the syslog server to receive logs.
r2(config)#**logging trap info**	Sets the logging level for messages sent to the syslog server.
r2(config)#**logging source-interface e0**	Defines the IP address that appears in the syslog messages stored on the syslog server.
r2#**show logging**	Shows the status of all logging functions.

SNMP is part of the TCP/IP protocol suite and is designed for the management of network devices. SNMP has three security models: v1, v2c, and v3. SNMP v3 offers a greater degree of security than v1 and v2c because of its capability to perform improved authentication, SNMP message integrity, and message encryption.

SNMP v1 and v2c use the concept of managers and agents. Managers are centralized workstations deployed for the purpose of managing SNMP agents on network devices by using gets (reading configuration and status information) and sets (writing new parameters to configuration). SNMP v3 uses the concept of engines and applications combined into SNMP entities.

Within each SNMP security model (v1, v2c, and v3), there are three security levels: noauth (community string passwords), auth (MD5 or SHA-1 authentication and message integrity), and priv (DES encryption). SNMP v1 and v2c support only the noauth security level with their use of community strings for access to read-only (ro) and read-write (rw) get and set functions. Community strings are the equivalent to passwords, and having a router's rw community string is equivalent to having its enable password. SNMP v1 and v2c security models do not use any advanced authentication or encryption in contrast to SNMP v3 which offers the auth security level for authentication and message integrity. SNMP v3 optionally adds encryption of the SNMP communications with the priv security level.

Securing Catalyst Switches

The following bullets are the broad issues when securing layer 2 switches:

- Protect administrative switch access:
  - Use SSH or other secure management protocols.
  - Disable the "enable" password. Use a strong "enable secret" unique to each switch.
- Protect the management port:
  - Create unique administrative user accounts in the local security database or in a Cisco Secure ACS AAA server. Define administrative access levels (the same as routers, 0–15) for each user. Use strong passwords.
  - Set EXEC timeout to terminate idle connections.
  - Use a logon warning banner.
  - Manage switches via OOB channels whenever possible.
  - Use a strong and unique password on every switch.
- Disable unused services.
- Protect access to SNMP and HTTP services with ACLs.

The following are some high-level guidelines for improving access port and trunk port security:

- Do not assign any port to VLAN 1, the default "management" segment.
- Assign all unused ports to an unused VLAN pruned from all active trunks.
- Shut down all unused ports.
- Be careful when assigning **portfast** status to a port, otherwise undesirable topology loops might occur.
- For trunks, assign dedicated VLAN numbers as the native VLAN number. Otherwise, if a trunk and a VLAN segment share the same number, hosts on the segment can cross the trunk without 802.1q tagging. This might not be desirable.
- For trunks, allow only the VLANs that must traverse the trunk. Prune all other VLANs.

Mitigating Layer 2 Attacks

In contrast to routers that operate at layer 3, switches are layer 2 devices that have one or more configured broadcast networks individually known as VLANs. VLANs are independent network segments that are unaware of each other's existence even when they are within the same switch. Hosts on separate VLANs can communicate only with each other if a layer 3 routing process can route them. Layer 2 switches use Ethernet MAC addresses for communication. Switches learn the MAC address of each connected device and populate its Content Address Memory (CAM) table. When the switch needs to send a frame to MAC "Y," it refers to its CAM table. If it finds an entry for MAC Y, it also finds its port and forwards the frame. If it does not find Y's MAC, it will not know its port and the switch floods the frame out all ports. Hosts that are not Y discard the frame, but when Y receives it, it replies to the original sender. The switch notes this and updates its CAM table with an entry marking Y's MAC and port for future reference. This precludes the need for future frame flooding to Y. An attacker can compromise these normal switch functions unless appropriate Layer 2 safeguards are put in place.

CAM tables support a finite number of entries. If an attacker uses a technique (for example, the macof attack utility) designed to overload the CAM table, the switch can no longer accept new entries; thus the switch floods all new frames out all ports and acts like a hub. Then the attacker can analyze all VLAN unicast conversations. To mitigate this condition, use the commands in the following table.

Port Security Commands	Command Explanation
r7(config-if)#**switchport port-security**	Enables port security features.
r7(config-if)# **switchport port-security mac-address** *mac_address*	Specifies an allowed MAC address for the interface.
r7(config-if)#**switchport port-security maximum 2**	Sets max number of MAC addresses allowed on switch port preventing an attacker from overloading the CAM table. This example hardcodes 1 MAC and allows for 1 dynamic.
r7(config-if)#**switchport port-security aging time 5**	Deletes the dynamically learned address after five minutes of inactivity. This also prevents attacking devices from constantly switching its MAC address by throttling the change interval.
r7(config-if)#**switchport port-security violation restrict**	Sends an error trap when maximum MAC count exceeded or when an unknown MAC is encountered.

MAC spoofing occurs when attackers misuse ARP functions to steer traffic usually destined for the target (and proper) host to their host. Attackers accomplish this with gratuitous ARPs (gARPs) that are unsolicited ARP broadcasts containing the IP address of the target host and the attacker's MAC address. The gARP causes all receiving hosts to incorrectly update their ARP table with an entry that pairs the target's IP address with the attacker's MAC address. Similarly the switch incorrectly updates its CAM table, and when any host needs to send a packet to the target's IP, the switch forwards the packet to the attacker. This causes a man-in-the-middle condition.

To mitigate these conditions, use the commands listed and described in the table that follows to hardcode MAC addresses to ports and limit the number of dynamically learned addresses. More advanced configurations, which are not depicted in the examples, also use dynamic ARP inspection and DHCP snooping techniques.

Port Security Commands	Command Explanation
r8(config-if)#**switchport port-security**	Enables port security features.
r8(config-if)#**switchport port-security mac-address** *mac_address*	Hardcodes the connected host's MAC address for the interface to prevent an attacker from claiming a new and different (spoofed) MAC.
r8(config-if)#**switchport port-security maximum 1**	Sets the maximum number of MAC addresses allowed on a switch port preventing an attacker from claiming a new MAC address. The setting of 1 in this example prevents the learning of any new MACs.
r8(config-if)#**switchport port-security violation shutdown**	Port shuts down when maximum MAC count exceeded.

Switchport violation modes include:

- **Protect**—When the maximum MAC count is exceeded, frames are dropped from unknown MACs. The switch does not notify and the port remains operational.

- **Restrict**— When the maximum MAC count is exceeded, frames are dropped from unknown MACs. The switch sends a trap to notify and the port remains operational.

- **Shutdown**— When the maximum MAC count is exceeded, the interface goes into "err-disable" (shutdown) mode, sends a trap, and turns off the port LED.

Types of MAC addresses include:

- **Static secure**—Manually configured MAC addresses on a port. 1–132 possible manual MACs.

- **Dynamic secure**—Dynamically learned but nonpermanent upon switch restart.

- **Sticky secure**—Dynamically learned and becomes part of the startup-config if running-config is saved before switch restart.

An attacker connected to a VLAN on a switch might desire to attack a host residing on another VLAN within the switch. If layer 3 routing is present, the attacker might use this path. If layer 3 routing to the destination VLAN does not exist or effective controls are in place, the attacker might alternatively use a VLAN hopping attack as his vector to the target. The attack system can craft frames with 802.1q tags containing the VLAN ID of the target system's VLAN. By doing so, the frames are received by the switch and then placed into the target VLAN. Likewise, an attack host might try to behave like a switch and negotiate trunking from its interface to the switch. When this trunk is allowed, the attacker can send and receive traffic among VLANs.

The interface-level command, **switchport mode access**, mitigates these exposures by disabling the capability for a port to become a trunk. The default is the dynamic desirable setting that can allow a switchport to become a trunk.

Spanning Tree Protocol (STP) is a layer 2 process that uses special frames called Bridge Protocol Data Units (BPDU) to guard against looped topologies. Connected switches identify one switch as the root bridge and block all other redundant data paths. By attacking the STP, an attacker attempts to pose as a root bridge to intercept frames. Forged BPDU frames can cause switches to begin spanning-tree recalculations. If the attacker has two interfaces connected to the layer 2 network (for example, two wired, two wireless, or a wired and wireless) and successfully becomes the root bridge, the system can be used to forward the network's data while snooping it.

The BPDU filter commands prevent ports from sending or receiving BPDUs either globally or at the interface level.

The BPDU Guard features disable a **portfast** designated port if a BPDU is received requiring manual intervention to re-enable it.

The Root Guard feature is designed to enforce the root bridge connection point in the network. If a device sends a BPDU to try to become the root bridge, Root Guard blocks it. When a device ceases sending BPDUs that might normally make it the root, Root Guard unblocks the port automatically. Root Guard should be enabled on all ports except the one that connects the root bridge.

Cisco commands that mitigate these exposures include the following:

Command	Description
r1(config-if)#**spanning-tree bpdufilter enable**	Prevents a port from sending or receiving bridge protocol data units (BPDUs) that is a mechanism used in spanning tree to elect a root bridge. This can be applied to all interfaces connecting directly to client PCs.
r1(config)#**spanning-tree portfast bpdufilter default**	Enables BPDU filtering on all PortFast-enabled ports and prevents the switch port connected to end stations from sending or receiving BPDUs.
r1(config-if)#**spanning-tree bpduguard enable**	Puts a port in the error-disabled state when it receives a BPDU. Intervention is required to re-enable the port.
r1(config-if)#**spanning-tree guard root**	Root Guard does not allow the port to become a STP root port.

The purpose of private VLANs is to prevent communication among hosts within the same VLAN segment. This is often desirable to prevent one infected host on a segment from attacking and exploiting another host on that same segment. Layer 3 controls, such as filtering and firewalling at the segment's gateway, cannot prevent the host-to-host infection because the hosts will communicate directly and not via the gateway.

Cisco switch platforms and IOS support private VLANs at different granularity levels. At the least granular level, "private VLAN edge" defines access and trunk ports to be either protected or unprotected, has local significance to the switch itself, and communicates only in these ways:

- Unprotected ports can talk to unprotected ports.
- Protected ports can talk to unprotected ports.
- Protected ports cannot talk to protected ports.

At a more granular level, "private VLANs" define the following port types within a layer segment:

- **Promiscuous**—Can communicate with all other ports.

- **Isolated**—Can communicate only with promiscuous ports.

- **Community**—Can communicate only with other fellow community ports and promiscuous ports.

VLAN proxy attacks attempt to circumvent private VLAN controls by altering frame addressing, so that Host A can communicate with Host B via Router 1 even though security policy does not allow direct A to B communication. Attackers craft and send a frame containing their valid source IP and MAC addresses to the destination IP address of the target. Instead of specifying Host B's MAC (policy controls would disallow the flow), they use the MAC address of the local gateway router. The private VLAN controls are unlikely to block access to the gateway router, so the switch forwards the frame to the router because the crafted frame specified the router's MAC. The router receives the frame, sees that the destination IP is Host B, rewrites the frame with the target's valid MAC address, and resends the data to the target.

By using a layer 3 ACL to prevent hosts in a given IP range from sending packets to hosts within that same IP range, the router can drop the crafted frames. Implementation of layer 3 access lists can occur on some Cisco layer 2 switches if it is supported by the IOS version.

```
access-list 101 remark Private VLAN attack
access-list 101 remark Place inbound on gateway port
access-list 101 remark Next line allows clients to talk to a server at .17
 on the same segment
access-list 101 permit ip 10.5.5.0 0.0.0.255 host 10.5.5.17
access-list 101 remark Next line prevents all other intra VLAN communication
access-list 101 deny  ip 10.5.5.0 0.0.0.255 10.5.5.0 0.0.0.255
access-list 101 permit  ip any any
```

IBNS

Identity-Based Network Services (IBNS) technology improves security by allowing users and devices access to a network only if they present valid authentication credentials. By using IBNS, enforcing a policy disallowing end point device access to network resources until it successfully authenticates is possible. After authentication, IBNS can stipulate authorization settings to limit a device's capabilities.

IBNS benefits include:

- Allowing different people to use the same PC and have different capabilities

- Ensuring that users receive only their designated privileges, no matter how they are logged onto the network

- Reporting unauthorized access

IBNS, which operates at layer 2 on both wired and wireless networks, uses 802.1x/EAP, the IEEE standard for port-level strong user authentication, and the following components:

- An end device, for example, Linux server

- An 802.1x-aware switch or wireless access point

- A RADIUS authentication server that supports 802.1x and the chosen authentication (EAP) type

- A user database on the RADIUS server or connected to it (external Windows AD, Novell Directory, and others)

The following mandatory components, all of which must be 802.1x-capable, constitute the parts of the IEEE 802.1x/EAP specification:

- **Supplicant**—The physically or wirelessly connected end device (PC, printer, IP phone) needing network access.

- **Authenticator**—The switch or wireless access point to which the supplicant physically connects (the chokepoint). Acts as the proxy (middle man) for authentication messages flowing between the supplicant and authentication server. Acts as the client to the authentication server.

- **Authentication Server**—The RADIUS server that uses its own user database or an external one to perform the centralized authentication.

The following figure illustrates a generic EAP (IBNS) process and how EAP messages flow during the authentication process.

High-Level EAP Flow

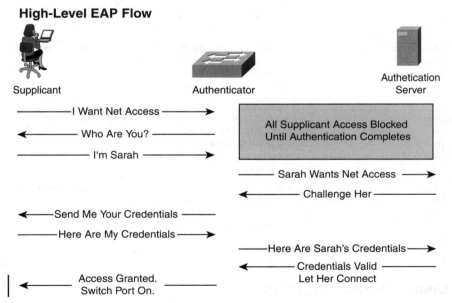

Use 802.1x to secure access to the network in both wired and wireless environments. The following table illustrates the commands related to enabling 802.1x authentication.

Task Step	Description	IOS Command
Step 1—Enable AAA (required)	Global command. Enable AAA.	`aaa new-model`
Step 2—Specify the 802.1x method (required)	Global command. Create an 802.1x authentication method list.	`aaa authentication dot1x {default} method1 [method2...]`
Step 3—Turn on 802.1x (required)	Interface command. Enable 802.1x for each port requiring it.	`dot1x port-control auto`
Step 4—Define the RADIUS server (required)	Global command. Specify the RADIUS server used for 802.1x.	`radius-server host {hostname ¦ ip-address} auth-port port-number key string`
Step 5—Enable periodic client reauthentication (optional)	Enable periodic re-authentication of the client. Disabled by default. 3600 second default if enabled.	`dot1x re-authentication` `dot1x timeout re-authperiod seconds`
Step 6—Define the client quiet period (optional)	Global command. The number of seconds that the switch remains in the quiet state following a failed authentication exchange with the client. Default = 60 seconds.	`dot1x timeout quiet-period seconds`
Step 7—Changing the switch-to-client retransmission time (optional)	The number of seconds that the switch waits for a response to an EAP-request identity frame from the client before resending the request. Default = 30 seconds.	`dot1x timeout tx-period seconds`
Step 8—Setting the switch-to-client frame-retransmission number (optional)	The number of times that the switch sends an EAP-request identity frame to the client before restarting the authentication process. Default = 2.	`dot1x max-req count`
Step 9—Allow multiple hosts on a port as required (optional)	Interface command. Allows multiple hosts (clients) on an 802.1X-authorized port. Only one of the attached hosts needs successfully authorization to grant all hosts network access.	`dot1x multiple-hosts`

Cisco Security Appliances

Cisco Security Appliance Series (PIX 500 Series and ASA 5500 Series devices) represent The Cisco network-based firewall solutions designed for protection of networks from external or internal threats. These systems combine typical firewall features, such as stateful inspection and network address translation with additional services such as VPN, IPS, and flexible access control utilizing AAA services.

Firewall Technologies

Network firewalls are devices that monitor network activity and manage the flow of traffic among different networks by permitting or denying packets based on configured security policies on the device.

Currently, most firewalls use one of the following three architectures:

- **Packet filtering**—Operates at the network or transport layer of the OSI model and uses static packet-header information to enforce access lists permitting or denying traffic into and out of a network. For example, a router configured with simple access lists.

  Packet filtering firewalls provide limited security, are usually inexpensive, and typically perform well. However, they have the following shortcomings:

  — They are easily defeated when someone sends arbitrary or spoofed packets that fit the ACL criteria.

  — They are not effective in blocking fragmented packets designed to bypass the filters.

  — They require increasingly complex ACLs as security policies evolve and are difficult to implement and maintain.

  — They have trouble with protocols and applications utilizing dynamic ports, such as multimedia applications.

- **Proxy server**—Operates at higher layers of the OSI model (typically layers 5–7) and requests connections on behalf of a client between the inside of the firewall and the outside network. By peeking into higher layers of the OSI model, proxy server firewalls provide better protection against network threats. However, the deeper inspection provided by proxy server firewalls requires much greater processing overhead relative to packet filtering firewalls.

  Proxy server firewalls provide much better security than packet filtering firewalls, but they have the following other shortcomings:

  — They are a single point of failure.

  — They are intimately involved with the applications that operate through them, so it is difficult to add support for new services and applications to the firewall.

  — They perform more slowly or require significantly faster hardware.

- **Stateful packet filtering**—Provides improved packet filtering capabilities by maintaining a stateful session flow table that includes the source and destination addresses, port numbers, TCP sequencing information, and additional flags for each TCP or UDP connection associated with that particular session. The firewall uses this information to more intelligently enforce ACLs. For example, it can identify and allow return traffic that is part of an existing session originated from the inside.

  Stateful packet filtering firewalls, which include Cisco security appliances, combine the benefits of packet-filtering firewalls and proxy server firewalls and eliminate their shortcomings.

Cisco Security Appliances

Cisco security appliances consist of the PIX 500 Series and ASA 5500 Series. Both product series are stateful packet-filtering devices with the following features:

- **Stateful packet inspection**—To establish a session, information about the connection must match the information in the table.

- **Proprietary operating system**—Eliminates security vulnerabilities of available general operating systems.

- **Cut-through proxy operation**—A user-based authentication method for both inbound and outbound connections that provides better performance than that of a proxy server.

- **Application-aware inspection**—Inspects packets at layers above the network layer to improve security and protect against application-layer threats.

- **Modular policies**—Allows application of different policies based on specific traffic flows through the firewall.

- **Virtual private networking**—Provides secure and inexpensive connectivity options for site-to-site and remote-access scenarios.

- **Security context (virtual firewalls)**—A single security appliance can be carved into multiple virtual firewalls, each with their own unique set of security policies, interfaces, and administrative domains.

- **High availability (failover)**—Provides device redundancy by allowing one appliance to back up another in an active/active or active/standby configuration.

- **Transparent firewall**—The appliance operates in a bridging mode and does not require introduction of additional networks to implement.

- **Web-based management**—Adaptive Security Device Manager (ASDM) provides browser-based management of Cisco security appliances.

Cisco PIX and ASA Security Appliance Families

The Cisco family of security appliances consist of the PIX 500 Series security appliances, the ASA 5500 Series security appliances, and the PIX Firewall Services Module (FWSM) blades for Catalyst 6500 Series switches and 7600 Series routers.

PIX 500-Series Security Appliances

The PIX 500 Series consists of five models:

- PIX 501

- PIX 506E

- PIX 515E

- PIX 525

- PIX 535

PIX 515E, 525, and 535 models include expansion slots used for additional Fast Ethernet interfaces, Gigabit Ethernet interfaces (PIX 525 and 535 models only), or hardware-based IPSec acceleration cards, such as the VPN Accelerator Plus (VAC+) card (all three models currently ship with a VAC+ card preinstalled). These models also provide high availability capabilities with active/standby and active/active failover functionality (active/active requires PIX Security Appliance release 7.0 software). In addition, a special PIX FWSM blade is available for the Catalyst 6500 Series switches and the 7600 Series routers.

The following table compares the different PIX 500 series models.

Model	Features and Specifications	Appropriate Use
PIX 501	Small desktop unit Two 10/100BASE-T interfaces (includes integrated 10/100 4-port switch). No failover support. Not supported with Cisco PIX Security Appliance release 7.0 software.	All-in-one security and VPN device for remote offices and small-to-medium size networks.
PIX 506E	Small desktop unit. Two 10/100BASE-T physical interfaces. Two VLANs (release 6.3(4) required). No failover support. Not supported with Cisco PIX Security Appliance release 7.0 software.	Remote offices and small-to-medium size networks with minimal hosting.
PIX 515E	1U rack-mount unit. Expansion slots. Up to six physical interfaces (three with a restricted license). Up to 25 VLANs (10 with a restricted license). Up to five security contexts (requires an unrestricted license). Failover support (active/active, active/standby). 2000 IPSec tunnels.	Medium-to-large networks requiring high availability and performance.
PIX 525	2U rack-mount unit. Expansion slots. Up to 10 physical interfaces (six with a restricted license). Up to 100 VLANs (25 with a restricted license). Up to 50 security contexts (requires an unrestricted license). Failover support (active/active, active/standby).	Large- to enterprise-size networks requiring high availability, expandability, and performance.
PIX 535	3U rack-mount unit. Expansion slots on multiple buses. Up to 14 physical interfaces (eight with a restricted license). Up to 150 VLANs (50 with a restricted license). Up to 50 security contexts (requires an unrestricted license). Failover support (active/active, active/standby).	ISP or enterprise networks requiring maximum performance.

continues

Model	Features and Specifications	Appropriate Use
FWSM	Runs in Catalyst 6500 Series switches and 7600 Series routers. 1000 VLANs per module. Up to 100 security contexts (two included, additional contexts require upgraded licenses). Failover support (inter- and intra-chassis). No VPN or IPS functionality included (IPSec is supported for secure device management).	ISP or enterprise networks requiring maximum performance.

ASA 5500 Series Security Appliances

ASA 5500 Series security appliances use the Cisco Adaptive Identification and Mitigation (AIM) architecture and provide multilayered security by combining the functionality of PIX 500 Series firewalls, Cisco 4200 Series intrusion prevention systems, and Cisco VPN 3000 Series concentrators.

A Security Services Module (SSM) can upgrade ASA 5500 Series security appliances. SSM modules provide additional security capabilities without impacting performance utilizing dedicated security coprocessors. The ASA 5500 Series currently consists of three models:

- ASA 5510
- ASA 5520
- ASA 5540

The following table compares the different ASA 5500 series models.

Feature	Cisco ASA 5510	Cisco ASA 5520	Cisco ASA 5540
Form Factor	1U rack-mount unit.	1U rack-mount unit.	1U rack-mount unit.
Integrated Network Ports	3 + 1 Management Port (5 Fast Ethernet with an upgraded license).	4-Gigabit (Gb) Ethernet, 1 Fast Ethernet.	4-Gb Ethernet, 1 Fast Ethernet.
VLANs	Zero (10 with upgraded license).	25	100
Security Contexts	Not supported.	Two (10 with an upgraded license).	Two (50 with an upgraded license).
High Availability	Active/standby with upgraded license.	Active/active and active/standby.	Active/active and active/standby.
System Bus	Multibus architecture.	Multibus architecture.	Multibus architecture.
Appropriate Use	Remote office or SMB security and VPN gateway.	Enterprise and SMB head-end security and VPN gateway.	Enterprise head-end security and VPN gateway.

Security Appliance Licensing

Cisco security appliances can be purchased with different licenses to accommodate varying security needs and budget constraints.

PIX 500 Series security appliances provide the following license options:

- **Unrestricted**—This option provides maximum memory and interfaces (physical and virtual), and it provides security contexts and failover capability.

- **Restricted**—This option provides limited memory and interfaces (physical and virtual). It does not provide security contexts and failover capability.

- **Failover Active/Standby**—This option provides active/standby failover functionality when used with another PIX with an unrestricted license (two PIX devices with unrestricted licenses can also function as an active/standby failover pair).

- **Failover Active/Active**—This option provides active/active failover functionality when used with another PIX with an unrestricted license (two PIX devices with unrestricted licenses can also function as an active/active failover pair).

PIX 501 and 506E security appliances do not support Cisco PIX Security Appliance release 7.0 software, security contexts, or failover functionality. PIX 506E is only available with a single unlimited-user license. PIX 501 can be obtained with licenses for 10-user, 50-user, or unlimited user counts.

In addition to the licenses listed, PIX security appliances also include licensing options for the number of security contexts and VPN encryption strengths. PIX 515E, 525, and 535 appliances with unrestricted licenses support two security contexts and can be licensed to enable additional security contexts up to the supported number for each platform. VPN encryption licenses include:

- **DES**—56-bit DES encryption.

- **3DES/AES**—168-bit triple DES or 128-bit, 192-bit, or 256-bit AES encryption.

Similarly, ASA 5500 Series security appliances can be obtained with different licenses. The following table lists the license options for ASA 5500 Series security appliances.

Feature	ASA 5510 Licenses		ASA 5520 Licenses		ASA 5540 Licenses		
	Base	Security +	Base	VPN +	Base	VPN +	VPN Premium
Interfaces	3 Fast Ethernet	5 Fast Ethernet	4-gb Ethernet, 1 Fast Ethernet	4-Gb Ethernet, 1 Fast Ethernet	4-Gb Ethernet, 1 Fast Ethernet	4-Gb Ethernet, 1 Fast Ethernet	4-Gb Ethernet, 1 Fast Ethernet
VLANs	Zero	10	25	25	100	100	100
IPSec VPN Peers	50	150	300	750	500	2,000	5,000
Active/ Standby Failover	N/A	Yes	Yes	Yes	Yes	Yes	Yes
Active/ Active Failover	N/A	N/A	Yes	Yes	Yes	Yes	Yes

continues

Feature	ASA 5510 Licenses		ASA 5520 Licenses		ASA 5540 Licenses		
GTP/GPRS Inspection	N/A	N/A	With GTP license	With GTP license	With GTP license	With GTP license	With GTP license
Security Contexts	N/A	N/A	Two (up to 10 with additional contexts licenses)	Two (up to 10 with additional contexts licenses)	Two (up to 50 with additional contexts licenses)	Two (up to 50 with additional contexts licenses)	Two (up to 50 with additional contexts licenses)

Configuring Cisco Security Appliances from the Command-Line Interface

Cisco security appliances use a command-line interface (CLI) based on and similar to the Cisco IOS and operate in one of four administrative access modes:

- **Unprivileged mode**—This mode is available when you first access the security appliance via Telnet, SSH, or the console (also referred to as the User mode). Only restricted settings are viewable in this mode and the prompt displays a > character.

- **Privileged mode**—Issuing the **enable** command from the unprivileged mode and providing the appropriate enable password accesses this mode. This mode displays a # prompt and provides access to all privileged and unprivileged commands.

- **Configuration mode**— Issuing the **configure terminal** command from while in privileged mode accesses this mode. The mode displays a **(config)#** prompt (or other appropriate subcommand prompt) and provides access to security appliance configuration commands.

- **Monitor mode**— Disrupting the security appliances normal flash boot sequence accesses this mode; troubleshooting or image updates via TFTP are its primary uses.

Enter a question mark (**?**) from the CLI prompt to access the online help information and display all available commands (a list of available commands is different based on the current access mode). Enter a question mark after a command to display the next required syntax element for that command. For example, type **access-list ?** from the configuration mode to determine the next required input for the **access-list** command:

```
fw(config)# access-list ?
configure mode commands/options:
 WORD < 241 char Access list identifier
 alert-interval  Specify the alert interval
                 for generating syslog
                 message
                 106001 which alerts that
                 the system has reached a
                 deny
                 flow maximum. If not
                 specified, the default
                 value is 300 sec
 deny-flow-max  Specify the maximum number
                 of concurrent deny flows
                 that can
```

```
                  be created. If not
                  specified, the default
                  value is 4096
```

Use the **help** command to display online help information about available commands and their specific syntax. It is necessary to issue the **help** command followed by the command of the desired help information. For example:

```
fw(config)# help access-list
USAGE:
Extended access list:
    Use this to configure policy for IP traffic through the firewall
[no] access-list <id> [line <line_num>] [extended] {deny ¦ permit}
{<protocol> ¦ object-group <protocol_obj_grp_id>} {host <sip> ¦ <sip>
<smask> ¦ object-group <network_obj_grp_id>} [el]
[output truncated]
```

Security Appliance CLI Configuration

The Cisco security appliances provide an optional interactive initial boot setup for non-configured devices (factory setting) and allow CLI configuration of additional settings. Discussion of the use of a GUI configuration tool appears later in this section.

Key configuration tasks for Cisco security appliances include the following:

- Preconfigure with interactive initial boot setup
- Set console timeout
- Set banner
- View and save configuration
- Erase configuration (if required)
- Reload configuration from Flash memory
- Back up and restore configuration
- Set TFTP parameters
- Configure name-to-IP address maps

Initial Interactive Boot Setup

When a nonconfigured security appliance boots up for the first time, it displays a series of interactive prompts to configure basic settings on the appliance. Using the **setup** command also begins this interactive configuration process. After initiation, terminate this process by answering **no** to the first question. The following example illustrates a typical interactive setup sequence:

```
Pre-configure Firewall now through interactive prompts [yes]? yes
Firewall Mode [Routed]: routed
Enable password [<use current password>]: <Enter>
Allow password recovery [yes]? yes
Clock (UTC):
 Year [2005]: <Enter>
 Month [Aug]: <Enter>
 Day [10]: <Enter>
 Time [18:12:45]: <Enter>
```

```
Inside IP address: 10.1.1.1
Inside network mask: 255.255.255.0
Host name: fw
Domain name: cisco.com
IP address of host running Device Manager: 10.1.1.12

The following configuration will be used:
Enable password: <current password>
Allow password recovery: yes
Clock (UTC): 18:12:45 Aug 11 2005
Firewall Mode: Routed
Inside IP address: 10.1.1.1
Inside network mask: 255.255.255.0
Host name: fw
Domain name: cisco.com
IP address of host running Device Manager: 10.1.1.12

Use this configuration and write to flash? yes
INFO: Security level for "inside" set to 100 by default.
```

The primary design of the initial boot setup is to preconfigure the security appliance for further configuration using the ASDM. The security appliance requires this preconfiguration before ASDM can connect to it.

Console Timeout Configuration

By default, security appliance console sessions do not time out. For increased security, configure the appliance to terminate an inactive consoled session after a specified timeout period expires using the **console timeout** command. For example, to terminate console sessions after 15 minutes of inactivity, use the following command:

```
fw(config)# console timeout 15
```

Banner Configuration

Three types of banner messages can be configured:

- **EXEC**—Used to display a banner whenever an EXEC process begins
- **Login**—Used to display a banner before the display of username and password login prompts
- **MOTD**—Used to display a Message-Of-The-Day (MOTD) banner

Use the **banner** command and the appropriate option (**exec**, **login**, or **motd**) to configure all three types of banner messages.

Configuration File Management Commands

Specific CLI commands are available to view current startup or running configurations on the security appliance and to save the running configuration to flash memory. Keep in mind that configuration changes made to the security appliances are not automatically saved to flash memory and are lost if the appliance is rebooted without saving the running configuration.

The following commands are accessible primarily in the privileged or configuration modes.

Command	Function
`show running-config`	Displays current running configuration on the console.
`show startup-config`	Displays current startup (saved on flash) configuration on the console.
`write memory`	Writes current running configuration to the flash memory (startup).
`write terminal`	Same as **show running-config** command, displays the current running configuration.
`copy running-config startup-config`	Same as **write memory** command, writes the current running configuration to memory.
`clear configure all`	Clears the running configuration on the security appliance.
`write erase`	Clears the startup configuration on the security appliance.
`reload`	Reloads the security appliance.
`dir`	Displays the contents of flash memory.

Configuration Backup and Restore Commands

Security appliance configuration can be backed up to or restored from a TFTP server over the network using the **write net** and **configure net** commands. The **write net** command writes a copy of the current running configuration file to a file on a TFTP server, whereas the **configure net** command reads a configuration file from a TFTP server and merges it with the current running configuration file on the security appliance. For example:

```
fw(config)# write net 10.1.1.12:/myconfig.txt
fw(config)# configure net 10.1.1.12:/myconfig.txt
```

Use the **tftp-server** command to simplify the syntax of **write net** and **configure net** commands by defining the TFTP server IP address and filename and path only once. The following example shows the use of the **tftp-server** command:

```
fw(config)# tftp-server inside 10.1.1.12 myconfig.txt
fw(config)# write net
fw(config)# configure net
```

Host Name-to-IP Address Mapping

Use the **name** command to map specific host names to IP addresses. This feature allows the use of host names instead of IP addresses in other CLI commands and generally improves the readability of the security appliances configuration.

```
fw(config)# name 10.1.1.2 inside-tftp
```

Security Appliance Security Levels

Cisco security appliances implement a security algorithm based on:

- Allowing outbound connections by default (connections originating from internal or more-protected networks to external or less-protected networks).

NOTE FWSM does not allow any traffic among interfaces by default. Explicitly allow traffic flow, even from an interface with a higher security level to an interface with a lower security level.

- Stateful connection control, ensuring that return traffic is valid.

- Making TCP sequence numbers more difficult to predict (and attack) by randomizing the initial TCP sequence number.

To allow outbound connections (or conversely disallow inbound connections) correctly, assign an appropriate security level to each interface (physical or logical) as shown in the following figure.

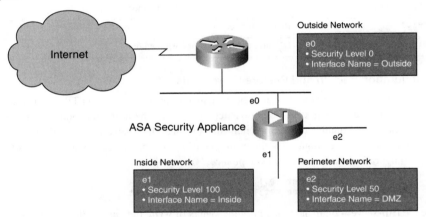

Consider the following rules when configuring security levels:

- Security levels range from 0–100.

- Security level 100 is the most secure interface and is assigned to the "inside" interface by default.

- Security level 0 is the least secure interface and is assigned to the "outside" interface by default.

- Traffic from an interface with a higher security value, for example 90, to a lower security value, for example 50, is allowed by default (can be blocked with an appropriate ACL).

- Traffic from an interface with lower security value, for example 30, to a higher security value, for example 70, is disallowed by default (can be allowed with an appropriate ACL).

- Traffic between two interfaces with the same security value is disallowed by default (can be allowed using the **same-security-traffic** command).

Transport Protocols

Cisco security appliances primarily deal with inbound and outbound transmissions over two protocols:

- **TCP**—Connection-oriented protocol and relatively easy to inspect properly.
- **UDP**—Connectionless protocol, and thus more difficult to inspect properly.

TCP connection steps are as follows:

1 A TCP SYN packet from an inside host is received and a translation slot is created. The embedded TCP information is then used to create a connection slot.

2 The connection slot is marked as embryonic (a half-open TCP session before completion of a three-way handshake).

3 Initial sequence number of the connection is randomized and the packet is forwarded onto the outgoing interface.

4 SYN/ACK packet from the destination host is matched against the connection slot and is allowed to return to the inside host if found to be legitimate.

5 The inside host completes the three-way handshake with an ACK packet.

6 The connection slot is marked as connected and data is sent. The embryonic counter is then reset for this connection.

UDP transactions are processed in the following manner:

1 The first IP packet from an inside host is received and a translation slot is created. The embedded UDP information is then used to create a UDP connection slot.

2 The security appliance maintains the UDP connection slot for the duration of the user-configurable UDP timeout (two minutes by default). When the UDP connection slot is idle for more than the configured UDP timeout, it is deleted from the connection table.

3 By maintaining a UDP "connection" in this manner, the security appliance can perform a stateful inspection of the UDP packets that are received from the destination host within the UDP timeout period.

4 The data is sent back to the inside host.

Connections and Translations

To better understand how Cisco security appliances process inbound and outbound transmissions, note the following differences between translations and connections:

- Translations occur at the IP layer of the TCP/IP protocol stack.
- Connections occur at the transport layer of the TCP/IP stack.
- There can be many connections using a single translation.

Use the **show conn** and **show xlate** commands respectively to display current connection and translation slots on the security appliance. The **show local-host** command displays more detailed information about connections and translations on a per host basis.

Network Address Translation

The security appliance's NAT function translates a real (local) IP address on one interface to a mapped (global) IP address on another interface as shown in the following figure.

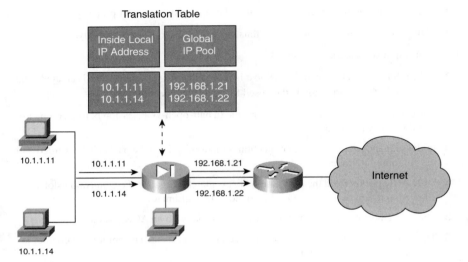

Cisco security appliances provide four main types of address translation:

- **Dynamic inside translation**—Internal host addresses are dynamically translated to a pool of addresses on the external or less secure interface. Dynamic translation is appropriate for outbound services, such as web browsing.

- **Static inside translation**—This type of translation provides a permanent one-to-one mapping between a local (real) host IP address and a global (mapped) IP address on the less secure interface. Static translations are typically used to provide access to services such as a web or FTP server.

- **Dynamic outside translation**—External host addresses are dynamically translated to a pool of addresses on the internal or more secure interface. Configured using the **nat** command with keyword **outside**.

- **Static outside translation**—This type of translation provides a permanent one-to-one mapping between an external (mapped) host IP address and a local (real) IP address on the more secure interface.

Port Address Translation

NAT provides address translation based only on IP addresses and requires a global IP address for every translated local IP address. Port Address Translation (PAT) can use a single global IP address to translate thousands of local IP addresses. To properly distinguish conversations between internal and external hosts, PAT uses unique source port numbers for each translation (to the same global IP address) as shown in the following figure.

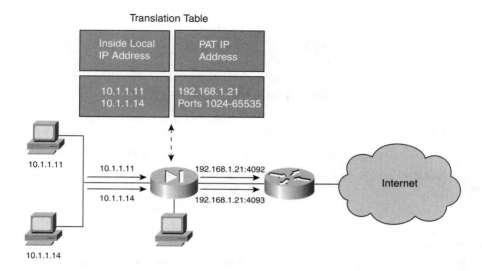

Note the following about PAT:

- PAT and NAT can be used together (PAT can back up NAT global pools).
- PAT can use the interface address to further reduce IP address requirements.
- With PAT, up to about 64,000 inside hosts can use one IP address.
- Multiple PAT addresses can be configured to allow additional hosts.
- PAT maps source port numbers to a single IP address.
- PAT secures transactions by hiding the inside source address through the use of a single IP address on the outside.

Basic Security Appliance Operational Configuration

Before any traffic can traverse the Cisco security appliance, a minimum basic configuration is required. Specifically, the following minimum configurations are required:

- Interface settings for at least two interfaces.
- A valid address translation policy (with ASA 5500 Series and PIX Security Appliances running release 7.0 software this is not required unless **nat-control** is enabled).
- A default route.

Use the following primary configuration commands for basic configuration for the security appliance:

- **hostname**—Assigns a hostname to the security appliance.
- **interface**—Enters interface configuration subcommand mode. It is also used to create logical interfaces.

- **nameif**—Assigns a name to the interface.

- **ip address**—Assigns an IP address to the interface.

- **security level**—Assigns the security level for an interface.

- **speed**—Specifies the connection speed for an interface.

- **duplex**—Specifies the duplex setting for an interface.

- **nat-control**—Enables or disables address translation policy requirement (NAT control is disabled by default in Security Appliance release 7.0 software).

- **nat**—Configures address translation for one or more hosts on a specific interface.

- **global**—Configures a pool of one or more global IP addresses for use with the **nat** command.

- **route**—Defines a static route or the default route for the appliance.

Interface Configuration

Interfaces are configured from the interface configuration subcommand mode. Use the **interface** command to enter this mode. The following example configures interface Ethernet 2 as a DMZ interface with an IP address of 172.16.1.1 and a security value of 50:

```
fw(config)# interface ethernet 2
fw(config-if)# nameif DMZ
fw(config-if)# ip address 172.16.1.1 255.255.255.0
fw(config-if)# security-level 50
fw(config-if)# speed 100
fw(config-if)# duplex full
fw(config-if)# no shut
```

Similar to IOS routers, interfaces are shut down by default and must be enabled using the **no shut** command. In addition, if speed and duplex settings are not explicitly configured, use auto-negotiation.

Logical interfaces are created as subinterfaces on a physical interface. For example, to create a logical interface on Ethernet 2 with VLAN 10, use the following commands:

```
fw(config)# interface ethernet2.1
fw(config-subif)# vlan 10
```

This command sequence creates the interface and enters its configuration mode. Other configuration tasks are the same as physical interfaces including configuration of the IP address, interface name, and security level.

By default, the outside interface is assigned a security value of zero and the inside interface is assigned a security value of 100. If the security values on other configured interfaces are not explicitly specified, a default security value of zero is assigned.

Network Address Translation

With Cisco Security Appliance release 7.0 software, an address translation policy is not required to allow traffic flow through the appliance (as was the case in previous software versions). However, if **nat-control** is enabled, then a valid address translation policy is required (similar to 6.3 and earlier releases of the software).

Configure NAT using the **nat** and **global** commands. Use the **global** command to configure an address or pool of addresses used with NAT or PAT on an interface. The **nat** command configures address translation on a specific interface for single or multiple hosts. Local (real) IP addresses are translated to a single or multiple global (mapped) IP addresses (configured with the **global** command) on the specified interface.

The following example shows a basic NAT configuration using **nat** and **global** commands:

```
fw(config)# global (outside) 1 192.168.1.20-192.168.1.30
fw(config)# nat (inside) 1 0.0.0.0 0.0.0.0
```

To view the configuration on the security appliance, use the **show running-config nat** and **show running-config global** commands. Use the **show xlate** command to view currently used translation slots.

Default Route

The last required step for basic configuration is a default route. Use the **route** command to configure the default route as shown in this example:

```
fw(config)# route outside 0.0.0.0 0.0.0.0 192.168.1.1
```

Syslog Configuration

Configure logging on the security appliance to generate and record syslog messages. Specify the syslog server and logging level and use the following **logging** commands to enable logging:

```
fw(config)# logging host inside 10.1.1.11
fw(config)# logging trap errors
fw(config)# logging timestamp
fw(config)# logging on
```

Cisco security appliance logging levels are as follows:

- **0–emergencies**—System unusable messages
- **1–alerts**—Take immediate action
- **2–critical**—Critical condition
- **3–errors**—Error message
- **4–warnings**—Warning message
- **5–notifications**—Normal but significant condition
- **6–informational**—Information message
- **7–debugging**—Debug messages and log FTP commands and WWW URLs

show Commands

Display various configuration settings and examine the status of the Security Appliance using the following **show** commands:

- **show memory**—Displays current memory utilization status on the appliance
- **show cpu usage**—Displays CPU utilization status based on five-second, one-minute, and five-minute intervals

- **show conn**—Displays current connections on the appliance
- **show version**—Displays information about hardware configuration, licensing, and the current running software version on the appliance
- **show ip address**—Displays configured IP addresses on the appliance interfaces
- **show interface**—Displays detailed information about each appliance interface (physical and logical)
- **show nameif**—Displays configured names and security levels for each interface
- **show running-config nat**—Displays the current NAT configuration on the security appliance
- **show running-config global**—Displays the current global configuration on the security appliance
- **show xlate**—Displays the current translation slots on the security appliance

Use the **ping** command to test and verify network connectivity

Cisco Adaptive Security Device Manager

Cisco ASDM is a browser-based configuration and monitoring tool designed for management of PIX and ASA security devices. ASDM offers a simple graphical interface and does not require extensive CLI experience from the administrator.

ASDM Features

ASDM is a Java-based application that is accessed as a downloadable Java applet or downloaded and locally installed on the management workstation for faster startup.

ASDM 5.0 provides support for PIX 500 Series and ASA 5500 series devices running security appliance 7.0 software. PIX 501 and 506E are not supported with security appliance 7.0 software and cannot run ASDM 5.0.

All communications between the ASDM and the security appliance are SSL-encrypted to ensure security.

Single Context mode supports five ASDM sessions per security appliance. Multiple Context mode supports five ASDM sessions per context up to a maximum of 32 sessions per physical security appliance.

ASDM Requirements

ASDM 5.0 operation requires the following:

- DES or 3DES activation key to support SSL encryption
- Java plug-in 1.4.2 or 1.5.0 (Microsoft JVM is not supported)
- Enabling JavaScript and Java on the browser
- Enabling SSL support on the browser

- Security Appliance software version 7.0

- ASA 5500 Series or PIX 500 Series security appliance (PIX 501 and 506E excluded)

If PIX Security Appliance software version 6.3 or earlier is running, use the appropriate version of the PIX Device Manager (PDM):

- Software version 6.0 or 6.1: Use PDM 1.0 or 1.1.

- Software version 6.2: Use PDM 2.0 or 2.1.

- Software version 6.3: Use PDM 3.0.

ASDM 5.0 supports the Windows, Sun Solaris, and Linux platforms with the following requirements:

- Minimum Windows requirements:

  — Windows 2000 (Service Pack 3) or Windows XP operating systems.
  — Internet Explorer 6.0 with Java Plug-in 1.4.2 or 1.5.0, or
  — Netscape Communicator 7.1, or 7.2, with Java plug-in 1.4.2 or 1.5.0.
  — Pentium or Pentium-compatible processor running at 450 MHz or higher.
  — Minimum 256 MB of RAM.
  — 1024 x 768-pixel display with at least 256 colors.
  — Windows 3.1, 95, 98, ME, or NT4 are not supported.

- SUN Solaris requirements:

  — Sun Solaris 2.8 or 2.9 running CDE Window Manager.
  — SPARC microprocessor.
  — Mozilla 1.7.3 with Java plug-in 1.4.2 or 1.5.0.
  — Minimum 256 MB of RAM.
  — 1024 x 768 pixel display with at least 256 colors.

- Linux requirements:

  — Red Hat Linux 9.0 or Red Hat Linux WS, version 3 running GNOME or KDE.
  — Mozilla 1.7.3 with Java Plug-in 1.4.2 or 1.5.0.
  — Minimum 256 MB of RAM.
  — 1024 x 768-pixel display with at least 256 colors.

Configuring the Security Appliance to Use ASDM

Before using ASDM to manage the security appliance, configure the following:

- Time (**clock set** command)

- hostname (**hostname** command)

- Domain name (**domain-name** command)

- Inside interface IP address (**ip address** command) of the security appliance

Enable the internal HTTP server and allow HTTP access to the security appliance from the workstation or subnet:

```
fw(config)# http 10.1.1.11 255.255.255.255 inside
fw(config)# http server enable
```

Accessing ASDM

After completion of the initial configuration on the security appliance, access ASDM using the URL https://*asa_ip_address* on a supported browser. For example:

```
https://10.1.1.1
```

After the launch of ASDM, the display of the Home screen occurs, as illustrated in the following figure.

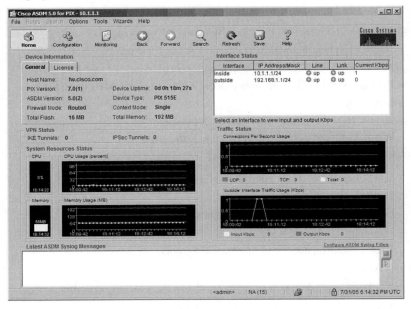

The ASDM Home screen includes the following sections:

- **Menu bar**—Provides access to File, Options, Tools, Wizards, and Help menu items.

- **Main toolbar**—Provides access to Home, Configuration, Monitoring windows, and search, context-sensitive help, and save functions. If the security appliance operates in multi-context mode, context-specific toolbar items are added, including the Context button (provides access to user contexts), context drop-down menu (allowing selection of individual named contexts), and the System button (selects the system execution space).

- **Device Information box**—Uses General and License tabs to display security appliance information. The General tab displays information about the security appliance hardware and software in use. The License tab displays encryption level and licensed features on the security appliance.

- **VPN Status box**—Displays the number of IKE and IPSec tunnels established on the security device.

- **System Resources Status box**—Displays CPU and memory usage graphs.

- **Interface Status box**—Displays interface-specific information, including IP address and mask, line and link status, and current kbps.

- **Traffic Status box**—Displays TCP and UDP connections graphs.

- **Latest ASDM Syslog Messages box**—Displays the most recent 10 system messages generated by the security appliance.

ASDM Configuration

The ASDM provides several wizards to greatly simplify configuration tasks on the security appliance. Wizards available include:

- Startup Wizard
- VPN wizards
  - Site-to-site VPNs
  - Remote-access VPNs

As shown in the following figure, access the main configuration page to perform standard configurations.

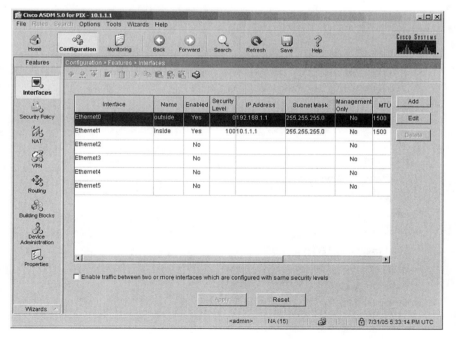

Features that can be configured on this page include:

- Interfaces. Configure logical and physical interfaces (**Configuration > Features > Interfaces**)
- Security Policy (**Configuration > Features > Security Policy**)
  - Access Rules
  - AAA Rules
  - Filter Rules
  - Service Policy Rules
  - Ethertype Rules (transparent firewall mode)
- NAT (**Configuration > Features > NAT**)
  - Translation Rules
  - Translation Exemption Rules
- VPN (**Configuration > Features > VPN**)
  - General VPN Options
    VPN System Options
    Client Update
    Tunnel Group
    Group Policy
    Default Tunnel Gateway
  - IKE
    Global Parameters
    Policies
    Certificate Group Matching (Policy and Rule)
  - IPSec
    IPSec Rules
    Tunnel Policy
    Transform Sets
    Pre-Fragmentation
  - IP Address Management
    Assignment
    IP Pools
  - Load Balancing (ASA 5500)
  - WebVPN (ASA 5500)
    WebVPN Access
    Servers and URLs
    Port Forwarding
    Homepage
    Proxies

WebVPN AAA

NetBIOS Servers

ACLs

— E-Mail Proxy (ASA 5500)

- IPS (**Configuration > Features > IPS**)

  — Sensor Setup

  Network

  Allowed Hosts

  SSH

  Certificates

  Time

  Users

  — Interface Configuration

  Interfaces

  Interface Pairs

  Bypass

  Traffic Flow Notifications

  — Analysis Engine

  Virtual Sensor

  Global Variables

  — Signature Definitions

  Signature Variables

  Signature Configuration

  Custom Signature Wizard

  Miscellaneous

  — Event Action Rules

  Event Variables

  Target Value Rating

  Event Action Overrides

  Event Action Filters

  General Settings

  — Blocking

  Blocking Properties

  Device Login Profiles

  Blocking Devices

  Router Blocking Device Interfaces

  Cat 6K Blocking Device Interfaces

  Master Blocking Sensor

— SNMP

   SNMP General Configuration

   SNMP Traps Configuration

— Auto Update

— Restore Defaults

— Reboot Sensor

— Shut Down Sensor

— Update Sensor

— Licensing

- Routing (**Configuration > Features > Routing**)

  — Static Route

  — RIP

  — Proxy ARPs

  — OSPF

     Setup

     Interface

     Static Neighbor

     Virtual Link

     Filtering

     Redistribution

     Summary Address

  — Multicast

     IGMP (Protocol, Access Group, Join Group, and Static Group)

     PIM (Protocol, Rendezvous Points, Route Tree, and Request Filter)

     MRoute

- Building Blocks (**Configuration > Features > Building Blocks**)

  — Hosts/Networks

  — Inspect Maps (FTP, GTP, HTTP, MGCP, SNMP)

  — TCP Maps

  — Time Ranges

- Device Administration (**Configuration > Features > Device Administration**)

  — Device

  — Password

  — AAA Access

  — User Accounts

  — Banner

— Console
— ASDM/HTTPS
— Telnet
— Secure Copy
— Secure Shell
— Management Access
— SMTP
— SNMP
— ICMP Rules
— TFTP Server
— Clock
— NTP
— Boot Image/Configuration
— FTP Mode
— Certificate
— Key Pair
— Trustpoint
— Configuration
— Import
— Export
— Authentication
— Enrollment
— Import Certificate
— Manage Certificates

- Properties (**Configuration > Features > Properties**)
  — AAA Setup
    AAA Server Group
    AAA Servers
    Auth. Prompt
  — Advanced
    Anti-Spoofing
    Connection Settings
    Fragment
    TCP Options
    Timeouts
  — ARP Inspection (Transparent Firewall mode)
  — ARP Static Table

- Bridging (Transparent Firewall mode)

  MAC Address Table

  MAC Learning
- Auto Update
- DHCP Services

  DHCP Server

  DHCP Relay
- DNS Client
- Failover—Single Mode
- Failover—Multiple Mode, Routed
- Failover—Multiple Mode, Transparent
- History/Metrics
- HTTP/HTTPS
- IP Audit

  IP Audit Policy

  IP Audit Signature
- Logging

  Logging Setup

  Event Lists

  Logging Filters

  Syslog Setup

  Syslog Servers

  E-Mail Setup
- Priority Queue
- Management IP
- SSL
- SUNRPC Server
- URL Filtering

ASDM Monitoring

Click on the Monitoring button on the Main toolbar to access ASDM monitoring functions (see the following figure).

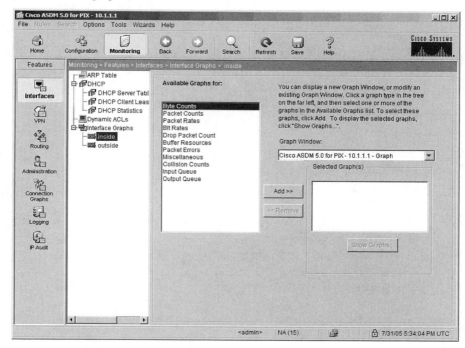

Specific monitoring features accessible from this page include:

- Interfaces
  - ARP Tables
  - DHCP

    DHCP Server Table

    DHCP Client Lease Information

    DHCP Statistics
  - Dynamic ACLs
  - Interface Graphs
- VPN
  - VPN Statistics

    Sessions

    Encryption Statistics

    Protocol Statistics

    Global IKE/IPSec Statistics

Crypto Statistics
— VPN Connections Graphs
IPSec Tunnels
- Routing
  — Routes
  — OSPF LSAs (Type 1, 2, 3, 4, 5, 7)
  — OSPF Neighbors
- Administration
  — ASDM/HTTPS Sessions
  — Telnet Sessions
  — AAA Local Locked Out
  — SSH Sessions
  — Authenticated Users
  — AAA Servers
  — CRL
  — DNS Cache
  — System Graphs (Blocks, CPU, and Memory)
  — Failover (Status and Graphs)
- Connection Graphs
  — Xlates
  — Perfmon
- Logging
  — Live Log
  — Log Buffer
- IP Audit

Securing Networks with Host- and Network-Based IPS

IPSs are designed to identify malicious and anomalous transactions within hosts and networks and at the option of the administrator take appropriate steps to terminate the activity to prevent system damage. This section provides an overview of Cisco intrusion prevention technology, network IPS command line and GUI-based setup and configuration, CSA HIPS, and HIPS management.

Introducing IPS

Part of the defense in-depth concept is the monitoring of communications on critical network segments with network IPS in addition to implementing software agent HIPS on all servers and desktops simultaneously. Cisco network IPSs are physical hardware devices (stand alone and devices modules) that monitor traffic on the network media for attacks, such as reconnaissance probes, improper use of network services, known exploits, and DoS. The Cisco HIPS product is the CSA that is a centrally-managed software agent resident on each host. CSA monitors the behavior of internal application and host processes and is designed to disallow transactions that exceed the bounds of a defined security policy.

The following table weighs the advantages and disadvantages of both detection technologies.

	Advantages	**Disadvantages**
Network IPS	Observes and interprets flows within one or more segments.	Cannot interpret encrypted data.
	Evaluates the extent of attacks by identifying the number of affected hosts.	Fragmented traffic can be difficult to reconstruct and analyze.
	Operating system is independent.	As the network becomes larger, monitoring everything can be difficult to scale.
Host IPS	Determines attack success or failure.	HIPS provides only the local view of attacks and not the big picture.
	Fragmented attacks are not an issue because IP stack reassembles them.	HIPS must support all the OS types and versions in use.
	Encrypted traffic is not an issue because the host will decrypt it.	

IDS and IPS network sensors are two variations of the technology and have the following qualities:

- Off the wire and router syslog data evaluation seeking malicious and unauthorized activity

- Definable actions in response to inappropriate network use

The main differences between Cisco network IDS and IPS are:

Network IPS	**Network IDS**
An inline-mode security control. IPS devices can be deployed in IDS mode if needed.	A promiscuous-mode security control that taps the network.
Positioned directly in the packet forwarding path as a layer 2 repeater. Analyzes data as it travels between two interfaces.	Positioned outside of the packet stream but receives a copy of each packet from the switch for analysis *and* detection.
Can *prevent* the first and subsequent attack packets from reaching their target by dropping them inline, resetting TCP connections, and blocking.	Can prevent *some* attack packets from reaching their target by resetting TCP connections and blocking. Because IDS is outside of the forwarding path, one or more attack packets might reach the target before the activation of the response action to prevent the subsequent packets.

Attacks are classified in four ways:

- **False positive**—Nonmalicious traffic causes an alarm.

- **False negative**—Malicious traffic does not generate an alarm. Either the signature is not configured correctly or the system does not have the facility to detect and alert on the situation.

- **True positive**—Malicious traffic generates an alarm.

- **True negative**—Nonmalicious traffic does not cause an alarm.

The technologies upon which Cisco IDS and IPS are based are as follows:

- **Profile-based detection (also known as anomaly detection)**—Uses a statistical baseline definition of activity types and levels considered normal for network and fires alerts as events cause conditions to exceed these bounds.

- **Signature-based detection (also known as misuse detection and pattern matching)**— Requires the creation of a "signature" containing bit patterns that describe an attack. When observation of the patterns on the wire occurs, the signature fires.

- **Protocol analysis detection**—Takes signature detection a step further by auditing the way particular protocols are *supposed* to behave according to RFC standards and compares them to how they are *actually* operating on the wire and fires an alert if they behave in a non-standard way.

A signature is described as a set of conditions that depict an intrusive event. Sensors ship with more than 1000 built-in signatures designed to describe misuse. Cisco periodically produces new signatures as the isolation and identification of new attacks occurs.

Sensor signature engines are the internal software processes designed to examine the many types of flows that occur on a network with the purpose of spotting unauthorized activity. Each engine is optimized to examine a particular type of communication and each signature is assigned to a particular engine. Thus each engine supports a general category of signatures meant to inspect communications in a particular way.

IPS 5.0 uses the following signature engines:

- **AIC**—Deep analysis of web and FTP traffic to prevent abuse of embedded protocols within HTTP and to watch for illegal use of FTP commands.

- **ATOMIC**—Inspects individual packets for abnormality:

  — ATOMIC.IP—Combines layer 3 and layer 4 functions for inspection of fields, flags, and payloads at any of these points within the packet using Regular Expression (Regex).

  — ATOMIC.ARP—Inspects the layer 2 ARP protocol for abnormalities and misuse.

- **FLOOD**—Detects ICMP and UDP floods directed toward individual hosts and networks.

- **META**—Provides the "intelligence" for event correlation as one or more engines note alerts within a finite time interval.

- **NORMALIZER**—Handles communications fragmented at the IP layer or segmented at the TCP layer to detect attacks that are spread across packets.

- **SERVICE**—Inspects specific network service protocols that operate at layers 5, 6, and 7:

  — **DNS**—Inspects DNS (TCP and UDP) traffic.

  — **FTP**—Inspects FTP traffic.

  — **GENERIC**—Inspects custom services and their payloads.

- **H225**—Inspects VoIP call signaling setup and termination traffic for standards compliance.
- **HTTP**—Inspects HTTP traffic.
- **IDENT**—Inspects IDENT (client and server) traffic.
- **MSRPC**—Inspects Microsoft RPC traffic, which is used extensively in Microsoft networks for inter-host communication.
- **MSSQL**—Inspects Microsoft SQL traffic.
- **NTP**—Inspects NTP traffic.
- **RPC**—Inspects RPC traffic.
- **SMB**—Inspects Microsoft SMB traffic.
- **SNMP**—Inspects SNMP traffic.
- **SSH**—Inspects SSH traffic.

- **STATE**—Tracks the state machines of SMTP, LPR, and Cisco device logins. Verifies proper transitions through states and alarms when a state transition is violated.

- **STRING**—Searches on Regex strings based on ICMP, TCP, or UDP protocol.

- **SWEEP**—Detects single or multi protocol ICMP, TCP, and UDP reconnaissance activity like Nessus scans.

- **TRAFFIC.ICMP**—Analyzes nonstandard protocols and attack traffic that use ICMP as their vector (TFN2K, LOKI, and DDoS variants).

- **TROJAN**—Inspects for non-ICMP, nonstandard protocol variants like the well-known BO2K and TFN2K exploits.

The following table summarizes analysis techniques used by IPS engines.

	Analysis Techniques	What the Sensor is Doing...
Signature Detection	Simple Pattern Matching	Looking for a particular string of characters in a single packet.
	Stateful Pattern Matching	Looking for a particular string of characters across multiple packets.
	Heuristic Analysis	Using statistical analysis to determine if combinations of observed communications amount to an attack.
Protocol Analysis Detection	Protocol Decode Analysis	Interpreting a protocol (or service) like a host would and analyzing for abnormal use of it or exploitation of known vulnerabilities.
	Protocol Anomaly	Looking for deviations from standard RFC protocol use.
Profile Detection	Statistical Anomaly Analysis	Attempting packet flood detection by noting large increases in traffic flow above what it considers normal based on previous levels.

Signatures have the following configurable parameters:

- REGEX string pattern matching

- Response actions

- Alarm summarization

- Threshold configuration

- Anti-evasion detection

Define signature parameters to accurately identify misuse and minimize false positives. In contrast to IDS analysis, which is passive and external to data flow, IPS analysis, which is in-line, must be accurate. If the hardware incorrectly drops frames instead of forwarding them, disruption of sessions is likely.

Built-in signatures can be modified (tuned) for an environment and new unique signatures can be created if required. Signature facts:

- A tuned signature is a signature with one or more modified built-in signature parameters.

- A custom signature is a new signature built from scratch or based upon a copy of a built-in signature.

- A signature can have subsignatures to describe variations of an exploit.

- Active signatures can be enabled or disabled during sensor tuning activities. If a signature is not currently enabled, the misuse it describes is not identified. Not all the 1000+ signatures are enabled by default.

- Signatures can be removed from the pool of available signatures by retiring them. Doing so saves sensor memory resources.

- Detailed information about each signature can be obtained from The Cisco Network Security Database (NSDB).

Engines have master and local tunable parameters. Master parameters are more global in nature and a modified setting flows across all engines. Local parameters are those specific to an engine. Some parameters are protected, meaning they cannot be changed for a built-in signature. However, creating a copy of the built-in signature generates a new custom signature. All signatures need required parameters.

Tuning activities include:

- Enabling and disabling signatures

- Modifying alarm severity levels

- Changing signature parameters

- Specifying event actions based on risk rating by using event action overrides

- Removing certain events that are known to happen in the environment using event action filters

- Creating alarm channel event filters

When a signature "fires" or is "triggered," a match between observed network activity and some definition of misuse found within a signature occurs. Signatures can be configured for multiple response actions when they are triggered:

- Droping attacker packets inline (IPS mode only)

- Terminating a TCP session by sending a RST to the attacker and target (victim)

- Blocking the attacker by instructing an edge router or PIX to dynamically modify an ACL

- Restricting attacker access to an entire operational domain by blocking the attacker at multiple entry points through the use of master blocking sensors

- Creating session IP logs to capture attack communications for later forensic analysis

IPS alarm facts:

- All enabled signatures have alarms (alerts) turned on by default.

- Each signature is assigned to one of the following configurable alert severity categories:
  - Informational
  - Low
  - Medium
  - High

- The sensor's Event Store database stores all alerts.

- The event console applications in the IPS Device Manager (IDM) and the CiscoWorks VMS component, Monitoring Center for Security, query a sensor's Event Store for alerts using Security Device Event Exchange (SDEE) on an ad-hoc basis or continually for "real-time" monitoring. The client management station always pulls data from the sensor as opposed to the sensor pushing the data.

The Cisco IPS hardware systems are all based on Linux, share a common code base, and come in several form factors including:

- "NM" modules for Cisco routers

- Modules for the Catalyst 6500 and Catalyst 7600 switch chassis lines

- AIP-SSM for the ASA lines

- Dedicated IPS hardware appliances

Only IDS capabilities are available in Sensor software version 4.1 and older, Cisco IOS Software Release 12.0 to 12.2, and PIX 5.2 and later. IPS capability is available in Sensor software version 5.0 and later and IOS 12.3 and later.

The following table details IPS hardware. Specifications are subject to change.

Sensor Hardware	Modules			Appliances
Product	NM-CIDS	AIP-SSM	IDSM-2	IPS 4215/4240/4255
Platform	Select Cisco routers	ASA	6500/7600 chassis	Dedicated standalone appliance
Throughput Performance (Mbps)	45	150 to 450 depending on ASA chassis	500 per module	80/250/600
Inline prevention?	No	Yes	Yes	Yes
Promiscuous detection?	Yes	Yes	Yes	Yes

The following technical factors affect sensor model selection:

- The required media (10/100/1000/copper/fiber) types.

- The required monitoring performance.

- The required response actions. For example, if inline drops are required, IPS must be deployed using a sensor that supports it.

- Whether the network runs within a chassis allowing for direct integrated monitoring within the chassis as opposed to a stand alone appliance.

Sensor deployment considerations:

- How many sensors are necessary for the environment?

- Where should sensors be placed?

- How will sensors be monitored and managed?

- How will sensors and management consoles communicate through the network infrastructures particularly firewalls?

For managing sensors, Cisco recommends a 5:1 (or less) sensor to GUI ratio for the IDM and a 300:1 (or less) sensor to GUI ratio for the CiscoWorks VMS Management Center for Intrusion Detection System Sensors (IDS MC).

Consider using host and network IPS on the following types of networks:

- Key internal segments, such as dedicated server segments and high-value, critical hosts.

- Segments that receive remote VPN connections. Analysis must be performed post-decryption.

- Segments that serve as Extranet boundaries between business partners or major organizational divisions.

- Segments between the perimeter gateway and the Internet for analysis of traffic that the firewall correctly allows but that might still contain malicious code. Note that placing IPS on the untrusted side of a firewall might generate more alarms than is useful.

Sensor CLI Configuration

Configure network sensors using a CLI or through one of several GUI interfaces including IDM and IDS MC.

Use the following methods to access the sensor CLI:

- Via direct connection of a keyboard and monitor to a sensor (not available on some models).
- Via the command and control network interface using:
  - SSH
  - Telnet (disabled by default)
- Via serial console cable.

Initial CLI configuration of a sensor via a console cable or direct keyboard connection is necessary (and required) before using SSH or a GUI interface for more advanced, detailed configurations. Regardless of the way accessed, use the sensor CLI for the following activities:

- Initialization
  - IP addressing
  - Trusted host access lists
  - User account creation
- Configuration
  - Engine tuning
  - Event actions
- Administration
  - Backing up and restoring a configuration.
  - Re-imaging a sensor
- Troubleshooting
  - Pinging
  - Statistics query

The CLI supports the following configuration modes:

- **Privileged EXEC mode**—The base level after authenticating for initializing, rebooting, displaying settings. Prompt = **sensor#**.

- **Global configuration mode**—Allows configuration settings for user accounts, SSH settings, upgrade/downgrade, and re-imaging. Features several interface configuration submodes. Enter via privileged EXEC mode. Prompt = **sensor(config)#**.

Other CLI modes accessed from within global configuration mode include:

- Service mode
- Interface command-control configuration mode
- Interface group configuration mode
- Interface sensing configuration mode

- Virtual sensor configuration mode
- Alarm channel configuration mode
- Tune micro engines mode
- Tune alarm channel mode

Create sensor user accounts and assign them to a predefined user account role for the purpose of controlling authorization privileges. With the exception of the "Service" role, multiple users can be assigned to a given role. The following table details user account roles.

Privilege	User Account Role			
	Administrator	Operator	Viewer	Service
Can log into the IDM interface.	x	x	x	
Can log into the CLI interface.	x	x	x	
Provides bash shell root access via a CLI interface.				x
Low-level OS access for Cisco TAC use only.				x
Can su to root user.				x
Only one account can have this role.				x
Can create and edit Service account role.	x			
Adding and deleting users. Password administration.	x			
Assigning Ethernet interfaces to a virtual sensor.	x			
Enabling and disabling Ethernet interfaces.	x			
Generating SSH keys and digital certs.	x			
Modifying sensor address.	x			
Defining permitted hosts.	x			
Tuning signatures.	x	x		
Managing blocking devices.	x	x		
View events.	x	x	x	
Changing own password.	x	x	x	x

An initialization is the process of defining sensor operational parameters. The CLI **setup** command is a script that lets you define the following:

Step 1   Assign a hostname.

Step 2   Assign the IP and subnet mask of command and control interface.

Step 3   Assign the sensor's default gateway.

Step 4   Enable Telnet server (default disabled) if desired though not recommended.

Step 5   Assign the web server port (default 443/tcp).

Step 6   Specify the trusted host ACL of systems permitted to interact with the sensor.

Step 7   Set the time and date and NTP settings.

Step 8   Modify the virtual sensor configuration (vs0) by assigning unused interfaces as either single promiscuous or inline monitoring pairs. Note that this step is done as part of IPS 5.0 **setup** but is a separate activity in IDS 4.1.

NOTE   All the preceding settings can be altered at a later time using the IDM GUI.

IDM

The IDM is a web-based Java GUI application used for configuring and managing one sensor at a time via its network command and control interface. Each sensor has an embedded web server daemon to which authorized administrators can connect for configuring and maintaining the system. A sensor must have been previously configured with an IP address via the CLI and the workstation where launching IDM must be part of the sensor's trusted host list. Only then can the administrator communicate with the sensor from a web browser using either HTTP or for more security SSL and Transport Layer Security (TLS).

High-level IDM features and benefits include:

- Secure web architecture using SSL/TLS communication
- Task-based web GUI
- General sensor configuration and management
- Signature configuration, customization, and creation
- Sensor event monitoring
- Access to the NSDB, a complete description of signatures, exploits, vulnerabilities, and benign triggers
- Online help
- Sensor restart and power down
- Restoring sensor settings to factory defaults

Cisco Security Agent

CSA is a distributed (centrally controlled) personal firewall and HIPS. It is software-designed to protect server and workstation endpoints from attacks by identifying and optionally preventing unwanted behavior caused by known and previously unknown ("Day Zero") threats from recognized and unrecognized systems. The following list describes the major CSA functions:

- Behavior-based intrusion detection and prevention of attacks, such as:
  - Buffer overflows and worms
  - Application masquerade

- Distributed personal firewall functionality for enforcing inbound and outbound port blocking

- Active content sandbox creation to isolate Java, JavaScript, and ActiveX applications used in potential web-based attacks

- Application behavior and version tracking protection to ensure that an application does not perform behavior outside of its scope.

- Local and global application activity correlation.

- Operating system component integrity

- Audit log consolidation

CSA complements signature-based AV software and is effective at identifying Day Zero exploits before attack signatures exist to describe them. CSA does not rely on signatures and does not inspect content but rather analyzes system behavior for abnormal activity. CSA agents have the ability to correlate a series of host events that comprise an exploit, report these abnormal events to a central management host, and have the management host create new policy for all other distributed agents to make them "aware" of new and potentially dangerous conditions.

Most organized attacks follow a stepped progression. The five phases of an attack are:

Step 1   Probe

An attacker performs reconnaissance to identify vulnerable targets and exploitable services using techniques that include but are not limited to ping scans, application port scans, OS fingerprinting, social engineering, and network sniffing.

Step 2   Penetrate

The attacker attempts to transfer software code aimed at exploiting a weakness discovered during the Probe phase to a target host. Attack vectors vary and are dependent on the type of system, the services it offers, and its level of hardening. Attack vectors often include buffer overflows, ActiveX, Common Gateway Interface (CGI), lack of OS patching, DNS and other service vulnerabilities, and email viri.

Step 3   Persist

After the successful launch of an exploit into memory, attackers often attempt to ensure their exploitation persists on the host even after a system reboot. The attackers achieve this by modifying system files, making Windows registry or UNIX rc file changes, and installing new code that processes upon reboot.

Step 4   Propagate

Attackers often use a compromised host as a beachhead to reach further into an organization by attacking other targets from the first host. Propagation vectors include the distribution of attacks within email, uploading files to other systems using unprotected file shares, NFS, or FTP services, active web connections, and file transfers via Internet Relay Chat (IRC).

Step 5   Paralyze

The final phase of an attack occurs when the true damage is done. Depending on the attack, data might be erased or secretly changed, systems can be crashed, information can be stolen, and distributed DoS (DDoS) attacks can be launched.

The techniques used in the Probe and Penetrate phases vary because of the constant development of new attack vectors. Accordingly, it is difficult to identify attacks until containment and development of a signature to describe the behavior occur. In contrast, the techniques used in the latter three steps, Persist, Propagate, and Paralyze, are limited in number and easily identified when processed at the host level. For example, if an exploit requires the creation of a rogue service account, this action is easy to identify.

The two components of a CSA deployment are:

- **CSA MC**—A component of the CiscoWorks VMS platform. It is the central management console for all CSA agents comprised of a web server, database, and a web front end. CSA MC does the following:
  - Groups hosts by function or security requirements.
  - Configures unique security policy by group, also know as Agent kits.
  - Distributes policies to hosts via logon scripts, software deployment products, emailed URL links, or software image replication.
  - Maintains security violation logs.
- **CSA host software**—This component uses optional "no user interaction" features to silently and transparently deploy onto Windows and UNIX hosts. CSA host software does the following:
  - Activates an Agent kit security policy designed at the CSA MC and deployed to specific hosts or groups of hosts.
  - Registers automatically with the CSA MC after installation.
  - In contrast to signature-based detection, CSA uses behavior-based technology that provides "Zero Update" prevention by monitoring internal host system kernel calls and seeking policy violations caused by known and unknown attacks.
  - Prevents disallowed behavior or when deployed in host IDS mode ("test" mode), optionally allows disallowed behavior and logs the event to the CSA MC.
  - Caches the latest security policy received from the CSA MC.
  - Polls the CSA MC at periodic intervals for policy updates.
  - Communicates with the CSA MC via SSL.

The following describe the mechanics of CSA:

- CSA agents and Agent kit policies are installed onto hosts. Note that local administrator or root privileges are required to install CSA locally.
- CSA inserts shims into the OS to intercept all calls to the host's file system, network interfaces, Windows Component Object Model (COM), Windows registry, and UNIX rc files.

- The various behaviors are intelligently analyzed for validity based upon the Agent kit policy deployed to that host.

- Operations are either allowed or denied.

The Intercept Correlate Rules Engine (INCORE), which is the OS shim, uses the following four interceptors to examine host behavior:

- **File system**—All read/write requests to OS-specific and application-specific files

- **Network**—All inbound and outbound network requests

- **Configuration**—Read/write requests to the Windows registry or Unix rc files

- **Execution space**—Maintains the integrity of each application's dynamic runtime environment by examining memory read and write requests and blocks requests when an application does not own a resource or when one application is attempting to inject data into another application's memory space

CSA host software offers an "application sandbox" function that is an execution space where untested and suspect programs can run with less than normal system resource access. A combination of the file system, configuration, and execution space interceptors provide this function.

As depicted in the following table, CSA combines several traditional security functions into one product by using the capabilities of the four interceptors in various combinations.

Security Function	Interceptor Type			
	Network	**File System**	**Configuration**	**Execution Space**
Distributed firewall	x			
Host IDS	x			x
Application sandbox		x	x	x
Network worm prevention	x			x
File integrity monitor		x	x	

A CSA's decision to allow or deny a behavior is based upon the Agent kit policy administrators design within the CSA MC and propagated to each CSA agent. Organizations design CSA policy based upon their risk tolerance and the assets they are protecting. Security policies can be permissive, restrictive, or somewhere in between. Generally, permissive policies deny malicious behavior and allow all other actions, whereas restrictive policies allow only required actions and deny all others.

The five areas that a CSA policy must address are as follows:

- Protection of application executables by preventing writing to executables

- Restriction of application processes by defining what applications and their spawned child processes can and cannot do

- Protection of application specific data by restricting access to important data

- Controlling network access by restricting inbound and outbound communication flow

- Protecting application registry keys by restricting key writing to only the processes that require it

Deploying HIPS with the CSA MC

CSA MC centralizes the control of CSA agents from a web-based console. The high-level CSA MC configuration steps are as follows:

Step 1   Install CSA MC.

Step 2   Create groups to which hosts will be associated based upon their security needs.

Step 3   Build and distribute Agent kits for each group.

Step 4   Register agents with the CSA MC (this occurs automatically).

Step 5   Configure group-specific CSA security policies.

Step 6   Attach security policies to groups.

Step 7   Generate security policy-based rules, so that the agents receive the policies and rules.

The CSA MC features role-based administration by multiple administrators. The roles are as follows:

- **Configure**—Provides full read and write access to all CSA MC functions

- **Deploy**—Provides full-read and partial-write access to CSA MC functions including managing hosts and groups, attaching policies, creating Agent kits, scheduling software updates, and performing all monitoring actions

- **Monitor**—Provides monitoring personnel with read-only access to the all CSA MC functions. Administrators can create reports, alerts, and event sets

The CSA MC ships with several default Agent kit security policies designed to meet the generalized security needs of:

- Servers

- Workstations

- The VMS server (where CSA MC resides) itself

Cisco recommends using these policies as the basis for custom policies and not to modify the default policy itself.

Groups consist of hosts that have similar security needs and one or more of the following qualities:

- The same type of function (web server, mail server)

- The same organizational business unit

- The same geographical location

- Some unique importance to the organization

Agent kits are designed around these common group needs and deployed to the hosts within the groups. By using groups, administrators can apply identical policies within a group, apply alerts and event set parameters consistently across a group, and demonstrate the effectiveness of Agent kit policies by using the CSA "test mode." Test mode applies a policy but does not enforce it. It instead logs an event that would have been usually denied. Note that Windows and Unix hosts cannot be in the same group.

It is possible to verify the current host CSA status for the following areas:

- **Active**—Identifies if the host is polling the CSA MC on a regular basis

- **Protected**—Identifies if a host is protected. An unprotected host is not part of any group or is part of a group with no security policy

- **Latest Software**—Identifies when a host is not running the latest CSA software

- **Test Mode**—Identifies when a host is running in test mode and policies are not enforced.

- **Last Poll**—Indicates the last time a host polled the CSA MC

With CSA MC, any changes to existing configurations require a save to the database and subsequent "generate rules" to distribute these changes to the affected agents

IPSec VPNs

A VPN provides secure, reliable, encrypted connectivity over a shared, public network infrastructure such as the Internet. Because the infrastructure is shared, connectivity is provided at lower cost than by existing dedicated private networks.

Cisco VPN products primarily rely on the IPSec. IPSec is a collection of protocols developed by the Internet Engineering Task Force (IETF) to provide standards-based security at the IP layer.

This section provides a general overview of the IPSec protocol and its operation and presents an introduction to Cisco VPN products, including the Cisco VPN 3000 Concentrator and the Cisco VPN Software Client.

IPSec

IPSec acts at the network layer, protecting and authenticating IP packets among IPSec devices (peers), such as PIX and ASA security appliances, Cisco routers, Cisco VPN 3000 Concentrators, the Cisco VPN Software client, and other IPSec-compliant products. IPSec is a framework of open standards and is not bound to a specific encryption or authentication protocol. As such, IPSec can work with multiple encryption schemes and extend easily when newer and better algorithms become available.

IPSec uses the underlying encryption and authentication algorithms to provide the following critical functions:

- **Data confidentiality**—Encryption of packets before transmission across network.

- **Data integrity**—IPSec receiver authenticates IPSec peers and packets sent by the IPSec sender to ensure that no altering of data occurs during transmission.

- **Data origin authentication**—IPSec receiver authenticates the source of the IPSec packets sent. This service depends on the data integrity service.

- **Anti-replay**—IPSec receiver detects and rejects replayed packets, helping prevent spoofing and man-in-the-middle attacks.

IPSec Security Protocols

IPSec consists of the following primary components:

- **Authentication Header (AH)**—A security protocol that provides authentication and optional replay-detection services. AH uses IP Protocol number 51.

- **Encapsulating Security Payload (ESP)**—A security protocol that provides data confidentiality and protection with optional authentication and replay-detection services. ESP uses IP protocol number 50.

- **Security Association (SA)**—Secure connections among IPSec peers based on a specific set of cryptography parameters negotiated by the peers to secure and protect information transfer.

IPSec Modes of Operation

IPSec, and more specifically ESP and AH, are configured to operate in two different modes:

- **Tunnel mode**—Tunnel mode for ESP encrypts the entire IP packet, including the original header, and tacks on a new unencrypted IP header. For AH, Tunnel mode adds a new IP header to the entire original IP packet, including the original header. This entire new packet is authenticated. See the following figure for an illustration of Tunnel mode.

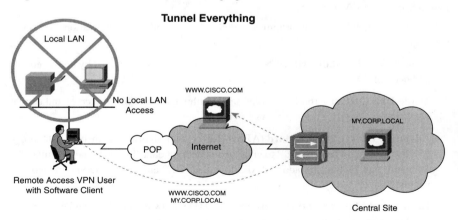

- **Transport mode**—Transport mode leaves the original IP header intact and inserts a new ESP or AH header after the IP header. When using ESP, only the original IP payload is encrypted. With AH, the entire new packet is authenticated. Because a new IP header is not added, there is less overhead with Transport mode. See the following figure for an illustration of Transport mode.

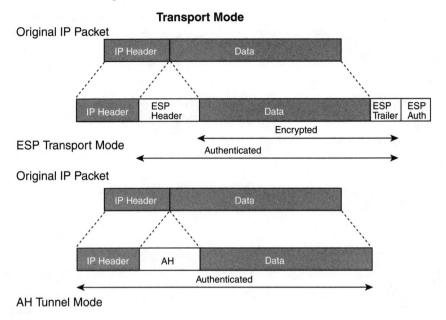

IPSec-Supported Algorithms

IPSec relies on the following algorithms to implement encryption, authentication, and key exchange:

- **Data Encryption Standard (DES)**—56-bit encryption algorithm used by ESP to encrypt and decrypt data.

- **Triple-DES (3DES)**—168-bit encryption algorithm used by ESP to encrypt and decrypt data.

- **Advanced Encryption Standard (AES)**—New cipher algorithm with 128-, 192-, or 256-bit encryption used by ESP to encrypt and decrypt data. The National Institute of Standards and Technology adopted AES to replace DES and 3DES encryption algorithms.

- **Hash-Based Message Authentication Code- (HMAC) variant Message Digest 5 (MD5)**—Uses a 128-bit shared key secret to provide message authentication.

- **HMAC-Variant Secure Hash Algorithm 1 (SHA-1)**—Uses a 160-bit shared key secret to provide message authentication. SHA-1 provides stronger authentication relative to MD5, but with additional processing overhead.

- **Diffie-Hellman (DH)**—DH is a public-key cryptography protocol that enables two parties to establish a shared secret key over an insecure communications channel.

- **RSA (Rivest, Shamir, and Adelman)**—Asymmetrical encryption algorithm used for encryption and decryption. Because asymmetrical encryption algorithms are processor-intensive, RSA is typically used for peer authentication only.

Peer Authentication

IPSec peers use several methods for peer authentication:

- **Pre-Shared Keys**—Uses a shared secret key known to both peers to authenticate the peers.

- **RSA Signatures**—With RSA signatures, uses digital certificates issued by a Certificate Authority (CA) to authenticate IPSec peers. This method requires more resources to implement, but it is more secure and scalable than pre-shared keys.

- **Encrypted Nonces**—This method requires each IPSec peer to generate a pseudorandom number (nonce) that is then encrypted and sent to other peers. Peers use the encrypted initiator and responder nonces, the DH key, and the initiator and responder cookies to generate authentication keys. A hash algorithm is used with this authentication key and device-specific information to generate a hash. This hash is then sent to the other peer. The remote peer authenticates this peer if an independent hash process produces the same results.

- **DSA (Digital Signature Algorithm)**—DSA is a U.S. government endorsed public key algorithm for digital signatures. DSA is primarily used for peer authentication.

Security Associations

Security associations are unidirectional or bidirectional connections established among IPSec peers and are uniquely identified by the IPSec protocol in use, the remote peer's address, and a 32-bit random number called the security parameter index (SPI).

- IPSec SAs are unidirectional. Therefore, peers must establish two unidirectional SAs.

- IKE SAs are bidirectional and require only a single SA between two peers.

- SAs are protocol-specific. Therefore if using both protocols, ESP and AH require separate SAs ,.

- Each SA is valid for duration of its lifetime, which is established during the negotiation process. The lifetime can be specified by time or the amount of traffic traversing the tunnel. After the SA lifetime expires reestablishment of the SA must occur.

The IPSec SAs are a compilation of the SA Database (SAD) and Security Policy Database (SPD). SAD specifies the SA destination IP address, IPSec protocol used, and the SPI number. The SPD defines the security services applied to the SA, specific encryption and authentication algorithms to be used, negotiation mode, and key lifetime.

During SA negotiations and setup, the IPSec peers must exchange and authenticate keys to establish the identity of the other peer and setup the appropriate SA. This mechanism relies on the following protocols:

- Internet Key Exchange (IKE).

- Internet Security Association and Key Management Protocol (ISAKMP).

- ISAKMP uses the IKE protocol for key exchange, but the two protocols are synonymous in Cisco VPN configurations.

To succeed in establishing an IPSec tunnel, peers must agree on a matching set of IPSec-related algorithms and variables. The following terms are important during this negotiation:

- **ISAKMP policies**—ISAKMP policies are specific combinations of algorithms and variables used Internet Key Exchange (IKE) to establish common policies among IPSec peers as shown in the following figure.

Only Tunnel Networks in the List

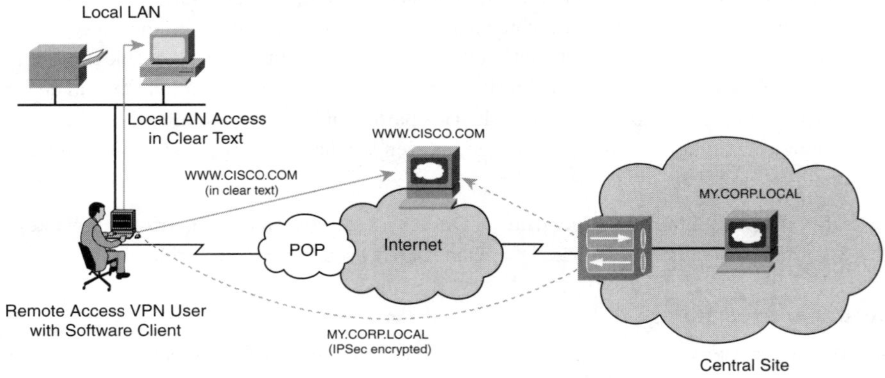

ISAKMP policies define variables such as:

— Encryption algorithm (DES, 3DES, AES)

— Hash algorithm (MD5, SHA-1)

— Authentication method (pre-share keys, RSA signatures, DSA signatures, and XAUTH variations)

— Key Exchange (DH group 1, 2, 5, or 7)

— Security Association lifetime (in seconds or bytes)

— Protocol used (ESP or AH)

— Operation mode (tunnel or transport)

- **Transform sets**— A transform set is a specific combination of message authentication and encryption algorithms used by IPSec peers. Configuration of multiple transform sets is possible on each IPSec peer.

- **Crypto maps**—Crypto maps define the combination of variables used by IPSec peers during IPSec SA negotiations. Specifically, crypto maps define:
  - Interesting traffic (traffic that protected by IPSec) using crypto ACLs
  - Peer identification
  - Transform sets to use
  - IPSec SA lifetime (optional)
  - Perfect Forward Secrecy (optional)

Key Management

IKE relies on two mechanisms for secure key exchange and management:

- **DH**—DH is a public-key cryptography algorithm used by IKE that allows two peers to establish a secret key over an insecure communications channel. DH supports various key lengths and encryption algorithms through its pre-defined groups. Operation of DH can be summarized as follows:
  - Each peer generates a public and a private key pair. The private key is kept secret and is never shared.
  - Each peer calculates a public key from its private key. Only the public key is exchanged over the insecure channel among the peers.
  - Each peer then combines the other peer's public key with its own private key and computes the same shared secret number.
  - The shared secret number is converted into a shared secret key.
  - The shared secret key is used to establish a secure communications channel among the peers (it is never exchanged over an insecure channel).
- **CA**—CA is a trusted entity that issues digital certificates.

How IPSec Works

IPSec operates according to the following steps:

Step 1   **Interesting traffic**—The VPN devices must first determine which traffic to protect. For every inbound and outbound datagram, the following three conditions might pertain:

    Apply IPSec

    Bypass IPSec

    Discard the datagram

Step 2   **IKE Phase 1**—During this phase, an initial secure communications channel is established (IKE bidirectional SA). IPSec peers use this channel for IKE Phase 2 negotiations, not to send user data. IKE Phase 1 can occur in the following modes:

- **Main mode**—This mode includes three two-way exchanges among peers:

- **First exchange**—IKE algorithms and hashes are negotiated. ISAKMP policies are used to improve performance by avoiding the large number of possible combinations of individual variables.

- **Second exchange**—DH protocol generates a shared secret key that is used to generate encryption keys for the secure communications channel.

- **Third exchange**—In this exchange, identity of the peer is authenticated and the secure communications channel is established for subsequent IKE transmissions.

- **Aggressive mode**—This mode reduces the number of exchanges by generating the DH pair on the first exchange, but without identity protection.

Step 3   **IKE Phase 2**—Matching unidirectional IPSec SAs are negotiated and established during IKE Phase 2 negotiations. The tunnel is now ready for user traffic. IKE Phase 2 does the following:

- Negotiates IPSec transform sets and security parameters

- Establishes matching unidirectional IPSec SAs

- Renegotiates the SAs when their lifetime expires

- Optionally performs additional DH exchange (perfect forward secrecy)

Step 4   **Data transfer**—IPSec peers send data defined as interesting according to the parameters defined by the crypto ACLs and negotiated in IPSec SAs.

Step 5   **Tunnel termination**—Termination of SAs occurs if their lifetime expires or when they are deleted.

Cisco VPN Overview

Construction of VPNs occurs in one of the following three implementation scenarios:

- Remote-access VPNs

- Site-to-site VPNs

- Firewall-based VPNs

Remote-Access VPNs

Remote-access VPNs connect remote dialup users to their home gateways through an ISP. Remote users need to first connect to the VPN using DSL, cable, or standard dialup connections. Cisco VPN software client establishes an encrypted tunnel to the VPN concentrator at the central site. The following figure illustrates a remote-access VPN topology.

Remote-Access VPN

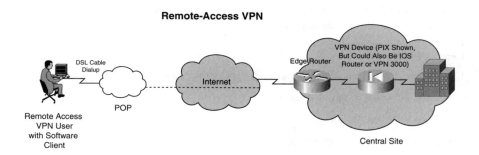

Site-to-Site VPNs

Site-to-site VPNs connect corporate sites over the Internet, replacing costlier WAN options such as leased lines and frame relay. Site-to-site VPNs are implemented using hardware devices at each end of the tunnel. This type of VPN can also connect networks among business partners to create an extranet. The following figure illustrates a site-to-site VPN topology.

Site-to-Site VPN

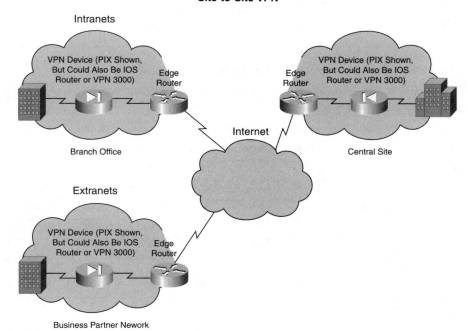

Firewall-Based VPNs

Firewall-based VPNs do not represent a different type of VPN. Instead, they refer to site-to-site or remote-access VPNs built using The Cisco firewall devices including the PIX 500

Series and ASA 5500 Series security appliances. Using this option, businesses can deploy VPNs using firewalls they already own.

Cisco VPN Hardware

Cisco offers VPN functionality on several different hardware and software platforms including:

- Cisco VPN 3000 Concentrators
- Cisco VPN-enabled routers
- Cisco PIX and ASA security appliances
- Cisco hardware and software VPN clients

The following table identifies the most appropriate use for each type of VPN device offered by Cisco Systems:

VPN Product	Remote-Access VPN	Site-to-Site VPN
VPN 3000 Concentrator	Primary role.	Secondary role.
VPN-Enabled Routers	Secondary role.	Primary role.
PIX and ASA Security Appliances	Uses existing security appliances to implement remote-access VPN.	Uses existing security appliances to implement site-to-site VPN.

Cisco VPN 3000 Concentrator Series Hardware Overview

The Cisco VPN 3000 Concentrator Series consists of several different models to meet a variety of requirements and budgets.

The Cisco VPN 3000 Concentrator Series include the models detailed in the following table:

Feature	3005	3015	3020	3030	3060	3080
Height	1 U	2 U	2 U	2 U	2 U	2 U
Performance (Mbps)	4	4	50	50	100	100
Simultaneous IPSec Users	200	200	750	1500	5000	10000
Simultaneous WebVPN Users	50	75	200	500	500	500
Max Site-to-Site Sessions	100	100	500	500	1000	1000
Network Interfaces	2	3	3	3	3	3
Encryption Method	SW	SW	HW	HW	HW	HW
Memory (MB)	32/64 (fixed)	128	256	128/256	256/512	256/512
Dual Power Supplies	No	Option	Option	Option	Option	Included
SEP Modules	0	0	1	1	2	4
Redundant SEP	--	--	Option	Option	Option	Included
Upgradeable?	No	Yes	No	Yes	Yes	No

Except for VPN 3005 Concentrator, all other models in the series use the same 2U chassis and are differentiated by the installed hardware encryption modules, power supplies, and expandability. All models include unlimited client licenses.

Models 3020 and higher support the use of a hardware Scalable Encryption Processor (SEP) for improved throughput.

Software Clients

Version 4.x is the latest version of the Cisco software VPN client and provides the following major features:

- The virtual adapter provides better compatibility with PPPoE stacks and fewer conflicts with other VPN clients, such as the Microsoft L2TP/IPSec client.

- Support for Microsoft Windows 98/ME/NT 4.0/2000/XP, Linux, Solaris, and Macintosh.

- AES support.

- Common GUI for Windows and Macintosh clients.

- Personal Firewall (Windows platform only).

- Split tunneling and split DNS.

- Load balancing and backup server support.

- Intelligent peer availability detection (DPD).

- Simple Certificate Enrollment Protocol (SCEP).

- Data compression (LZS).

- Auto Initiation.

- Startup before logon.

- Application Launcher.

Firewall Features

Cisco VPN client for Windows provides a built-in stateful firewall feature to enhance the security of the host system. Enable the feature in one of three ways:

- **Stateful Firewall (always on)**—The enduser enables or disables this mode, and it is effective with or without an established VPN tunnel.

- **Central Policy Protection (CPP)**—Use this mode for implementations requiring centralized policy management and enforcement.

- **Are You There (AYT)**—When an administrator configures AYT, the concentrator polls the client during initial logon and periodically thereafter. If the client firewall is not detected, the concentrator can be configured to refuse or drop the connection.

Auto Initiation

Auto Initiation provides the capability to automatically start a VPN connection based on the client's connected network. Use this option to secure clients on wireless LANs (WLANs) that have some inherent security weaknesses.

Hardware Clients

Cisco VPN 3002 Hardware Client is an Easy VPN client and essentially performs the same functions as the software VPN client. The hardware client is a good choice when connecting multiple users from a remote location and provides the following additional capabilities:

- The VPN tunnel is established on the hardware and there is no need to load and run the software client on each host.
- Auto Update features.

Cisco supports Easy VPN Remote functionality on several other hardware platforms in addition to the VPN 3002 Hardware Client, including:

- Cisco PIX 501 and 506E security appliances with software version 6.3 or greater
- Easy VPN Remote routers (800, UBR900, 1700, and 1800 Series IOS routers)

Operation Modes

SOHO environments or small branch offices requiring access to centralized resources typically use the Cisco VPN 3002 Hardware Client. The hardware client operates in one of two modes to provide the most appropriate type of service:

- **Client mode**—In this mode, the clients behind the Hardware Client are not directly accessible from the central site. Instead, the Hardware Client uses PAT and the addresses of the individual hosts behind it remain hidden. This mode requires a single private IP address allocated to the Hardware Client. Client mode causes VPN connections to be started by traffic from the Hardware Client side, so resources are used only on demand.
- **Network Extension mode**—In Network Extension mode, the clients behind the Hardware Client are accessible from the central site. Translation of the IP addresses of the clients does not occur in this mode. Consequently, allocation of an appropriate number of IP addresses is necessary when using Network Extension mode.

VPN 3002 Hardware Client is commonly used in the Network Extension mode, as it provides most of the benefits of a site-to-site VPN. However, note that only a single subnet can be accessed behind the 3002 Hardware Client (for example, a router cannot be placed behind the 3002 Hardware Client to route multiple subnets through the tunnel).

Configuring Remote-Access VPNs with Pre-Shared Keys on Cisco 3000 Concentrator

This section presents an overview of remote-access VPNs configured using pre-shared keys (digital certificates can also configure remote-access VPNs).

There are two kinds of pre-shared keys:

- **Unique**—Typically used with site-to-site VPNs where a unique pre-shared key is tied to a specific IP address (IPSec peer). Unique pre-shared keys are more secure but are unsuitable for remote-access VPNs because client IP addresses are typically dynamic and likely to change frequently.

- **Group**—A group pre-shared key is used for remote-access VPNs and is associated with a specific group name. The group can be the base group or any other group defined by the administrator.

The Cisco VPN software client must be loaded on the systems accessing the VPN remotely. The Software client provides the following major services:

- Negotiates IPSec parameters to establish the tunnel

- Performs user authentication with user and group names and passwords or digital certificates

- Manages security keys for encryption and decryption

- Enforces centralized policies about access rights and firewall settings

- Authenticates, encrypts, and decrypts data

Users and Groups

Cisco VPN 3000 Concentrators use user- and group-based policies to simplify configuration of settings appropriate for different groups of remote-access users.

A default base group is available and the administrator can create additional groups. Apply base group settings to all newly created groups initially. Then modify the settings on each group as required to implement the appropriate security policy for each group of users.

Assign users to any available group configured on the VPN 3000 Concentrator.

In addition to internal users and groups, the Cisco VPN 3000 Concentrators support external directories and authentication servers such as RADIUS or Active Directory. Larger implementations typically rely on external directories.

The VPN concentrator uses the following order to check authentication parameters when establishing a remote-access VPN connection:

User parameters—If any parameters are missing, then the system looks at group parameters.

Group parameters—If any parameters are missing, then the system looks at IPSec tunnel-group parameters.

IPSec tunnel-group parameters—IPSec tunnel-group parameters are the parameters of the IPSec group used to create the tunnel. If any parameters are missing, then the system looks at base-group parameters.

Default base-group parameters—Default base-group parameters are the default settings applied to all other groups when they are first created.

Based on the described authentication order, you should configure group and user settings in the following order:

Base-group parameters—Configure general settings on the base group.

Group parameters—Modify specific settings on a group that should be different from previously configured base-group settings.

User parameters—Modify specific settings for an individual user that should be different from the rest of the group.

Network Authentication

Cisco VPN 3000 Concentrators support the following two types of authentication:

- **Concentrator authentication**—Controls user rights and privileges as they relate to the concentrator.

- **Network authentication (Xauth)**—Controls access to the corporate network. Network authentication is referred to as Extended Authentication (Xauth).

Initial Configuration for Remote Access

Use the following required steps to configure the Cisco VPN 3000 Concentrator for remote access (assuming the concentrator has only factory settings):

Step 1   **General System Settings**—From the console, set the system time, date, and time zone.

Step 2   **Ethernet 1**—From the console, configure the Ethernet 1 interface with an appropriate IP address on the local network. The remaining steps are performed using a browser, using the IP address configured for Ethernet 1 interface in this step.

Step 3   **IP Interfaces**—Each interface is configured with the following parameters:

- **Disabled**—Select to disable the interface.
- **DHCP Client**—Select to obtain the IP address, subnet mask, and default gateway from DHCP.
- **Static IP Address**—Select to configure static IP address and subnet mask.
- **Public Interface check box**—Check to make a public interface.
- **MAC Address**—This is the physical address and display only. You cannot change this value.
- **Filter**—Select a default or custom filter.
- **Speed**—Set the speed (10, 100, 10/100 auto).
- **Duplex**—Set duplex (Half, Full, Auto).
- **MTU**—Specify the maximum transmission unit in bytes, between 68 and 1500. Default is 1500 bytes.
- **Public Interface IPSec Fragmentation Policy**—This setting determines how the concentrator handles fragmentation of packets exceeding the MTU when using this interface.

Step 4   **System Information**—Configures basic information such as device name, contact name, time, DNS servers, domain name, and the default gateway.

Step 5   **Protocols**—Enable desired tunneling protocols (IPSec, PPTP, L2TP)

Step 6   **Address Assignment**—Specify the method of assigning addresses to client from one of the following four options:

- **Use Client Address**—Uses the IP address supplied by the client.

- **Use Address from Authentication Server**—Uses an IP address from an authentication server, such as CSACS.

- **Use DHCP**—Uses DHCP to obtain an IP address for the client.

- **Use Address Pools**—Uses internal address pools configured on the VPN Concentrator.

Step 7   **Authentication**—Select an authentication method using the following variables:

- **Server Type**—Choose RADIUS, NT Domain, SDI (SecurID server), Kerberos/ Active Directory, or Internal Server.

- **Additional Settings**—Depending on the type of server chosen in the preceding step, the address of the authentication server and other server type-dependent information might need specification.

Step 8   **Internal Authentication Server Database**—If using the internal authentication server, populate the internal user database including the group name and password.

Step 9   **Admin Password**—Specify the administrative password for the device.

Step 10   **Save the Configuration**—Save the configuration on the concentrator to maintain settings after a reboot.

IKE Proposals

For proper operation of remote-access VPNs, configure appropriate IKE proposals on the Cisco VPN 3000 Concentrator. IKE proposals are a specific combination of IKE variables including:

- Authentication mode

- Authentication Algorithm

- Encryption Algorithm

- DH group

- Lifetime (data- or time-based)

IKE proposals perform the same function as the transform sets discussed earlier. When a client attempts to connect to the VPN Concentrator, it sends an IKE proposal to the concentrator. The concentrator looks for a matching IKE proposal on its list to make the connection.

The order of configuration of the IKE proposals on the concentrator is important. If remote-access-specific proposals (names beginning with CiscoVPNClient) are not at the top of the list, Unity clients might not be able to successfully connect.

Group Configuration

Configure group settings via **User Management > Groups from the Web-Based Interface.** Configure the settings for the Base Group or specific groups that are created. The Base Group sets the default group settings initially applied to any newly created group. Each group's settings can then be further modified with the following seven tabs:

- General tab
- IPSec tab
- Client Config tab
- Client FW tab
- HW Client tab
- PPTP/L2TP tab
- WebVPN tab
- NAC tab

Major settings configured on these tabs include such items as:

- Group name and password
- Number of simultaneous logins allowed
- DNS and WINS settings to be delivered to clients
- IPSec SA
- Tunnel type
- Authentication method
- IPComp settings
- Mode Configuration
- Banner
- NAT-T and IPSec over UDP/TCP settings
- Backup Server lists
- Split Tunneling and Split DNS settings
- Firewall requirement settings
- PPTP and L2TP settings

Split Tunneling

Split tunneling is one of the significant options during remote-access VPN configuration and worth a brief review. When configuring remote-access VPNs, configure the concentrator to:

- **Tunnel Everything**—This option sends all traffic through the IPSec tunnel. This option is typically considered more secure, but it is costly in terms of bandwidth and processing overhead imposed on the central site. The following figure illustrates full-tunneling configuration where the IPSec tunnel protects all traffic, including Internet sites (Cisco.com in this example).

Tunnel Everything

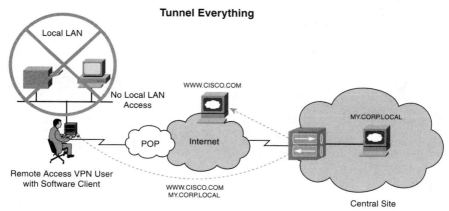

- **Allow Networks in List to Bypass the Tunnel**—With this option, all traffic is sent through the IPSec tunnel except traffic destined for the local LAN networks in the bypass list. The following figure illustrates this type of configuration where the local network is accessed in clear text while all other traffic is accessed through the IPSec tunnel.

Tunnel Everything Except Local LAN Traffic

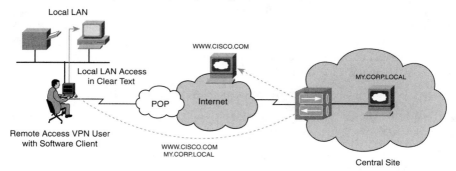

- **Only Tunnel Networks in the List**—With this option, only traffic destined for specified networks is sent through the IPSec tunnel. All other traffic (typically internet browsing traffic) is sent in clear text. This option lowers the impact on the central site's bandwidth and CPU utilization. A built-in network ("VPN Client Local LAN [Default]") is defined to allow local LAN access. The following figure illustrates split-tunneling configuration where users access only corporate resources through the IPSec tunnel. Internet sites (Cisco.com in this example) is accessed in clear text.

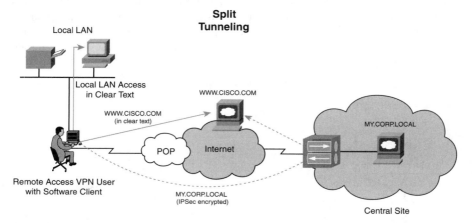

Split DNS

Split DNS defines internal DNS servers for name resolution of resources accessed through the IPSec tunnel and ISP-assigned DNS servers for all other DNS requests. If name resolution for an IPSec-protected resource is required, the DNS query is sent through the IPSec tunnel to a corporate DNS server for name resolution. Clear text DNS requests are resolved by the ISP-assigned DNS servers. Split DNS is used in conjunction with split tunneling.

Cisco VPN Software Client for Windows

The VPN Software Client terminates the VPN tunnel on the remote client PC. The software provides the capability to create multiple profiles, or "connection entries," which allow the remote host to connect to different concentrators and VPN headends as necessary. However, only one connection can be active at any time. To connect using an alternate profile, disconnect from the current active connection first.

Create connection entries using the following primary configuration tabs:

- **Authentication**—Group name and password or digital certificate information is configured in this tab.

- **Transport**—Transparent tunneling (IPSec over UDP or TCP) settings and local LAN access options are configured here.

Keep in mind that settings configured here must also be configured and permitted on the concentrator to have any effect. In other words, if the VPN 3000 Concentrator is configured to disallow local LAN access, enabling the local LAN access option on the VPN Software Client will not override the settings on the concentrator and local LAN access is not possible.

- **Backup Servers**—Backup servers are configured here for redundancy.

- **Dialup**—This tab allows you to specify a default Microsoft Dial-Up Networking or other third-party connection for the VPN Software Client. With this setting configured, if the client starts and no active Internet connection is present, the VPN client uses the configured dialup entries to make a connection to the Internet automatically.

Preconfiguration of the Client for Distribution   To facilitate the distribution of the VPN Software Client in the enterprise, several options are available to preconfigure certain settings for installation and initial configuration of the client.

- Use oem.ini to enable or disable silent installation and specify automatic reboot after installation.

- Use vpnclient.ini to configure startup settings such as:
  — Default connection entry
  — Log settings
  — Simple Mode or Advanced Mode operation
  — Stateful firewall settings

- Use profile (.pcf) files to define authentication, transport, backup servers, and dialup settings for each profile.

Set MTU Application   One of the issues that software clients might have to deal with is IP fragmentation and the MTU size. When IP packets are tunneled using other protocols such as IPSec or GRE, the additional headers and trailers that other protocols add can increase the packet size to more than the typical MTU of 1500 bytes. The VPN Concentrator must then fragment the packets to reduce the size and comply with the MTU settings. Certain protocols used with remote-access connections, such as PPPoE used with DSL and cable services, also impact packet size and can have an effect on fragmentation.

One method to reduce fragmentation and its impact on applications affected is to configure a smaller MTU setting for traffic that traverses the IPSec tunnel. The Cisco VPN Software Client automatically sets an MTU setting of 1300 bytes. This setting allows approximately 200 additional bytes for use by various protocols that might be in use (such as PPPoE, ESP, AH, and others).

If additional changes are necessary, use the SetMTU utility to set the MTU size to an appropriate value. Keep in mind that setting the MTU at too low a value impacts the network performance negatively.

Backup Servers, Load Balancing, and Reverse Route Injection

Cisco VPN 3000 Concentrators include redundancy and load balancing capabilities designed for high availability applications. This section presents these features and the reverse route injection function of the concentrator.

Cisco VPN Client Backup Servers

Backup servers provide redundancy by specifying additional concentrators that clients can connect to if their primary concentrator is not available.

The list of backup servers can be configured on the concentrator, the hardware client, or the software client. Depending on the configuration settings on the concentrator, the list of backup servers configured on clients might or might not be used. Up to 10 servers can be configured in order of highest to lowest priority.

Backup Server Configuration on Concentrator   Backup servers on the concentrator are configured on the Client Config tab in Group setup. Three options are available:

- **Use Client Configured List**—This option allows the client to use its own list of backup servers.

- **Disable and Clear Configured List**—This option disables the backup server feature and instructs the clients to clear their list of backup servers.

- **Use List Below**—This option instructs the clients to use the list of backup servers configured on the concentrator and replaces any list that might already be configured on the clients.

Backup Server Configuration on Clients   You can also configure lists of backup servers on the Hardware Client and the Software Client. If the setting on the concentrator is "Use Client Configured List," the local list configured on the client is used to locate backup servers.

Backup servers on the VPN 3002 Hardware Client are configured in **Configuration > System > Tunneling Protocols > IPSec**.

Backup servers on the VPN Software Client are configured via the Backup Servers tab of the application.

Cisco VPN Client Load Balancing

Load balancing provides the capability of distributing sessions across multiple concentrators to improve performance. The clients must meet the following requirements for load balancing:

- VPN Software Client version 3.5 or higher
- VPN Hardware Client version 3.5 or higher

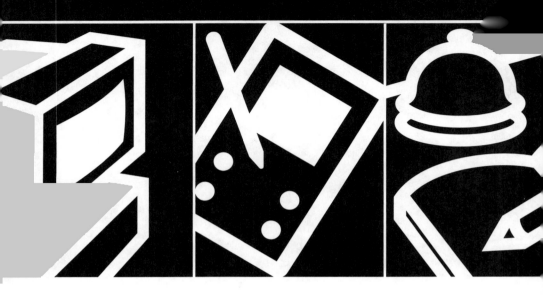

Part II

Securing Cisco Networks with Routers and Switches (SNRS) Flash Cards

The flash cards in this part of the book prepare you for the Securing Cisco Networks with Routers and Switches (SNRS) exam (642-502) to achieve your CCSP certification. Over 250 more questions for this section of the book can be found on the CD-ROM accompanying this book. The flash cards address specific topic areas for this exam and are organized as follows:

- **Section 1: Security Fundamentals**—Tests your knowledge of security concepts including policy, attacks, and threats.

- **Section 2: Device Access and Basic Security**—Tests your knowledge of router and switch access modes, secure and insecure protocols used for device management, RFCs used in filtering, and device logging.

- **Section 3: AAA Concepts and Device Configuration**—Tests your knowledge of authentication, authorization, and accounting (AAA) and Cisco Secures Access Control Servers for advanced authentication.

- **Section 4: Cisco IOS Firewall Security**—Tests your knowledge of the Cisco IOS firewall features, capabilities, and configuration procedures and commands.

- **Section 5: Layer 2 Device Security**—Tests your knowledge of Layer 2 attacks and ways to mitigate them, Identity Based Network Services (IBNS) systems, and 802.1x/Extensible Authentication Protocol (EAP) authentication.

- **Section 6: Cisco Security Device Manager**—Tests your knowledge of Security Device Manager (SDM) installation procedures and requirements, its architecture, and configuration procedures with SDM.

- **Section 7: Building Basic IPSec VPNs Using Cisco Routers**—Tests your knowledge of VPN technologies and related protocols, and evaluates your familiarity with commands and procedures for configuration of VPNs using pre-shared keys.

- **Section 8: Building Cisco IOS-Based VPNs Using Certificate Authorities**—Tests your knowledge of commands and procedures for configuration of VPNs with certificate authorities (CA).

- **Section 9: Cisco IOS Remote Access Using Cisco Easy VPN**—Tests your familiarity with commands and procedures to configure remote access VPNs on Cisco IOS routers. Cisco VPN Software Client and Easy VPN topics are also covered.

Section 1
Security Fundamentals

Question 1

Effective network security begins with what?

Question 2

Name two types of network security threats.

Question 3

Describe an unstructured threat.

Question 1 Answer

Effective network security begins with a security policy, which is a format statement of an organization's rules concerning the use of technology and the treatment of information assets that each employee must follow. Each employee should be obligated to adhere to the security policy.

Question 2 Answer

Network security threats include:

- Unstructured threats
- Structured threats
- External threats
- Internal threats

Question 3 Answer

An unstructured threat comes from inexperienced individuals, also known as script kiddies, who use hacking tools widely available on the Internet.

Question 4

Describe an internal threat.

Question 5

Describe an IP spoofing attack.

Question 6

What type of attack is a slow network scan?

Question 4 Answer

Threats from individuals with authorized access to the network with an account on a server or physical access to the wire is an internal threat. Examples include disgruntled employees who currently work at the organization, former employees, or nonemployees who are on site, such as contract workers.

Question 5 Answer

IP spoofing is an attack whereby the attacker attempts to impersonate a trusted IP address, so that the target accepts communications from him.

Question 6 Answer

This is a reconnaissance information scan because it is an unauthorized attempt to map a network topology.

Section 2
Device Access and Basic Security

Question 1

Name three router CLI modes.

Question 2

How many privileged access levels are there? Which are the most privileged?

Question 3

Name two insecure application protocols often used in the management of routers.

Question 1 Answer

Router command-line modes include:

- ROM monitor
- User EXEC
- Privileged EXEC
- Configuration mode

Question 2 Answer

There are 16 privileged access levels, which consist of levels 0 through 15, and 15 is the most privileged.

Question 3 Answer

Two insecure application protocols often used in the management of routers are:

- Telnet
- SNMP

Question 4

What protocol and port is used by Secure Shell as its default?

Question 5

Why is Telnet insecure?

Question 6

When enabling SSH on a router, what is the first command that must run before all other SSH-related commands?

Question 4 Answer

TCP port 22

Question 5 Answer

Telnet is insecure because usernames, passwords, and all data are sent in clear text between the client and the end device. This data is subject to sniffing and unauthorized re-use.

Question 6 Answer

ip domain-name yourdomain.com

Question 7

What is RFC 1918's significance?

Question 8

What range is a Class E network?

Question 9

Which event level is more severe: level 5 or level 3?

Question 7 Answer

RFC 1918 specifies non Internet-routable addresses for internal use within organizational network infrastructure. They are also called private addresses.

Question 8 Answer

248.0.0.0 /5

Question 9 Answer

Level 3 (Error) is more severe than level 5 (Notification).

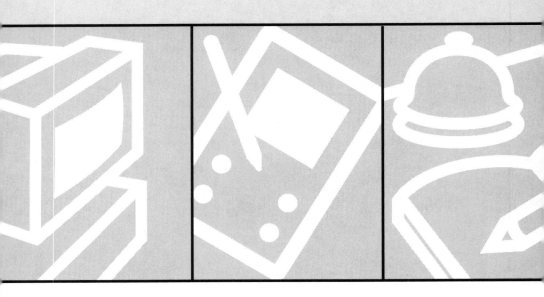

Section 3
AAA Concepts and Device Configuration

Question 1

What does the acronym AAA stand for?

Question 2

Describe the function of AAA?

Question 3

Which command enables AAA on a router?

Question 1 Answer

AAA stands for:

- Authentication
- Authorization
- Accounting

Question 2 Answer

AAA is a service that defines who can access the system, what each user is authorized to do with the system, and it provides an auditable accounting trail of user activities while they are connected.

Question 3 Answer

The command is **aaa new-model**.

Question 4

If the command aaa authentication login default local enable is in a router configuration, where will the router first look for privileged EXEC access credentials?

Question 5

Which part of AAA dictates what a user is allowed to do?

Question 6

Provide an example command that records within the NAS the start and stop times of a user's EXEC session.

Question 4 Answer

It first looks in its local database of usernames and passwords.

Question 5 Answer

Authorization

Question 6 Answer

One viable command is **aaa accounting exec start-stop group tacacs.**

Question 7

What does CSACS stand for?

Question 8

Which advanced authentication standard does CSACS support for wireless supplicant network access?

Question 9

What operating systems does CSACS support?

Question 7 Answer

Cisco Secure Access Control Server

Question 8 Answer

802.1X/EAP

Question 9 Answer

Windows 2000 Server (Service Pack 4) or Windows Server 2003—
Enterprise or Standard Edition

Section 4
Cisco IOS Firewall Security

Question 1

What is the function of CBAC?

Question 2

What is a state table?

Question 3

Does CBAC inspect ICMP?

Question 1 Answer

The function of CBAC is to provide stateful firewalling among two or more segments that terminate on or traverse a CBAC-enabled router or switch.

Question 2 Answer

A state table maintains connection information for sessions going through the firewall, as allowed by the security policy implemented.

Question 3 Answer

CBAC supports inspection of ICMP with Cisco IOS Software Release 12.2(15)T or later. TCP and UDP protocols can be inspected only with earlier versions of IOS.

Question 4

How does CBAC control traffic on the IOS router?

Question 5

What is the TCP SYN wait time and what is its default global value?

Question 6

What commands are used to globally define TCP and UDP idle times?

Question 4 Answer

CBAC dynamically modifies ACLs applied to an interface to permit or deny return traffic based on the specific configuration of the IOS firewall.

Question 5 Answer

TCP SYN wait time is the period in seconds that the IOS firewall waits for a half-open session to establish before it is dropped and removed from the session table. Its default value is 30 seconds.

Question 6 Answer

The commands **ip inspect tcp idle-time** and **ip inspect udp idle-time** globally define the time in seconds that the IOS firewall maintains a TCP or UDP session in its session table without any activity.

Question 7

What are the default TCP and UDP global idle times?

Question 8

What is the default global DNS timeout value, and what command is used to modify it?

Question 9

What settings are configured if you use the ip inspect max-incomplete high command?

Question 7 Answer

Default global idle times for TCP and UDP are 3600 and 30 seconds, respectively.

Question 8 Answer

The default global DNS timeout period is 5 seconds. Use the **ip inspect dns-timeout** command to modify its value.

Question 9 Answer

The command **ip inspect max-incomplete high** globally defines the absolute limit for the number of existing half-open TCP or UDP connections. When the number of existing half-open connections exceeds this limit, existing half-open connections are deleted to accommodate new connections, as necessary. The default value is 500.

Question 10

Your Microsoft Exchange server experiences Internet mail problems after you enable CBAC's SMTP inspection on your router. What can cause this, and how can you fix the problem?

Question 11

You can use CBAC's SMTP and ESTMP inspections simultaneously; true or false?

Question 12

What is PAM?

Question 10 Answer

Microsoft Exchange uses Extended Simple Mail Transport Protocol (ESMTP) for Internet mail. If you use IOS version 12.3(7)T or greater, you can use ESTMP inspection with Microsoft Exchange. With earlier versions of IOS, you must disable SMTP inspection.

Question 11 Answer

False. You cannot use SMTP or ESMTP inspections simultaneously. To enable either inspection, you must first disable the other inspection if it is enabled on the router.

Question 12 Answer

Port to Application Mapping (PAM) is used to customize various TCP and UDP ports for different network applications and services, and allows CBAC to inspect applications on nonstandard ports. For example, if a web server is configured to operate on port 8080 instead of 80, you can configure CBAC to inspect the HTTP traffic on this nonstandard port using PAM.

Question 13

You want to use CBAC to inspect HTTP traffic from a development site that runs on TCP port 8000. What feature of CBAC must you use to accomplish this task?

Question 14

What command is used to configure a CBAC inspection list?

Question 15

What command configures Java inspection rules?

Question 13 Answer

Port-to-application mapping, or PAM, is the feature that allows CBAC to inspect applications on nonstandard ports. To allow CBAC inspection of HTTP traffic on TCP port 8000, the following command is used:

```
router(config)# ip port-map http port 8000
```

Question 14 Answer

Use the **ip inspect name** command to configure CBAC inspection lists.

Question 15 Answer

You can enable Java inspection using the **ip inspect name** command, protocol name **http,** and the optional keyword **java-list.** A standard ACL can be specified to permit Java applets from friendly sites.

Question 16

Describe authentication proxy.

Question 17

Making the assumption that a router at 209.165.200.225 is fully set up to allow user A to use authentication proxy, what is the first thing user A needs to do to get access to his destination?

Question 18

What device dictates which hosts the remote user that uses authentication proxy services can access?

Question 16 Answer

Authentication proxy provides dynamic per-user authentication and authorization to users who are required to pass through a router to get to services on its other side.

Question 17 Answer

Open a browser and type in the URL address to the desired web destination. For example: http://www.cisco.com. The router will handle the creation of access list entries to allow the access to cisco.com.

Question 18 Answer

The AAA NAS server stores a user access profile associated with the user, and this profile contains access control entries that enforce which hosts and networks he can access.

Question 19

What is a proxyacl?

Question 20

What privilege level must each authentication proxy user have to successfully use the proxy authentication services?

Question 21

Can a user start an authentication proxy session to a router via an encrypted tunnel?

Question 19 Answer

A proxyacl is an access control entry within a user's AAA NAS profile that defines a host or network that a user can access.

Question 20 Answer

Each user profile on the AAA NAS must be set to privilege level 15.

Question 21 Answer

Yes, HTTPS can provide the router with username and password information, though this is possible only if the IOS version on the router supports this cryptographic feature.

Question 22

Which AAA router command is required for authentication proxy authorization?

Question 23

What does the acronym IPS stand for?

Question 24

Define network misuse.

Question 22 Answer

The command **aaa authorization auth-proxy default group tacacs** specifies that the router should use a configured TACACS+ servers for user authorization.

Question 23 Answer

Intrusion prevention system

Question 24 Answer

Network misuse is any activity the security policy implicitly or explicitly forbids.

Question 25

How does IOS IPS identify attacks?

Question 26

Name the two event alarm mechanisms for IOS IDS and the two alarm mechanisms for IOS IPS?

Question 27

What is an IDS Director?

Question 25 Answer

IOS IPS examines packet flows inline as they traverse through the router to identify attacks. To be identified, the attack signature and an IPS policy with a signature must be enabled, and the IPS policy must be applied to an interface through which the packet flows.

Question 26 Answer

IOS IDS supports Syslog and Post Office Protocol, and IOS IPS supports Syslog and SDEE.

Question 27 Answer

An IDS Director is the name of a Post Office Protocol-based central IDS management server. It can receive event alarms from IDS-enabled devices, such as IOS IDS-capable routers.

Question 28

The IPS function can analyze packet flows in what direction from an interface?

Question 29

Which IOS intrusion technology components can be tuned?

Question 30

List four IOS IPS engine types.

Question 28 Answer

The IPS function can analyze packet flows from both inbound and outbound.

Question 29 Answer

Unlike the enterprise-class Cisco Secure IPS, IOS IDS signatures cannot be individually tuned. However, IOS IPS signatures can be tuned. Both IOS IDS and IPS signatures can be enabled or disabled, which affect overall router performance, especially with compound signatures that require more computing resources.

Question 30 Answer

IOS IPS signatures analysis engines include:

- Layer 3 IP protocol
- TCP
- UDP
- IP options
- ICMP
- HTTP
- DNS
- SMTP
- FTP
- RPC

Section 5
Layer 2 Device Security

Question 1

What is a CAM table?

Question 2

Which switch command disables the ability for an interface to become a trunk?

Question 3

What is the purpose of a private VLAN?

Question 1 Answer

A CAM table is the content addressable memory on a switch where the MAC address(es) connected to each port are stored. It allows the switch to know where packets must be forwarded to get to their destination.

Question 2 Answer

The **switchport mode access** command

Question 3 Answer

A private VLAN is meant to control host-to-host data traffic within a broadcast network. A VLAN is a broadcast network.

Question 4

Why is a DHCP address depletion attack a threat?

Question 5

What does IBNS stand for, and what is its purpose?

Question 6

What is 802.1X?

Question 4 Answer

A DHCP address depletion attack is a threat because if no dynamic addresses are available in the pool to legitimate hosts, these hosts cannot gain network access; therefore, it causes a denial-of-service condition.

Question 5 Answer

Identity Based Networking Security (IBNS) technology improves security because it allows users and devices access to a network only if they present valid authentication credentials.

Question 6 Answer

The IEEE standard for strong port-level user authentication

Question 7

What is the difference between 802.1X and EAP?

Question 8

What communication is blocked by the authenticator before valid authentication of the supplicant?

Question 9

Which EAP type requires only user passwords, is simple to deploy, and provides two-way authentication?

Question 7 Answer

802.1X is the access model for host-to-host communication, and it consists of the authentication messaging. Extensible Authentication Protocol (EAP) is the authentication system that is sent within the 802.1X messages.

Question 8 Answer

Before valid supplicant authentication, all network communication is blocked, except 802.1X messages, CDP, and STP.

Question 9 Answer

LEAP, which stands for Lightweight Extensible Authentication Protocol

Question 10

Which EAP type relies on PACs?

Question 11

Which EAP types are referred to as EAP within EAP technologies?

Question 12

Name three EAP types supported by CSACS.

Question 10 Answer

EAP-FAST

Question 11 Answer

EAP-TLS and PEAP

Question 12 Answer

The following are EAP types supported by CSACS:

- EAP-MD5
- EAP-TLS
- LEAP
- PEAP
- EAP-FAST

Section 6
Cisco Security Device Manager

Question 1

What happens if you install SDM on a router with an unsupported IOS version?

Question 2

What must be enabled on the router to support operation of SDM on the router?

Question 3

What command is used to install SDM on a router via TFTP?

Question 1 Answer

SDM fails to launch until the router is upgraded to a supported version of IOS software.

Question 2 Answer

HTTP and HTTPS server support should be enabled on the router if you use the following commands:

```
Router(config)# ip http server
Router(config)# ip http secure-server
```

Question 3 Answer

Use the following command:

```
Router# copy tftp://<tftp-server ip-address>/sdm.tar flash:
```

Question 4

What protocols does SDM use to communicate with the IOS device?

Question 5

List the SDM primary interface elements?

Question 6

List the SDM-compatible browsers.

Question 4 Answer

SDM uses Telnet and SSH to communicate with the IOS device.

Question 5 Answer

SDM interface primary elements include the menu bar, the toolbar, the mode indicator, and the taskbar.

Question 6 Answer

The SDM-compatible browsers are:

- Netscape version 4.79 on all supported operating systems, except Windows 98

- Netscape version 7.1 or 7.2

- Internet Explorer version 5.5 or later

Question 7

How many IOS devices can be simultaneously administered using SDM?

Question 8

What protocol is used by SDM to deliver configuration commands to an IOS router?

Question 9

What command is used to disable the finger service in IOS?

Question 7 Answer

An instance of SDM can configure a single IOS device. Multiple instances of SDM can run on the same PC to administer different routers.

Question 8 Answer

SDM uses HTTP or HTTPS to deliver commands to IOS devices with software versions 12.3M or 12.3T. With earlier IOS versions, SDM uses RPC to deliver configuration commands to the router.

Question 9 Answer

The finger service can be disabled if you use either the **no ip finger** or **no service finger** command.

Question 10

Why should you disable router services not critical to your operational environment?

Question 11

Which command prevents an incoming IP packet from defining a route it wants to use instead of the route in the router's routing table?

Question 12

Why is it a good idea to synchronize each router's clock with a trusted NTP source?

Question 10 Answer

Router services provide theoretical and actual attack vectors, and if they are not needed, you should turn them off.

Question 11 Answer

The **no ip source-route** command

Question 12 Answer

Synchronizing all network devices to a trusted NTP source ensures that logged events have the correct time stamp. It also ensures that digital certificates, if they are in use, do not have operational issues.

Section 7
Building Basic IPSec VPNs
Using Cisco Routers

Question 1

IPSec SAs are bidirectional; true or false?

Question 2

List the three commonly used key lengths with AES encryption.

Question 3

What does interesting traffic mean as it relates to VPN configurations?

Question 1 Answer

False. IPSec SAs are unidirectional. Two unidirectional SAs are required for a bidirectional tunnel.

Question 2 Answer

AES encryption uses 128-bit, 192-bit, or 256-bit encryption keys.

Question 3 Answer

Interesting traffic is typically selected using an access control list (crypto ACL), and it is defined as the traffic that IPSec protects.

Question 4

What protocol uses bidirectional SAs?

Question 5

In which IPSec mode is an ESP header inserted between the IP header and the encrypted payload?

Question 6

Which IPSec mode does not require host-based encryption?

Question 4 Answer

IKE SAs

Question 5 Answer

In Transport mode, an ESP header is inserted between the IP header and the encrypted payload.

Question 6 Answer

In Tunnel mode, encryption occurs between VPN devices terminating the IPSec tunnel, and the hosts are not required to perform encryption.

Question 7

Which devices are compatible with the VPN Services Module?

Question 8

List the four primary tasks required for IPSec configuration with IKE pre-shared keys.

Question 9

What command is used to display the current IKE policies configured on an IOS router?

Question 7 Answer

VPNSM can be deployed in 7600 series routers and Catalyst 6500 switches.

Question 8 Answer

Step 1   Prepare for IKE and IPSec.

Step 2   Configure IKE.

Step 3   Configure IPSec.

Step 4   Test and verify.

Question 9 Answer

The following command displays the current IKE policies configured on an IOS router:

```
Router# show crypto isakmp policy
```

Question 10

What command is used to display the current IPSec transform sets configured on an IOS router?

Question 11

What command is used to enable IKE?

Question 12

What command is used to create a new IKE policy on an IOS router?

Question 10 Answer

The following command displays the current IPSec transform sets configured on an IOS router:

```
Router# show crypto ipsec transform-set
```

Question 11 Answer

The following command enables IKE:

```
Router(config)# crypto isakmp enable
```

Question 12 Answer

The following command creates a new IKE policy on an IOS router:

```
Router(config)# crypto isakmp policy priority
```

Question 13

What is the default IKE peer authentication method?

Question 14

What command is used to configure pre-shared key peer authentication method in IKE?

Question 15

What command is used to configure a pre-shared key that IPSec peers can use?

Question 13 Answer

Cisco IOS uses RSA signatures as the default peer authentication method.

Question 14 Answer

The **crypto isakmp policy** command first creates the IKE policy. After the policy is created and you are in the ISAKMP configuration mode, you can specify pre-shared key peer authentication using the following command:

```
Router(config-isakmp)# authentication pre-share
```

Question 15 Answer

Pre-shared keys are configured using the following command:

```
Router(config)# crypto isakmp key key-name {address peer-address
[subnet-address] | hostname peer-hostname}
```

Question 16

What command is used to display and verify configured IKE policies?

Question 17

How many transforms can be specified in a transform set?

Question 18

What command is used to set the global IPSec SA lifetime on a router?

Question 16 Answer

Configured IKE policies can be displayed using the following command:

```
Router# show crypto isakmp policy
```

Question 17 Answer

Up to three transforms can be specified as part of a single transform set.

Question 18 Answer

The following command sets the global IPSec SA lifetime on a router:

```
Router (config)# crypto ipsec security- association lifetime seconds
```

Section 8
Building Cisco IOS-Based VPNs
Using Certificate Authorities

Question 1

What is a CA?

Question 2

What is a PKCS #7?

Question 3

What is a PKCS #10?

Question 1 Answer

Certificate Authorities (CA) are trusted entities that issue, administer, and revoke digital certificates (via CRLs) that are used to authenticate IPSec peers.

Question 2 Answer

Public-Key Cryptography Standard #7 (PKCS #7) is an RSA standard certificate format used to encrypt, sign, and package enrollment messages.

Question 3 Answer

Public-Key Cryptography Standard #10 (PKCS #10) is an RSA standard syntax used for certificate requests.

Question 4

What is SCEP?

Question 5

Which command is used to minimize memory usage on the IOS device when you configure VPNs with CA?

Question 6

What settings must be configured on the router before CA support can be configured?

Question 4 Answer

Simple Certificate Enrollment Protocol (SCEP) is a common protocol created by Cisco, VeriSign, Entrust, Microsoft, Netscape, and Sun Microsystems to provide a standard method to submit requests, download certificates and CRLs, and manage certificate lifecycles.

Question 5 Answer

The **crypto ca certificate query** command prevents storage of certificates and CRLs on the router to minimize memory usage (certificates and CRLs are retrieved from the CA).

Question 6 Answer

Before you configure CA support on a router, the time, date, host name, and domain name of the router must be configured.

Question 7

What command is used to declare a CA?

Question 8

How do you specify the URL used by the IOS device to enroll with the CA?

Question 9

Provide the IOS command used to authenticate the CA.

Question 7 Answer

The following command declares a CA:

```
Router(config)# crypto ca trustpoint ca-name
```

Question 8 Answer

From the CA configuration mode prompt, the following command specifies the URL used to enroll with the CA:

```
Router(ca-trustpoint)# enrollment URL [http: ¦ https:]url
```

Question 9 Answer

Use the following IOS command to authenticate a CA:

```
Router(config)# crypto ca authenticate ca-name
```

Question 10

Which command is used to request a certificate from a CA?

Question 11

Which command displays configured CA settings on the router?

Question 12

What command is used to configure IKE with CA support?

Question 10 Answer

Use the following command to request a certificate from a CA:

```
Router(config)# crypto ca enroll ca-name
```

Question 11 Answer

Use the following command to display configured CA certificates:

```
Router# show crypto ca certificates
```

Question 12 Answer

After an IKE policy is configured using the **crypto isakmp policy** command, use the **authentication rsa-sig** command to specify IKE with certificate support.

Section 9
Cisco IOS Remote Access Using Cisco Easy VPN

Question 1

What are the two main components of the Cisco Easy VPN?

Question 2

What does split tunneling mean?

Question 3

List a security concern associated with split tunneling?

Question 1 Answer

Cisco Easy VPN consists of two components:

- Cisco Easy VPN Remote
- Cisco Easy VPN Server

Question 2 Answer

With split tunneling enabled, remote clients are configured to route Internet-bound traffic directly to the Internet in clear text, which eliminates the need for all traffic to pass through the encrypted tunnel.

Question 3 Answer

With split tunneling enabled, remote clients maintain a clear-text connection to the Internet while connected to the corporate network. If the split-tunneled client is compromised, it can provide a backdoor into the corporate network.

Question 4

What command is used to configure an IP address pool?

Question 5

What command configures RRI, and where is this command relevant?

Question 6

What command is used to configure IKE dead peer detection (DPD)?

Question 4 Answer

Use the **ip local pool** command to create an IP address pool.

Question 5 Answer

Use the **reverse route** command to configure reverse route injection (RRI). This command is available from the dynamic crypto map configuration mode (available after issuing the **crypto dynamic-map** command).

Question 6 Answer

You can configure the router to send IKE DPD messages with the **crypto isakmp keepalive** command in the global configuration mode.

CCSP: Securing Cisco Networks with Routers and Switches (SNRS) Quick Reference Sheets

Please note that there is some overlap of content in the Cisco CCSP certification courses and corresponding exams. We chose to make each section of this book stand on its own, and we covered the material for each exam independently, so that you can focus on each exam without the need to reference a common topic from a different exam's section. Because of this, you might notice redundant coverage of topics in certain sections of this book.

Security Fundamentals

This section broadly describes fundamental technology security concepts including security policies, the Cisco Security Wheel, why policies are created, security threats, and sample network attacks.

What Is a Security Policy?

Network security must be a continuous process to be effective and must always be built around a security policy. A policy is defined first and the processes and procedures to support that policy are designed around it. RFC 2196, *Site Security Handbook*, describes a security policy as, "…a formal statement of the rules by which people who are given access to an organization's technology and information assets must abide."

Security policies can be as simple as one to a few documents or they can consist of many documents that describe every aspect of security for that organization. The organization's business needs and any governmental regulations to which it must comply direct the level of policy detail. A comprehensive security policy describes some of the following concepts in writing:

- A definition of organizational information and physical assets and their relative values.

- Risk to those assets based upon threats and the likelihood the threats will occur.

- The implementation of safeguards (Security Wheel Step 1), and the degree of implementation needed to mitigate the effect of threats to assets.

- The requirements placed upon users when they interact with the organization's technology systems, such as acceptable use policies.

- How safeguards are to be monitored for effectiveness, periodically tested, and systematically improved (Security Wheel Steps 2, 3, and 4, respectively).

Cisco Security Wheel

A continuous security policy process is most effective because it promotes retesting and reapplying updated security measures on a constant basis. The Security Wheel provides a four-step process to promote and maintain network security:

Step 1   **Secure**—Implement security safeguards to prevent unauthorized access to network systems. For example: Firewalls, encryption, system hardening, and authentication, authorization, and accounting (AAA).

Step 2   **Monitor**—Monitor the network for security policy violations using tools such as a real-time intrusion prevention system and detailed logs of system activity.

Step 3   **Test**—Evaluate the effectiveness of the security safeguards in place by performing periodic tests such as system vulnerability analysis and application and operating system hardening review.

Step 4   **Improve**—Improve overall security by collecting and analyzing information from the monitoring and testing phases to make judgments on ways to make security more effective.

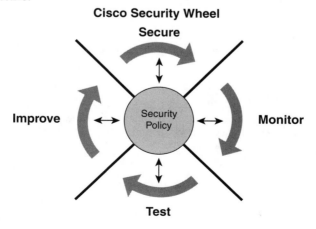

Cisco Security Wheel

Reasons for Creating a Security Policy

As we increasingly use computers and networks in our daily lives, not only do we benefit by the technology, we also become accustomed to unfailing availability. However, threats often exist that can disrupt systems. Networked systems must be designed and implemented with security in mind because most contemporary systems are interlinked or "open" in contrast to a previous time when systems were "closed" islands. This interlinking, often demanded by business processes and information exchange, increases the system vulnerabilities' risk of attack and exploitation by threats. Comprehensive network security safeguards are needed because attacks to systems have become easier for two reasons:

- Software development tools and easy-to-use operating systems provide attackers with a basis to develop attack tools.

- The Internet allows attackers to not only distribute attack tools and related attack techniques but also gain the necessary connectivity required for the attack.

If Information Technology (IT) systems are mission-critical to an organization's business, then formal security policy is especially important. If an organization suffers from a devastating loss of data because of an attack, fire, or other kind of outage, the effects on the business can be quite detrimental. Effective security policy forms a framework to avoid security problems and recover faster should they occur.

Security Threat Types

There are four ways to categorize threats to network security:

- **Unstructured threats**—Threats primarily from inexperienced individuals using hacking tools available on the Internet (script kiddies).

- **Structured threats**—Threats from hackers who are more motivated and technically competent. They usually understand network system designs and vulnerabilities, and they can create hacking scripts to penetrate network systems.

- **External threats**—Threats from individuals or organizations working outside your company who do not have authorized access to your computer systems or network. They work their way into a network mainly from the Internet or dialup access servers.

- **Internal threats**—Threats from individuals with authorized access to the network with an account on a server or physical access to the wire (typically disgruntled current or former employees or contractors).

Network Attacks

At a high level, three ways to categorize attacks are:

- **Reconnaissance attacks**—Attempts to map your network topology and the hosts within.

- **Access attacks**—Attempts to gain access to data and to spy upon, change, or destroy those resources.

- **Denial of Service (DoS) attacks**—Attempts on system availability and integrity that aim to disable and make the resources unavailable for legitimate purposes.

The following list defines various network attack types:

- **Application layer attacks**—The exploitation of well known or esoteric flaws in server applications and services.

- **DoS**—Barraging a network or hosts with more connection requests or data than can normally be handled for the purpose of permanently or temporarily denying access to systems, services, or applications; for example, SYN floods or Address Resolution Protocol (ARP) depletion.

- **Man-in-the-middle**—Attackers intercept two-way client and server communications for the purposes of information theft, alteration, DoS, reconnaissance, or trust exploitation.

- **IP spoofing**—Attackers attempt to impersonate a trusted IP address, so that the target accepts their communications.

- **ARP spoofing**—Attackers attempt to impersonate the Media Access Control (MAC) address of a trusted host to redirect IP communications.

- **Network reconnaissance**—An attempt to discover and map systems, services, vulnerabilities, and publicly available information about target systems. This is often a prelude to more sophisticated attacks.

- **Port redirection**—A trust exploitation attack that occurs when attackers that do not have direct access to an end target use an intermediate host (that the end target trusts) as a launching point.

- **Password attacks**—An attempt to gain account access by obtaining the corresponding password.

- **Trust exploitation**—Attackers take advantage of the fact that other hosts will trust one host that has been compromised, potentially allowing unauthorized access.

- **Unauthorized access**—Internal or external attacks that occur when people attempt access to systems or applications to which they have not been granted access.

- **Viruses, Trojan horse, phishing, pharming, and spam attacks**—Malicious code and trust exploitation targeted at workstations, servers, and users of these systems.

Device Access and Basic Security

The following sections address management methods and good security practices when managing Cisco devices.

Configuration Modes

The following are command-line modes for IOS-based routers and switches:

- **ROM Monitor**—The reduced functionality IOS mode to which a device boots if the system IOS image is missing or corrupt, or if an administrator purposely runs a break sequence via the serial console.

- **User EXEC mode**—The default IOS shell with limited command access.

- **Privileged EXEC mode**—Commonly referred to as "enable" mode, this shell can allow access to all IOS commands.

- **Configuration modes**
  - Global configuration—Allows global configuration settings.
  - Interface configuration—Allows configuration settings for individual interfaces.
  - Line configuration—Allows configuration settings for vty, console, and aux ports.

Privilege Levels

There are 16 levels of access defined by the numeric range 0–15. Zero is the most restrictive level and 15 is the most permissive level that grants the user full system privileges. Custom privilege levels that define permitted commands can be customized and tied to a logon account. There are three default access levels as follows:

- **Privilege level 0**—Includes the **disable, enable, exit, help**, and **logout** commands.

- **Privilege level 1**—Includes all user-level commands at the router# prompt.

- **Privilege level 15**—Includes all enable-level commands at the router# prompt.

Administrative Access Types

The following table describes the major protocols, both secure and insecure, commonly used to manage network-connected devices. Regardless of the management protocols in use, it is recommended that network accessible devices use access control lists (ACLs) whenever possible to selectively specify the permitted remote device source addresses. Note that not all options are available for all IOS revisions.

Protocol Name	Secure?	Used For	Standard Port and Protocol	Description	Notes
Secure Shell (SSH)	Yes	Command-line configuration management.	22/tcp	Authenticated and encrypted remote access to devices.	Used as a secure substitute to Telnet.
Telnet	No	Command-line configuration management.	23/tcp	Clear text remote access to devices.	Passwords and data can be intercepted with a network sniffer.
HTTPS (SSL)	Yes	GUI-based configuration management via the SDM.	443/tcp	Authenticated and encrypted remote access to devices.	Used as a secure substitute to HTTP.
HTTP	No	GUI-based configuration management via the SDM.	80/tcp	Clear text web protocol.	Passwords and data can be intercepted with a network sniffer.
Secure Copy (SCP)	Yes	Data transfer.	22/tcp	Tunneled in SSH.	Used as a secure substitute to TFTP.

Protocol Name	Secure?	Used For	Standard Port and Protocol	Description	Notes
Trivial File Transfer Protocol (TFTP)	No	Data transfer.	69/udp and >1023/udp	Clear text data transfer.	Common way to upload or download images and configurations.
Simple Network Management Protocol (SNMCP) version 1 and 2c	No	Device management.	161/udp, 162/udp	Read-only and read-write device access and management.	Use complex, non-default community strings.
SNMP version 3	Yes	Device management.	161/udp, 162/udp	Read-only and read-write device access and management with added security.	Helps prevent exposure to interception by using encryption.

Enabling Secure Shell (SSH)

SSH is a security protocol that has many uses including transmitting insecure protocols within SSH tunnels. As a command-line application, SSH is a secure alternative to Telnet. To enable the use of SSH on a router, the IOS revision must have the cryptographic components to support it.

SSH-Related Command	Explanation
`ip domain-name yourdomain.com`	Define the domain name that will become a component of the certificate.
`crypto key generate rsa general-keys modulus 2048`	Generate a crypto keypair. Note that several options exist for generating keys.
`ip ssh {various options}`	Various options exist for how ssh is to run. This is one example.
`Line vty 0 4` `    transport input ssh`	Turn on the ability to use ssh for vty access.

NOTE   The Cisco Security Device Manager (SDM) section discusses secure GUI-based router management via HTTPS.

Using ACLs to Filter Traffic

An access list filters data traffic by one or more parameters, such as IP address, IP protocol, and port number. Use IP access lists to limit which hosts can interact with a device, including the specific services allowed. ACLs are applied inbound or outbound on interfaces and vty lines and sequentially evaluate traffic as it leaves or enters the interface. Types of ACLs include:

- **Standard ACL**—Numbered from 1 to 99, these ACLs permit or deny based on the source address only. For example, ACL 2 and ACL 3:

```
access-list 2 permit host 209.165.200.225
access-list 2 deny any log
access-list 3 deny any
```

- **Extended Numbered ACL**—Numbered from 100 to 199 and 2000 to 2699 these IP ACLs permit or deny based on source and destination IP addresses as well as layer 4 protocols (Internet Control Message Protocol [ICMP], TCP, UDP, Enhanced Interior Gateway Routing Protocol [EIGRP], Encapsulating Security Payload [ESP], and others) and ports. For example:

```
access-list 2102 permit tcp host 209.165.200.225 10.5.5.0 0.0.0.255 eq ssh
access-list 2102 permit udp host 209.165.200.226 10.5.5.0 0.0.0.255 eq 500
access-list 2102 permit esp host 209.165.200.226 10.5.5.0 0.0.0.255
access-list 2102 permit icmp host 209.165.200.225 10.5.5.0 0.0.0.255
  echo-reply
access-list 2102 deny ip any any log
```

- **Extended Named ACL**—Similar to numbered ACLs, but they use names as identifiers. For example:

```
ip access-list extended production-inbound-acl
  permit tcp host 209.165.200.225 10.5.5.0 0.0.0.255 eq ssh
  permit udp host 209.165.200.226 10.5.5.0 0.0.0.255 eq 500
  permit esp host 209.165.200.226 10.5.5.0 0.0.0.255
  permit icmp host 209.165.200.225 10.5.5.0 0.0.0.255 echo-reply
  deny ip any any log-input
```

ACLs must be applied to an interface and the traffic direction specified (in or out) for filtered evaluation to occur. The following example applies an access list to the E0/0 interface and evaluates inbound traffic:

```
configure terminal
  interface ethernet0/0
  ip access-group production-inbound-acl in
  exit
```

Virtual terminal (vty), console, and aux line connections should have ACLs and other settings applied to secure access. The examples that follow use access lists 2 and 3 in the previous bullets:

Command	Explanation
`line vty 0 4`	Used for SSH and Telnet access to router. Enter configuration for vty lines 0–4. Note that devices might have more than five vty lines. Ensure all vty lines are secure.
`access-class 2 in`	Apply access list 2 for inbound traffic.
`access-class 3 out`	Apply access list 3 for outbound traffic. In this example, a user with an SSH or Telnet session to the device will not be able to establish another outbound SSH or Telnet to another host.
`transport input telnet ssh`	Allow only incoming Telnet and SSH connections.
`transport output none`	Do not allow outbound administrative connections.
`exec-timeout 5 0`	Timeout connections after 5 minutes of inactivity.
`login local`	Challenge connection attempts by using the local username and password database.
`line con 0`	Used for serial-line access to the router via the console port. Enter configuration for the console line.
`exec-timeout 2 30`	Timeout inactive connections after 2.5 minutes.

Command	Explanation
`login local`	Challenge connection attempts by using the local username and password database.
`line aux 0`	Used for modem access to the router. Often seen as an insecure backdoor and thus disabled. Enter configuration for the aux line.
`transport input none`	Disallow incoming protocols. This configuration effectively disables the use of the aux.
`login local`	Challenge connection attempts by using the local username and password database.
`exec-timeout 0 1`	Timeout connections after one second of inactivity.
`no exec`	Disables all EXEC sessions to the router via aux port.

Other administrative services, such as HTTP and SNMP, should use access lists to permit a limited set of hosts access to the device.

Command	Explanation
`access-list 5 permit host 10.1.230.4` `access-list 5 deny any log`	Create the ACL defining a central management host as permitted. Deny all other hosts.
`snmp-server community This!saC0mplexpas5word ro 5`	Define the read-only SNMP string and specify that ACL 5 should be used to limit access to the router's snmp processes.
`snmp-server community wgg^$**&djJjk rw 5`	Define the read-write SNMP string and specify that ACL 5 should be used to limit access to the router's snmp processes.
`no ip http server` `ip http secure-server`	Disable the onboard http server. Enable the secure HTTPS server. Only available with certain IOS revisions.
`ip http access-class 5`	Define which hosts are allowed access to this management interface by using ACL 5.
`ip http authentication local`	Use the local user database to challenge connection attempts. Use remote Cisco Secure ACS AAA server if available.

IP Spoof Filtering

IP spoofing occurs when an attacker poses as a trusted party and uses a trusted source address. Spoofing filters should be placed within access lists that separate administrative domains and the Internet perimeter.

- Use RFC 1918 filtering to prevent non-Internet-routable IANA (www.iana.org) reserved addresses from being the source addresses within egress or ingress Internet traffic. These network ranges include:
  - 10.0.0.0 /8 (10.0.0.0 through 10.255.255.255)
  - 172.16.0.0 /12 (172.16.0.0 through 172.31.255.255)
  - 192.168.0.0 /16 (192.168.0.0 through 192.168.255.255)
- Use RFC 2827 antispoofing features when:
  - Filtering to prevent routable ingress traffic from the ISP destined for networks you do not control.

— Filtering to prevent routable ingress traffic from the ISP sourced with IP addresses you control internally that were not initially sourced internally.

— Filtering to prevent routable egress traffic to your ISP with source addresses for networks you do not control internally.

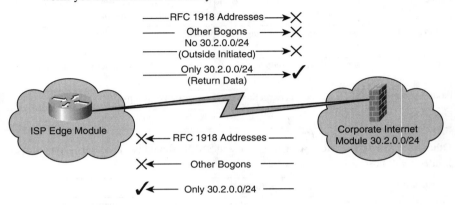

- Filter other bogon network ranges that you should not route across network boundaries, such as the following:

  — IANA unallocated addressing, such as 248.0.0.0 /5, 5.0.0.0 /8, and 72.0.0.0 /5.
  — Class D Multicast—224.0.0.0 /4 (EIGRP routing updates use Class D space and inaccurate filtering will break them.)
  — Class E—240.0.0.0 /5
  — Historical Broadcast—0.0.0.0 /8
  — Broadcast—255.255.255.255 /32
  — Test Net—192.0.2.0 /24
  — Link Local—169.254.0.0 /16
  — And others identified on the IANA website

- Filter ports and protocols (especially insecure ones) that should never cross a network boundary. For example:

  — TFTP
  — SNMP
  — Telnet

Event Logging

Use event logging to record device events. A number tagged on a logging event denotes the level of seriousness. Whereas Level 6 is an "informational" message, Level 1 is highly severe and requires immediate attention. The figure that follows is a review of logging levels and logging destination commands. Preceding a command with **no** disables any logging destination.

NOTE Regardless of the level at which you log, the messages to be logged will include those at the specified level plus all levels more severe. For example, when logging at level 6 (informational), levels 6–0 are logged.

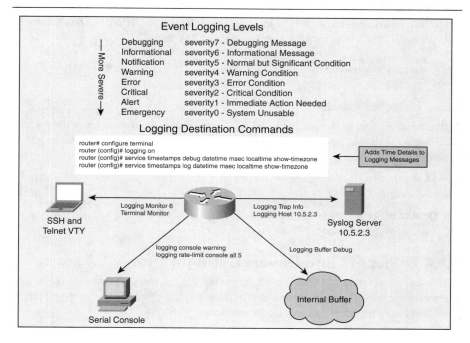

Routing Security

Router neighbor authentication protects the integrity of a routed system by preventing a legitimate router from accepting and recombining unauthorized or malicious routing updates from attackers. Routing protocols that can use MD5 authentication schemes to verify authorized neighboring routers include the following:

- RIP
- OSPF
- EIGRP
- BGP
- ISIS

NOTE Use the **passive-interface** command for each routing protocol to disable a router's capability to announce routing updates from an interface where announcements are unnecessary or a security risk.

Banners

Banners should be crafted in conjunction with the requirements of your legal authority. In general, state that unauthorized use is prohibited and always use banners to warn people trying to log on that they must have proper authorization to administer the device. Furthermore, do not include information that succinctly identifies the system owner, otherwise an attacker will instantly know the correct target has been reached. For example:

```
banner login ^C
Notice: Unauthorized access to this system is prohibited!!
^C
```

Denial of Service Attacks

Traffic floods are attacks that attempt to exhaust host resources by overwhelming them with more data requests than can normally be handled. Routers include the following Cisco IOS features to control traffic volume:

- **TCP intercept**—Monitors and brokers the TCP handshaking process between a client and server.

- **Quality of Service (QoS)**—QoS access-rate settings control traffic flow and have the capability to drop packets beyond preset thresholds.

AAA Concepts and Device Configuration

AAA encompasses a suite of Cisco device commands that help administrators control who can access a resource, provide resource authorization to permit the actions of authenticated users, and keep a record of the connected user's actions.

AAA Overview

AAA (triple A) is an acronym standing for:

- **Authentication**—Who are you? Prove your identity.

- **Authorization**—With what resources are you allowed to interact?

- **Accounting**—When logged in, what did you do?

Each of these security subsystems defines, respectively, who can access the system by introducing per user authentication, the authorization each user has after the system has approved their logon, and an auditable accounting trail of their activities when connected.

AAA is configured on client devices, such as routers, switches, and wireless access points (network devices). Client devices communicate with a central network access server (NAS), such as a Cisco Secure Access Control Server (CSACS). CSACS is a software product that centralizes AAA over one or more servers to improve load sharing and redundancy. Do not confuse the AAA client device concept with the end user as it is not the same in this context. Client devices are configured to direct all end-user activities related to authentication, authorization, and accounting to an NAS. Using either the TACACS+ or RADIUS protocol, the client sends authentication requests to the NAS. The NAS verifies the username and password against its own user databases or against a remote database it is configured to reference, such as an LDAP server, Windows directory server, or SecuredID server. The NAS replies to the client device with a success or failure response. When the user authenticates successfully, the NAS indicates this with one or more authorization attributes to the client. Additionally, the NAS might send session attributes to the client to provide additional security and control of privileges like an ACL or IP addressing information.

The uses of AAA include the following:

- AAA of administrators that require administrative access to network devices.
- AAA of employees that use applications routed through a router and terminating on another host.
- 802.1X authentication for wired and wireless LANs.
- End-user, self-service password changes.

Network Device Authentication Methods

The following describes administrative access authentication methods for devices like routers and switches:

- **Line password**—Set within the line vty and line console configurations. When the correct password is entered, the user is granted access to the User EXEC mode (router> prompt).
- **Enable secret password**—Set within the global configuration. When the user enters the correct password from User EXEC mode, the user receives access to the privileged EXEC mode (router# prompt).
- **Local user database**—Usernames, passwords, and privilege levels set within the device's global configuration.
- **External user database**—Usernames, passwords, and privilege levels reside on an external NAS. Local router configuration redirects authentication queries to the external database.

Basic AAA Configuration Process

Basic AAA implementation implies the use of a local user database (as opposed to a central NAS) and router commands that instruct the system to refer to the local database.

Router with Local
AAA Database

AAA-Related Command	Explanation
`username superuser privilege 15 password 3#gMOpic!!`	Create local user "superuser" with all IOS command privileges.
`aaa new-model`	Enable the AAA access control model for the device.
`aaa authentication login default local enable`	Authentication—For all interfaces, use the local user database by default for privileged EXEC mode. If this fails use the local enable secret password.
`aaa authentication login NO_AUTHENT none`	Authentication—There is no challenge for a username with interfaces that specify NO_AUTHENT (example) for authentication.
`aaa authorization exec default local if-authenticated`	Authorization—If properly authenticated, give the user a privileged EXEC shell.
`aaa authorization exec NO_AUTHOR none`	Authorization—Give a privileged EXEC shell with properly authenticated users for interfaces specifying NO_AUTHOR.
`aaa authorization commands 15 local if-authenticated`	Authorization—If properly authenticated, give the user access to all commands.
`aaa authorization commands 15 NO_AUTHOR none`	Authorization—Give access to all commands if properly authenticated interfaces specify NO_AUTHOR.
`line con 0`	Line console 0 configuration commands follow:
`login authentication NO_AUTHENT`	Use the NO_AUTHENT authentication profile specified above or con 0 access. Do not use the local user database.
`authorization exec NO_AUTHOR`	Use the NO_AUTHOR authorization exec profile for con 0 access.
`authorization commands 15 NO_AUTHOR`	Use the NO_AUTHOR authorization command profile for con 0 access.

NAS AAA Configuration Process

More complex AAA implementation implies the use of a remote NAS user database to which the network device forwards authentication requests.

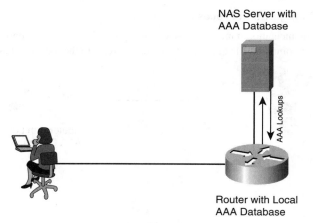

NAS Server with
AAA Database

AAA Lookups

Router with Local
AAA Database

The following table is a set of example commands to enable AAA using local router commands and a remote NAS.

NOTE For a complete listing of AAA commands, refer to the Cisco documentation online at Cisco.com.

AAA-Related Command	Explanation
`username supertech privilege 15 password dsJeys2!eW`	Create local user "supertech" with all privileges.

`tacacs-server host 10.200.200.2`
 	
`radius-server host 10.200.200.44`
	IP address of NAS. Use one or the other.

`tacacs-server key cOmplex!Key`
 	
`radius-server key fhj7rsas9eo2`
	Shared key (password) that identifies this device as legitimate to the NAS.

`aaa new-model`	Enable the AAA access control model for the device.
`aaa authentication banner *Unauthorized use is strictly prohibited*`	Echoes this warning banner at the initial username challenge.
`aaa authentication login default group tacacs local enable`	Authentication—For all interfaces, use the TACACS+ server by default. If this fails, use the local user database. If this fails, use the enable secret password.
`aaa authentication login NO-TACACS none`	Authentication—Interfaces specify NO-TACACS for authentication do not challenge for a username.
`aaa authorization exec default group tacacs if-authenticated`	Authorization—If properly authenticated by TACACS, give the user a privileged EXEC shell.
`aaa authorization exec NO-AUTH none`	Authorization—Give a privileged EXEC shell to properly authenticated interfaces that specify NO-AUTH.
`aaa authorization commands 15 default group tacacs`	Authorization—Give users at this privilege level access to all commands by default.
`aaa authorization commands 15 NO-AUTH none`	Authorization—Give properly authenticated interfaces that specify NO-AUTH access to all commands.
`aaa accounting exec start-stop group tacacs`	Accounting—Records both start and stop times for privileged EXEC shell sessions.
`aaa accounting commands 15 default stop-only group tacacs`	Accounting—Records the commands processed in the privilege EXEC shell by users at the specified privilege level. Sends a "stop" accounting notice at the end of the requested user process.

AAA Debug Commands

debug commands assist in troubleshooting configuration problems. For example:

- Why is user "drocque" not able to fully connect?

- Is the client device (router) able to connect to the RADIUS server?

- What accounting messages are going to the TACACS server at 192.168.253.76?

debug can be turned on for a subset of the router process and the associate messages is logged to the destination of your choice as long as the destination specifies the event level debug.

NOTE Take extreme care when using debugging commands because too many messages can overwhelm a system. This is especially true when directing debug output to a serial console.

The following output shows a partial list of available TACACS+, RADIUS, and AAA debugging commands. Full command output is truncated.

```
router#debug aaa ?
  accounting            Accounting
  authentication        Authentication
  authorization         Authorization
  ...truncated command list...
router#debug aaa authorization
AAA Authorization debugging is on
router#debug radius ?
  accounting       RADIUS accounting packets only
  authentication   RADIUS authentication packets only
  brief            Only I/O transactions are recorded
  ...truncated command list...
router#debug radius accounting
Radius protocol debugging is on
Radius protocol brief debugging is off
Radius protocol verbose debugging is off
Radius packet hex dump debugging is off
Radius packet protocol (authentication) debugging is off
Radius packet protocol (accounting) debugging is on
Radius elog debugging debugging is off
Radius packet retransmission debugging is off
Radius server fail-over debugging is off
Radius elog debugging debugging is off
router#debug tacacs ?
  accounting        TACACS+ protocol accounting
  authentication    TACACS+ protocol authentication
  authorization     TACACS+ protocol authorization
  events            TACACS+ protocol events
  ...truncated command list...
router#debug tacacs authorization
TACACS+ authorization debugging is on
router#undebug all
All possible debugging has been turned off
```

Cisco Secure ACS (CSACS) for Windows Product Overview

CSACS is a centralized NAS that runs on the Windows platform with the following features:

- Automatic service monitoring, database synchronization, and user data import tools

- LDAP and ODBC user authentication support

- 802.1X authentication support
- Downloadable IP ACL support
- Device command-set authorization
- User and administrative access reporting
- Dynamic quota generation
- Time restrictions support
- User and device group profiles
- Cisco Trust Agent, Network Admission Control (NAC) integration
- X.509 Certification Revocation List (CRL) checking
- Cisco Security Agent (host IDS) integration

CSACS hardware and OS requirements include:

- Pentium III processor, 550-MHz or faster.
- 256-MB RAM and 250-MB+ free disk space (a large local user database might push this minimum limit higher)
- Minimum graphics resolution of 256 colors at 800 x 600 lines
- Windows 2000 Server (Service Pack 4) or Windows Server 2003, Enterprise or Standard Edition

---

NOTE Consult Cisco.com for the latest system requirements and performance statistics.

CSACS system performance statistics include:

- Performance capabilities are server specification dependent. Faster CPU and more RAM equals better performance.
- CSACS can support 100,000 users or more using distributed load sharing.
- Maximum number of simultaneously supported AAA clients (routers, switches, and access points) is approximately 5000.

Services on the computer running CSACS include the following:

- **CSAdmin**—Administrative HTML interface
- **CSAuth**—Authentication services
- **CSDBSync**—External RDBMS synchronization
- **CSLog**—Accounting and system activity logging service
- **CSMon**—CSACS performance monitoring, recording, and notification
- **CSTacacs**—TACACS+ AAA clients to CSAuth communication service
- **CSRadius**—RADIUS AAA clients to CSAuth communication service

The following table details CSACS features and their default service protocols and ports:

CSACS Feature	Protocol/Port
RADIUS authentication and authorization	udp/1645, udp/1812
RADIUS accounting	udp/1646, udp/1813
TACACS+	tcp/49
CiscoSecure database replication	tcp/2000
RDBMS synchronization with synchronization partners	tcp/2000
User-changeable password web application	tcp/2000
Logging	tcp/2001
Administrative HTTP default port (configurable to tcp/1024 to tcp/65535)	tcp/2002

CSACS server types:

- **Primary Cisco Secure ACS**—A CSACS that sends replicated database components to other CSACSs

- **Secondary Cisco Secure ACS**—A CSACS that receives replicated database components from a primary

Database replication features:

- Creation of complete or partial CSACS configuration replicas that AAA clients reference if the primary fails.

- Control replication timing and schedules to keep replicas updated.

- Securely transport configuration data among CSACSs.

CSACS can authenticate users against multiple external user directory database types. The following list describes several CSACS service and database interactions:

- If no external user databases are defined, CSACS will use its internal database.

- If a Windows user database is defined, the CSACS must be part of the Windows domain directory. Incoming credential checks pass on to a trusted domain directory.

- If an LDAP user database is defined, CSACS will pass the request via a TCP network connection to the correct LDAP.

- If a third-party token server is defined, CSACS first finds the username and then forwards the authentication request to the token server for verification.

The following table compares TACACS+ and RADIUS protocols:

Point of Comparison	TACACS+	RADIUS
Intended purpose	Device management (router, switch, and WAP).	User access control (802.1X authentication, IOS firewall authentication proxy).
Transport protocol	TCP—connection-oriented.	UDP—connectionless.

Point of Comparison	TACACS+	RADIUS
Encryption	Full packet encryption between the client and NAS.	Encrypts the shared secret password between the client and NAS.
AAA architecture	Separate control of each service: authentication, authorization, and accounting.	Authentication and authorization combined as one service.
RFC	1492.	2138, 2139, 2865, and 2869.

Cisco IOS Firewall Security

Cisco provides firewall, intrusion prevention, and authentication proxy security capabilities in its IOS-based routers as part of an overall industry trend toward multi-purpose network appliances.

IOS Firewall Feature Set Components

The Cisco IOS Firewall feature set comprises these main components:

- **Context Based Access Control (CBAC)**—Provides stateful packet inspection and access control capabilities.

- **Authentication Proxy**—Provides dynamic per-user authentication and authorization to network resources.

- **Intrusion Prevention System (IPS)**—Cisco IOS IPS provides signature-based intrusion detection and prevention.

- **Port-to-Application Mapping (PAM)**—Allows inspection of supported applications on non-standard ports.

These components are enabled individually or in combination on many Cisco routers and layer 3 switch platforms. These features increase router memory and CPU utilization, so before turning them on, consider their impact on overall performance.

CBAC

Similar to the functionality provided by Cisco PIX Firewall, CBAC improves IOS' standard ACLs by adding stateful inspection of TCP and UDP packets and utilizing application layer information to intelligently protect the network from many attacks. By utilizing session state information, CBAC can determine if incoming packets are part of sessions that were initiated were initiated from another segment, and dynamically modifies the ACLs to temporarily allow return traffic. CBAC also adds features to identify and mitigate denial-of-service and IP fragmentation attacks.

Authentication Proxy

Authentication proxy provides granular controlled access to network resources on a per-user basis. Authentication proxy adds a temporary access control entry to an interface to allow session flows after the requesting user successfully authenticates to a user database. Without this feature, access control can be applied based only on IP addresses or on a per-interface basis (applied to all inbound or outbound traffic on a particular interface), and an administrator must perform it interactively.

IPS

The IPS feature adds another layer of security as it provides signature-based intrusion prevention and intrusion detection (depending on the version of IOS in use) directly within IOS-based routers. IOS IDS and IPS feature a smaller database of signatures and fewer capabilities compared to Cisco Secure IPS dedicated appliances, but they can be an attractive security feature for remote offices where the cost justification of larger systems is difficult.

Using CBAC to Protect Users from Attack

Cisco IOS ACLs

CBAC provides better security than ACLs alone (stateful packet inspection), but it relies on ACLs as the mechanism that ultimately permits or denies specific traffic from passing through an interface. Keep the following in mind regarding ACLs:

- ACLs can provide basic packet filtering based on:
  - Source and destination IP addresses
  - Source and destination ports
  - Specific protocol used (such as TCP, UDP, ICMP, IP, and so on)
- Packets are checked against each ACL statement in order (top to bottom) until a match is found. If two statements define traffic that affects the same packet, the one higher up in the ACL takes precedence.
- Every ACL includes an implicit deny all as its last statement. If a packet does not match any of the statements in the ACL, the implicit deny all applies and the packet is discarded.

How CBAC Works

CBAC protects the network in the following ways:

- **Performing packet inspection**—TCP, UDP, and application-layer protocols are inspected. For application-layer protocols that require special handling, programming CBAC's behavior helps to accommodate session flow across the firewall boundary.

- **Maintaining a state table with session state information**—Permits return traffic for sessions initiated from the inside while blocking other inbound traffic on an external interface.

- **Preventing DoS attacks**—Accomplished by defining the threshold against the number of half open TCP and UDP sessions in total, in a specified period of time, or per host.

- **CBAC**—Resets the session, blocks all SYN packets temporarily to guard against SYN floods, and generates alert messages.

- **Dynamically modifying ACLs**—Temporarily changes the ACLs applied to an interface with top-inserted reflexive entries to permit or deny traffic based on the specific configuration of the IOS Firewall. These ACLs are not saved to the NVRAM and expire when sessions are torn down (TCP) or timeout (TCP and UDP).

Supported Protocols

CBAC provides special handling support for TCP, UDP, and major application-layer protocols. When configuring CBAC, inspection can be enabled for any combination of the supported protocols from the following list:

- TCP
- UDP
- CU-SeeMe (only the White Pine version)
- FTP
- H.323 (such as NetMeeting and ProShare)
- HTTP (Java blocking)
- ICMP
- Microsoft NetShow
- UNIX R-commands (such as rlogin, rexec, and rsh)
- RealAudio
- Real Time Streaming Protocol (RTSP)
- Remote Procedure Call (RPC) (Sun RPC, not DCE RPC)
- Simple Mail Transport Protocol (SMTP) and Extended Simple Mail Transport Protocol (ESMTP) (ESTMP support requires IOS version 12.3(7)T or greater)
- SQL*Net
- StreamWorks
- TFTP
- VDOLive

NOTE CBAC does not provide support for IP Security (IPSec) packet inspection.

Alerts and Audit Trails

CBAC can be configured to generate event-based alerts and audit trails. Alerts and audit trail information can be sent to a syslog for reporting and auditing purposes and can be configured on a per-protocol basis. Information sent to the syslog server typically includes:

- Time stamps
- Source address/port
- Destination address/port
- Transmitted bytes

Configuring CBAC

Configuration of CBAC consists of the following primary tasks:

- Select the interface and direction for inspection.
- Configure ACLs on the interface.
- Configure the global timeouts and thresholds (optional).
- Define an inspection rule.
- Apply the inspection rule to the interface.
- Configure logging and audit trail (optional).
- Test and verify CBAC configuration.

Select the Interface and Direction for Inspection

When applying CBAC, you must decide which interface to use and in what direction. For each interface, the "internal" side is the trusted or more secure side (where sessions originate and return traffic is permitted). Conversely, the external interface is the untrusted side and sessions that originate there are blocked.

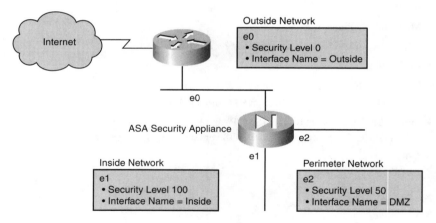

You can configure CBAC inbound, outbound, or in both directions on an interface. For example, the preceding figure shows a scenario where the configuration of CBAC is in the inbound direction on interface S1. If the configuration of CBAC was in the outbound direction on interface S1, the Internet would effectively be considered the internal network.

Configure ACLs on the External Interface

Use the **access-list** command to block all traffic that should not originate from the external side. The simplest scenario is when you do not want any traffic to originate from the external side:

```
Router(config)# access-list 101 deny ip any any
```

If you want to allow ICMP traffic and access to a web server at 10.1.1.11, the ACL would be as follows:

```
Router(config)# access-list 101 permit icmp any any
Router(config)# access-list 101 permit tcp any host 10.1.1.11 eq www
Router(config)# access-list 101 deny ip any any
```

Configure Global Timeouts and Thresholds

Global timeouts and thresholds can be changed to modify the behavior of the IOS Firewall and its DoS mitigation characteristics. You change them by modifying the following variables:

- TCP SYN and FIN wait times

- TCP, UDP, and Domain Name System (DNS) idle times

- Half-open (embryonic) TCP connection limits (global and host-specific)

The settings are applied globally to all sessions. Default values are used if you do not specify a value.

TCP SYN and FIN Wait Times   Use the following commands to configure TCP SYN and FIN wait times:

Command	Explanation
`ip inspect tcp synwait-time` *seconds*	Globally defines the time in seconds that the IOS firewall waits for a half-open session to establish before it drops the session and removes it from the session table.
`no ip inspect tcp synwait-time`	Globally resets the SYN wait time back to its default of 30 seconds.
`ip inspect tcp fynwait-time` *seconds*	Globally defines the time in seconds that the IOS firewall maintains a TCP session in its session table after a FIN exchange.
`no ip inspect tcp fynwait-time`	Globally resets the FYN wait time back to its default of 5 seconds.

TCP, UDP, and DNS Idle Times   Use the following commands to configure TCP, UDP, and DNS idle times:

Command	Explanation
`ip inspect {tcp ¦ udp} idle-time` *seconds*	Globally defines the time in seconds that the IOS Firewall maintains a TCP or UDP session in its session table without any activity.
`no ip inspect {tcp ¦ udp} idle-time`	Globally resets the TCP or UDP idle times back to their default values of 3600 seconds (TCP) and 30 seconds (UDP).
`ip inspect dns-timeout` *seconds*	Globally defines the time in seconds that the IOS Firewall manages a DNS lookup without any activity.
`no ip inspect dns-timeout`	Globally resets the DNS timeout period back to its default value of 5 seconds.

Global Half-Opened Connection Limits A high number of half-open TCP (embryonic) or UDP connections can indicate a DoS attack. CBAC considers UDP traffic (a connectionless protocol) as half open when no return traffic is detected. Global limits on half-open connections are used to fine-tune CBAC's DoS mitigation characteristics.

Use the following commands to configure global half-open connection limits:

Command	Explanation
`ip inspect max-incomplete high` *number*	Globally defines the absolute limit on number of existing half-open TCP or UDP connections. When the number of existing half-open connections exceeds this limit, existing half-open connections are deleted to accommodate new connections as necessary. Default value is 500.
`ip inspect max-incomplete low` *number*	When the maximum absolute limit set by keyword **high** is exceeded, CBAC deletes existing half-open TCP or UDP connections until the low limit set by the keyword **low** is reached. Default value is 400.
`ip inspect one-minute high` *number*	Globally defines the limit on number of new half-open TCP or UDP connections (in a one-minute period). When the number of new half-open connections (per minute) exceeds this limit, existing half-open connections are deleted to accommodate new connections as necessary. Default value is 500.
`ip inspect one-minute low` *number*	When the one-minute rate limit set by keyword **high** is exceeded, CBAC deletes existing half-open TCP or UDP connections until the low limit set by the keyword **low** is reached. Default value is 400.

Half-Opened Connection Limits by Host In addition to global settings, CBAC can limit half-open TCP connections on a per-host basis. The following command allows further fine tuning of CBAC's DoS mitigation characteristics by defining per-host limits:

`ip inspect tcp max-incomplete host` *number* `block-time` *minutes*

Command Parameter	Explanation
`host` *number*	Defines the limit on number of half-open TCP connections with the same destination host in a range of 1–250. When the number of half-open connections with any single host exceeds this limit, existing half-open connections with the host are deleted to accommodate new connections. The **block-time** setting determines the manner in which existing connections are deleted. Default value is 50.

Command Parameter	Explanation
`block-time` *minutes*	When the maximum per-host limit exceeds the limit set by keyword **host**, CBAC deletes existing half-open TCP connections with that host to accommodate new connections. If **block-time** is set to zero, CBAC deletes the oldest existing half-open TCP connection by that host to accommodate every new connection request (thus keeping the total the same). If **block-time** is set to a value higher than zero, CBAC deletes all existing half-open TCP connections with that host and blocks new connections from the host until block time expires. Default **block-time** value is zero.

Port-to-Application Mapping

PAM allows customization of various TCP and UDP ports for different network applications and services. After it is configured, PAM allows CBAC to inspect applications on non-standard ports. For example, if you configure a web server to operate on port 8080 instead of 80, you can configure CBAC to inspect the HTTP traffic on this nonstandard port using PAM.

You can also configure PAM on a per-host or per-subnet basis using an appropriately constructed ACL.

User-Defined Port Mapping   To configure user-defined port mapping, use the **ip port-map** command with the following syntax:

> `ip port-map` *appl_name* `port` *port_num* [`list` *acl_num*]

Command Parameter	Explanation
`ip port-map` *appl_name*	The argument **appl_name** specifies the name of the CBAC-supported application that is inspected on a nonstandard port.
`port` *port_num*	The argument **port_num** identifies the nonstandard port CBAC must use to inspect application specified.
`list` *acl_num*	Optional keyword **list** used to specify an ACL (**acl_num**) to configure PAM on a per-host or per-subnet basis.

Defining Application Protocols Inspection Rules

CBAC is configured using the **ip inspect name** command. After configuration, CBAC is applied to an interface for inbound or outbound inspection.

Application Protocols Inspection Rules   CBAC supports inspection of the protocols and applications listed in the following table.

Supported Application or Protocol	Command Keyword
TCP	**tcp**
UDP	**udp**
CU-SeeMe	**cuseeme**

continues

Supported Application or Protocol	Command Keyword
FTP commands and responses	**ftp-cmd**
FTP tokens	**ftp-tokens**
H.323 (versions 1 and 2)	**h323**
HTTP	**http**
IMAP	**imap**
Microsoft NetShow	**netshow**
POP3	**pop3**
RealAudio	**realaudio**
Remote procedure call	**rpc**
Real Time Streaming Protocol	**rtsp**
Session Initiation Protocol	**sip**
Simple Mail Transfer Protocol	**smtp**
Skinny Client Control Protocol (SCCP)	**skinny**
Structured Query Language*Net (SQL*Net)	**sqlnet**
StreamWorks	**streamworks**
TFTP	**tftp**
UNIX r-commands (rlogin, rexec, and rsh)	**rcmd**
VDOLive	**vdolive**

Use the following command to configure CBAC for inspection of any of the supported applications and protocols:

```
ip inspect name inspection-name protocol [alert {on | off}] [audit-trail {on
| off}][reset] [secure-login] [timeout seconds]
```

Command Parameter	Explanation
`ip inspect name`	Command to configure CBAC.
`inspection-name`	Specific name for the configuration of the inspection rule set.
`protocol`	Name of CBAC-supported application or protocol that is inspected as part of the rule set.
`alert {on ¦ off}`	Optionally enables or disables alerts on a per-protocol basis. If not specified, global alert settings defined by **ip inspect alert-off** command are in effect.
`audit-trail {on ¦ off}`	Optionally enables or disables audit trail on a per-protocol basis. If not specified, global audit trail settings defined by **ip inspect audit trail** command are in effect.
`reset`	Optional keyword used to reset the TCP connection if the client enters a non-protocol command before authentication is complete.
`secure-login`	Optional keyword to specify encryption for authentication for a user at a non-secure location.

Several protocols and applications have additional protocol-specific keywords when used with the **ip inspect name** command. A discussion of the protocols and specific keywords follows.

Java Inspection Rules   Java-specific inspection rules are configured using the command:

```
ip inspect name inspection-name http [java-list access-list] [alert {on |
off}] [audit-trail {on | off}] [timeout seconds]
```

Use the standard http inspection with the keyword **java-list to enable the java** inspection. Specify a standard ACL to permit java applets from friendly sites.

RPC Applications Inspection Rules   Use the following command to configure RPC-specific inspection rules:

```
ip inspect name inspection-name rpc program-number number [wait-time
minutes] [alert {on | off}] [audit-trail {on | off}] [timeout seconds]
```

Use the protocol name **rpc to enable RPC inspection**. Use the RPC-specific keyword **program-number** to permit a specific program number. The optional keyword **wait-time** specifies the time in minutes that the firewall allows subsequent connections from the same source address and to the same destination address and port. The default wait-time value is zero.

IP Packet Fragmentation Inspection Rules   Use the following command to configure the inspection rules for IP fragmentation:

```
ip inspect name inspection-name fragment [max number timeout seconds]
```

To enable the fragmentation inspection, use protocol name fragment and the keyword **max**. Keyword **max** specifies the maximum number of unassembled packets (packets that arrive at the router interface before the initial packet for a session) for which CBAC allocates state information (structures). Allowable range for maximum state entries is 50–10000, with a default value of 256.

Router Interface Inspection Rules and ACLs

After an inspection rule set is configured, it is applied to an interface using the **ip inspect** command to enable CBAC. The appropriate application of inspection rules and ACLs effectively enables CBAC. The ACL blocks all traffic and CBAC dynamically modifies the ACL to allow return traffic it deems safe based on the configured inspection rules.

In general, consider the following when applying CBAC:

- To interface where traffic originates:

  — Apply inbound ACL to allow permissible traffic (optional)
  — Apply inspection rule (**ip inspect**) in the inbound direction to inspect the desired traffic
- To all other interfaces:

  — Apply inbound ACL to deny all traffic (protocols not inspected by CBAC might be permitted)

The command syntax is as follows:

```
ip inspect inspection-name {in | out}
```

The value for *inspection-name* is the name of the previously configured inspection rule set. Keyword **in** specifies inspection on inbound traffic. Keyword **out** specifies inspection on outbound traffic.

Testing and Verifying CBAC

After CBAC is configured and operational, you can use the appropriate **show** or **debug** commands to verify configuration and operational parameters or to troubleshoot problems.

Use the **show ip inspect** command to display and verify inspection rule configuration with the following syntax:

```
show ip inspect {name inspection-name | config | interfaces | session [detail]
 | all}
```

Command Parameter	Explanation
name inspection-name	Displays configuration for inspection rule with the name *inspection-name*.
config	Shows the complete CBAC inspection configuration.
interfaces	Shows interface configuration for specified inspection rules and access lists.
session [detail]	Shows existing sessions for the named CBAC inspection rule set. Optional keyword **detail** displays additional details about these sessions.
all	Shows all CBAC configuration and all existing sessions currently tracked and inspected by CBAC.

Use the **debug ip inspect** command to display debug messages about IOS firewall events with the following syntax:

```
debug ip inspect {function-trace | object-creation | object-deletion | events
 | timers | protocol | detailed}
```

Command Parameter	Explanation
function-trace	Displays messages about software functions called by CBAC.
object-creation	Displays messages about software objects created by CBAC.
object-deletion	Displays messages about software objects deleted by CBAC.
events	Displays messages about CBAC software events, including information about CBAC packet processing.
timers	Displays messages about CBAC timer events such as when an idle timeout occurs.
protocol	Displays protocol-specific messages for CBAC-inspected protocol events, including details about the packets of the protocol.
detailed	Displays detailed information for all the other enabled CBAC debugging.

Cisco IOS Firewall Authentication Proxy

If users need to get to services outside of the local network, authentication proxy provides dynamic per-user authentication and authorization via the chokepoint (gateway) router. When valid credentials are supplied to the gateway router performing the proxy function, access control entries specific to that user that dictate the hosts and networks the user can access are transparently configured on the router. These entries, which are placed in the router's inbound and outbound ACLs, provide the proper "holes" necessary for communications, so that the user can get to the proper services as defined by the security policy. After a configurable period of inactivity, the user's ACLs and credentials are removed from the proxy. Subsequent access by the user requires re-authentication.

NOTE   Use the authentication proxy for internal users to access external networks or for external users to access internal networks. The proxy function temporarily ties an authenticated user's current source IP address to access control entries, so that the source IP can access the specified hosts.

How Authentication Proxy Works

Step 1   A user opens a browser and specifies a destination URL. For example: http:// www.cisco.com.

Step 2   The router checks for the source IP address from which the user requested the connection to see if another session is active. If the connection already exists, the user's traffic is automatically let through. If no connection exists, the router prompts the user for username and password credentials.

Step 3   When the user submits the credential, the router sends them to the AAA server for authentication.

Step 4   If authentication succeeds, the AAA server uploads the user's authorization profile to the router that defines the hosts the user can access.

Step 5   The authorization profile becomes a series of access control entries (ACE) specific to each user placed into the following ACLs:

- The inbound ACL on the interface to which the user will send traffic in order for it to get to its destination.

- The outbound ACL (if it exists) on the interface through which traffic will flow to get to its destination.

NOTE   The CBAC firewall function will also produce dynamic reflexive ACL entries for return traffic. See the CBAC section for details.

Authentication Proxy Configuration

Step 1   Perform AAA router configuration. Reference the techniques described in the "NAS AAA Configuration Process" section. The following commands show the use of AAA for the auth-proxy function:

```
aaa authentication login default group {radius I tacacs}
aaa authorization auth-proxy default group {radius I tacacs}
aaa accounting auth-proxy default group {radius I tacacs}
```

Step 2 Perform AAA NAS user profile configuration on a Cisco Secure ACS server. The following commands define per-user access profiles and associated access control entries.

Only **permit proxyacl** entries are permitted in the NAS:

```
proxyacl#1=permit tcp any host 209.165.200.225 eq 80
proxyacl#2=permit udp any host 209.165.200.226 eq 53
```

The source IP address within the proxyacl's must be set to **any**. The router will replace **any** with the authenticated user's current IP address.

All users must have privilege level 15.

```
priv-lvl=15
```

Step 3 Perform router HTTP server configuration. Note that as shown in the latter two commands that follow, some IOS revisions support HTTPS.

```
ip http server
ip http authentication aaa
ip http secure-server
ip http secure-trustpoint
```

Step 4 Perform router authentication proxy configuration. The **auth-cache-time** sets the idle timeout in minutes, so if it expires because of inactivity, the removal of the user authentication entries and dynamic ACL entries occurs. The **ip auth-proxy name** command associates HTTP traffic with auth-proxy functions. The last two commands that follow apply the functions to an interface.

```
ip auth-proxy auth-cache-time 60
ip auth-proxy name APPROVED-USERS http
interface e0/1
 ip auth-proxy APPROVED-USERS
```

Cisco IOS Intrusion Prevention System and IOS Intrusion Detection

Networks that use firewalls with tight rules are not necessarily immune to exploitation because attacks can still be embedded within traffic identified as acceptable. For example: firewalls often allow HTTP (web) traffic, but the traffic can still contain malicious code embedded deep within the packet payload. In another example: violations of security policy often include network reconnaissance probing, unauthorized topology information collection, and attacks on FTP, SMTP, and DNS services.

Both IOS Intrusion Prevention Systems (IPS) and IOS Intrusion Detection Systems (IDS) are intrusion analysis solutions that identify policy violations through the use of predefined data patterns (signatures) that describe attacks. These features are embedded functions within a router's IOS code and use the router's CPU for processing. Their purpose is to deeply analyze the contents of the packets flowing through a router and to identify known network misuse and attacks. A router's capability to perform IDS or IPS depends on the router model and the IOS revision.

The IOS intrusion analysis products are a subset of the Cisco appliance-based IPS products, the latter of which offers more features, speed, and flexibility. The IOS features are a complement to rather than a replacement for the enterprise-scale Cisco Secure IPS appliances. IOS IPS/IDS identifies the most common attacks using a subset of signatures and is often used at locations where a full blown IPS is too expensive or cannot be managed effectively.

IOS IDS is an older approach to packet inspection. It has the follow features:

- Monitoring happens in the packet processing path.

- When a signature match occurs, the following response actions are possible:
    - Send an alert
    - Drop the traffic
    - Reset the TCP connection

- Signatures describing known attacks number approximately 100.

- Signatures fall into one of the following four analysis engines:
    - Info Atomic
    - Info Compound
    - Attack Atomic
    - Attack Compound

- Signatures cannot be modified.

- Signatures can be enabled or disabled.

- Logs signature matches to management hosts with either syslog (udp/514) or Post Office Protocol (tcp/45000) or both. Post Office Protocol was deprecated in IOS 12.3(14)T.

Informational signatures relate to one or more packets associated with reconnaissance and information gathering. Attack signatures relate to one or more packets associated with an acute system attack. An atomic signature results when the attack can be observed within a single packet. A compound signature results when the attack happens over a period of time and involves a sequence of steps and multiple packets. Tracking compound attacks requires the router to maintain the state of the offending packet flow for further evaluation. Compound signatures can adversely affect memory and CPU load because of their complexity. In contrast, atomic signatures have a negligible performance affect.

IOS IPS introduced in Cisco IOS Software Release 12.3(8)T is a newer approach to packet inspection and has the following features:

- IOS IPS replaces IOS IDS.

- Monitoring happens in the packet processing path.

- When a signature match occurs the following response actions are possible:
    - Send an alert
    - Drop the traffic
    - Reset the TCP connection

- Signatures describing known attacks number more than 750.

- Signature updates are copied to flash as a Signature Definition File (SDF) and can be activated on the fly. No reboot is required.

- Signatures fall into one of the following ten analysis engines:

  — Layer 3 IP Protocol
  — TCP
  — UDP
  — IP Options
  — ICMP
  — HTTP
  — DNS
  — SMTP
  — FTP
  — RPC

- Signatures can be modified or newly created using the Security Device Manager 2.0 and newer or CiscoWorks VMS IDS Management Center 2.3 or newer.

- Signatures can be enabled or disabled.

- Logs signature matches to syslog management hosts (udp/514) or prepares alerts for queries by Security Device Event Exchange (SDEE) clients over tcp/80 (HTTP) or tcp/443 (SSL/TLS).

NOTE   Newer IOS revisions use SDEE to communicate events to clients using the HTTP or HTTP over SSL and TLS protocols. The router is an SDEE provider and acts as an HTTP server. Management host clients are SDEE initiators and pull IPS alerts from the router. A router's IP HTTP server must be activated.

How IPS Works

The following list describes the high points of IOS IPS functions:

- Examines packet flows inline as they traverse through the router.

- Allows for one outbound or one inbound traffic evaluation policy per interface with support for multiple policies per router.

- Uses inbound policies to evaluate traffic for signature matches before evaluation by any inbound ACL. Evaluates outbound policies as they leave the router, which implies that attacks have reached the router internals.

- Inspects packet sequentially through a series of modules.

  — IP (for example, misuse of IP options)
  — ICMP, UDP, or TCP depending on the protocol used in the flow (for example, misuse of layer 4 flags)

— Applications (for example, misuse of DNS or HTTP application RFC standards)

TIP For the purposes of remembering the inspection order, it can be helpful to think of inspection as occurring from the outer portion of the packet's layer 3 (IP) portion inward to the layer 4 (TCP, UDP, and ICMP) portions and then on in toward the payload where application-specific data resides.

- Takes any supported and configured action upon a signature match, to include:
  - Alarm
  - Drop
  - TCP Reset (applies to TCP flows only)
- Allows for reduction of false positives by using standard access lists to prevent the evaluation of specific hosts by an entire IPS security policy or a single signature.

IDS Configuration

The following table lists important command-line interface (CLI) commands to enable IOS IDS on a router.

IOS IDS Command	Explanation
`ip audit smtp spam 250`	Turn on IP auditing for SMTP by limiting the number of email recipients within one message. The default number of 250 is configurable.
`ip audit po max-events 100`	Set the maximum number of events that can sit in the IDS event queue before being sent to the IDS Director event server. Prevents over utilization of memory. The default number of 100 is configurable.
`ip audit notify nr-director` `ip audit notify log`	Specify the sending of IDS events to the IDS Director and/or a syslog server.

`ip audit po local hostid 101 orgid 200`
`ip audit po remote hostid 100 orgid 200 rmtaddress 10.4.4.3 localaddress 10.3.7.7`
`ip audit po protected {protected ip address range}`
	If using an IDS Director management host, set the Post Office communication parameters. Hostid's are unique and Orgid's are the same. Identify the IP addresses considered to be on the "inside" (protected side) of your network.

`ip audit info action alarm drop reset` `ip audit attack action alarm drop reset`	Specify any or all the possible actions that will occur by default; the default action is Alarm (send an event).
`ip audit signature {signature id number} disable`	Disable any signatures you do not want or need; enter as many as needed.
`ip audit name HQ-AUDIT info` `ip audit name HQ-AUDIT attack`	Create an audit rule.
`interface e0/1` `ip audit HQ-AUDIT {in ¦ out}`	Apply the audit rule to an interface.

IPS Configuration

The following table lists important CLI commands for performing key but limited configuration to a router's IPS function. The router's GUI-based SDM or CiscoWorks VMS supports complete IPS configuration.

Command	Explanation
`ip ips name acmeIPS`	Specifies an IPS rule by name. In this case, the rule is named acmeIPS.
`ip ips sdf location disk1:attack-drop.sdf`	Specifies the location of the SDF file that contains instructions for how the IPS handles signature matches.
`ip ips notify sdee`	Specifies that SDEE will be used for event alarms.
`ip http server`	Enables the HTTP server, necessary for SDEE events to be pulled by a client.
`ip ips signature signature-id delete`	Deletes a specified signature from the global pool of signatures. Conserves CPU by eliminating unneeded signatures.
`ip ips signature signature-id disable`	Disables a specified signature. The router still analyzes traffic for these signature matches, but when it observes the pattern it will not take action.
`interface GigabitEthernet0/1` `ip ips acmeIPS in`	Applies an IPS rule to the interface. One rule per interface. Apply in or out.

Layer 2 Device Security

The following sections address layer 2 device security:

- Layer 2 Attacks and Mitigation
- Access Port and Trunk Security
- Identity-Based Networking Services
- Configuring 802.1X Port-Based Authentication

Layer 2 Attacks and Mitigation

Layer 2 attacks occur at the data link layer that traditionally has had little to no security mechanisms. The exploitation of switches occurs in a variety of ways and leaves end devices potentially vulnerable. To mitigate layer 2 attack effectiveness, Cisco created specific security controls. Because every Cisco platform does not offer all prevention mechanisms, it is important to verify that your hardware and IOS version supports the safeguards you wish to implement. The following sections describe layer 2 attacks and ways to mitigate them.

Content Addressable Memory (CAM) Table Overflow

By their design, switches are multiport bridges. Unicast conversations between two devices on a segment (VLAN) are invisible to all other connected devices. Attackers physically connected to a switch segment might desire to intercept and analyze other conversations within their VLAN. To do this, they can use a CAM table overflow attack. A switch's CAM table maintains the MAC addresses associated with each physical port. By maintaining the table, the switch knows to which port it must forward frames so they can get to their destination. CAM tables support a finite number of entries. If attackers use a technique designed to overload the CAM table, the switch can no longer accept new entries, thus the switch will flood all new frames out all ports. The attackers can then analyze all VLAN unicast conversations. The following table describes how to enable layer 2 port security for the switch and set several parameters to prevent CAM table attacks from adversely affecting the switch.

Command	Description
switchport port-security	Interface command. Enables port security features
switchport port-security max-mac-count 1	Interface command. Sets maximum number of MAC addresses allowed on switch port that prevents an attacker from overloading the CAM table.
switchport port-security aging time 5	Interface command. Deletes the dynamically learned address after five minutes of inactivity. This also prevents an attacking device from constantly switching its MAC address by throttling the change interval.

VLAN Hopping

Attackers connected to a VLAN on a switch might desire to attack a host that resides on another VLAN within the switch. If layer 3 routing is present, the attackers might be able to use this path. If layer 3 routing to the destination VLAN does not exist or effective controls are in place, the attackers might alternatively be able to use a VLAN hopping attack as their vector to the target. The attack system can craft frames with 802.1q tags that contain the VLAN ID of the target system's VLAN. By doing so, the switch receives the frames and then they potentially are placed into the target VLAN. Likewise an attack host might try to behave like a switch and negotiate trunking from its interface to the switch. If trunking is allowed, the attacker can send and receive traffic among all VLANs on the switch.

A switchport's default mode is the **dynamic desirable** setting that allows the port to become a trunk if the client side attempts to negotiate it as such. Allowing a port to be a trunk exposes the network to layer 2 attacks. To prevent a port from becoming a trunk, you should configure it as an access port. Access ports do not use trunk tagging and are only members of a single VLAN thus mitigating some layer 2 threats. To configure a port as an access port use the following interface command on each switchport:

```
switchport mode access
```

Spanning Tree Protocol Manipulation

Spanning Tree Protocol (STP) is a layer-2 process that uses special frames called Bridge Protocol Data Units (BPDU) to guard against looped topologies. Connected switches identify one switch as the root bridge and block all other redundant data paths. By attacking the Spanning-Tree Protocol (STP), attackers attempt to pose as a root bridge to intercept frames. Forged BPDU frames can cause switches to begin spanning-tree recalculations. If the attackers have two interfaces connected to the layer 2 network (for example, two wired, two wireless, or a wired and wireless) and successfully become the root bridge, they can use their system to forward the network's data while snooping it.

The BPDU filter commands prevent ports from sending or receiving BPDUs either globally or at the interface level. The BPDU guard features automatically disable a portfast designated port if the port receives a BPDU from the connected host. This condition requires manual intervention to re-enable the port. The design of the root guard feature enforces the root bridge connection point in the network. If a device sends a BPDU to try to become the root bridge, root guard blocks it. When a device ceases sending BPDUs that might normally make it the root, root guard unblocks the port automatically. Enable root guard on all ports except the one that connects the root bridge.

Cisco commands that mitigate these exposures include the following:

Command	Description
`spanning-tree bpdufilter enable`	Interface command. Prevents a port from sending or receiving BPDUs that are mechanisms used in spanning tree to elect a root bridge. This can be applied to all interfaces that connect directly to client PCs.
`spanning-tree portfast bpdufilter default`	Global command. Enables BPDU filtering on all Port Fast-enabled ports and prevents the switch port connected to end stations from sending or receiving BPDUs.
`spanning-tree bpduguard enable`	Interface command. Puts a port in the error-disabled state when it receives a BPDU. Intervention is required to re-enable the port.
`spanning-tree guard root`	Interface command. Root guard does not allow the port to become a STP root port.

MAC Address Spoofing

The Address Resolution Protocol (ARP) is a way for hosts to match destination IP and MAC addresses for the proper framing and sending of communications. ARPs occur when host X needs to communicate to host Y and X has Y's IP address but not the corresponding MAC address. Attackers can misuse ARP functions to steer traffic to a false destination by improperly matching the target's IP address with the attacker's MAC address. Attackers accomplish this with gratuitous ARPs (GARPs) that are unsolicited ARP broadcasts containing the incorrect IP-to-MAC pairing. The GARP causes all receiving hosts to incorrectly update their ARP table with the incorrect information. Similarly the switch incorrectly updates its CAM table, thus when any host needs to send a packet to the target's IP, the switch forwards the packet to the attacker causing a man-in-the-middle condition.

To mitigate these conditions, several Cisco commands are used to hard code MAC addresses to ports. These commands include: limiting the number of dynamically learned addresses, specifying the ports to which only valid Dynamic Host Configuration Protocol (DHCP) servers connect, and verifying ARP broadcasts by referencing a DHCP snooping database.

Command	Description
`switchport port-security`	Interface command. Enables port security features.
`switchport port-security mac-address` *mac_address*	Interface command. Hardcodes the connected host's MAC address for the interface to prevent spoofing. Often considered difficult to scale.

Command	Description
`switchport port-security max-mac-count 1`	Interface command. Sets the maximum number of MAC addresses allowed on switch port to prevent an attacker from overloading the CAM table. The specified number less the hardcoded MACs equals the quantity of allowed dynamic MACs.
`ip dhcp snooping`	Interface command. Signifies the interface as a port connecting a legitimate DHCP server.
`ip dhcp snooping vlan 39-44`	Global command. Specifies the VLANs configured for DHCP snooping.
`ip arp inspection options`	Global command. Dynamic ARP Inspection (DAI) determines the validity of an ARP based on the valid IP to MAC address bindings stored in the DHCP snooping database.

Private VLANs

The purpose of private VLANs is to prevent communication among hosts within the same VLAN segment. This is often desirable to prevent one infected host on a segment from attacking and exploiting another host on that same segment. Layer 3 controls like filtering, and firewalling at the segment's gateway cannot prevent the host-to-host infection because the hosts communicate directly and not via the gateway.

Cisco switch platforms and IOS allow for private VLANs with different levels of control. A "Private VLAN Edge" implementation is one where ports are either "protected" (by executing the **switchport protected** interface command) or "unprotected" (by leaving an interface at its default). PVLAN edge implementations can only communicate in the following ways:

- Unprotected ports can talk to unprotected ports

- Protected ports can talk to unprotected ports

- Protected ports cannot talk to protected ports

If two servers connect to protected ports they cannot communicate at layer 2.

More advanced switch platforms offer even more granularity in PVLAN implementation. These PVLANs control not only host-to-host communication within a broadcast domain but also IP communication at layer 3 and/or layer 4 (for example, TCP port 80, UDP port 69) using VLAN ACLs (VACLs). There are three types of PVLAN ports:

- **Promiscuous**—A device connected to a promiscuous port can communicate with all other interfaces in the broadcast domain. Often gateway routers connect to these ports.

- **Isolated**—An isolated port has complete layer 2 separation from the other ports within the same broadcast domain except promiscuous ports.

- **Community**—Community ports can communicate among themselves and with promiscuous ports.

IntraVLAN Proxy Attacks

VLAN proxy attacks attempt to circumvent private VLAN controls by altering frame addressing, so that Host A can communicate with Host B via Router 1 even though security policy does not allow direct A to B communication. The attackers craft and send a frame containing their valid source IP and MAC addresses to the destination IP address of the target. Instead of specifying Host B's MAC (policy controls would disallow the flow), they use the MAC address of the local gateway router. Because the private VLAN controls are unlikely to block access to the gateway router, the switch forwards the frame to the router as the crafted frame specified the router's MAC. The router receives the frame, sees that the destination IP is Host B, rewrites the frame with the target's valid MAC address, and retransmits the data to the target.

By using a layer 3 ACL to prevent hosts in a given IP range from sending packets to hosts within that same IP range, the router can drop the crafted frames. Layer 3 access lists are implemented on some Cisco layer 2 switches.

```
access-list 101 remark Private VLAN attack
access-list 101 remark Place inbound on gateway port
access-list 101 remark Next line allows clients to talk to a server at .17
 on the same segment
access-list 101 permit ip 10.5.5.0 0.0.0.255 host 10.5.5.17
access-list 101 remark Next line prevents all other intra VLAN communication
access-list 101 deny   ip 10.5.5.0 0.0.0.255 10.5.5.0 0.0.0.255
access-list 101 deny   ip any any
```

DHCP Address Depletion

Attackers can exhaust an available DHCP address pool by repeatedly broadcasting DHCP requests with multiple spoofed MAC addresses. When the pool is depleted, legitimate hosts cannot obtain an IP address. Furthermore, the attackers can set up a DHCP server on their host that responds to new DHCP requests from network clients. This rogue address pool can cause clients to use the attacker as their gateway, effectively causing a man-in-the-middle condition.

Command	Description
`ip dhcp snooping`	Prevents DHCP starvation by filtering rogue DHCP messages. Multiple options exist.
`switchport port-security max-mac-count 1`	Discussed previously. Helps to control the number of MAC addresses on a port to mitigate this attack.

VTP Attacks

VLAN Trunking Protocol (VTP) is a layer 2 protocol used to maintain VLAN configuration consistency among switches within a related grouping (VTP domain). If effective precautions are not taken, a rogue switch can inject spurious VTP VLAN information into the infrastructure causing mass reconfiguration of the network.

Process the following commands on a main switch:

Command	Description
`core-switch(config)#vtp domain shmoo`	Assigns VTP domain name.

Command	Description
`core-switch(config)#`**`vtp password`** `w4andh2`	Assigns VTP domain password. Other switches in the VTP domain must use this password too.
`core-switch(config)#`**`vtp mode server`**	Sets mode to server indicating that VTP configuration information cannot be overwritten.

Access Port and Trunk Security

The following are guidelines for improving access and trunk port security:

- Do not assign any port to VLAN 1, the default "management" segment.

- Assign all unused ports to an unused VLAN pruned from all active trunks.

- Shutdown all unused ports.

- Be careful when assigning **portfast** status to a port because undesirable topology loops can occur.

- For trunks, assign dedicated VLAN numbers as the native VLAN number. Otherwise, if a trunk and a VLAN segment share the same number, hosts on the segment can cross the trunk without 802.1q tagging. This might not be desirable.

- For trunks, only allow the VLANs that must traverse the trunk. Prune all other VLANs.

Identity-Based Networking Services (IBNS)

IBNS Overview

IBNS technology improves security by allowing users and devices access to a network only if they present valid authentication credentials. After authentication, IBNS can stipulate authorization settings to limit a device's capabilities. IBNS operates at layer 2 on both wired and wireless networks by using 802.1X/Extensible Authentication Protocol (EAP), the IEEE standard for port-level strong user authentication, and the following components:

- A client device. For example, Windows PC, Linux server, printer, wirelessly connected PDA.

- An 802.1X-aware switch or wireless access point.

- A RADIUS authentication server (NAS) that supports 802.1x and your chosen authentication EAP type. Note that TACACS+ is not supported for 802.1X.

- A user directory on the RADIUS server or one with which the RADIUS server can communicate, such as Active Directory or an LDAP directory.

NOTE   Historically the term network logon was a logon to a file server directory via a workstation. With IBNS, this term is actually more accurate because users are first validated to gain access to the physical network and a logon to a file server directory often follows.

By using 802.1X/EAP for authentication, you can enforce a policy that disallows end-point device access to network resources until successfully authenticated. 802.1X/EAP provides the following services in support of IBNS:

- User identification (the user might be a human or a device)
- Centralized authentication
- Wired and wireless LAN access
- Centralized wireless key management

Cisco IBNS adds capabilities above and beyond standard 802.1X/EAP authentication with custom extensions when using Cisco Secure ACS as the authentication server. Extensions include:

- User and device automatic VLAN assignment based on authentication. For example, when Margaret in the Pharmacy Department authenticates, she is always placed into VLAN 33. When Russell in the Dispatching Department authenticates, he is always placed into VLAN 99. These both happen even if they shared the same PC.
- Single MAC address port security compatibility to prevent hub-connected devices from "riding" the valid authentication of another user.
- VoIP compatibility to allow low-level VoIP frames to flow before authentication.
- Automatic guest VLAN assignment for devices lacking compatible 802.1X support.
- High availability 802.1X to prevent network lockout should an authentication device fail.
- Dynamic and custom ACL assignment to the port based upon the supplied authentication credentials. As users log on and off, the per-port ACLs will change based on their group assignment.

How 802.1X/EAP Works

802.1X/EAP is a modular technology comprised of both 802.1X for message exchange and Extensible Authentication Protocol (EAP) for authentication. Originally defined in RFC 2284, it separates message exchanges from the authentication process itself, making it "extensible" because the two are independent of the other. As new authentication mechanisms are developed the message exchanges can remain the same. Think of 802.1X as the access model for host-to-host communication and EAP as the authentication system.

The following are mandatory components that comprise the IEEE 802.1X/EAP specification and must be 802.1X-capable:

- **Supplicant**—The physically or wirelessly connected end device (PC, printer, and IP phone) needing network access.
- **Authenticator**—The switch or wireless access point to which the supplicant physically connects (the chokepoint). Acts as the proxy (middle man) for authentication messages flowing between the supplicant and authentication server. This device is the client to the authentication server.
- **Authentication Server**—The RADIUS server that performs the centralized authentication using its own user database or an external one.

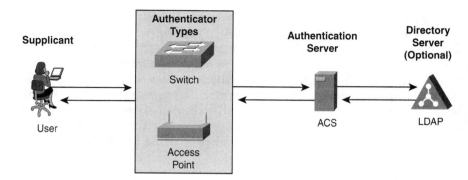

To gain network access, the supplicant must support 802.1X/EAP either directly within the OS or by using a supplicant application from a third-party. The IOS running on the authenticator must support and be configured for 802.1X/EAP. The authentication server must support the required EAP types.

Before a valid end point (supplicant) authentication, select communication protocols related to administrative network operations are not blocked but all other communications are. An unauthenticated port is said to be an uncontrolled port (also called an open port or a port in an unauthorized state) and will only pass frames related to 802.1X, Cisco Discovery Protocol (CDP), and Spanning Tree Protocol (STP). A port is said to be a controlled port (or a port in an authorized state) after valid end-point authentication and only then does it have the capability to pass all traffic types when not limited by an ACL. During the authentication process, one of many EAP methods might be used.

The following graphic describes a generic EAP process and how EAP messages can flow during the authentication process:

High-Level EAP Flow

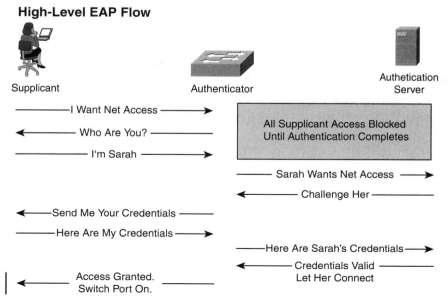

An EAP flow begins either by the authenticator or by the supplicant during conditions like a network transition from link-down to link-up or when the switch receives an EAPOL start frame. The switch or access point sends an initial identity request frame followed by one or more requests for authentication information. Upon receipt of the frames, an 802.1X-enabled client responds with an EAP identity response frame. If the client does not receive an EAP request identity frame, it can start authentication by sending an EAPOL-start frame, which prompts the switch to request the client's identity. If the client supports 802.1X but the access device does not, the client's EAPOL frames are dropped because it does not understand them. The client then transmits traffic as if the access device's port is in a controlled state essentially skipping 802.1X authentication.

Additional terms:

- **EAPOL**—EAP encapsulation over LAN for wired networks.
- **EAPOW**—EAP encapsulation over wireless for wireless networks.
- **EAP Start**—Start of the EAP exchange.
- **EAP Success**—Authentication succeeded.
- **EAP Failure**—Authentication failed.

EAP Types

The EAP types offer different levels of security and complexity. Choosing an EAP type should be driven by the organization's security needs. EAP supports several authentication methods including the following:

- Static usernames and passwords
- Public key authentication (digital certificates on smart cards or other secure repository)
- Token card one-time passwords
- Kerberos

For greater security, several EAP types feature two-way authentication where the client authenticates the server and the server authenticates the client. EAP types that only use one-way authentication only authenticate the client to the server.

Each EAP-type's authentication message flow is unique. The following list describes several EAP types:

- EAP-MD5
    - Referenced in RFC 2284 (802.1X) standard
    - Supplicant authentication: CHAP password hash
    - One-way authentication
    - Weak security from challenge passwords
- LEAP (Lightweight Extensible Authentication Protocol)
    - Developed by Cisco for wireless network authentication
    - Supplicant authentication: MS-CHAPv1 password hash

- Security quality based upon password strength; susceptible to dictionary attacks
- Two-way authentication
- Low management overhead

- EAP-FAST (EAP Flexible Authentication via Secure Tunneling)

    - Developed by Cisco as a successor to LEAP
    - Uses shared secret Protected Access Credential Keys (PAC-Key) performed once during client provisioning
    - Uses the PAC to establish a secure tunnel for key exchange
    - Two-way authentication
    - Supplicant authentication: EAP-SIM, EAP-OTP, EAP-GTC, and MS-CHAPv2

- EAP-TLS (EAP Transport Layer Security)

    - Strong authentication security level
    - Based upon SSLv3 (TLS 1.0)
    - Uses client-side and server-side certificates
    - Often used by EAP-within-EAP technologies (for example, PEAP, and EAP-TTLS)
    - Requires a Public Key Infrastructure (PKI)
    - Two-way authentication
    - Supplicant authentication: public key certificate
    - High overhead for processing

- EAP-TTLS (EAP Tunneled Transport Layer Security)

    - Strong authentication security level
    - Developed by Funk Software and Certicom
    - Builds an encrypted TLS tunnel between Supplicant and authenticator before user credentials pass to the authentication server
    - Supplicant authentication: CHAP, PAP, MS-CHAP(v2), another EAP
    - Competes against PEAP
    - Uses server digital certificates and client passwords
    - Low management overhead

- PEAP (Protected EAP)

    - Strong authentication security level for wireless networks
    - Developed by Cisco, Microsoft, and RSA
    - Can be described as an EAP within an EAP. For example:
      PEAP-EAP-TLS (server certificates/client certificates or smartcards)
      PEAP-EAP-MS-CHAPv2 (server certificates/client passwords)
    - Builds an encrypted TLS tunnel between the supplicant and authenticator for the inner EAP process to operate more securely
    - Two-way authentication
    - Supplicant authentication: any other EAP

— Competes with EAP-TTLS

— Low management overhead

Cisco Secure ACS (CSACS) and EAP

CSACS is a key component in the 802.1X/EAP authentication process and can serve as a flexible authentication server platform.

In addition to the authentication-related features, CSACS provides the following features:

— When users are not found in the built-in user database, authentication of unknown users occurs with external user databases.

— Ability to configure user accounts using an external data source.

— Proxy of authentication requests to other AAA servers.

— Self-signed server certificate generation when a proper Certificate Authority (CA) is not available.

— Certificate revocation list (CRL) lookups during EAP-TLS authentication.

CSACS supports the following varieties of EAP:

- EAP-MD5

- EAP-TLS

- LEAP

- PEAP

- EAP-FAST

In addition to its built-in user database, interfacing of CSACS can occur with a variety of external user authentication databases including the following:

- Windows User Database (NT and Active Directory)

- Generic LDAP implementations

- Novell NetWare Directory Services (NDS)

- Open Database Connectivity (ODBC) compliant relational databases

- RSA SecurID one-time password token servers

- RADIUS compliant token servers

The following table describes authentication database types that can interface with Cisco Secure ACS and the supported EAP types you might use in conjunction with them.

Authentication Database Types	LEAP	EAP-MD5	EAP-TLS	PEAP (EAP-GTC)	PEAP (EAP-MS-CHAPv2)	EAP-FAST Phase Zero	EAP-FAST Phase Two
CSACS (built-in user database)	X	X	X	X	X	X	X
Windows NT	X			X	X	X	X

Authentication Database Types	LEAP	EAP-MD5	EAP-TLS	PEAP (EAP-GTC)	PEAP (EAP-MS-CHAPv2)	EAP-FAST Phase Zero	EAP-FAST Phase Two
Windows Active Dir	X		X	X	X	X	X
LDAP			X	X			X
Novell NDS				X			X
ODBC	X	X	X	X	X	X	X
LEAP Proxy RADIUS Server	X			X	X	X	X
OTP Token Servers				X			

Configuring 802.1X Port-Based Authentication

802.1X is used to secure access to the network in both wired and wireless environments. This section illustrates how to secure a wired network with advanced authentication.

Supported Switch Port Types

The following port types support 802.1X:

- Layer 2 static-access ports
- Layer 3 routed ports

The following port types do not support 802.1X:

- Trunk ports
- Dynamic ports
- Dynamic-access ports
- EtherChannel ports
- Secure ports
- Switch Port Analyzer (SPAN) destination ports

802.1X interface configuration variations:

Command	Description

`access-switch(config)#`
`dot1x port-control`
`force-authorize`
	Interface command (default). Disables 802.1X authentication by forcing it to the "authorized" state regardless of whether the client tries 802.1X or not.

`access-switch(config)#`
`dot1x port-control`
`force-unauthorize`
	Interface command. Causes a port to remain in the unauthorized state. No authentication takes place but the port is not usable.

`access-switch(config)#` `dot1x port-control auto`	Interface command. Enables 802.1X authentication. Port begins in the unauthorized state and transitions to authorized once valid credentials are supplied.

802.1X Port-Based Authentication Switch Configuration Tasks

The following table illustrates the commands related to enabling 802.1X authentication.

Task Step	Description	IOS Command
Step 1—Enable AAA (required).	Global command. Enable AAA.	`aaa new-model`
Step 2—Specify the 802.1X method (required).	Global command. Create an 802.1X authentication method list.	`aaa authentication dot1x {default} method1 [method2...]`
Step 3—Turn on 802.1X (required).	Interface command. Enable 802.1X for each port requiring it.	`dot1x port-control auto`
Step 4—Define the RADIUS server (required).	Global command. Specify the RADIUS server used for 802.1X.	`radius-server host {hostname ¦ ip-address} auth-port port-number key string`
Step 5—Enable periodic client reauthentication (optional).	Global command. Enable periodic reauthentication of the client. Disabled by default. 3600 seconds default if enabled.	`dot1x re-authentication` `dot1x timeout re-authperiod seconds`
Step 6—Define the client quiet period (optional).	Global command. The number of seconds that the switch remains in the quiet state following a failed authentication exchange with the client. Default = 60 seconds.	`dot1x timeout quiet-period seconds`
Step 7—Change the switch-to-client retransmission time (optional).	Global command. The number of seconds that the switch waits for a response to an EAP-request identity frame from the client before retransmitting the request. Default = 30 seconds.	`dot1x timeout tx-period seconds`
Step 8—Set the switch-to-client frame-retransmission number (optional).	Global command. The number of times that the switch sends an EAP-request identity frame to the client before restarting the authentication process. Default = 2.	`dot1x max-req count`
Step 9—Allow multiple hosts on a port as required (optional).	Interface command. Allows multiple hosts (clients) on an 802.1X-authorized port. Only one of the attached hosts must have successful authorization for the granting of network access to all hosts.	`dot1x multiple-hosts`

Use the following commands to track 802.1X statistics.

Description	IOS Command
Display 802.1X statistics	`show dot1x statistics`
Display 802.1X operational status	`show dot1x`

Cisco Security Device Manager

In addition to the familiar command-line interface available for configuration of IOS devices, Cisco provides a simple browser-based management tool called Security Device Manager

(SDM). SDM is a Java-based application that requires a compatible Java Virtual Machine (JVM) and browser for proper operation.

SDM Overview

SDM provides an alternative management interface to administrators who are less familiar with IOS CLI commands. It also provides a series of wizards to simplify various configuration and management tasks.

Through the use of wizards, SDM simplifies otherwise complex configuration tasks including:

- LAN and WAN interface configuration
- Firewall and ACL configuration
- LAN-to-LAN and remote access virtual private networks (VPN)
- Routing and NAT
- IOS intrusion prevention
- QoS

In addition, SDM provides a comprehensive security audit wizard to simplify the task of auditing the security configuration on an IOS device. This tool compares the configuration of an IOS device to recommended settings by Cisco Technical Assistance Center and identifies noncompliant settings. It also provides suggestions to address any security configuration issues it identifies.

Typical workflow when using SDM to configure a new IOS device is as follows:

1 Configure LAN parameters.

2 Configure WAN and routing parameters.

3 Configure firewall and security parameters.

4 Configure VPN parameters.

5 Perform security audit.

SDM Software

SDM comes preinstalled on Cisco 1800, 2800, and 3800 series routers. Installation of SDM can also occur on existing routers with supported hardware and software. Specific supported series include:

- 800 Series
- 1700 Series
- 2600 Series
- 2800 Series
- 3600 Series
- 3700 Series

- 3800 Series

- 7000 Series

The minimum IOS version required to run SDM depends on the router platform and model in use. Latest information on minimum IOS versions that support SDM operation with each router platform is available on Cisco.com. SDM is compatible with most, but not all, hardware modules that can be installed on various router platforms. An updated list of hardware modules supported by SDM is also available on Cisco.com.

SDM requires a PC with a Pentium III or faster processor and any of the following supported operating systems:

- Microsoft Windows XP Professional

- Microsoft Windows 2003 Server Standard Edition (Advanced Server is not supported)

- Microsoft Windows 2000 Professional with Service Pack 4 or higher (Windows 2000 Advanced Server is not supported)

- Microsoft Windows ME

- Microsoft Windows 98 Second Edition

- Microsoft Windows NT 4.0 Workstation with Service Pack 4 or higher

Japanese, Simplified Chinese, French, German, Spanish, and Italian language support is also available when used with one of the following operating systems:

- Microsoft Windows XP Professional with Service Pack 1 or later

- Microsoft Windows 2000 Professional with Service Pack 4 or later

In addition, SDM requires one of the following compatible browsers:

- Netscape version 4.79 on all supported operating systems except Windows 98

- Netscape version 7.1 or 7.2

- Internet Explorer version 5.5 or later

Finally, SDM requires SUN Java Runtime Environment (JRE) version 1.4.2_05 or later or Microsoft JVM version 5.0.0.3810 or later.

SDM Installation

To install SDM, you must complete the following five tasks:

- Task 1—Download SDM image from Cisco.com.

- Task 2—Prepare router for SDM installation.

- Task 3—Upgrade router IOS image if necessary.

- Task 4—Copy SDM files to router flash memory.

- Task 5—Start SDM.

Task 1—Download SDM Image   SDM is preinstalled on several router series, but it can also be installed on any supported platform. Obtain the latest version of SDM at http://www.cisco.com/cgi-bin/tablebuild.pl/sdm and install it on a supported router. Expand the downloaded file and place it on a TFTP server. The SDM files include the following:

- sdm.tar

- ips.tar

- home.tar

- home.html

- home.shtml (required for Cisco 7200 and Cisco 7300 routers)

- attack-drop.sdf

- sdmconfig-*modelnum*.cfg

Task 2—Prepare Router for SDM Installation   Before installation of the SDM files, prepare the router as follows:

Step 1   Enable HTTP and HTTPS server support:

```
Router(config)#ip http server
Router(config)#ip http secure-server
```

Step 2   Configure HTTP authentication method (local authentication shown here):

```
Router(config)#ip http authentication local
Router(config)#username username privilege 15 password 0 password
```

Step 3   Configure SSH and Telnet for local login and privilege level 15:

```
Router(config)#line vty 0 4
Router(config-line)# privilege level 15
Router(config-line)# login local
Router(config-line)# transport input telnet ssh
```

Step 4   Optionally enable buffer logging:

```
Router(config)#logging buffered 51200 warning
```

Task 3—Upgrade Router IOS Image if Necessary   If the router's IOS image is not supported by SDM, install a supported version before the installation of SDM. Use the **copy tftp flash** command to copy IOS images from a TFTP server to the router.

Task 4—Copy SDM Files to Router Flash Memory   Use the **copy tftp flash** command to copy the appropriate SDM files to the flash memory of the router:

```
Router# copy tftp://<tftp server IP address>/sdm.tar flash:
```

Answer **no** when prompted to erase flash to avoid erasing the entire flash memory contents (including the IOS image).

Use the **copy tftp flash** command to copy all SDM files listed previously.

Task 5—Start SDM   Use the following URL to access the router at its IP address:

```
https://<router IP address>
```

SDM is accessible from the Cisco Router and Security Device Manager link in the left panel on the IOS home page that appears at this address.

SDM User Interface

SDM's interface consists of the following primary elements:

- **Menu Bar**—Provides access to File, Edit, View, Tools, and Help menus.

- **Toolbar**—Provides access to SDM wizards, operating modes, refresh, save, and online help. SDM operates in one of three modes:

  — **Home**—Provides basic information about the router's hardware, software, and configuration.

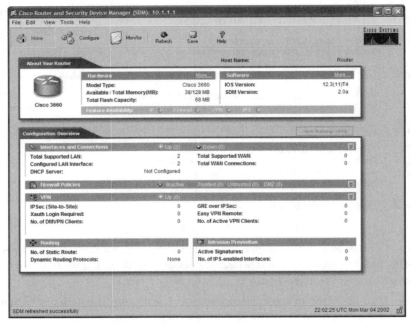

  — **Configure**—Provides access to configuration pages and wizards.

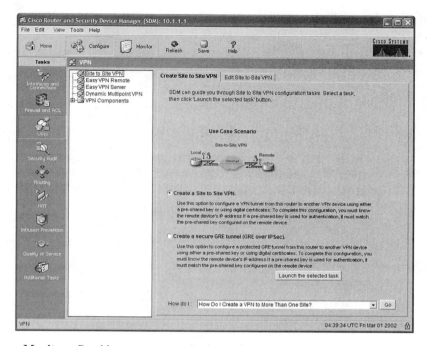

— **Monitor**—Provides access to monitoring tools.

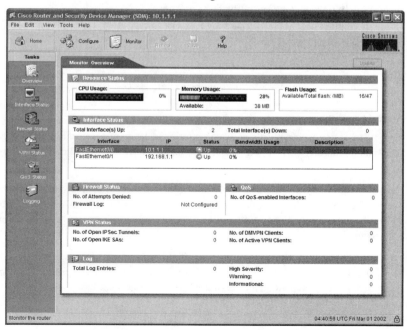

- **Mode Indicator**—Displays the current operation mode, date and time, and browser security at the bottom of the window.

- **Task Bar**—Available on the left side of the screen in configure and monitor modes and provides access to various configuration and monitoring tools and wizards.

SDM Wizards

In addition to normal configuration screens, SDM provides task-based wizards to simplify and streamline common configuration tasks. Specifically, SDM provides the following configuration wizards:

- Start-up wizard to configure basic router setting including:
  - Default username and password
  - LAN interface settings
  - WAN interface settings
  - DHCP Server configuration
  - Security configuration
- LAN wizard to configure Ethernet LAN interfaces.
- WAN wizard to configure various WAN interfaces.
- Firewall wizards to configure basic and advanced IOS firewall settings.
- VPN wizards to configure site-to-site VPNs, Dynamic Multipoint VPNs (DMVPN), and Easy VPN Remote and Server settings.
- Security Audit wizard and One-Step Lockdown to perform security audits and lock down a router with little effort.
- IPS wizard to configure IOS IPS settings.
- QoS wizard to configure QoS settings on the router.

Advanced Configuration

Although wizards greatly simplify many configuration tasks, they cover only a subset of all the potentially configured settings on IOS devices and are not the best choice for creating highly customized configurations.

SDM provides many advanced screens to allow administrators easy access to all configuration settings on IOS devices. These advanced configuration screens cover areas not covered by SDM wizards, such as routing and NAT settings, and provide additional configuration options for areas covered by wizards, such as VPN or firewall configurations.

Click the edit tab on SDM to access advanced configuration settings for tasks with wizards. The following figure shows the site-to-site VPN configuration screen. Access the corresponding wizard by clicking the button labeled **Launch the selected task**.

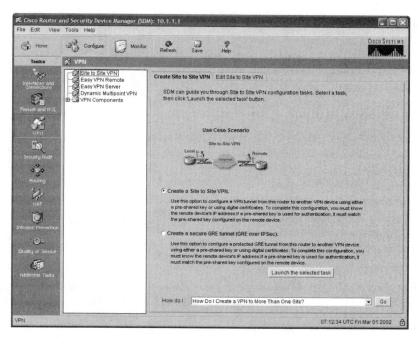

Click the tab labeled **Edit Site to Site VPN** to access advanced configuration settings. Tasks without wizards simply display the advanced settings page as shown with the Routing configuration page.

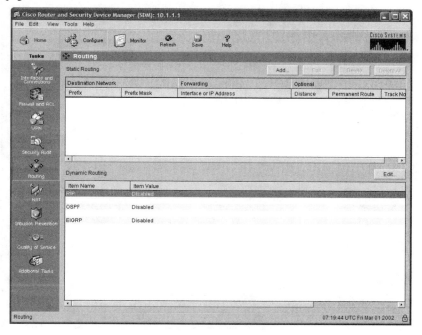

Settings configured using the advanced configuration screens exclusively include:

- Routing
- NAT (basic configuration possible using WAN Wizard)
- Router Properties (Network Time Protocol [NTP], logging, SNMP, date, and time)
- Router Access (local user account, management access, VTY, and SSH)
- DHCP (can be configured as part of LAN Wizard)
- DNS
- ACLs (basic configuration possible using Firewall Wizard)
- AAA settings
- Inspection Rules (basic configuration possible using Advanced Firewall Wizard)
- Local Pools (basic configuration possible using LAN Wizard)
- Reset to factory settings

Routing and NAT settings are accessed using their respective icons in the taskbar. Access to other settings is available using the **Additional Tasks** icon in the taskbar.

A separate IPS-specific manager accessed through SDM manages the IPS settings. The following figure shows the IPS configuration manager and the IPS Signatures task page.

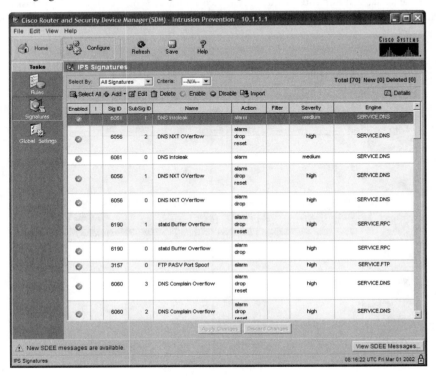

Security Audit

SDM's Security Audit and One-Step Lockdown features are some of the best ways to evaluate the security configuration of IOS routers and to fix settings not in compliance with Cisco TAC best practices. The following figure illustrates how to access these features using the **Security Audit** icon in the configuration **taskbar**.

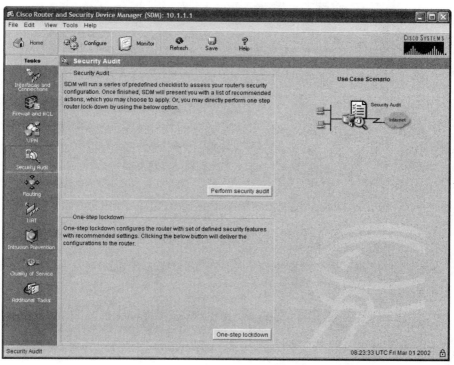

Click the link labeled **Perform security audit** on this page to start the Security Audit Wizard. The wizard operation is as follows:

1 Security Audit Wizard prompts the user to specify the inside (trusted) and outside (untrusted) interfaces.

2 Security Audit Wizard displays a list of security settings currently configured on the router and how they compare with Cisco recommended settings. If the configured settings match recommended settings, status is shown as Passed. If they are different, the setting is marked with a red X and its status is shown as Not Passed.

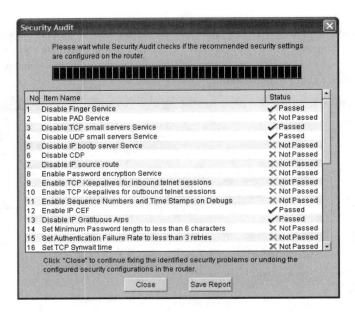

3 A remediation window displays settings marked Not Passed and provides a check box next to each setting labeled Fix it.

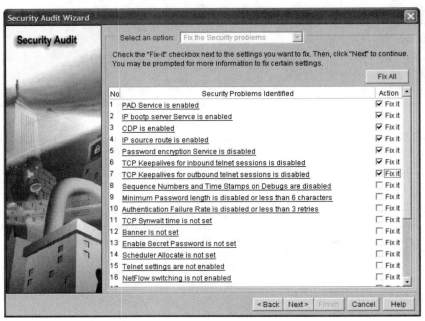

4 The administrator can now allow Security Audit to correct settings individually or click the button labeled Fix All to select all identified non-compliant settings.

5 Security Audit asks for additional information that might be required to correct certain settings.

6 Specified settings are modified on the router.

The One-Step Lockdown feature further simplifies this process by eliminating the interactive steps required with Security Wizard. It determines what settings are not compliant with Cisco best practices and corrects them all in a single step.

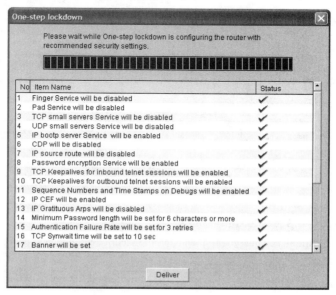

When used properly, both tools can increase the security of IOS devices in any network. An overview of recommended security settings follows.

Disable Unused Router Services and Interfaces

By default, Cisco routers enable certain insecure services and settings often for the support of legacy environments as listed in the table that follows. If the mode of these settings has no bearing on your environment, you should harden them accordingly. Note that various versions of IOS have these various settings in a default secure mode.

Feature	Description	Recommended Action	IOS Command
Bootp service	Bootp allows the router to act as an IOS image server for other routers booting up.	Disable.	`no ip bootp server`
Cisco Discovery Protocol (CDP)	Proprietary layer 2 protocol between Cisco devices.	If CDP is not needed, disable it globally.	`no cdp run`

continues

Feature	Description	Recommended Action	IOS Command
Finger service	A *nix user lookup service allowing the remote listing of users.	Unauthorized persons do not need to know this, disable it.	`no ip finger` `no service finger`
HTTP service	Web-based administrative router access.	Disable if not used. If required, use via out-of-band channels and secure access with ACLs. Use secure HTTP if offered by IOS.	`no ip http server`
Nagle service	A traffic congestion control algorithm for Telnet to reduce number of packets sent during sessions.	Enable Nagle.	`service nagle`
PAD service	X.25 packet assembly/disassembly (PAD) service.	Disable.	`no service pad`
TCP small servers	Standard TCP network services: echo, daytime, chargen, and so on.	A legacy feature exploited by attacks.	`no service tcp-small-servers`
UDP small servers	Standard UDP network services: echo, discard, and so on.	A legacy feature exploited by attacks.	`no service upd-small-servers`

Globally-Applied Security Commands

From **config terminal**, consider the following global security commands if they are not critical to operations:

Feature	Description	Recommended Action	IOS Command
Classless routing	Router forwards packets without a specific route.	Disable and rely on specific routes otherwise data can be sent via undesirable paths.	`no ip classless`
Configuration automatic load	Upon boot up, router attempts loading IOS from a network bootp server.	Disable.	`no service config` `no boot network`
DNS	Routers can perform DNS name resolution for host names in the configuration.	Generally, disable a router's capability to be a DNS client.	`no ip domain-lookup` `no ip name-server`
Identification (auth) protocol	Allows any host to ask the router who it is.	Disable.	`no ip identd`
IP source routing	An IP feature that allows packets with a predefined route override local routes.	Disable.	`no ip source-route`
Simple Network Managment Protocol (SNMP)	SNMP enables remote set and query of configuration information.	Disable if not used; otherwise use complex community strings and restrict access with ACLs.	`no snmp-server`

Interface Security Commands

From **config terminal** then **interface e0/1** (for example, interface), consider the following security commands applied at the interface or line level if they are not critical to operations.

Feature	Description	Recommended Action	IOS Command
IP directed broadcast	Potential DoS activity that sends broadcasts to all hosts on a network.	Disable.	`no ip directed-broadcast`
IP mask reply	ICMP mask replies can be used in reconnaissance activities to echo the network mask.	Disable on all interfaces.	`no ip mask-reply`
IP redirects	An attacker can use an ICMP redirect to modify a local routing table.	Disable on all interfaces.	`no ip redirect`
IP unreachable notifications	ICMP unreachables can be used in reconnaissance activities to notify senders of incorrect IP addresses.	Disable on all interfaces.	`no ip unreachable`
NTP	A router can act as a time server or client. Use to synchronize log time entries with other devices.	Disable on all interfaces except the ones that communicate with authorized NTP systems.	`ntp disable`
Proxy ARP interface command	When enabled, router can serve as a proxy intermediary between hosts on two different networks and allow undesirable communication among segments.	Disable on all interfaces.	`no ip proxy-arp`
Shutdown interfaces	Shutdown unused interfaces to prevent unwanted use.	Apply to all unused interfaces.	`shutdown`

Password Security Commands

The following commands relate to securing passwords:

Feature	Description	Recommended Action	IOS Command
Password encryption service	Presents the hash of the actual password when the configuration is displayed.	Always enable.	`service password-encryption`
Enable password	Compared to the "enable secret" password, the enable password is cryptographically weak.	Always disable.	`no enable password`
Enable secret password	More difficult to break than the enable password.	Always enable.	`enable secret`

Building Basic IPSec VPNs Using Cisco Routers

VPN Overview

A VPN offers secure, reliable, encrypted connectivity over a shared, public network infrastructure such as the Internet. Because the infrastructure is shared, connectivity is provided at lower cost than by existing dedicated private networks.

Benefits of VPNs

VPNs provide the following benefits:

- **Cost Savings**—Using the public network (Internet), VPNs provide cost effective connectivity solutions and can eliminate more expensive traditional WAN implementations.

- **Improved Communications**—VPNs provide greater access to telecommuters at home and on the road using broadband connections such as DSL and cable, as well as standard dialup.

- **Security**—VPNs use advanced encryption and authentication protocols to protect data from unauthorized access.

- **Scalability**—VPNs allow customers to add capacity with less overhead.

- **Wireless Network Security**—VPNs provide advanced security to wireless networks.

IPSec

IPSec acts at the network layer, protecting and authenticating IP packets between IPSec devices (peers), such as PIX firewalls, Cisco routers, the Cisco VPN client, and other IPSec-compliant products. IPSec is a framework of open standards and is not bound to a specific encryption or authentication protocol. As such, IPSec can work multiple encryption schemes and extends easily when newer and better algorithms become available.

IPSec uses the underlying encryption and authentication algorithms to provide the following functions:

- **Data confidentiality**—Packets are encrypted before transmission across network.

- **Data integrity**—IPSec receiver authenticates IPSec peers and packets sent by the IPSec sender to ensure no altering of the data during transmission.

- **Data origin authentication**—IPSec receiver authenticates the source of the IPSec packets sent. This service depends on the data integrity service.

- **Anti-replay**—IPSec receiver can detect and reject replayed packets to help prevent spoofing and man-in-the-middle attacks.

IPSec Security Protocols

IPSec uses the following security protocols:

- **Authentication Header (AH)**—A security protocol that provides authentication and optional replay-detection services. AH uses IP Protocol number 51.

- **Encapsulating Security Payload (ESP)**—A security protocol that provides data confidentiality and protection with optional authentication and replay-detection services. ESP uses IP protocol number 50.

IPSec Modes of Operation

IPSec, and more specifically ESP and AH, is configured to operate in two different modes:

- **Tunnel mode**—Tunnel mode for ESP encrypts the entire IP packet, including the original header, and tacks on a new unencrypted IP header. For AH, tunnel mode adds a new IP header to the entire original IP packet, including the original header. This entire new packet is authenticated.

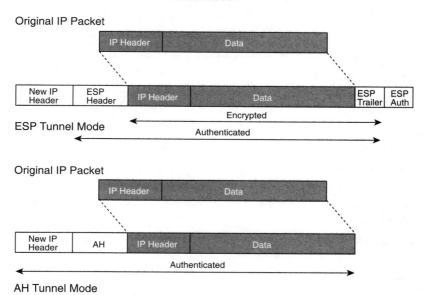

Tunnel Mode

- **Transport mode**—Transport mode leaves the original IP header intact and inserts a new ESP or AH header after the IP header. When using ESP, only the original IP payload is encrypted. With AH, the entire new packet is authenticated.

Transport Mode

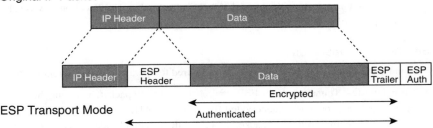

ESP Transport Mode

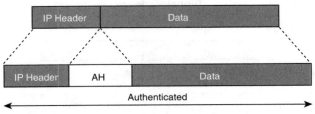

AH Tunnel Mode

IPSec-Supported Algorithms

IPSec relies on the following algorithms to implement encryption, authentication, and key exchange:

- **Data Encryption Standard (DES)**—56-bit encryption algorithm used by ESP to encrypt and decrypt data.

- **Triple-DES (3DES)**—168-bit encryption algorithm used by ESP to encrypt and decrypt data.

- **Advanced Encryption Standard (AES)**—New cipher algorithm with 128-, 192-, or 256-bit encryption used by ESP to encrypt and decrypt data. The National Institute of Standards and Technology adopted AES to replace DES and 3DES encryption algorithms.

- **Hash-based Message Authentication Code- (HMAC) variant Message Digest 5 (MD5)**—Uses a 128-bit shared key secret to provide message authentication.

- **HMAC-variant Secure Hash Algorithm 1 (SHA-1)**—Uses a 160-bit shared key secret to provide message authentication. SHA-1 provides stronger authentication relative to MD5 but with additional processing overhead.

- **Diffie-Hellman (DH)**—DH is a public-key cryptography protocol that enables two parties to establish a shared secret key over an insecure communications channel.

- **RSA (Rivest, Shamir, and Adelman)**—Asymmetrical encryption algorithm used for encryption and decryption. Because asymmetrical encryption algorithms are processor-intensive, RSA is typically used for peer authentication only.

Peer Authentication

Cisco IOS provides three methods for IPSec peer authentication:

- **Pre-shared keys**—A shared secret key known to both peers is used to authenticate the peers.

- **RSA signatures**—With RSA signatures, digital certificates issued by a Certificate Authority (CA) are used to authenticate IPSec peers. This method requires more resources to implement, but it more secure and scalable than pre-shared keys.

- **RSA encrypted nonces**—This method requires each IPSec peer to generate a pseudorandom number (nonce) that is then encrypted and sent to other peers. Peers use the encrypted initiator and responder nonces, the DH key, and the initiator and responder cookies to generate authentication keys. A hash algorithm is used with this authentication key and device-specific information to generate a hash. This hash is then sent to the other peer. The remote peer authenticates this peer if an independent hash process produces the same results.

Security Association

To succeed in establishing an IPSec tunnel, peers must agree on a matching set of IPSec-related algorithms and variables. The following terms are important during this negotiation:

- **Internet Security Association and Key Management Protocol (ISAKMP) policies**—ISAKMP policies are specific combinations of algorithms and variables used by Internet Key Exchange (IKE) to establish common policies between IPSec peers. ISAKMP policies define variables such as:

  — Encryption algorithm (DES, 3DES, AES)
  — Hash algorithm (MD5, SHA-1)
  — Authentication method (pre-share or RSA signatures)
  — Key Exchange (Diffie-Hellman group 1, 2, 5, or 7)
  — Security Association lifetime (in seconds or bytes)
  — Protocol used (ESP or AH)
  — Operation mode (Tunnel or Transport)

Parameter	ISAKMP Policy 1	ISAKMP Policy 2
Encryption Algorithm	3DES	3DES
Hash Algorithm	SHA-1	SHA-1
Authentication Method	Pre-Share	Pre-Share
Key Exchange	1024-bit D-H	1024-bit D-H
IKE SA Lifetime	86,400 Seconds	86,400 Seconds

- **Transform sets**—A transform set is a specific combination of message authentication and encryption algorithms used by the IOS router. You can configure multiple transform sets on the IOS router.

- **Crypto maps**—Crypto maps define the combination of variables used by IPSec peers during IPSec security association (SA) negotiations. Specifically, crypto maps define:
  - Interesting traffic (traffic that is protected by IPSec) using crypto ACLs
  - Peer identification
  - Transform sets to use
  - IPSec SA lifetime (optional)
  - Perfect Forward Secrecy (optional)

- **SA**—An SA is a unidirectional or bidirectional association established between IPSec peers and is uniquely identified by the IPSec protocol in use, the remote peer's address, and a 32-bit random number called the security parameter index (SPI).
  - IPSec SAs are unidirectional. Therefore, two unidirectional SAs must be established between peers.
  - IKE SAs are bidirectional and require only a single SA between two peers.
  - SAs are protocol-specific. Therefore, ESP and AH require separate SAs, if both protocols are being used.
  - Each SA is valid for the duration of its lifetime established during the negotiation process. The lifetime is specified by time or the amount of traffic traversing the tunnel. The SA must be reestablished after the SA lifetime expires.

To establish a match during the negotiation process, each peer compares the list of ISAKMP policies offered by the other peer with its own list. ISAKMP policies are used to improve performance by avoiding the large number of possible combinations of individual variables. The peers establish the IKE SA when they find matching policies.

During SA negotiations and setup, the IPSec peers must exchange and authenticate keys to establish the identity of the other peer set up appropriate SA. This mechanism relies on the following protocols:

- IKE

- ISAKMP

ISAKMP uses the IKE protocol for key exchange, but the two protocols are synonymous in Cisco VPN configurations.

Key Management

IKE relies on two mechanisms for secure key exchange and management:

- DH—DH is a public-key cryptography algorithm used by IKE that allows two peers to establish a secret key over an insecure communications channel.

- CA—CA is a trusted entity that issues digital certificates.

How IPSec Works

The primary operation steps for IPSec are as follows:

Step 1   **Define interesting traffic**—*Interesting traffic* is selected using an ACL and is defined as the traffic that is protected by IPSec.

Step 2   **IKE Phase 1**—During this phase, an initial secure communications channel is established (IKE bidirectional SA). IPSec peers use this channel for IKE Phase 2 negotiations, not to transmit user data. IKE Phase 1 can occur in the following modes:

- **Main Mode**—This mode includes three two-way exchanges between peers:

  — **First Exchange**—IKE algorithms and hashes are negotiated. ISAKMP policies are used to improve performance by avoiding the large number of possible combinations of individual variables.

  — **Second Exchange**—DH protocol is used to generate a shared secret key that is then used to generate encryption keys for the secure communications channel.

  — **Third Exchange**—In this exchange, identity of the peer is authenticated and the secure communications channel is established for subsequent IKE transmissions.

- **Aggressive mode**—This mode reduces the number of exchanges by generating the DH pair on the first exchange but without identity protection.

Step 3   **IKE Phase 2**—Matching unidirectional IPSec SAs are negotiated and established during IKE Phase 2 negotiations. The tunnel is now ready for user traffic. IKE Phase 2 does the following:

- Negotiates IPSec transform sets and security parameters

- Establishes matching unidirectional IPSec SAs

- Renegotiates the SAs when their lifetime expires

- Optionally performs additional DH exchange (perfect forward secrecy)

Step 4   **Data transfer**—IPSec peers transmit data defined as interesting in Step 1 according to the parameters negotiated in IPSec SAs.

Step 5   **Tunnel termination**—SAs are terminated if their lifetime expires or when they are deleted.

Cisco VPN Router Models

Cisco provides VPN models of its routers to address the needs of a diversified marketplace. Smaller routers such as the 800 series are aimed at home office or telecommuter uses, 1800 and 2800 series are designed for branch office applications, and the 3700 and 3800 series are designed to meet the requirements of medium to large companies. At the high end, Cisco 7100 series routers and Catalyst 6500 switches are designed to address the needs of large enterprise network implementations.

Higher-end implementations include hardware-based encryption engines to improve performance. For mid-range routers, the following modules are available:

- **AIM-VPN/BPII**—Basic performance AIM for 2600 and 2800 series routers

- **AIM-VPN/EPII**—Enhanced performance AIM for 2600 and 2800 series routers

- **AIM-VPN/HPII**—High performance AIM for 3660, 3700, and 3800 series routers

Acceleration modules are also available for high end 7100, 7200, 7300, and 7400 series routers and Catalyst 6500 switches:

- **VPN Acceleration Module (VAM)**—Provides compression and encryption for 7100 and 7200 series routers

- **Integrated Service Module (ISM)**—Accelerated performance for 7100 series routers

- **Integrated Service Adapter (ISA)**—For 7140 and 7200 series routers

- **VPN Services Module (VPNSM)**—For Catalyst 6500 switches and 7600 series routers

The following table lists the current Cisco router families or models that support VPN functionality.

Model	Max Tunnels	Performance (3DES/ AES Mbps)	Hardware Encryption
800	50	7/2	None
1700	100	15/NA	VPN Module

Model	Max Tunnels	Performance (3DES/ AES Mbps)	Hardware Encryption
2600XM	800	22/22	AIM-VPN/EPII-PLUS
2691	1000	150/150	AIM-VPN/EPII-PLUS
2800	2000	66/66	Onboard VPM
2800	2000	150/150	AIM-VPN/EPII-PLUS
3745	2000	190/190	AIM-VPN/HPII-PLUS
3800	700	180/180	Onboard VPN
3800	2000	185/185	AIM-VPN/HPII-PLUS
7200	5000	280/280	VAM
7301	5000	379/379	VAM
7600 and Catalyst 6500	8000	1.9-Gbps/ NA	VPN Services Module

Configuring IPSec for IKE Pre-Shared Keys

IPSec configuration consists of four primary tasks:

Step 1   Prepare for IKE and IPSec.

Step 2   Configure IKE.

Step 3   Configure IPSec.

Step 4   Test and verify.

The tables in this section summarize the pecific steps involved with each task and the corresponding IOS commands. The following table lists the steps involved in Task 1, preparing for IKE and IPSec.

Task Step	Description	IOS Command
Step 1—Determine IKE (IKE Phase 1) policy.	Determine the IKE policies that will be configured between IPSec peers including key distribution method, authentication method, peer IP addresses or hostnames, encryption algorithm, hash algorithm, and IKE SA lifetime.	Not applicable
Step 2—Determine IPSec (IKE Phase 2) policy.	Determine IPSec policy parameters that will be negotiated by IPSec peers detailing IPSec algorithms and parameters for optimal security and performance (configured as transform sets), peer details, traffic to be protected, and manual or IKE-initiated SAs.	Not applicable
Step 3—Check the current configuration.	Determine current router configuration and existing IPSec policies and transform sets that must be considered when planning the new configuration.	Router# **show running-config** Router# **show crypto isakmp policy** Router# **show crypto ipsec transform-set** Router# **show crypto map**

continues

Task Step	Description	IOS Command
Step 4—Ensure the network works without encryption.	Verify connectivity between peers using the **ping** command.	`Router# ping ip_address`
Step 5—Ensure ACLs are compatible with IPSec.	Ensure existing ACLs (on perimeter routers, the PIX security appliances, or other routers) do not block IPSec traffic.	`Router# show access-lists` `pix# show access-lists`

After the successful completion of the preceding steps, you can move to Task 2, configuring the IKE policy. The IKE policy specifies a set of parameters IPSec peers use during IKE Phase 1 negotiations. These parameters include:

- Encryption Algorithm (DES, 3DES, AES 128, AES 192, or AES 256)

- Integrity (hash) Algorithm (SHA-1 or MD5)

- Peer Authentication Method (pre-shared keys, RSA-encrypted nonces, or RSA signatures)

- DH Key Exchange Group (group 1 [768-bit], group 2 [1024-bit], or group 5 [1536-bit])

- SA Lifetime (any number of seconds)

The following table lists the individual steps involved in IKE configuration task and provides corresponding IOS commands.

Task Step	Description	IOS Command
Step 1—Enable or disable IKE.	Enable or disable IKE.	`Router (config# crypto isakmp enable` `Router (config# no crypto isakmp enable`
Step 2—Create IKE policies.	Create IKE policies.	`Router (config# crypto isakmp policy priority` (creates policy and enters ISAKMP configuration mode as indicated by the changed prompt text) `Router (config-isakmp)# authentication [pre-share ¦ rsa-encr ¦ rsa-sig]` (default is rsa-sig, specify **pre-share** for IKE with pre-shared keys) `Router (config-isakmp)# encryption [aes [128 ¦ 192 ¦ 256] ¦ des ¦ 3des]` (default is **des**, aes and **3des** provides stronger security) `Router (config-isakmp)# group [1 ¦ 2 ¦ 5]` (default is **group 1**, but **group 5** provides strongest security and is recommended when using AES encryption) `Router (config-isakmp)# hash [md5 ¦ sha]` (default is **sha**, which provides stronger security) `Router (config-isakmp)# lifetime seconds` (default is 86,400 seconds)
Step 3—Configure pre-shared keys.	Configure pre-shared keys.	`Router (config)# crypto isakmp key key-name`
Step 4—Verify the IKE configuration.	Verify the IKE configuration.	`Router# show crypto isakmp policy`

With an appropriate IKE policy configured, Step 3 defines a suitable IPSec policy. Parameters specified as part of an IPSec policy include:

- IPSec Transform Sets defining AH and ESP encryption and compression algorithms
- Global IPSec SA Lifetimes specifying the time SAs remain valid before they must be renogtiated.
- Crypto ACLs defining traffic that will be encrypted
- Crypto maps defining sets of IPSec parameters used by IPSec peers to set up SAs

The following table lists the individual steps involved in the IPSec configuration task and provides corresponding IOS commands.

Task Step	Description	IOS Command

Step 1—Configure transform set suites.	Configures transform set suites used by IPSec peers during SA negotiations. Up to three transforms are configured in each set.	`Router (config)#` **`crypto ipsec`** **`transform-set`** `transform-set-name` `transform1` [`transform2` [`transform3`]]
		Possible transforms include:
		
		`ah-md5-hmac`
		`ah-sha-hmac`
		`esp-3des`
		`esp-aes (128, 192, 256)`
		`esp-des`
		`esp-md5-hmac`
		`esp-null`
		`esp-seal`
		`esp-sha-hmac`
		`comp-lzs`

Step 2—Configure global IPSec SA lifetimes.	Configures global IPSec SA lifetime in seconds.	`Router (config)#` **`crypto ipsec security-association lifetime`** `seconds`
Step 3—Create crypto ACLs.	Uses extended IP ACLs to define the traffic that will be encrypted.	`Router (config)#` **`access-list`** `access-list-number` {**`deny`** ¦ **`permit`**} `protocol source source-wildcard destination destination-wildcard` [**`precedence`** `precedence`] [**`tos`** `tos`] [**`log`**]

continues

Task Step	Description	IOS Command
Step 4—Create crypto maps.	Creates crypto maps that group sets of IPSec parameters including transform sets, peer addresses, crypto ACLs, PFS, and SA-specific lifetime.	Router (config)# **crypto map** *map-name sequence-number* [**ipsec-manual** ¦ **ipsec-isakmp** [**dynamic** *dynamic-map-name* ¦ **profile** *profile-name*]] (use with **ipsec-isakmp** to create crypto map with ISAKMP and enter crypto map configuration mode)
		Router (config-crypto-map)# **match address** *acl-name*
		Router (config-crypto-map)# **set peer** *peer-address*
		Router (config-crypto-map)# **set pfs** [**group1** ¦ **group2** ¦ **group5**]
		Router (config-crypto-map)# **set transform-set** *transform-set-name*
		Router (config-crypto-map)# **set security-association lifetime** *seconds*
Step 5—Apply crypto maps to interfaces.	Applies crypto maps to an interface to activate IPSec on the interface.	Router (config)# **Interface** *interface-name*
		Router (config-if)# **crypto map** *map-name*

The last step involves testing and verification of IPSec configuration as outlined in the following table:

Task Step	Description	IOS Command
Step 1—Display IKE policies, key, and established SAs.	Display configured IKE policies, key, or active SAs with the **show crypto isakmp policy** commands.	Router # **show crypto isakmp policy** Router # **show crypto isakmp key** Router # **show crypto isakmp sa**
Step 2—Display transform sets.	Display configured transform sets with the **show crypto ipsec transform-set** command.	Router # **show crypto ipsec transform-set**
Step 3—Display IPSec SAs.	Display the current state of IPSec SAs with the **show crypto ipsec sa** command.	Router # **show crypto ipsec sa**
Step 4—Display crypto maps.	View configured crypto maps with the **show crypto map** command.	Router # **show crypto map** [*map-name* ¦ **interface** *interface-name*]
Step 5—Enable debug for IPSec.	Debug IKE and IPSec traffic with the **debug crypto ipsec** and **debug crypto isakmp** commands.	Router # **debug crypto ipsec** Router # **debug crypto isakmp**

Building Cisco IOS-Based VPNs Using Certificate Authorities

VPNs built using certificates to authenticate IPSec peers are more secure and scalable compared to those using pre-shared keys. CAs manage the distribution and revocation of digital certificates and allow for highly secure and scalable implementations.

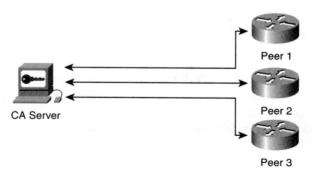

CA operation comprises several steps:

Step 1   Client (IOS device in this case) that wishes to authenticate with a CA creates a public and a private key using appropriate key-generation software.

Step 2   The client creates an unsigned X.509v3 certificate that includes its ID and the public key created in Step 1 among other things.

Step 3   Client sends certificate created in Step 2 to the CA using a secure method.

Step 4   The CA creates a signature using a hash of the X.509v3 certificate from the client and encrypts it using the CA's private key. CA attaches this signature to the certificate and returns the signed certificate (identity certificate) to the client. The client stores this identity certificate for use until it expires. The CA also sends its own digital certificate that includes it public key. The client uses this certificate as its root certificate.

Step 5   The client uses its signed identity certificate to authenticate with other IPSec peers. Peers authenticate the identify certificates using the CA's public key stored in their root certificate.

Step 6   The CA can also revoke a certificate. Clients can check certificates against a Certificate Revocation Lists (CRL) maintained by the CA to determine if a certificate is valid or revoked.

Supported CA Standards

Cisco IOS supports the following CA standards:

- **IKE**—Commonly used with pre-shared keys but can also work with CAs.

- **Public-Key Cryptography Standard #7 (PKCS #7)**—An RSA standard certificate format used to encrypt, sign, and package enrollment messages.

- **Public-Key Cryptography Standard #10 (PKCS #10)**—An RSA standard syntax used for certificate requests.

- **RSA keys**—RSA standard public key cryptography system comprised of a public and private key pair.

- **X.509v3**—X.500 standard digital certificate format used as digital identification cards between devices.

- **CA interoperability**—Interoperable CAs can communicate with IOS devices and provide digital certificate to the devices using Simple Certificate Enrollment Protocol (SCEP).

Simple Certificate Enrollment Protocol

SCEP is a common protocol created by Cisco, VeriSign, Entrust, Microsoft, Netscape, and Sun Microsystems to provide a standard method to submit requests, download certificates and CRLs, and manage certificate lifecycles. It uses manual authentication or authentication based on a pre-shared key.

Supported CA Servers

Cisco IOS software supports the following CA servers:

- VeriSign Private Certificate Services (PCS) and OnSite Service

- Entrust Technologies Entrust/PKI

- BeTrusted UniCERT Certificate Management System

- Microsoft Windows Certificate Services (SCEP functionality requires installation of SCEP Add-on for Certificate Services)

Configuring CA Support

Configuration of CA support on IOS devices includes the following five primary tasks:

Step 1   Prepare for IKE and IPSec.

Step 2   Configure CA support.

Step 3   Configure IKE for IPSec.

Step 4   Configure IPSec.

Step 5   Test and verify.

The following tables summarize the specific steps involved with each task and the corresponding IOS commands. The next table lists the steps involved in Task 1, preparing for IKE and IPSec.

Task Step	Description	IOS Command
Step 1—Plan for CA support.	Determine the CA server details including the type of CA server used, its IP address, administrator contact information, and other relevant settings.	Not applicable
Step 2—Determine IKE (IKE Phase 1) policy.	Determine the IKE policies between IPSec peers based on the number and location of the peers.	Not applicable
Step 3—Determine IPSec (IKE Phase 2) policy.	Identify IPSec peer details such as IP addresses and IPSec modes to allow configuration of crypto maps.	Not applicable

Task Step	Description	IOS Command
Step 4—Check the current configuration.	Determine current router configuration and existing IPSec policies and transform sets that must be considered when planning the new configuration.	Router# **show running-config** Router# **show crypto isakmp policy** Router# **show crypto ipsec transform-set** Router# **show crypto map**
Step 5—Ensure the network works without encryption.	Verify connectivity between peers using the **ping** command.	Router# **ping ip_address**
Step 6—Ensure ACLs are compatible with IPSec.	Ensure existing ACLs (on perimeter routers, the PIX security appliances, or other routers) do not block IPSec traffic.	Router# **show access-lists** pix# **show access-lists**

Task 2 configures CA support on the IOS device as outlined in the following table.

Task Step	Description	IOS Command
Step 1—Manage NVRAM usage (optional).	Specify that certificates and CRLs should not be stored locally but retrieved from the CA when needed.	Router (config)# **crypto ca certificate query**
Step 2—Set the router time and date.	Set the router time and date.	Router (config)# **clock timezone zone hours-offset** Router# **clock set hh:mm:ss day month year**
Step 3—Set router host and domain names and add a CA server entry.	Set host name and domain name for the router and create a CA server entry in the router's host table.	Router (config)# **hostname router-name** Router (config)# **ip domain-name router-domain-name** Router (config)# **ip host ca-name ca-ip-address**
Step 4—Generate an RSA key pair.	Generate an RSA key pair (public and private keys).	Router (config)# **crypto key generate rsa general-keys modulus mod-size**
Step 5—Declare a CA.	Declare the CA on the IOS router.	Router (config)# **crypto ca trustpoint** *ca-name* (declares the CA and enters CA config mode) Router (ca-trustpoint)# **enrollment URL** [**http:** ¦ **https:**]*url* (specifies the RUL for enrollment with CA) Router (ca-trustpoint)# **enrollment mode ra** (sets registration authority mode if required) Router (ca-trustpoint)# **crl query** *URL* (specifies the URL to obtain CRLs) Router (ca-trustpoint)# **enrollment retry-period** *minutes* (sets number of minutes [1-60] the router waits before resending a certificate request to the CA) Router (ca-trustpoint)# **enrollment retry-count** *number* (specifies how many times [1-100] the router resends a certificate request to the CA without receiving a certificate)

continues

Task Step	Description	IOS Command
Step 6— Authenticate the CA.	Authenticate the CA to verify that it is valid.	Router (config)# `crypto ca authenticate ca-name`
Step 7—Request certificate.	Obtain router's identity certificate from the CA.	Router (config)# `crypto ca enroll ca-name`
Step 8—Save configuration.	Save the CA configuration on router.	Router # `copy running-config startup-config`
Step 9—Monitor and maintain CA interoperability.	Complete optional steps to monitor and maintain interoperability (requesting a CRL, deleting router's RSA keys, deleting certificates from the configuration, and deleting peer's public keys as applicable).	Router (config)# `crypto ca crl request ca-name` Router (config)# `crypto key zeroize rsa` Router # `show crypto ca certificates` Router (config)# `crypto ca certificate chain ca-name` Router (config)# `no certificate certificate-serial-number` Router (config)# `crypto key pubkey-chain rsa` Router (config)# `no named-key key-name` Router (config)# `no addressed-key key-address`
Step 10—Verify the CA support configuration.	Verify the CA support configuration.	Router # `show crypto ca certificates` Router # `show crypto key mypubkey ¦ pubkey-chain rsa`

Task 3 configures IKE on the IOS device as outlined in the following table.

Task Step	Description	IOS Command
Step 1—Enable or disable IKE.	Enable or disable IKE.	Router (config# `crypto isakmp enable` Router (config# `no crypto isakmp enable`
Step 2—Create IKE policies.	Create IKE policies.	Router (config# `crypto isakmp policy` *priority* (creates policy and enters ISAKMP configuration mode as indicated by the changed prompt text) Router (config-isakmp)# `authentication [pre-share ¦ rsa-encr ¦ rsa-sig]` (default is `rsa-sig`) Router (config-isakmp)# `encryption [aes [128 ¦ 192 ¦ 256] ¦ des ¦ 3des]` (default is `des`, `aes` and `3des` provides stronger security) Router (config-isakmp)# `group [1 ¦ 2 ¦ 5]` (default is `group 1`, but `group 5` provides strongest security and is recommended when using AES encryption) Router (config-isakmp)# `hash [md5 ¦ sha]` (default is `sha`, which provides stronger security) Router (config-isakmp)# `lifetime` *seconds* (default is 86,400 seconds)
Step 3—Set IKE identity.	Set the IKE identity to address or hostname.	Router (config)# `crypto isakmp identity [address ¦ hostname]`
Step 4—Verify the IKE configuration.	Verify the IKE configuration.	Router# `show crypto isakmp policy`

Task 4 configures IPSec on the IOS device as outlined in the following table.

Task Step	Description	IOS Command
Step 1— Configure transform set suites.	Configures transform set suites used by IPSec peers during SA negotiations. Up to three transforms can be configured in each set.	Router (config)# **crypto ipsec transform-set** *transform-set-name transform1* [*transform2* [*transform3*]] Possible transforms include: ah-md5-hmac ah-sha-hmac esp-3des esp-aes (128, 192, 256) esp-des esp-md5-hmac esp-null esp-seal esp-sha-hmac comp-lzs
Step 2— Configure global IPSec SA lifetimes.	Configures global IPSec SA lifetime in seconds.	Router (config)# **crypto ipsec security- association lifetime** *seconds*
Step 3—Create crypto ACLs.	Uses extended IP ACLs to define the traffic that will be encrypted.	Router (config)# **access-list** *access-list-number* {**deny** ¦ **permit**} *protocol source source-wildcard destination destination-wildcard* [**precedence** *precedence*] [**tos** *tos*] [**log**]
Step 4—Create crypto maps.	Creates crypto maps that group sets of IPSec parameters including transform sets, peer addresses, crypto ACLs, PFS, and SA-specific lifetime.	Router (config)# **crypto map** *map-name sequence-number* [**ipsec-manual** ¦ **ipsec-isakmp** [**dynamic** *dynamic-map-name* ¦ **profile** *profile-name*]] (use with **ipsec-isakmp** to create crypto map with ISAKMP and enter crypto map configuration mode) Router (config-crypto-map)# **match address** *acl-name* Router (config-crypto-map)# **set peer** *peer-address* Router (config-crypto-map)# **set pfs** [**group1** ¦ **group2** ¦ **group5**] Router (config-crypto-map)# **set** transform-set transform-set-name Router (config-crypto-map)# **set security-association lifetime** *seconds*
Step 5—Apply crypto maps to interfaces.	Applies crypto maps to an interface to activate IPSec on the interface.	Router (config)# **Interface** *interface-name* Router (config-if)# **crypto map** *map-name*

The last step involves testing and verification of IPSec configuration as outlined in the following table.

Task Step	Description	IOS Command
Step 1—Display IKE policies and established SAs.	Display configured IKE policies and active SAs using the **show crypto isakmp policy** commands.	Router#`show crypto isakmp policy` Router#`show crypto isakmp sa`
Step 2—Display transform sets.	Display configured transform sets using the **show crypto ipsec transform-set** command.	Router#`show crypto ipsec` `transform-set`
Step 3—Display IPSec SAs.	Display the current state of IPSec SAs using the **show crypto ipsec sa** command.	Router#`show crypto ipsec sa`
Step 4—Display crypto maps.	View configured crypto maps with the **show crypto map** command.	Router#`show crypto map` [*map-name* ¦ `interface` *interface-name*]
Step 5—Enable debug for IPSec and CA.	Debug IKE and IPSec and CA events using the **debug crypto** commands.	Router#`debug crypto ipsec` Router#`debug crypto isakmp` Router#`debug crypto key-exchange` Router#`debug crypto pki`

Cisco IOS Remote Access Using Cisco Easy VPN

Easy VPN is Cisco's proprietary VPN based on the Cisco Unified Client Framework. It is based on open standards such as IKE and IPSec with additional Cisco proprietary protocols and mechanism aimed at simplifying the configuration, deployment, and management of remote access VPNs. Cisco Easy VPN consists of two components:

- Cisco Easy VPN Remote
- Cisco Easy VPN Server

It is typically used for remote access VPNs using the Cisco VPN software client and an Easy VPN Server device such as VPN 3000 Concentrators, Cisco IOS devices, and PIX Firewalls. It can also be used to connect Easy VPN Server devices with IOS devices (as well as VPN 3000 and PIX devices) functioning as Easy VPN Remote devices to build site-to-site VPNs with simpler configuration and management than traditional IPSec site-to-site VPNs.

Cisco Easy VPN Server

The Cisco Easy VPN Server allows Cisco IOS routers, PIX security appliances, and VPN 3000 Concentrators to function as VPN head-end devices to Cisco Easy VPN Remote devices in site-to-site or remote-access VPNs. Easy VPN Servers can push security policies defined at the central site to Easy VPN Remote devices, allowing centralized management of VPN devices and ensuring the deployment of up-to-date policies before a connection is allowed. Cisco Easy VPN Servers can also terminate VPN tunnels started by clients running the Cisco VPN Client software on a variety of supported operating systems.

The following devices support Easy VPN Server functionality (please check Cisco.com for the most up-to-date information as this list is likely to change with evolving Cisco product portfolios):

- Cisco IOS devices including 800, 1700, 1800, 2600, 2800, 3600, 3700, 3800, 7200, 7300, and 7500 Series routers

- Cisco PIX security appliance models 535, 525, and 515E

- Cisco ASA 5500 Series security appliances

- Cisco VPN 3000 Concentrators

Easy VPN Servers support the following functionality:

- **Mode Configuration Version 6 support**—Supports IKE Mode Configuration (MC).

- **XAUTH Version 6 support**—Allows the Server to request extended authentication information from the Remote device using ISAKMP.

- **IKE Dead Peer Detection (DPD) support**—Keepalive scheme allowing IPSec peers to determine if the other peer is still "alive." DPD removes orphaned connections from the server.

- **Split tunneling**—Remote clients can be configured to route Internet-bound traffic directly to the Internet in clear text, removing the overhead of having all traffic pass through the encrypted tunnel.

- **Initial contact**—A remote device can be refused a connection request if an existing connection entry appears for it on the server (because of a sudden disconnection). Initial Contact prevents this problem by implementing an initial-contact message sent by Remote devices during the initial connection attempt.

- **Group-based policy control**—Defines policy attributes such as IP addresses, DNS, and split tunneling on a per-group or per-user basis.

Easy VPN Servers support the following IPSec attributes:

- HMAC-MD5

- HMAC-SHA1

- Pre-shared keys

- RSA signatures

- DSA signatures

- DH Group 2, 5, and 7

- IKE encryptions DES and 3DES

- IPSec encryptions AES and Null

- IPSec Tunnel mode

- LZS payload compression

- Enhanced Serial Port

The following IPSec attributes are unsupported by Easy VPN Servers:

- DSS authentication
- DH Group 1
- AH
- IPSec Transport mode
- PFS
- Manual Key authentication

Cisco Easy VPN Remote

Cisco Easy VPN Remote devices can establish connections with Easy VPN Servers and receive security policies upon a VPN tunnel connection with the server, thus minimizing configuration requirements at the remote location.

Easy VPN Remote devices are also significantly simpler to configure than traditional IPSec VPN devices, further simplifying their deployment and reducing their implementation costs. The following devices provide Easy VPN Remote functionality (please check Cisco.com for the most up-to-date information as this list is likely to change with evolving Cisco product portfolios):

- Cisco VPN Client 3.6 or greater
- Cisco VPN 3002 Hardware Client version 3.6 or greater
- Cisco PIX Firewall 501 and 506E with software version 6.3 or greater
- Easy VPN Remote Routers (800, UBR900, 1700, and 1800 Series)

Modes of Operation

Easy VPN Remote devices (excluding VPN Software clients) function in one of two modes:

- **Client mode**—In this mode, the clients behind Easy VPN Remote are not directly accessible from the central site. Instead, the remote device uses port address translation (PAT) and the addresses of the individual hosts behind it remain hidden. This mode requires a single private IP address allocated to the remote device. Client mode causes the start of VPN connections by traffic from the Easy VPN Remote side, so resources are used only on demand.

- **Network extension mode**—In network extension mode, the clients behind the Easy VPN Remote device are accessible from the central site. The IP addresses of the clients are not translated in this mode. Consequently, allocate an appropriate number of IP addresses when using the network extension mode. Note that only a single subnet can be accessed behind the Easy VPN Remote Client (for instance, you cannot place a router behind a 3002 Hardware Client to route multiple subnets through the tunnel).

Overview of Cisco Easy VPN Operation

The following steps outline the Easy VPN Remote connection process:

Step 1   **Initiate IKE Phase 1**—Peers authenticate each other using pre-shared keys or certificates.

Step 2   **Establish the IKE SA**—SA parameters are negotiated to determine a common set.

Step 3   **Accept the SA**—Peers agree on an SA proposal and the Easy VPN Server authenticates the device.

Step 4   **Username and password challenge is processed**—The server prompts the user for a username and password and authenticates the user by checking the information against a AAA server using protocols, such as RADIUS or TACACS+.

Step 5   **Mode configuration**—IKE MC begins and the remote client receives the downloaded configuration parameters.

Step 6   **The RRI process is initiated**—Reverse Route Injection process adds a static entry to the Server router's route table for the connected Remote client.

Step 7   **Connection is completed with IKE Quick Mode**—IKE Quick Mode begins to complete IPSec SA negotiations and establishment.

Configuring the Easy VPN Server

The following table outlines the steps for configuration of the Easy VPN Server.

Task Step	Command Description and Example
Step 1—Create an IP address pool.	Create an IP address pool using the **ip local pool** command: `Router (config)# ip local pool mypool 10.1.1.128 10.1.1.254`
Step 2—Configure group policy lookup.	Configure group policy lookup using **aaa new-model** and **aaa authorization network** commands: `Router (config)# aaa new-model` `Router (config)# aaa authorization network auth-access local` (specifies network access authorization using a method name and enables use of local if server is unavailable)

Step 3—Create IKE policy for Remote VPN Client access.	Configure the IKE policy for Easy VPN Remote clients using the **crypto isakmp**, **authentication pre-share**, **encryption**, and **group configuration** commands: `Router (config)# crypto isakmp enable`
	`Router (config)# crypto isakmp policy 10`
	`Router (config-isakmp)# authentication pre-share`
	`Router (config-isakmp)# encryption 3des`
	`Router (config-isakmp)# group 2`
	`Router (config-isakmp)# hash sha`

continues

Task Step	Command Description and Example
Step 4—Define group policy for mode configuration push.	Define a group policy for mode configuration by creating the group profile and configuring the IKE pre-shared key, DNS servers, WINS servers, domain DNS server, and specifying the local IP address pool: `Router (config)# crypto isakmp client configuration group mc-group` (creates the group profile) `Router (config-isakmp-group)# key cisco123` (creates IKE pre-shared key) `Router (config-isakmp-group)# dns 10.1.1.10 10.1.1.11` (defines DNS servers used by clients in group) `Router (config-isakmp-group)# wins 10.1.1.12 10.1.1.13` (defines WINS servers used by clients in group) `Router (config-isakmp-group)# domain cisco.com` (specifies domain name used in DNS search order) `Router (config-isakmp-group)# pool mypool` (specifies a configured IP Pool to use with this group)
Step 5—Create a transform set.	Create transform sets for the Easy VPN Remote clients using the **crypto ipsec transform-set** command: `Router (config)# crypto ipsec transform-set my-transform-set esp-3des esp-sha-hmac`

Step 6—Create a dynamic crypto map with RRI.	Creates the dynamic crypto map with RRI by creating a dynamic crypto map, assigning a transform set to the crypto map, and enabling RRI:
	`Router (config)# crypto dynamic-map my-dyno-map 1`
	`Router (config-crypto-map)# set transform-set my-transform-set`
	`Router (config-crypto-map)# reverse route` (enables RRI)

Step 7—Apply mode configuration to the dynamic crypto map.	Apply mode configuration in global configuration mode to a dynamic crypto map by configuring the router to respond to mode configuration requests, enabling IKE queries for group policy lookup, and applying changes to the dynamic crypto map: `Router (config)# crypto map my-dyno-map client configuration address respond` (Router now responds to MC requests) `Router (config)# crypto map my-dyno-map isakmp authorization list auth-access` (enables IKE querries for group policy lookup) `Router (config)# crypto map my-dyno-map 1 ipsec-isakmp dynamic my-dyno-map`

Step 8—Apply a dynamic crypto map to the router interface.	Apply the created dynamic crypto map to the Easy VPN Server router's outside interface with the **interface** and **crypto map** commands in the global configuration mode:
	`Router (config)# Interface f0/1`
	`Router (config)# crypto map my-dyno-map`

Step 9—Enable IKE DPD.	Enable a Cisco IOS VPN gateway to send IKE DPD messages with the **crypto isakmp keepalive** command in the global configuration mode: `Router (config)# crypto isakmp keepalive 15 3` (IKE DPD packets send every 15 seconds with retires 3 seconds apart)

Task Step	Command Description and Example
Step 10—Configure XAUTH (optional).	Configure XAUTH on the Easy VPN Server router by enabling AAA login authentication, setting XAUTH timeout value, and enabling IKE XAUTH for the dynamic crypto map: Router (config)# **aaa authentication login auth-access local** (enables AAA authentication) Router (config)# **crypto isakmp xauth timeout 15** (specifies xauth time period in seconds) Router (config)# **crypto map my-dyno-map client authentication list auth-access** (enables XAUTH for the configured dynamic map,)
Step 11—Enable XAUTH save password option (optional).	Enable the XAUTH save password feature to allow the Easy VPN Remote to save and reuse the last validated username and password for reauthentication.
Step 12—Verify.	Verify the configuration with the **show running-config** command.

Configuring Easy VPN Remote for the Cisco VPN Client 4.x

The following table outlines the configuration of the Easy VPN Remote for Cisco VPN Client 4.x.

Task Step	Command Description
Step 1—Install Cisco VPN Client 4.x.	Install the Cisco VPN Client 4.x on a supported operating system.
Step 2—Create new client connection entries.	Create new connection entries on the client PC as shown in the figure following this table.
Step 3—Modify client options.	Select appropriate client options from the drop-down menu.
Step 4—Configure client general properties.	Select client options from the **Options** drop-down menu including: • Application Launcher (automatically start an application when a connection establishes). • Windows Logon properties (to optionally establish a VPN connection before logon to Windows, launch a third party application before logon to Windows, or automatically terminate the VPN session whenever logging off from Windows). • Enable or disable stateful firewall. • Choose Simple or Advanced modes. • Set preferences (Save window settings, Hide upon connect, Enable or disable tooltips, Enable or disable connect history display, Enable or disable accessibility options, Enable or disable connect on open).
Step 5—Configure client authentication properties.	Select the appropriate client authentication method from the menu radio buttons.
Step 6—Configure client connection properties.	Configure dialup or VPN client connection properties.
Step 7—Confirm client settings.	Confirm client settings including VPN client logs, MTU size, and connection status.

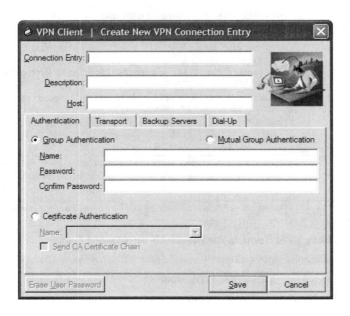

Configuring Cisco Easy VPN Remote for Access Routers

The following table outlines the configuration of the Easy VPN Remote for Cisco VPN Client 4.x.

Task Step	Command Description
Step 1—Configure the DHCP server pool.	Configure the DHCP server pool with the **ip dhcp pool, network, default-router, import all, lease, exit**, and **ip dhcp excluded-address** commands.
Step 2—Configure and assign the Cisco Easy VPN Client profile.	Configure and assign the Cisco Easy VPN client profile with the **crypto ipsec client ezvpn**, **group** *group-name* **key** *group-key*, **peer**, **mode**, and **exit** commands.
Step 3—Configure XAUTH password save (optional).	Configure the XAUTH password save with the **crypto ipsec client ezvpn**, and **username** *aaa-username* **password** *aaa-password* commands as appropriate.
Step 4—Start the VPN tunnel.	Start the VPN tunnel with the **crypto ipsec client ezvpn xauth** command.
Step 5—Verify the Cisco Easy VPN configuration.	Verify the Cisco Easy VPN configuration with the **show crypto ipsec client ezvpn** command.

Part III

CCSP: Securing Networks with PIX and ASA (SNPA) Flash Cards

The flash cards in this part of the book prepare you for the Securing Networks with PIX and ASA (SNPA) exam (642-522) toward achieving your CCSP certification. Over 300 more questions for this section of the book can be found on the CD-ROM accompanying this book. Over 300 more questions for this section of the book can be found on the CD-ROM accompanying this book. The flash cards address specific topic areas for this exam and are organized as follows:

- **Section 1: Cisco Security Appliance Technology and Features**—Tests your knowledge of firewall technologies and Cisco security appliance features and capabilities.

- **Section 2: Cisco PIX and ASA Security Appliance Families**—Tests your knowledge of Cisco Security Appliance series and features of individual models within each series.

- **Section 3: Cisco Security Appliance Basic Configuration**—Tests your knowledge of basic command-line interface configuration commands and procedures for Cisco security appliances.

- **Section 4: Translations and Connections**—Tests your general knowledge of TCP and UDP protocols and the security appliance's handling of these protocols, translation, and connections. Command-line interface (CLI) commands used to configure and monitor address translation are also covered.

- **Section 5: Access Control Lists and Content Filtering**—Tests your knowledge of access control lists (ACL) and content filtering capabilities of the security appliance. Configuration and monitoring commands are also included.

- **Section 6: Object Grouping**—Tests your knowledge of the object grouping feature of the security appliance and its configuration procedures and commands.

- **Section 7: Authentication, Authorization, and Accounting**—Tests your familiarity with AAA concepts and command-line interface configuration procedures and commands.

- **Section 8: Switching and Routing**—Tests your knowledge of the routing and switching features of the security appliance, and evaluates your knowledge of routing and switching configuration commands and procedures.

- **Section 9: Modular Policy Framework**—Tests your familiarity with the modular policy framework (MPF), which is a new feature of the Security Appliance Software 7.0.

- **Section 10: Advanced Protocol Handling**—Tests your knowledge of the advanced protocol handling features of Cisco security appliances. Commands and procedures for configuration of advanced protocol-handling features and enhanced inspection engine are also included.

- **Section 11: Virtual Private Network Configuration**—Tests your knowledge of general VPN concepts and technologies and the security appliance's support for VPNs.

- **Section 12: Configuring Security Appliance Remote Access Using Cisco Easy VPN**—Tests your knowledge of configuration commands used with Easy VPN configurations on the security appliance.

- **Section 13: WebVPN Configuration**—Tests your knowledge of the features and benefits of WebVPN and procedures for configuration of WebVPN on ASA 5500 Series appliances. WebVPN is a new SSL-based VPN option available with Security Appliance Software 7.0 and the ASA 5500 Series devices.

- **Section 14: Transparent Firewall**—Tests your knowledge of the features of transparent firewall mode and evaluates your knowledge of configuration commands required to enable and operate the security appliance in transparent firewall mode. Transparent firewall is a new feature available with Security Appliance Software 7.0.

- **Section 15: Security Contexts**—Tests your knowledge of security context and virtual firewall capabilities of the security appliances as well as the configuration procedures used to enable and operate multi-context mode.

- **Section 16: Failover**—Tests your knowledge of active/ active and active/passive failover requirements and configuration commands. Failover capabilities of the security appliances provide high-availability operation of the security appliance.

- **Section 17: Cisco Adaptive Security Device Manager**—Tests your knowledge of the features and requirements of the ASDM. Because of the GUI nature of ASDM, a limited number of configuration questions are included. Cisco ASDM is the GUI-based configuration and management tool Cisco provides for use with security appliances.

- **Section 18: Advanced Inspection and Prevention Security Services Module**—Tests your knowledge of currently available Security Services Modules (SSM) features—AIP-SSM-10 and AIP-SSM-20—as well as configuration requirements and procedures. SSMs are unique to the ASA 5500 Series security appliances.

- **Section 19: Security Appliance Management**—Tests your knowledge of various administrative access methods and your familiarity with the management features of the security appliance.

Section 1
Cisco Security Appliance Technology and Features

Question 1

What are the main three network firewall types?

Question 2

Which layers of the OSI model are used by proxy server firewalls?

Question 3

What are the drawbacks of proxy server firewalls?

Question 1 Answer

The three network firewall types are:

- Packet-filtering firewalls
- Proxy server firewalls
- Stateful packet-filtering firewalls

Question 2 Answer

Proxy server firewalls are application-aware and operate on layers 5 through 7 of the OSI model.

Question 3 Answer

The drawbacks of proxy server firewalls are:

- Single point of failure
- Difficult to add support for new applications and protocols
- High processing overhead

Section 2
Cisco PIX and ASA Security Appliance Families

Question 1

How many security contexts are available on security appliances that run unrestricted licenses?

Question 2

How many expansion slots are available on a PIX 525?

Question 3

How many expansion slots are available on a PIX 535?

Question 1 Answer

PIX 500 Series and ASA 5500 Series security appliances running unrestricted licenses support 2 security contexts. Additional security contexts up to the maximum supported on each model can be licensed. PIX 501, PIX 506E, and ASA 5510 security appliances do not support security contexts, regardless of the type of license on the appliance.

Question 2 Answer

PIX 525 includes three 32-bit, 33-MHz PCI expansion slots.

Question 3 Answer

The PIX 535 provides four 64-bit, 66-MHz PCI expansions slots and five 32-bit, 33-MHz PCI expansion slots for a total of nine.

Question 4

How many FWSM blades can be installed in one Catalyst 6500 switch?

Question 5

What is the maximum throughput performance for the FWSM?

Question 6

How many VLANs are supported by the FWSM?

Question 4 Answer

A maximum of four FWSM blades per chassis are supported.

Question 5 Answer

FWSM can operate at up to 5.5 Gbps throughput.

Question 6 Answer

FWSM supports up to 1000 VLANs.

Section 3
Cisco Security Appliance Basic Configuration

Question 1

What command displays the running configuration on the security appliance?

Question 2

What command is used to display the configured boot environment on the security appliance?

Question 3

What is the default security level applied to the inside interface?

Question 1 Answer

To display the current running configuration, the **show running-config** or **write terminal** commands are used.

Question 2 Answer

The **show bootvar** command displays the current boot environment.

Question 3 Answer

Inside interface is set at security level 100 by default, although its value can be changed by the user. Please note that with Security Appliance Software 6.x or earlier versions, the security level value of the inside interface is fixed at 100 and cannot be modified by the user.

Question 4

What command is used to allow traffic between two interfaces with the same security level?

Question 5

What command sets the interface name?

Question 6

What command designates an interface for management tasks?

Question 4 Answer

The **same-security-traffic** command can be used to enable traffic flow between interfaces with the same security level.

Question 5 Answer

The **nameif** command assigns a name to a physical or logical interface.

Question 6 Answer

The **management-only** command designates an interface for management purposes.

Section 4
Translations and Connections

Question 1

Why is TCP easier to inspect than UDP?

Question 2

What is the significance of a TCP SYN packet?

Question 3

What is a TCP three-way handshake?

Question 1 Answer

TCP is a connection-oriented protocol, and therefore easier to inspect, as conversations between internal and external hosts are more easily tracked in the session table of the security appliance.

Question 2 Answer

A TCP SYN packet signifies initiation of a new TCP connection.

Question 3 Answer

Use a three-way handshake to establish TCP connections, which includes a three-step exchange of SYN, SYN/ACK, and ACK packets between two hosts.

Question 4

At what layer of the TCP/IP protocol stack do translations occur?

Question 5

What command is used to configure the idle timeout period for dynamic address translation?

Question 6

What command is used to configure dynamic outside translation?

Question 4 Answer

Translations occur at the IP layer of the TCP/IP stack.

Question 5 Answer

The **timeout xlate** *hh:mm:ss* configures the address translation timeout period.

Question 6 Answer

To configure dynamic outside translation, use the **nat** command with the **outside** option keyword:

```
hostname(config)# nat (dmz) 1 10.1.1.0 255.255.255.0 outside
```

Section 5
**Access Control Lists and
Content Filtering**

Question 1

What command is used to create an access list?

Question 2

In what direction can access lists be applied to an interface on the security appliance?

Question 3

How is ACL editing performed?

Question 1 Answer

To configure access lists, use the **access-list** command.

Question 2 Answer

With Security Appliance Software version 7.0, access lists can be applied to inbound or outbound traffic on any security appliance interface.

Question 3 Answer

ACL editing is performed by using the **line** keyword and specifying a line number when adding new access control entries to the ACL. The new ACE is inserted into the ACL at the specified line number.

Question 4

What command is used to control ICMP traffic flow terminating on any of the security appliance interfaces?

Question 5

What command is used to control ICMP traffic flowing through the security appliance interfaces?

Question 6

How do you display the hit counts on an access list?

Question 4 Answer

The **icmp** command configures flow control for ICMP traffic that terminates on any of the security appliance interfaces.

Question 5 Answer

To control ICMP traffic flowing through the security appliance interfaces, use extended ACLs (**access-list** command).

Question 6 Answer

The **show access-list** command displays the currently configured access lists and the hit counts associated with each access control entry.

Section 6
Object Grouping

Question 1

What command is used configure network object groups?

Question 2

What command is used configure protocol object groups?

Question 3

What command is used configure ICMP object groups?

Question 1 Answer

The command **object-group network** is used to define network object groups.

Question 2 Answer

The command **object-group protocol** is used to define protocol object groups.

Question 3 Answer

The command **object-group icmp-type** is used to define ICMP type object groups.

Question 4

What command is used configure service object groups?

Question 5

What command is used to configure nested object groups?

Question 6

What command is used to display configured object groups?

Question 4 Answer

The command **object-group service** is used to define TCP, UDP, or TCP and UDP service object groups.

Question 5 Answer

The command **group-object** is used from the **object-group** subcommand menu to add (nest) an existing object group.

Question 6 Answer

The command **show running-config object-group** displays current configured object groups on the security appliance.

Section 7
Authentication, Authorization, and Accounting

Question 1

What types of authentication are available on the security appliance?

Question 2

What command is used to define a AAA server group?

Question 3

How is the authentication key for a AAA server defined?

Question 1 Answer

Three types of authentication are available on security appliances:

- Security appliance access authentication
- Cut-through proxy authentication
- Tunnel access authentication

Question 2 Answer

To define AAA server groups, use the **aaa-server** command:

```
fw(config)# aaa-server MYACS protocol tacacs+
```

Question 3 Answer

To define authentication keys for AAA servers, use the **key** command from the AAA server host subcommand menu:

```
fw(config-aaa-server-host)# key mykey
```

The key may also be defined when the AAA server is defined:

```
fw(config)# aaa-server MYACS protocol tacacs+
fw(config)# aaa-server MYACS (inside) host 10.1.1.11 mykey
```

Question 4

What command is used to enable access authentication to the security appliance?

Question 5

What command enables cut-through proxy authentication?

Question 6

What command enables command authorization on the security appliance?

Question 4 Answer

The **aaa authentication [serial| enable | telnet | ssh | http] console** command enables access authentication on the security appliance.

Question 5 Answer

The commands **aaa authentication match** or **aaa authentication include | exclude** enable access authentication on the security appliance.

Question 6 Answer

To configure command authorization, use the **aaa authorization command** command.

Section 8
Switching and Routing

Question 1

How is RIP configured on the security appliance?

Question 2

What version of RIP is required if you need to enable MD5 authentication of route updates?

Question 3

How many OSPF processes can be configured on the security appliance?

Question 1 Answer

Use the **rip** command to enable RIP on a per-interface basis.

Question 2 Answer

RIP Version 2 supports only MD5 authentication of route update packets.

Question 3 Answer

A maximum of two OSPF processes are supported.

Section 9
Modular Policy Framework

Question 1

What is an advantage of MPF?

Question 2

Name five of the protocols that can be inspected in a policy map?

Question 3

What command is used to configure a service policy?

Question 1 Answer

Modular Policy Framework (MPF) is a new feature of the security appliance 7.0 software that allows application of specific security policies based on defined traffic flows.

Question 2 Answer

Inspection is available for the following inspection services: CTIQBE, DNS, ESMTP, FTP, GTP, H323, HTTP, ICMP, ICMP error, ILS, MGCP, NetBIOS, PPTP, RSH, RTSP, SIP, SKINNY, SNMP, SQL*Net, SUNRPC, TFTP, and XDMCP.

Question 3 Answer

To configure service policies, use the **service-policy** command.

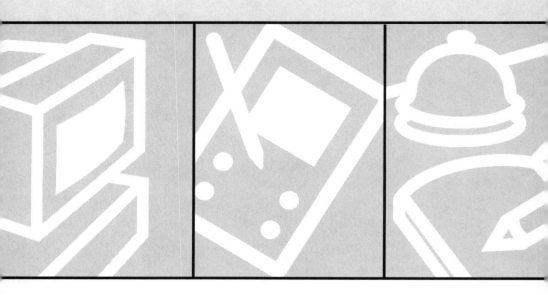

Section 10
Advanced Protocol Handling

Question 1

What command is used to configure advanced protocol handling capabilities of Cisco security appliances?

Question 2

How is a default inspected protocol disabled?

Question 3

What command is used to display current inspection policy on the security appliance?

Question 1 Answer

In Security Appliance 7.0 software, use the **inspect** command (similar to IOS routers) to accomplish advanced protocol handling configuration, and replace the older **fixup protocol** command used in previous versions of the software.

Question 2 Answer

To disable specific inspections on the default list, use the **no inspect** command in the inspection_default class-map subcommand menu (accessed in the global_policy policy-map subcommand menu).

Question 3 Answer

The **show running-config policy-map** command displays inspection policies.

Section 11
Virtual Private Network Configuration

Question 1

Which IP protocol is assigned to ESP?

Question 2

Which IP protocol is assigned to AH?

Question 3

Name the two modes of IPSec operation.

Question 1 Answer

IP protocol 50 is assigned to ESP.

Question 2 Answer

IP protocol 51 is assigned to AH.

Question 3 Answer

IPSec can operate in Tunnel or Transport modes.

Question 4

Which IPSec mode of operation leaves the IP header intact and inserts the ESP header after the IP header?

Question 5

Which IPSec mode of operation creates a new IP header?

Question 6

Which IPSec mode of operation does not require the host to perform any encryption?

Question 4 Answer

Transport mode leaves the original IP header intact and inserts a new ESP header after the IP header. When you use ESP in Transport mode, only the original IP payload is encrypted.

Question 5 Answer

Tunnel mode encrypts the entire IP packet, including the original header, and tacks on a new IP header.

Question 6 Answer

Tunnel mode is typically implemented between two VPN devices that perform encryption and decryption tasks, eliminating the need for the host to perform these operations.

Section 12
**Configuring Security Appliance
Remote Access Using Cisco
Easy VPN**

Question 1

What are the two main components of the Cisco Easy VPN?

Question 2

List the devices that can function as an Easy VPN Server.

Question 3

What does split tunneling mean?

Question 1 Answer

Cisco Easy VPN consists of two components:

- Cisco Easy VPN Remote
- Cisco Easy VPN Server

Question 2 Answer

Easy VPN Server functionality is supported by the following devices:

- Cisco ASA 5500 Series security appliances
- Cisco PIX security appliance models 535, 525, and 515E
- Cisco IOS devices, including 800, 1700, 1800, 2600, 2800, 3600, 3700, 3800, 7200, 7300, and 7500 Series routers
- Cisco VPN 3000 concentrators

Question 3 Answer

With split tunneling enabled, remote clients are configured to route Internet-bound traffic directly to the Internet in clear text, which removes the overhead needed for all traffic to pass through the encrypted tunnel.

Question 4

What is RRI?

Question 5

What command is used to configure an IP address pool?

Question 6

What command is used to create a dynamic crypto map?

Question 4 Answer

Reverse Route Injection (RRI) process adds a static entry to the Easy VPN Server route table for the connected Remote client.

Question 5 Answer

To create an IP address pool, use the **ip local pool** command.

Question 6 Answer

Use the **crypto dynamic-map** command to configure dynamic crypto maps.

Section 13
WebVPN Configuration

Question 1

What service is required on the security appliance for WebVPN operation?

Question 2

How is WebVPN enabled on a specific interface?

Question 3

What commands are used to create a WebVPN group policy?

Question 1 Answer

WebVPN uses the internal HTTP server on the security appliance. It must be enabled using:

```
fw(config)# http server enable
```

Question 2 Answer

After you use the **webvpn** command to enable WebVPN globally, you can use the command **enable** *interface_name* from the **webvpn** subcommand menu.

Question 3 Answer

Creation of a WebVPN group policy includes the following steps:

Step 1   To create a normal group policy, use the **group-policy** command.

Step 2   To access the group policy attributes subcommand menu, use the **group-policy attributes** command.

Step 3   To set the tunnel group protocol for WebVPN, use the **vpn-tunnel-protocol webvpn** command.

Section 14
Transparent Firewall

Question 1

At what layer of the OSI model does the transparent firewall operate?

Question 2

What command enables transparent firewall mode on the security appliance?

Question 3

What routing protocols are supported in transparent firewall mode?

Question 1 Answer

The transparent firewall mode is based on MAC addresses and operates on layer 2 of the OSI model.

Question 2 Answer

To enable transparent firewall mode, use the **firewall transparent** global command.

Question 3 Answer

Routing is not performed in the transparent firewall mode, and dynamic routing protocols are not supported in this mode.

Question 4

What command is used to configure the management IP address of a transparent firewall?

Question 5

What type of ACL is unique to the transparent firewall mode?

Question 6

What command is used to configure an EtherType ACL?

Question 4 Answer

To configure the management IP address, use the **ip address** command in the global configuration mode.

Question 5 Answer

EtherType ACLs are unique to the transparent firewall mode and are designed for nonIP traffic control.

Question 6 Answer

To configure EtherType ACLs, use the **access-list** command with the **ethertype** option keyword.

Section 15
Security Contexts

Question 1

What command is used to allocate an interface to a security context?

Question 2

What command is used to delete a security context?

Question 3

What command is used to enable single security context mode?

Question 1 Answer

Use the **allocate-interface** command from the system execution space to allocate an interface (physical or logical) to a specific security context.

Question 2 Answer

You can use the **no context** command to delete a security context.

Question 3 Answer

To enable single security context mode, use the command **mode single**.

Section 16
Failover

Question 1

What main types of failover are supported on Cisco security appliances?

Question 2

What failover primary configurations are available on Cisco security appliances?

Question 3

Which models of the PIX 500 Series security appliances do not support failover?

Question 1 Answer

Security appliances support two main types of failover:

- Hardware failover
- Standard failover

Question 2 Answer

Cisco security appliances support Active/Active and Active/Standby configurations (not all models support Active/Standby configuration, and some do not support any kind of failover).

Question 3 Answer

PIX 501 and 506E do not support any form of failover.

- **Broadcast ping**[md]The ping test consists of sending out a broadcast ping request.

Question 4

Which command enables failover?

Question 5

What command configures the failover link for stateful failover?

Question 6

What command configures the IP address used on the failover link?

Question 4 Answer

The global **failover** command enables failover on the security appliance.

Question 5 Answer

To configure the stateful failover link, use the **failover link** command.

Question 6 Answer

The command **failover interface ip** configures the IP addresses the peers use for the failover link.

Section 17
Cisco Adaptive Security Device Manager

Question 1

What version of the security appliance software is required when using ASDM 5.0?

Question 2

How many ASDM sessions are supported in single context mode?

Question 3

What version of the Microsoft JVM is supported with ASDM 5.0?

Question 1 Answer

ASDM 5.0 provides support for PIX 500 Series and ASA 5500 Series devices that run security appliance 7.0 software. PIX 501 and 506E are not supported with security appliance 7.0 software and cannot run ASDM 5.0.

Question 2 Answer

Five ASDM sessions per security appliance are supported in single context mode.

Question 3 Answer

Microsoft JVM is not supported with ASDM 5.0. Java plug-in 1.4.2 or 1.5.0 are required.

Section 18
Advanced Inspection and Prevention Security Services Module

Question 1

What are SSM modules?

Question 2

What is the default login information for AIP-SSM modules?

Question 3

What command is used to start the initialization process on the AIP-SSM modules?

Question 1 Answer

Security Services Modules are used with expansion slots available on ASA 5500 series security appliances. They are used to expand the security capabilities of the ASA appliances.

Question 2 Answer

Initial login into AIP-SSM uses a username of cisco and a password of cisco.

Question 3 Answer

The command **setup** starts the initialization process on the AIP-SSM module.

Section 19
Security Appliance Management

Question 1

Name the management access modes to the security appliance.

Question 2

What command is used to specify hosts or subnets with telnet access to the security appliance?

Question 3

What command is used to generate RSA keys used with SSH access?

Question 1 Answer

The following options exist for management access to the security appliance:

- Console
- Telnet
- SSH
- HTTPS (ASDM)

Question 2 Answer

To configure telnet access, use the **telnet** command:

```
fw(config)# telnet 10.1.1.0 255.255.255.0 inside
```

Question 3 Answer

Use the **crypto key generate rsa** command to accomplish the generation of RSA keys on the security appliance.

Question 4

What command is used to specify hosts or subnets with HTTP access to the security appliance?

Question 5

What command is used to specify a new activation key on the security appliance?

Question 6

What does the command no service password-recovery do?

Question 4 Answer

To configure HTTP access, use the **http** command:

```
fw(config)# http 10.1.1.0 255.255.255.0 inside
```

Question 5 Answer

To install a new activation key, use the **activation-key** command along with the appropriate four-element or five-element hexadecimal string that Cisco provides to you.

Question 6 Answer

With this command, password recovery can be performed only after all files in the flash memory are erased.

Securing Networks with PIX and ASA (SNPA) Quick Reference Sheets

Please note that there is some overlap of content in the Cisco CCSP certification courses and corresponding exams. We chose to make each section of this book stand on its own, and we covered the material for each exam independently, so that you can focus on each exam without the need to reference a common topic from a different exam's section. Because of this, you might notice redundant coverage of topics in certain sections of this book.

Cisco Security Appliance Technology and Features

Network firewalls are devices that monitor network activity and manage the flow of traffic between different networks by permitting or denying packets based on configured security policies on the device.

Currently, most firewalls use one of the following three architectures:

- **Packet filtering**—Operate at the network or transport layer of the OSI model and use static packet-header information to enforce access lists that permit or deny traffic into and out of a network. A router configured with a simple Access Control List (ACL) is an example.

  Packet-filtering firewalls provide limited security, are usually inexpensive, and typically perform well. However, they have the following shortcomings:

  — They can be easily defeated when someone sends arbitrary or spoofed packets that fit the ACL criteria.

  — They do not effectively block fragmented packets designed to bypass the filters.

  — They require increasingly complex ACLs as security policies evolve and are difficult to implement and maintain.

— They have trouble with protocols and applications that use dynamic ports, such as multimedia applications.

- **Proxy servers**—Operate at higher layers of the OSI model (typically layers 5 to 7) and request connections on behalf of a client between the inside of the firewall and the outside network. Because they peek into higher layers of the OSI model, proxy server firewalls provide better protection against network threats. However, the deeper inspection proxy server firewalls provide requires much greater processing overhead relative to packet-filtering firewalls.

Proxy server firewalls provide much better security than packet-filtering firewalls, although they have other shortcomings:

— They are a single point of failure.

— They are intimately involved with the applications that operate through them, so it is difficult to add support for new services and applications to the firewall.

— They perform more slowly or require significantly faster hardware.

- **Stateful packet filtering**—Provide improved packet filtering capabilities because they maintain a stateful session flow table that includes the source and destination addresses, port numbers, TCP sequencing information, and additional flags for each TCP or UDP connection associated with that particular session. The firewall uses this information to more intelligently enforce ACLs. For example, it can identify and allow return traffic that is part of an existing session originated from the inside.

Stateful packet filtering firewalls, such as Cisco security appliances, combine most of the benefits of packet-filtering firewalls and proxy server firewalls and eliminate their shortcomings.

Cisco Security Appliances

Cisco security appliances consist of the PIX and Adaptive Security Appliance (ASA) series. Both product series are stateful packet filtering devices with the following features:

- **Stateful packet inspection**—For a session to be established, information about the connection must match the information in the table.

- **Proprietary operating system**—Eliminates security vulnerabilities of available general operating systems.

- **Cut-through proxy operation**—A user-based authentication method for both inbound and outbound connections, which provide better performance than that of a proxy server.

- **Application-aware inspection**—Inspects packets at layers above the network layer to improve security and protect against application-layer threats.

- **Modular policies**—Allows application of different policies based on specific traffic flows through the firewall.

- **Virtual private networking**—Provides secure and inexpensive connectivity options for site-to-site and remote access scenarios.

- **Security context (virtual firewalls)**—A single security appliance can be carved into multiple virtual firewalls, each with their own unique set of security policies, interfaces, and administrative domains.

- **High availability (failover)**—Provides device redundancy because it allows one appliance to back up another in an active/active or active/standby configuration.

- **Transparent firewall**—The appliance operates in a bridging mode and does not require introduction of additional networks to implement.

- **Web-based management**—Adaptive Security Device Manager (ASDM) that provides browser-based management of Cisco security appliances.

Cisco PIX and ASA Security Appliance Families

The Cisco family of security appliances consists of the PIX 500 Series security appliances, the ASA 5500 Series security appliances, and the PIX Firewall Services Module (FWSM) blades for Catalyst 6500 Series switches and 7600 Series routers.

PIX 500-Series Security Appliances

The PIX 500 Series consists of five models:

- PIX 501
- PIX 506E
- PIX 515E
- PIX 525
- PIX 535

PIX 515E, 525, and 535 models include expansion slots that are used for additional Fast Ethernet interfaces, Gigabit Ethernet interfaces (PIX 525 and 535 models), or hardware-based IPSec acceleration cards, such as the VPN Accelerator Plus (VAC+) card (all three models currently ship with a VAC+ card preinstalled when purchased with an unrestricted license). These models also provide high availability capabilities with active/standby and active/active failover functionality (active/active requires PIX Security Appliance release 7.0 software). In addition, a special PIX FWSM blade is available for the Catalyst 6500 Series switches and the 7600 Series routers.

The following table compares the different PIX 500 Series models.

Model	Features and Specifications	Appropriate Use
PIX 501	Small desktop unit Built-in, four-port switch 133-MHz processor Two physical interfaces No failover support 7500 connections 60 Mbps throughput 3 Mbps 168-bit 3DES, 4.5 Mbps 128-bit AES IPSec throughput 10 IPSec tunnels Not supported with Cisco PIX Security Appliance release 7.0 software	All-in-one security and VPN device for remote offices and small-to-medium size networks.

Model	Features and Specifications	Appropriate Use
PIX 506E	Small desktop unit 300-MHz processor Two physical interfaces Two VLANs (release 6.3(4) or higher required) No failover support 25,000 connections 100 Mbps throughput 15 Mbps 168-bit 3DES, 30 Mbps 128-bit AES IPSec throughput 25 IPSec tunnels Not supported with Cisco PIX Security Appliance release 7.0 software	Remote offices and small-to-medium size networks with minimal hosting.
PIX 515E	1U rack-mount unit 433 MHz processor Two 32-bit, 33-MHz PCI expansion slots Up to six physical interfaces (three with restricted licenses) Up to 25 VLANs (ten with restricted licenses) Up to five security contexts (requires an unrestricted license) Failover support (active/active, active/standby) 130,000 connections 190 Mbps throughput 130 Mbps 168-bit 3DES, 130 Mbps 256-bit AES IPSec throughput 2000 IPSec tunnels	Medium-to-large networks requiring high availability and performance.
PIX 525	2U rack-mount unit 600 MHz processor Three 32-bit, 33-MHz PCI expansion slots Up to ten physical interfaces (six with restricted licenses) Up to 100 VLANs (25 with restricted licenses) Up to 50 security contexts (requires an unrestricted license) Failover support (active/active, active/standby) 280,000 connections 330 Mbps throughput 145 Mbps 168-bit 3DES, 135 Mbps 256-bit AES IPSec throughput 2000 IPSec tunnels	Large- to enterprise-size networks requiring high availability, expandability, and performance.
PIX 535	3U rack-mount unit 1-GHz processor Four 64-bit/66-MHz PCI expansion slots (bus 0 and 1) Five 32-bit, 33-MHz PCI expansion slots (bus 2) Up to 14 physical interfaces (eight with a restricted license) Up to 150 VLANs (50 with a restricted license) Up to 50 security contexts (requires an unrestricted license) Failover support (active/active, active/standby) 500,000 connections 1.65 Gbps throughput 425 Mbps 168-bit 3DES, 425 Mbps 256-bit AES IPSec throughput 2000 IPSec tunnels	ISP or Enterprise networks requiring maximum performance.

continues

Model	Features and Specifications	Appropriate Use
FWSM	Runs in Catalyst 6500 Series switches and 7600 Series routers Up to four modules per chassis 1000 VLANs per module Up to 100 security contexts (two included, additional contexts require upgraded licenses) Failover support (inter- and intra-chassis) 1 GB RAM 128 MB flash memory 1,000,000 connections 5.5 Gbps throughput No VPN or IPS functionality included (IPSec is supported for secure device management)	ISP or Enterprise networks requiring maximum performance.

ASA 5500 Series Security Appliances

ASA 5500 Series security appliances use the Cisco Adaptive Identification and Mitigation (AIM) architecture and provide multilayered security by combining the functionality of PIX 500 Series firewalls, Cisco 4200 Series intrusion prevention systems, and Cisco VPN 3000 Series concentrators.

You can use a Security Services Module (SSM) to upgrade ASA 5500 Series security appliances. SSM modules provide additional security capabilities without impacting performance using dedicated security coprocessors. Adaptive Inspection and Prevention Security Services Modules (AIP SSM) are currently available.

The ASA 5500 Series currently consists of three models:

- ASA 5510
- ASA 5520
- ASA 5540

The following table compares the different ASA 5500 Series models.

Feature	Cisco ASA 5510	Cisco ASA 5520	Cisco ASA 5540
Form Factor	1U rack-mount unit	1U rack-mount unit	1U rack-mount unit
Firewall Throughput	Up to 300 Mbps	Up to 450 Mbps	Up to 650 Mbps
Concurrent Threat Mitigation Throughput (Firewall + Anti-x Services)	Up to 150 Mbps with AIP-SSM-10	Up to 225 Mbps (with AIP-SSM-10) or 375 Mbps (with AIP-SSM-20)	Up to 450 Mbps with AIP-SSM-20
3DES/AES VPN Throughput	Up to 170 Mbps	Up to 225 Mbps	Up to 325 Mbps

Feature	Cisco ASA 5510	Cisco ASA 5520	Cisco ASA 5540
IPSec VPN Peers	50 (150 with upgraded license)	300 (750 with upgraded license)	500 (5000 with upgraded license)
WebVPN Peers	50 (150 with upgraded license)	300 (750 with upgraded license)	500 (2500 with upgraded license)
Concurrent Sessions	32,000 (64,000 with upgraded license)	130,000	280,000
New Sessions/ Second	6000	9000	20,000
Integrated Network Ports	3 + 1 Management Port (5 Fast Ethernet with upgraded license)	4 Gigabit Ethernet, 1 Fast Ethernet	4 Gigabit Ethernet, 1 Fast Ethernet
VLANs	0 (10 with upgraded license)	25	100
Security Contexts	Not supported	2 (10 with an upgraded license)	2 (50 with an upgraded license)
High Availability	Active/standby with upgraded license	Active/active and active/ standby	Active/active and active/ standby
SSM Expansion Slot	1	1	1
User Accessible Flash Slot	1	1	1
USB 2.0 Ports	2	2	2
Serial Ports	2 RJ-45, Console and Auxiliary	2 RJ-45, Console and Auxiliary	2 RJ-45, Console and Auxiliary
Memory	256 MB	512 MB	1024 MB
System Flash	64 MB	64 MB	64 MB
System Bus	Multi-bus architecture	Multi-bus architecture	Multi-bus architecture
Appropriate Use	Remote office or SMB security and VPN gateway	Enterprise and SMB head-end security and VPN gateway	Enterprise head-end security and VPN gateway

Security Appliance Licensing

Cisco security appliances can be purchased with different licenses to accommodate varying security needs and budget constraints.

PIX 500 Series security appliances provide the following license options:

- **Unrestricted**—Maximum memory and interfaces (physical and virtual) are provided. Security contexts and failover capability are also provided.

- **Restricted**—Limited memory and interfaces (physical and virtual) are provided. Security contexts and failover capability are not provided.

- **Failover Active/Standby**—Provides active/standby failover functionality when used with another PIX with an unrestricted license (two PIX devices with unrestricted licenses can also function as an active/standby failover pair).

- **Failover Active/Active**—Provides active/active failover functionality when used with another PIX with an unrestricted license (two PIX devices with unrestricted licenses can also function as an active/active failover pair).

PIX 501 and 506E security appliances do not support Cisco PIX Security Appliance release 7.0 software, security contexts, or failover functionality. PIX 506E is only available with a single unlimited-user license. PIX 501 can be obtained with licenses for 10-user, 50-user, or unlimited user counts.

In addition to the licenses listed, PIX security appliances also include licensing options for the number of security contexts and VPN encryption strengths. PIX 515E, 525, and 535 appliances with unrestricted licenses support two security contexts and can be licensed to enable additional security contexts up to the supported number for each platform. VPN encryption licenses include:

- **DES**—56-bit DES encryption

- **3DES/AES**—168-bit triple DES or 128-bit, 192-bit, or 256-bit AES encryption

Similarly, ASA 5500 Series security appliances can be obtained with different licenses. The following table lists the license options for ASA 5500 Series appliances.

Feature	ASA 5510 Licenses		ASA 5520 Licenses		ASA 5540 Licenses		
	Base	Security +	Base	VPN +	Base	VPN +	VPN Premium
Interfaces	3 Fast Ethernet	5 Fast Ethernet	4 Gigabit Ethernet, 1 Fast Ethernet	4 Gigabit Ethernet, 1 Fast Ethernet	4 Gigabit Ethernet, 1 Fast Ethernet	4 Gigabit Ethernet, 1 Fast Ethernet	4 Gigabit Ethernet, 1 Fast Ethernet
VLANs	0	10	25	25	100	100	100
IPSec VPN Peers	50	150	300	750	500	2000	5000
Active/ Standby Failover	N/A	Yes	Yes	Yes	Yes	Yes	Yes

Feature	ASA 5510 Licenses		ASA 5520 Licenses		ASA 5540 Licenses		
Active/Active Failover	N/A	N/A	Yes	Yes	Yes	Yes	Yes
GTP/GPRS Inspection	N/A	N/A	With GTP license	With GTP license	With GTP license	With GTP license	With GTP license
Security Contexts	N/A	N/A	Two (up to ten with additional context licenses)	Two (up to ten with additional context licenses)	Two (up to 50 with additional context licenses)	Two (up to 50 with additional context licenses)	Two (up to 50 with additional context licenses)

Cisco Security Appliance Basic Configuration

Cisco security appliances use a command-line interface based on and similar to the Cisco IOS and operate in one of four administrative access modes:

- **Unprivileged mode**—This mode is available when you first access the security appliance via Telnet, SSH, or the console (also referred to as the User mode). Restricted settings are only viewable in this mode and the prompt displays a ">" character.

- **Privileged mode**—This mode is accessed if you issue the **enable** command from the unprivileged mode and provide the appropriate enable password. This mode displays a "#" prompt and provides access to all privileged and unprivileged commands.

- **Configuration mode**—This mode is accessed when you issue the **configure terminal** command while in privileged mode. The mode displays a "(config)#" prompt (or other appropriate subcommand prompt) and provides access to security appliance configuration commands.

- **Monitor mode**—This mode is accessed when you disrupt the security appliance's normal flash boot sequence, and it is used primarily for troubleshooting or image updates via TFTP.

The following file management commands are accessible primarily in the privileged or configuration modes.

Command	Function
`show running-config`	Displays current running configuration on the console.
`show startup-config`	Displays current startup (saved on flash) configuration on the console.
`write memory`	Writes current running configuration to the flash memory (startup).
`write terminal`	Same as **show running-config** command, which displays the current running configuration.
`copy running-config startup-config`	Same as **write memory** command, which writes the current running configuration to memory.

continues

Command	Function
show history	Shows a list of previously entered commands.
clear configure all	Clears the running configuration on the security appliance.
write erase	Clears the startup configuration on the security appliance.
reload	Reloads the security appliance.
dir	Displays the contents of flash memory.
boot system flash:	When more than one image is stored on flash memory, it specifies the image the security appliance uses during the flash boot process.
show bootvar	Displays the current boot variable environment on the device.

Security Appliance Security Levels

Cisco security appliances implement a security algorithm based on:

- Allowing outbound connections by default (connections originating from internal or more-protected networks to external or less-protected networks)

- Stateful connection control, which ensures that return traffic is valid

- Making TCP sequence numbers more difficult to predict (and attack) by randomizing the initial TCP sequence number

Unlike other Cisco security appliances, the FWSM does not allow any connections by default. All connections, including connections from more secure networks to less secure networks, must be explicitly allowed by the administrator. To allow outbound connections (or conversely disallow inbound connections) correctly, you must assign an appropriate security level to each interface, physical, or logical.

ASA Security Levels

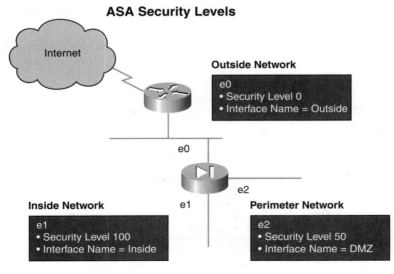

- Security levels range from 0 to 100.

- Security level 100 is the most secure interface and is typically reserved for the inside interface.

- Security level 0 is the least secure interface and is typically reserved for the outside interface.

- Traffic from an interface with a higher security value to a lower security value, for example 90 to 50, is allowed by default (it can be blocked with an appropriate ACL).

- Traffic from an interface with lower security value to a higher security value, for example 30 to 70, is disallowed by default (it can be allowed with an appropriate ACL).

- Traffic between two interfaces with the same security value is disallowed by default (use the **same-security-traffic** command to allow it).

Basic Configuration

Before any traffic can traverse the Cisco security appliance, a minimum basic configuration is required. Specifically, the following minimum configurations are required:

- Interface settings for at least two interfaces.

- A valid address translation policy (with ASA 5500 Series and PIX security appliances running release 7.0 software, this is not required unless **nat-control** is enabled).

- A default route.

The following primary configuration commands are used for basic configuration for the security appliance:

- **hostname**—Assigns a hostname to the security appliance.

- **interface**—Enters interface configuration subcommand mode. It is also used to create logical interfaces.

- **nameif**—Assigns a name to the interface.

- **ip address**—Assigns an IP address to the interface.

- **security level**—Assigns the security level for an interface.

- **speed**—Specifies the connection speed for an interface.

- **duplex**—Specifies the duplex setting for an interface.

- **nat-control**—Enables or disables address translation policy requirement (NAT control is disabled by default in release 7.0 software).

- **nat**—The **nat** command configures address translation for one or more hosts on a specific interface.

- **global**—Configures a pool of one or more global IP addresses for use with the **nat** command.

- **route**—Defines a static route or the default route for the appliance.

Interface Configuration

Interfaces are configured from the interface configuration subcommand mode. The **interface** command is used to enter this mode. The following example configures interface Ethernet 2 as a DMZ interface with an IP address of 172.16.1.1 and a security value of 50:

```
fw(config)# interface ethernet 2
fw(config-if)# nameif DMZ
fw(config-if)# ip address 172.16.1.1 255.255.255.0
fw(config-if)# security-level 50
fw(config-if)# speed 100
fw(config-if)# duplex full
fw(config-if)# no shut
```

If speed and duplex settings are not explicitly configured, auto-negotiation is used.

Logical interfaces are created as subinterfaces on a physical interface. For example, to create a logical interface on Ethernet 2 with VLAN 10, the following commands are used:

```
fw(config)# interface ethernet2.1
fw(config-subif)# vlan 10
```

This command sequence creates the interface and enters its configuration mode. Other configuration tasks are the same as physical interfaces including configuration of the IP address, interface name, and security level.

A management interface is configured using the **management-only** command (accepts management traffic only).

The **management-access** command configures an internal management interface and makes it accessible through an IPSec tunnel (an interface configured with the **management-access** command can accept nonmanagement traffic).

By default, the outside interface is assigned a security value of 0 and the inside interface is assigned a security value of 100. If the security values on other configured interfaces are not explicitly specified, a default security value of 0 is assigned.

Network Address Translation

With Cisco Security Appliance release 7.0 software, an address translation policy is not required to allow traffic flow through the appliance (as was the case in previous software versions). However, if **nat-control** is enabled, a valid address translation policy is required (similar to 6.3 and earlier releases of the software).

To configure NAT, use the **nat** and **global** commands. The **global** command is used to configure an address or pool of addresses used with NAT or PAT on an interface. The **nat** command configures address translation on a specific interface for single or multiple hosts. Local (real) IP addresses are translated to a single or multiple global (mapped) IP addresses (configured with the **global** command) on the specified interface.

The following example shows a basic NAT configuration that uses **nat** and **global** commands:

```
fw(config)# global (outside) 1 192.168.1.21-192.168.1.30
fw(config)# nat (inside) 1 0.0.0.0 0.0.0.0
```

Network Address Translation

Translation Table

Inside Local IP Address	Global IP Pool
10.1.1.11	192.168.1.21
10.1.1.14	192.168.1.22

To view the configuration on the security appliance, you use the **show running-config nat** and **show running-config global** commands. You can view the current translation slots using the **show xlate** command.

Default Route

The last required step for basic configuration is a default route. The default route is configured using the **route** command, as shown in this example:

```
fw(config)# route outside 0.0.0.0 0.0.0.0 192.168.1.1
```

Syslog Configuration

You can configure logging on the security appliance to generate and record syslog messages. If time-stamped entries are required, the **clock** command can be used to set the time on the appliance:

```
fw# clock set 15:30:00 jun 15 2005
```

Alternatively, clock synchronization with an NTP server is configured if you use the **ntp server** command:

```
fw(config)# ntp authentication-key 1 md5 cisco
fw(config)# ntp trusted-key 1
fw(config)# ntp server 10.1.1.14 key 1 source inside prefer
fw(config)# ntp authenticate
```

Next, the syslog server and logging level are specified, and you use the **logging** command to enable logging:

```
fw(config)# logging host inside 10.1.1.11
fw(config)# logging trap errors
fw(config)# logging timestamp
fw(config)# logging on
```

Cisco security appliance logging levels are as follows:

- **0**—**emergencies**—System unusable messages
- **1**—**alerts**—Take immediate action
- **2**—**critical**—Critical condition
- **3**—**errors**—Error message
- **4**—**warnings**—Warning message
- **5**—**notifications**—Normal, although significant condition
- **6**—**informational**—Information message
- **7**—**debugging**—Debug messages and log FTP commands and WWW URLs

The **logging message** command can be used to customize the severity level for a specific syslog message or to disable a specific syslog message. The following example disables logging for syslog message 501101 and changes the severity level of message 502101 to 3:

```
fw(config)# logging message 502101 level 3
fw(config)# no logging message 501101
```

The **logging emblem** command is used to instruct the appliance to use the EMBLEM format for syslog messages (typically used with CiscoWorks management servers). The **logging emblem** command modifies only the format of syslog messages stored and displayed on the security appliance. To use the EMBLEM format for syslog messages sent to a server (such as a CiscoWorks management server), the **format emblem** option is used when you define the syslog host, as shown in this example:

```
fw(config)# logging host inside 10.1.1.11 format emblem
```

Translations and Connections

This section covers network address translation features of the Cisco security appliances and presents an overview of how different transport protocols are handled.

Transport Protocols

Cisco security appliances primarily deal with inbound and outbound transmissions over two protocols:

- **TCP**—Connection-oriented protocol and relatively easy to inspect properly.
- **UDP**—Connectionless protocol, and therefore more difficult to inspect properly.

TCP connection steps are as follows:

Step 1   The first IP packet (SYN) from an inside host is received and a translation slot is created. The embedded TCP information is then used to create a connection slot.

Step 2   The connection slot is marked as embryonic (a half-open TCP session before completion of a "three-way handshake").

Step 3   Initial sequence number of the connection is randomized and the packet is forwarded onto the outgoing interface.

Step 4   SYN/ACK packet from the destination host is matched against the connection slot and is allowed to return to the inside host if found to be legitimate.

Step 5   The inside host completes the three-way handshake with an ACK packet.

Step 6   The connection slot is marked as connected and data is sent. The embryonic counter is then reset for this connection.

UDP transactions are processed in the following steps:

Step 1   The first IP packet from an inside host is received and a translation slot is created. The embedded UDP information is then used to create a UDP connection slot.

Step 2   The security appliance maintains the UDP connection slot for the duration of the user-configurable UDP timeout (2 minutes by default). When the UDP connection slot is idle for more than the configured UDP timeout, it is deleted from the connection table.

Step 3   By maintaining a UDP "connection" in this manner, the security appliance can perform a stateful inspection of the UDP packets that are received from the destination host within the UDP timeout period.

Step 4   The data is sent back to the inside host.

Connections and Translations

- Translations occur at the IP layer of the TCP/IP protocol stack.
- Connections occurs at the transport layer of the TCP/IP stack.
- There can be many connections if you use a single translation.

To display current connection and translation slots on the security appliance, use the **show conn** and **show xlate** commands respectively. The **show local-host** command displays more detailed information about connections and translations on a per host basis.

Network Address Translation

Cisco security appliances provide four main types of address translation:

- **Dynamic inside translation**—Internal host addresses are dynamically translated to a pool of addresses on the external or less secure interface. Dynamic translation is appropriate for outbound services, such as web browsing.

- **Static inside translation**—This type of translation provides a permanent one-to-one mapping between a local (real) host IP address and a global (mapped) IP address on the less secure interface. Static translations are typically used to provide access to services, such as a web or FTP server.

- **Dynamic outside translation**—External host addresses are dynamically translated to a pool of addresses on the internal or more secure interface. To configure them, use the **nat** command with keyword **outside**.

- **Static outside translation**—This type of translation provides a permanent one-to-one mapping between an external (mapped) host IP address and a local (real) IP address on the more secure interface.

A sample configuration for dynamic inside address translation is shown in the following example:

```
fw(config)# global (outside) 1 192.168.1.20-192.168.1.30
fw(config)# nat (inside) 1 0.0.0.0 0.0.0.0
```

Static translations are configured if you use the static command, as shown in the following example, where an internal host at 10.1.1.4 is statically translated to 192.168.1.10 on the outside interface:

```
fw(config)# static (inside,outside) 192.168.1.10 10.1.1.4 netmask
255.255.255.255
```

Supply the network address and appropriate subnet mask in the static statement to statically translate a subnet.

Identity NAT

Identity NAT involves the use of the **nat 0** command to disable address translation for a specific host or network.

The following example allows hosts inside the security appliance on the 10.1.1.0/24 network to appear on other interfaces of the security appliance without address translation:

```
fw(config)# nat (inside) 0 10.1.1.0 255.255.255.0
```

It's important to note that with identity NAT, only the local hosts may initiate connections.

NAT Exemption

The **nat 0** command can also be used with an ACL to exempt a specific traffic pattern from address translation, referred to as NAT exemption. NAT exemption is commonly used in VPN configurations to exempt tunnel-bound traffic from translation:

```
fw(config)# nat (inside) 0 access-list no_nat_vpn_traffic
```

Policy NAT

Policy NAT uses the **nat** or **static** commands along with an ACL, which allows address translation based on source and destination addresses. The following example demonstrates policy NAT where the same local addresses are translated to two different global pools, depending on the destination network for the traffic:

```
fw(config)# access-list policy-nat1 permit ip 10.0.0.0 255.255.255.0
172.20.0.0 255.255.0.0
fw(config)# access-list policy-nat2 permit ip 10.0.0.0 255.255.255.0
172.30.0.0 255.255.0.0
fw(config)# nat (inside) 1 access-list policy-nat1
fw(config)# nat (inside) 2 access-list policy-nat2
fw(config)# global (outside) 1 192.168.0.100-192.168.0.149
fw(config)# global (outside) 2 192.168.0.150-192.168.0.199
```

Port Address Translation

NAT provides address translation based only on IP addresses and requires a global IP address for every local IP address that is translated. PAT can use a single global IP address to translate thousands of local IP addresses. To properly distinguish conversations between internal and external hosts, PAT uses unique source port numbers for each translation (to the same global IP address).

Port Address Translation

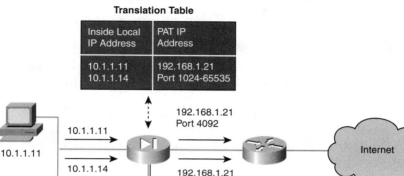

Translation Table

Inside Local IP Address	PAT IP Address
10.1.1.11	192.168.1.21
10.1.1.14	Port 1024-65535

- PAT and NAT can be used together (PAT can back up NAT global pools).

- PAT can use the interface address to further reduce IP address requirements.

- With PAT, one IP address can be used for up to about 64,000 inside hosts.

- Multiple PAT addresses can be configured to allow additional hosts.

- PAT maps source port numbers to a single IP address.

- PAT secures transactions because it hides the inside source address through the use of a single IP address on the outside.

Basic PAT configuration is shown in the following example:

```
fw(config)# global (outside) 1 192.168.1.21
fw(config)# nat (inside) 1 0.0.0.0 0.0.0.0
```

PAT can also use the IP address of the interface on the outside:

```
fw(config)# global (outside) 1 interface
```

Static PAT

Static PAT, or port redirection, allows access to different internal servers from the outside using the same IP address with different ports. For example, 192.168.1.11/80 can redirect internally to 10.1.1.11, while 192.168.1.11/21 can redirect to a different server at 10.1.1.12. This feature allows hosting of services on different internal servers using the same external IP address.

```
fw(config)# static (inside,outside) tcp 192.168.1.11 www 10.1.1.11 www
 netmask 255.255.255.255
fw(config)# static (inside,outside) tcp 192.168.1.11 ftp 10.1.1.12 ftp
 netmask 255.255.255.255
```

DNS Support

The translation commands **nat** and **static** can be used with the **dns** option to provide support for translation of IP addresses embedded in DNS records.

TCP Intercept and Connection Limits

DoS attack mitigation is provided by the TCP intercept and TCP and UDP connection limit functions available with nat and static commands. TCP intercept is enabled by limiting the number of embryonic connections per host using the emb_limit option. Maximum simultaneous TCP and UDP connection limits are enabled by specifying the values for tcp_max_conns and udp_max_conns options. If these settings are not specified, their values are set to 0, indicating unlimited embryonic connections per host and unlimited simultaneous TCP or UDP connections are allowed.

```
nat (real_interface) nat_id real_ip [mask [dns] [outside [[tcp] tcp_max_conns
[emb_limit] [norandomseq]]] [udp udp_max_conns]
static (real_interface,mapped_interface) {mapped_ip ¦ interface} {real_ip
[netmask mask]} ¦ {access-list access_list_name} [dns] [norandomseq
[nailed]] [[tcp] [tcp_max_conns [emb_limit]] [udp udp_max_conns]
```

Access Control Lists and Content Filtering

This section provides an overview of the security appliance ACL and content filtering capabilities.

Access Control Lists

ACLs are created using the **access-list** command and are then applied to an interface in the inbound or outbound direction using the **access-group** command. ACLs permit or deny the initial inbound or outbound packet on the interface based on the particular access control entries (ACE) configured.

```
fw(config)# access-list myacl extended permit tcp any host 192.168.1.21 eq
www
fw(config)# access-list myacl extended permit tcp any host 192.168.1.21 eq
ftp
fw(config)# access-list myacl extended deny ip any any
```

If no ACLs are applied to an interface, the default ASA policy is applied:

- Traffic from more secure interface to less secure interface is allowed.

- Traffic from less secure interface to more secure interface is disallowed.

To display configured access lists and counter information, use the **show access-list** command. To reset the counters, use the **clear access-list** acl_name **counters** command.

Time-based access lists are configured using the **access-list** command with the **time-range** option. A time range must be first configured using the **time-range** command.

To enable ACL logging, use the **log** keyword when you define the ACL.

By default, new ACE entries are added to the end of an ACL. ACL editing allows the addition of a new ACE entry at a specific location within an existing ACL. To edit an ACL, specify the line number for the new ACE entry using the **line** option with the **access-list** command.

icmp Command

ACLs are used to control the flow of ICMP traffic through the security appliance. To control ICMP traffic terminating on any of the security appliance interfaces, use the **icmp** command.

```
fw(config)# icmp permit any outside
fw(config)# icmp permit any inside
```

Malicious Active Code Filtering

To enable Java applet and ActiveX blocking, use the filter command with **activex** or **java** options as shown in the following example:

```
fw(config)# filter activex 80 0.0.0.0 0.0.0.0 0.0.0.0 0.0.0.0
fw(config)# filter java 80 0.0.0.0 0.0.0.0 0.0.0.0 0.0.0.0
```

URL Filtering

URL-filtering is possible with Websense or N2H2 services if you use the **filter** command and **url** option. Use the **url-server** command to configure the Websense or N2H2 servers.

```
fw(config)# url-server (inside) vendor websense host 10.1.1.11 protocol tcp
fw(config)# filter url 80 0.0.0.0 0.0.0.0 0.0.0.0 0.0.0.0 allow
```

The **allow** option in the preceding example instructs the appliance to allow access if the URL server is inaccessible.

Object Grouping

The object grouping feature groups network objects, such as hosts and services to simplify creation of ACLs. Object grouping reduces the number of ACL entries required to implement complex security policies.

There are several types of Object Groups:

- **Network**—Client hosts, server hosts, or subnets.
- **Protocol**—Uses keywords (**ah**, **eigrp**, **esp**, **gre**, **icmp**, **icmp6**, **igmp**, **igrp**, **ip**, **ipinip**, **ipsec**, **nos**, **ospf**, **pcp**, **pim**, **pptp**, **snp**, **tcp**, or **udp**) or an integer in the range 0 to 255 that represents an IP protocol number. Keyword **ip** is used to match any Internet protocol, including ICMP, TCP, and UDP.
- **Service**—TCP or UDP port numbers assigned to specific services or applications.
- **ICMP type**—ICMP message types that are permitted or denied access.

Configuring and Using Object Groups

Use the following steps to create object groups:

Step 1   Use the **object-group** command to enter the appropriate subcommand mode for the type of group you want to configure.

Step 2   In subcommand mode, define the members of the object group.

Step 3   (Optional) Use the description subcommand to describe the object group.

Step 4   Use the **exit** or **quit** command to return to configuration mode.

The following examples show several types of group object configurations:

```
fw(config)# object-group network myservers
fw(config-network)# network-object host 10.1.1.11
fw(config-network)# network-object host 10.1.1.14

fw(config)# object-group icmp-type myicmp
fw(config-icmp)# icmp-object echo
fw(config-icmp)# icmp-object echo-reply

fw(config)# object-group protocol myprotocols
fw(config-protocol)# protocol-object tcp
fw(config-protocol)# protocol-object ospf

fw(config)# object-group service web tcp
fw(config-service)# port-object eq www
fw(config-service)# port-object eq https
```

The following example shows an ACL entry that uses object groups:

```
fw(config)# access-list og_acl permit tcp any object-group myservers
object-group web
```

Nested Object Groups

Existing object groups can be combined (nested) in another object group to further simplify creation of object groups. For example, if an object group defines all web servers and another defines all FTP servers, a new object group can be created to define all web servers and FTP servers by nesting the existing object groups in the new group.

The **group-object** command is used from the object group configuration subcommand mode to nest existing object groups. Nested object groups must be of the same type as the parent object group.

```
fw(config)# object-group network webservers
fw(config-network)# network-object host 10.1.1.11
fw(config-network)# network-object host 10.1.1.14

fw(config)# object-group network ftpservers
fw(config-network)# network-object host 10.1.1.15
fw(config-network)# network-object host 10.1.1.16

fw(config)# object-group network ftp_and_web
fw(config-network)# group-object webservers
fw(config-network)# group-object ftpservers
```

To display configured object groups, use the **show running-config object-group** command.

Authentication, Authorization, and Accounting

Cisco security appliances provide support for authentication, authorization, and accounting (AAA) services. AAA provides the following functionality:

- **Authentication**—This service validates the identity of the user (who you are).

- **Authorization**—This service grants access to specific resources based on the identity of the user that authentication validates (what you can do).

- **Accounting**—This service tracks and records user activities (what you did).

Authentication is valid without authorization. Authorization is never valid without authentication.

AAA can be applied for access to the security appliance itself or access through the appliance. Specifically, three types of authentication are available on security appliances:

- Security appliance access authentication
- Cut-through proxy authentication
- Tunnel access authentication

Similarly, three types of authorization are available:

- Security appliance access authorization
- Cut-through proxy authorization
- Tunnel access authorization

And finally, three accounting types are available:

- Security appliance access accounting
- Cut-through proxy accounting
- Tunnel access accounting

Basic AAA implementations can use the local user database (using the default group LOCAL). More complex AAA implementations use a remote AAA server, such as the Cisco Secure Access Control Server (ACS) to which the security appliance forwards authentication requests.

AAA Configuration

General procedures for configuration of authentication, authorization, and accounting on Cisco security appliances are presented in this section.

Security Appliance Access Authentication

To configure authentication for access to the security appliance, you must:

- Use the **aaa-server** command to specify an AAA server group.
- Specify the authentication servers for the group that uses the **aaa-server** command.
- Configure authentication using this server for serial, telnet, ssh, http, or enable-mode access as necessary using the **aaa authentication** command.

```
fw(config)# aaa-server MYACS protocol tacacs+
fw(config-aaa-server-group)# max-failed-attempts 3
fw(config-aaa-server-group)# exit
fw(config)# aaa-server MYACS (inside) host 10.1.1.11
fw(config-aaa-server-host)# key mykey
fw(config-aaa-server-host)# exit
fw(config)# aaa authentication telnet console MYACS
```

Alternatively, the LOCAL group can be used to authenticate against the local user directory of the security appliance.

Users must be configured on the ACS for access to the security appliance. On the Cisco Secure ACS, you can add new users if you click on **User Setup** in the navigation bar.

You can add users to the local directory of the security appliance if you use the **username** command:

```
fw(config)# username myuser password mypassword privilege 15
```

To modify the authentication prompt that the security appliance displays, use the **banner** command.

Cut-Through Proxy Authentication

Authentication can be enabled for traffic flowing through the security appliance. To minimize the performance penalty of authenticating each and every packet traversing the interfaces, Cisco security appliances perform cut-through proxy authentication.

With cut-through proxy authentication, a user's initial traffic is authenticated against a configured AAA server group. Once authenticated, the security appliance allows direct traffic flow between the user and the server without further authentication (session state information is however maintained).

Cut-through proxy authentication can only be configured for FTP, Telnet, HTTP, or HTTPS sessions. The configuration procedure is as follows:

- Use the **aaa-server** command to specify a AAA server group.
- Use the **aaa-server** command to specify the authentication servers for the group.
- Use the **access-list** command to define the traffic pattern (source and destination addresses) that must be authenticated.
- Use the **aaa authentication match** command to configure authentication for this traffic.

The LOCAL group can be used instead of an AAA server to authenticate against the local user directory of the security appliance.

```
fw(config)# access-list ctp permit tcp any host 192.168.1.120 eq www
fw(config)# aaa authentication match ctp inside LOCAL
```

To configure cut-through proxy authentication, you can also use the **aaa authentication include** command:

```
fw(config)# aaa authentication include http inside 0.0.0.0 0.0.0.0
    192.168.1.120 255.255.255.255 LOCAL
```

Current authentication configuration is displayed with the **show uauth** and **show aaa-server** commands.

Authentication of non- Telnet, FTP, HTTP, or HTTPS traffic is possible if you use the **virtual telnet** and **virtual http** commands. With virtual Telnet or virtual HTTP, the user begins a telnet or http session to the virtual IP address on the security appliance and is prompted for authentication. After successful authentication, the user is allowed to begin non-Telnet, FTP, HTTP, or HTTPS traffic.

Use the **auth-prompt** command to modify the authentication prompt that the security appliance displays.

Tunnel Access Authentication

Tunnel access authentication is configured as follows:

- Use the **aaa-server** command to specify a AAA server group.

- Use the **aaa-server** command to specify the authentication servers for the group.

From the **tunnel-group** subcommand mode, use the **authentication-server-group** command to specify the AAA server group for the specific tunnel group.

```
fw(config)# tunnel-group mytunnel type ipsec-ra
fw(config)# tunnel-group mytunnel general-attributes
fw(config-general)# authentication-server-group MYACS
```

Authorization

After a user is authenticated, authorization determines what the user can do. Without authorization, the user has full access to resources after successful authentication. Authorization provides more granular access control because it allows the administrator to authorize access to specific resources on a per-user or per-group basis using one of two methods:

- **Classic user authorization**—Access rules are configured on the TACACS server and queried by the security appliance on demand.

- **Downloadable ACLs**—ACLs are configured on the RADIUS server and assigned to specific groups or users. They are then downloaded to the security appliance when the specific user or group is authenticated. Downloadable ACLs are only supported with RADIUS.

Authorization is configured on the security appliance if you use the **aaa authorization match** or **aaa authorization include | exclude** commands. Authorization configuration also requires appropriate settings on the TACACS server.

To configure command authorization on the security appliance itself, the **aaa authorization command** command is used:

```
fw(config)# aaa authorization command MYACS
```

The following example shows a configuration requiring TACACS authorization for telnet traffic through the security appliance to the outside interface:

```
fw(config)# access-list my-authz permit tcp any any eq telnet
fw(config)# aaa authorization match my-authz inside MYACS
```

The AAA server must then be configured with the appropriate authorization policies to complete the configuration. These settings are configured in the **Group Setup** screen (**Shell Command Authorization Set** and **Per Group Command Authorization**).

Downloadable ACLs are configured on the ACS on a per-user or per-group basis. They are created in the **Shared Profile Components** screen of the ACS and applied to a specific user or group from a drop-down menu listing previously configured downloadable ACLs in the **User Setup** or **Group Setup** screens.

Accounting

Similar to authentication and authorization, to configure accounting, you must specify an AAA server group, specify the AAA servers in the group, specify target traffic for accounting, and enable accounting on the security appliance. To enable accounting, use the **aaa accounting match** or **aaa accounting include | exclude** commands.

```
fw(config)# access-list my-account permit tcp any any eq telnet
fw(config)# aaa accounting match my-account outside MYACS
```

Switching and Routing

Cisco security appliances provide basic support for VLANs and routing protocols to better integrate with other networking devices and to improve functionality.

Virtual LANs

VLAN support was first introduced with PIX security appliance software version 6.3:

- With VLANs, security appliances can support many logical interfaces, in addition to physical interfaces available on each model.

- Only 802.1Q tagged VLANs are supported .

- VLANs are not supported on the PIX 501.

- In security appliance software version 7.0, logical interfaces are created as subinterfaces on a physical interface (trunk port).

To create a new logical interface, the **interface** command is used along with the physical interface number (trunk port), a dot, and a subinterface number between 1 and 4294967295. The subinterface number does not correspond to the VLAN number. After the logical interface is created, all other settings are configured with the same commands used with physical interfaces. Some settings, such as speed and duplex, are not configurable on a logical interface, and the corresponding commands are unavailable.

The following example shows a VLAN configuration:

```
fw(config)# interface ethernet2
fw(config-if)# nameif dmz-trunk
fw(config-if)# no security-level
fw(config-if)# speed 100
fw(config-if)# duplex full
fw(config-if)# no ip address
fw(config-if)# no shutdown
fw(config-if)# interface ethernet2.10
fw(config-subif)# vlan 10
fw(config-subif)# nameif DMZ1
fw(config-subif)# ip address 172.16.10.1 255.255.255.0
fw(config-subif)# security-level 50
fw(config-subif)# interface ethernet2.20
fw(config-subif)# vlan 20
fw(config-subif)# nameif DMZ2
fw(config-subif)# ip address 172.16.20.1 255.255.255.0
fw(config-subif)# security-level 60
```

VLANs

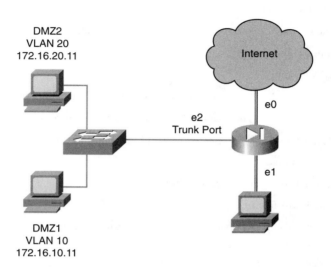

DMZ2
VLAN 20
172.16.20.11

Internet

e0

e2
Trunk Port

e1

DMZ1
VLAN 10
172.16.10.11

Routing

The security appliance provides support for static routes and RIP and OSPF dynamic routing protocols (OSPF support was introduced with PIX security appliance software version 6.3).

To create static routes, use the **route** command. For example:

```
fw(config)# route inside 10.20.30.0 255.255.255.0 10.1.1.100
```

A default route can be configured if you use the **route** command with the network and subnet field values of 0.0.0.0 (any any). For example, to create a default route to 192.168.20.1, use the following command:

```
fw(config)# route outside 0.0.0.0 0.0.0.0 192.168.20.1
```

Dynamic Routing

The security appliance supports RIP and OSPF dynamic routing protocols.

RIP   Support is included for RIP version 1 and version 2 (RIP version 2 adds support for route update multicasting and MD5 encrypted authentication). The security appliance can be configured to operate passively (listens for and learns RIP 1 or 2 updates, but does not broadcast routes) or in default mode (listens for and learns RIP 1 or 2 updates, can broadcast one of its interfaces as a default route).

To configure RIP support, use the **rip** command:

```
fw(config)# rip inside default version 2 authentication md5 mykey 1
```

OSPF PIX security appliance software version 6.3 introduced support for the OSPF routing protocol. OSPF provides route discovery and propagation and fast route convergence times via an industry standard protocol.

The following OSPF features are supported:

- Intra-area, inter-area, and external (Type 1 and Type 2) routes
- Virtual links
- OSPF LSA flooding
- Authentication for OSPF packets (cleartext and MD5 authentication)
- Designated Router (DR) or Area Border Router (ABR) functionality
- Limited Autonomous System Border Router (ASBR) functionality
- Route redistribution
- Stub areas and not so stubby areas (NSSA)
- ABR Type 3 LSA filtering
- Load balancing among a maximum of three peers on a single interface, using equal cost multipath routes (ECMP)

The following OSPF features are not supported:

- Point-to-point link/serial interface/nonbroadcast multiaccess (NBMA)
- OSPF on-demand circuit
- Flood reduction
- Redistribution of routes between non-OSPF routing protocols
- Policy routing

In addition, the following limitations exist:

- RIP and OSPF cannot run together on the same security appliance
- OSPF is not supported on the PIX 501
- You can configure a maximum of two OSPF processes

Configuration of OSPF requires the following:

- Use the **router ospf** command to create an OSPF process on the appliance
- Define the networks and areas in the OSPF subcommand mode
- Define other OSPF settings, such as authentication from the OSPF or interface subcommand modes

The following example shows an OSPF configuration with one process and MD5 authentication:

```
fw(config)# interface ethernet
fw(config-if)# ospf message-digest-key 1 md5 cisco
fw(config-if)# ospf authentication message-digest
fw(config-if)# interface ethernet
```

```
fw(config-if)# ospf message-digest-key 1 md5 cisco
fw(config-if)# ospf authentication message-digest
fw(config-if)# router ospf 1
fw(config-router)# network 10.1.1.0 255.255.255.0 area 0
fw(config-router)# network 192.168.1.0 255.255.255.0 area 1
fw(config-router)# area 0 authentication message-digest
fw(config-router)# area 1 authentication message-digest
```

Multicast

IP multicasting provides more efficient use of bandwidth because it provides for simultaneous delivery of a single transmission to multiple hosts. IP multicasting uses the range of addresses from 224.0.0.0 to 239.255.255.255 (some addresses in this range are reserved for administrative purposes or well-know services or protocols, such as certain routing protocols).

When configured properly, the security appliance can function as an Internet Group Management Protocol (IGMP) proxy and enable delivery of content from a source to a multicast host group separated by the security appliance. On the security appliances, IP multicast support is configured using the igmp command.

To allow internal hosts access to a multicast source on the outside:

- Enable multicast routing on the security appliance using the global **multicast-routing** command. This command enables IGMP and PIM on all interfaces on the security appliance by default.

- Optionally disable IGMP on an interface using the **no igmp** command from the interface subcommand menu.

- Optionally use the **igmp join-group** command on the inside interface subcommand mode to join the multicast group.

- Optionally control access to the multicast group using a standard or extended ACL to define the multicast traffic. Use the **igmp access-group** acl_name command in the outside interface's subcommand mode to apply the ACL to IGMP traffic.

- Use the **igmp forward** command on the inside interface subcommand mode.

- Optionally use the **igmp version** command to specify the IGMP version (default is version 2).

- Optionally use the **igmp query-interval** command to specify the frequency of the IGMP query messages (default is 125 seconds).

- Optionally use the **igmp query-timeout** command to specify the number of seconds that the security appliance waits to hear a query message before it becomes the designated multicast router and sends out the query messages (255 seconds by default).

- Optionally use the **igmp query-max-response-time** command to specify the maximum query response time for IGMP version 2 (default is 10 seconds).

Consider the following example configuration:

```
fw(config)# access-list myigmp permit udp any host 230.1.1.50
fw(config)# interface ethernet0
fw(config-if)# igmp access-group myigmp
```

```
fw(config-if)# interface ethernet1
fw(config-if)# igmp forward interface outside
fw(config-if)# igmp join-group 230.1.1.50
```

You can use the **mroute** command to specify a default route for multicast traffic when different default routes are required for multicast and unicast traffic.

Protocol Independent Multicast Sparse-Mode

PIM Sparse-mode multicast uses a rendezvous point (RP) instead of flooding the network to determine status of multicast group members. PIM Sparse-mode is most appropriate for:

- Groups with a small number of receivers
- Intermittent multicast traffic

To configure, the **pim rp-address** command is used to specify the rendezvous point:

```
fw(config)# pim rp-address 192.168.20.1
```

You can only enable PIM Sparse-Mode or IGMP forwarding individually, as both features cannot be enabled simultaneously.

Modular Policy Framework

Modular Policy Framework (MPF) is a new feature of the Security Appliance 7.0 software that allows application of specific security policies based on defined traffic flows.

To use MPF, these steps are required:

Step 1   Use the **class-map** command to define the traffic flow.

Step 2   Use the **policy-map** command to assign a security policy (actions) to the desired class of traffic.

Step 3   Use the **service-policy** command to enable a policy map on a global or per-interface basis.

The **class-map** command enters you in the class-map subcommand menu where different criteria can be used to define a class of traffic. The following tables lists and describes the criteria that you can use with the **class-map** command.

Match Criteria	Description
Access-list	Use a preconfigured access-list to match traffic.
Any	Keyword to specify matching all traffic.
Default-inspection-traffic	Matches the default inspection traffic, including CTIQBE (TCP 2748), DNS (UDP 53), FTP (TCP 21), GTP (UDP 2123,3386), H323-H225 (TCP 1720), H323 RAS (UDP 1718-1719), HTTP (TCP 80), ILS (TCP 389), MGCP (UDP 2427,2727), NetBIOS (UDP 137-138), RPC (UDP 111), RSH (TCP 514), RTSP (TCP 554), SIP (TCP 5060), SIP (UDP 5060), SKINNY (TCP 2000), SMTP (TCP 25), SQL*Net (TCP 1521), TFTP (UDP 69), XDMCP (UDP 177), and ICMP.

Match Criteria	Description
Differentiated service code point (DSCP)	Matches based on IETF-defined DSCP value in the TOS byte of the IP header.
Flow	Specifies a match based on the destination IP address within the tunnel-group (used in conjunction with a **match tunnel-group**).
Port	Matches traffic based on TCP or UDP destination port.
Precedence	Matches based on the precedence value of the TOS byte in the IP header.
RTP	Matches based on the RTP destination port.
Tunnel-group	Matches tunnel traffic.

For example, to match the tunnel traffic for a tunnel group named remote-tg, use the following commands:

```
fw(config)# class-map myclassmap
fw(config-cmap)# match tunnel-group remote-tg
fw(config-cmap)# match flow ip destination-address
```

To display configured class maps, use the **show running-config class-map** command. After a class-map is defined, the **policy-map** command is used to associate a specific policy or action to the class-map. The actions that might be assigned include:

- **Inspect**—Protocol inspection services (CTIQBE, DNS, ESMTP, FTP, GTP, H323, HTTP, ICMP, ILS, MGCP, NetBIOS, PPTP, RSH, RTSP, SIP, SKINNY, SNMP, SQL*Net, SUNRPC, TFTP, XDMCP)
- **IPS**—Intrusion prevention services
- **Police**—Rate-limit traffic for this class
- **Priority**—Strict scheduling priority for this class
- **Set**—Set QoS values or connection values

For example, to enable IPS on the class map defined in the previous example, the following commands are used:

```
fw(config)# policy-map mypolicymap
fw(config-pmap)# class myclassmap
fw(config-pmap-c)# ips inline fail-close
```

To display configured policy maps, use the **show running-config policy-map** command.

After the policy map is defined, the **service-policy** command is used to enable the policy map on a global or per-interface basis:

```
fw(config)# service-policy mypolicymap interface outside
```

or

```
fw(config)# service-policy mypolicymap global
```

Only a single global policy can be configured at any time. You must delete the current global policy before a new global policy is declared.

Advanced Protocol Handling

Advanced protocol-handling capabilities of Cisco security appliances allow them to properly inspect and secure protocols and applications that use dynamically assigned destination or source IP addresses or ports or operate at layer 4 or higher of the OSI model. The application inspection engine works with NAT.

In Security Appliance 7.0 software, to accomplish the advanced protocol handling configuration, use the **inspect** command (similar to IOS routers), which replaces the older **fixup protocol** command used in previous versions of the software. Pre-7.0 **fixup protocol** commands are accepted on security appliances with version 7.0 of the software, although the configuration is converted to an MPF-compatible format before it's saved to RAM or NVRAM.

By default, protocol inspection is enabled globally using the default inspection policy, which includes the following inspections:

- DNS
- FTP
- H323 H225
- H323 RAS
- NetBIOS
- RSH
- RTSP
- SKINNY
- ESMTP
- SQL*NET
- SUNRPC
- TFTP
- SIP
- XDMPC

Specific inspections can be disabled on the default list if you use the **no inspect** command, as shown in this example:

```
fw(config)# policy-map global_ policy
fw(config-pmap)# class inspection_default
fw(config-pmap-c)# no inspect sunrpc
```

The following additional inspections are not enabled by default and can be enabled using the **inspect** command:

- CTIQBE
- HTTP

- ICMP

- ICMP Error

- ILS

- MGCP

- PPTP

- SNMP

Inspection for supported protocols can also be enabled on non-standard ports. For example, to enable HTTP inspection on the nonstandard TCP port 8080, the following commands are used:

```
fw(config)# class-map http_8080
fw(config-cmap)# match port tcp eq 8080
fw(config-cmap)# policy-map global_policy
fw(config-pmap)# class http_8080
fw(config-pmap-c)# inspect http
```

Inspection settings for some protocols, such as DNS, can be modified. For example, to change the maximum-length of a DNS query allowed from the default value of 512 bytes to 1024 bytes, the following command is used:

```
fw(config)# policy-map global_policy
fw(config-pmap)# class inspection_default
fw(config-pmap-c)# inspect dns maximum-length 1024
```

A **show running-config policy-map** command output shows the added HTTP inspection on port 8080:

```
fw(config)# show running-config policy-map
!
policy-map global_ policy
 class inspection_default
  inspect dns maximum-length 1024
  inspect ftp
  inspect h323 h225
  inspect h323 ras
  inspect http
  inspect netbios
  inspect rsh
  inspect rtsp
  inspect skinny
  inspect esmtp
  inspect sqlnet
  inspect sunrpc
  inspect tftp
  inspect sip
  inspect xdmcp
 class http_8080
  inspect http
!
```

Security appliance software version 7.0 provides the ability to further customize inspection of several protocols. The **http-map**, **ftp-map**, **gtp-map**, **mgcp-map**, and **snmp-map** commands allow customization of inspection characteristics for each protocol. For example, the **http-map** command can be used to specify inspection based on specific content length, content type, header length, URL length, request method, transfer encoding type, or application firewall inspection (to discover exploits). You can specify an action of **allow**, **reset**, or **drop** when conditions exceed the criteria limits defined if you use the **http-map** command. You can also use the **log** option to enable or disable logging of events. Consider the following example configuration:

```
fw(config)# class-map myhttpport
fw(config-cmap)# match port tcp eq 80
fw(config)# http-map myhttpmap
fw(config-http-map)# content-length min 100 max 1000 action drop log
fw(config-http-map)# max-uri-length 150 action reset log
fw(config)# policy-map mypolicy
fw(config-pmap)# class myhttpport
fw(config-pmap-c)# inspect http myhttpmap
fw(config)# service-policy mypolicy interface outside
```

Virtual Private Network Configuration

A virtual private network (VPN) offers secure, reliable, encrypted connectivity over a shared, public network infrastructure, such as the Internet. Because the infrastructure is shared, connectivity can be provided at lower cost than by existing dedicated private networks.

Benefits of VPNs

VPNs provide the following benefits:

- **Cost Savings**—Using the public network (Internet), VPNs provide cost effective connectivity solutions and can eliminate more expensive traditional WAN implementations.

- **Improved Communications**—VPNs provide greater access to telecommuters at home and on the road using broadband connections, such as DSL and cable, as well as standard dialup.

- **Security**—VPNs use advanced encryption and authentication protocols to protect data from unauthorized access.

- **Scalability**—VPNs allow customers to add capacity with less overhead.

- **Wireless Network Security**—VPNs provide advanced security to wireless networks.

IPSec

IPSec acts at the network layer and protects and authenticates IP packets between IPSec devices (peers), such as PIX and ASA security appliances, Cisco IOS routers, Cisco VPN 3000 Concentrators, the Cisco VPN software client, and other IPSec-compliant products. IPSec is a framework of open standards and is not bound to a specific encryption or authentication protocol. Therefore, IPSec can work multiple encryption schemes and is easily extended when newer and better algorithms become available.

IPSec uses the underlying encryption and authentication algorithms to provide the following functions:

- **Data confidentiality**—Packets are encrypted before transmission across network.

- **Data integrity**—IPSec receiver authenticates IPSec peers and packets sent by the IPSec sender to ensure that the data has not been altered during transmission.

- **Data origin authentication**—IPSec receiver authenticates the source of the IPSec packets sent. This service depends on the data integrity service.

- **Anti-replay**—IPSec receiver can detect and reject replayed packets, which helps prevent spoofing and man-in-the-middle attacks.

IPSec Security Protocols

IPSec uses the following security protocols:

- **Authentication Header (AH)**—A security protocol that provides authentication and optional replay-detection services. AH was assigned IP Protocol number 51.

- **Encapsulating Security Payload (ESP)**—A security protocol that provides data confidentiality and protection with optional authentication and replay-detection services. ESP was assigned IP protocol number 50.

IPSec Modes of Operation

IPSec, and more specifically ESP and AH, is configured to operate in two different modes:

- **Tunnel mode**—Tunnel mode for ESP encrypts the entire IP packet, including the original header, and tacks on a new unencrypted IP header. For AH, tunnel mode adds a new IP header to the entire original IP packet (including the original header). This entire new packet is authenticated.

Tunnel Mode

Original IP Packet

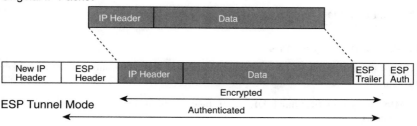

ESP Tunnel Mode

Original IP Packet

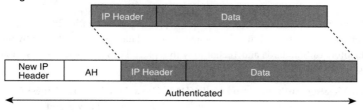

AH Tunnel Mode

- **Transport mode**—Transport mode leaves the original IP header intact and inserts a new ESP or AH header after the IP header. When using ESP, only the original IP payload is only encrypted. With AH, the entire new packet is authenticated. Because a new IP header is not added, there is less overhead with Transport mode.

Transport Mode

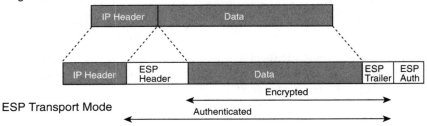

ESP Transport Mode

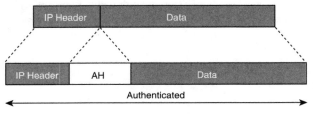

AH Tunnel Mode

IPSec-Supported Algorithms

IPSec relies on the following algorithms to implement encryption, authentication, and key exchange:

- **Data Encryption Standard (DES)**—56-bit encryption algorithm used by ESP to encrypt and decrypt data.

- **Triple-DES (3DES)**—168-bit encryption algorithm used by ESP to encrypt and decrypt data.

- **Advanced Encryption Standard (AES)**—New cipher algorithm with 128-, 192-, or 256-bit encryption used by ESP to encrypt and decrypt data. AES was adopted by the National Institute of Standards and Technology to replace DES and 3DES encryption algorithms.

- **Hash-based Message Authentication Code (HMAC) variant Message Digest 5 (MD5)**—Provides message authentication using a 128-bit shared key secret.

- **HMAC-variant Secure Hash Algorithm 1 (SHA-1)**—Provides message authentication using a 160-bit shared key secret. SHA-1 provides stronger authentication relative to MD5, although with additional processing overhead.

- **Diffie-Hellman (DH)**—DH is a public-key cryptography protocol that enables two parties to establish a shared secret key over an insecure communications channel.

- **RSA (Rivest, Shamir, and Adelman)**—Asymmetrical encryption algorithm used for encryption and decryption. Because asymmetrical encryption algorithms are processor-intensive, RSA is typically used only for peer authentication.

- **DSA (Digital Signature Algorithm)**—DSA is a U.S. government endorsed public key algorithm for digital signatures. DSA is primarily used for peer authentication.

Peer Authentication

Security Appliance Software version 7.0 provides three methods for peer authentication:

- **Pre-shared keys**—A shared secret key known to both peers is used to authenticate the peers.

- **RSA signatures**—With RSA signatures, digital certificates issued by a Certificate Authority (CA) are used to authenticate IPSec peers. This method requires more resources to implement, although it is more secure and scalable than pre-shared keys.

- **DSA signatures**—DSA signatures are similar to RSA signatures, although use digital certificates generated by the DSA signature algorithm. DSA signatures cannot be used for SSH or SSL.

Security Association

To successfully establish an IPSec tunnel, peers must agree on a matching set of IPSec-related algorithms and variables. The following terms are important during this negotiation:

- **ISAKMP policies**—Internet Security Association and Key Management Protocol (ISAKMP) policies are specific combinations of algorithms and variables used by Internet Key Exchange (IKE) to establish common policies between IPSec peers. ISAKMP policies define variables, such as:

  — Encryption algorithm (DES, 3DES, and AES)
  — Hash algorithm (MD5 and SHA-1)
  — Authentication method (pre-share, RSA signatures, or DSA signatures)
  — Key Exchange (Diffie-Hellman group 1, 2, 5, or 7)
  — Security Association lifetime (in seconds or bytes)

Parameter	ISAKMP Policy 1	ISAKMP Policy 2
Encryption Algorithm	3DES	3DES
Hash Algorithm	SHA-1	SHA-1
Authentication Method	Pre-Share	Pre-Share
Key Exchange	1024-Bit D-H	1024-Bit D-H
IKE SA Lifetime	86,400 Seconds	86,400 Seconds

- **Transform sets**—A transform set is a specific combination of message authentication and encryption algorithms that the security appliance uses. You can configure multiple transform sets on the security appliance.

- **Crypto maps**—Crypto maps define the combination of variables that IPSec peers use during IPSec Security Association (SA) negotiations. Specifically, crypto maps define:

  - Interesting traffic (traffic that is protected by IPSec) that uses crypto ACLs
  - Peer identification
  - Transform sets to use
  - IPSec SA lifetime (optional)
  - Perfect Forward Secrecy (optional)

- **Security Association (SA)**—An SA is a unidirectional or bidirectional association established between IPSec peers and is uniquely identified by the IPSec protocol in use, the remote peer's address, and a 32-bit random number called the security parameter index (SPI).

  - IPSec SAs are unidirectional. Therefore, two unidirectional SAs must be established between peers.
  - IKE SAs are bidirectional and only a single SA is required between two peers.
  - SAs are protocol-specific. Therefore, separate SAs are required for ESP and AH if both protocols are used.
  - Each SA is valid for duration of its lifetime, which is established during the negotiation process. The lifetime can be specified by time or the amount of traffic traversing the tunnel. The SA must be reestablished after the SA lifetime expires.

During SA negotiations and setup, the IPSec peers must exchange and authenticate keys to establish the identity of the other peer and setup the appropriate SA. This mechanism relies on the following protocols:

- IKE

- ISAKMP

ISAKMP uses the IKE protocol for key exchange, although the two protocols are synonymous in Cisco VPN configurations.

IKE relies on two mechanisms for secure key exchange and management:

- **Diffie-Hellman (DH)**—DH is a public-key cryptography algorithm used by IKE that allows two peers establish a secret key over an insecure communications channel.

- **Certificate Authority (CA)**—CA is a trusted entity that issues digital certificates.

How IPSec Tunnels Are Established

IPSec operates in the following manner:

- **IKE Phase 1**—During this phase, an initial secure communications channel is established (IKE bidirectional SA). IPSec peers use this channel for IKE Phase 2 negotiations, not to send user data. IKE Phase 1 can occur in the following modes:

  - **Main mode**—This mode includes three two-way exchanges between peers:

    First exchange—IKE algorithms and hashes are negotiated. ISAKMP policies are used to improve performance because it avoids the largest number of possible combinations of individual variables.

    Second exchange—DH protocol is used to generate shared secret key, which is then used to generate encryption keys for the secure communications channel.

    Third exchange—In this exchange, identity of the peer is authenticated and the secure communications channel is established for subsequent IKE transmissions.

  - **Aggressive mode**—This mode reduces the number of exchanges by generating the DH pair on the first exchange, but without identity protection.

- **IKE Phase 2**—Matching unidirectional IPSec SAs are negotiated and established during IKE Phase 2 negotiations. The tunnel is now ready for user traffic. IKE Phase 2 performs the following:

  - Negotiates IPSec transform sets and security parameters
  - Establishes matching unidirectional IPSec SAs
  - Renegotiates the SAs when their lifetime expires
  - Optionally performs additional DH exchange (perfect forward secrecy)

- **Data transfer**—IPSec peers send data defined as interesting according to the parameters defined by crypto ACLs and negotiated in IPSec SAs.

- **Tunnel termination**—SAs are terminated if their lifetime expires or when they are deleted.

Configuring IPSec for IKE Pre-Shared Keys

IPSec configuration consists of four primary tasks:

- Task 1—Prepare for IKE and IPSec
- Task 2—Configure IKE
- Task 3—Configure IPSec
- Task 4—Test and verify

Specific steps involved with each task and the corresponding security appliance commands are summarized in the sections that follow.

Task 1: Prepare for IKE and IPSec

The following table lists the steps involved in Task 1, preparing for IKE and IPsec.

Steps	Description	ASA Command Example
Step 1—Determine IKE (IKE Phase 1) Policy.	Determine the IKE policies that are configured between IPSec peers, including key distribution method, authentication method, peer IP addresses or hostnames, encryption algorithm, hash algorithm, and IKE SA lifetime.	Not applicable.
Step 2—Determine IPSec (IKE Phase 2) Policy.	Determine IPSec policy parameters that is negotiated by IPSec peers including transform sets, peer details, and traffic to be protected.	Not applicable.
Step 3—Ensure the Network Works Without Encryption.	Use the **ping** command to verify connectivity between peers.	`fw# ping ip_address`
Step 4—Permit IPSec packets to bypass ACLs.	Ensure existing configuration does not block IPSec traffic.	`Fw(config)# sysopt connection permit-ipsec`

After all these steps are successfully completed, you can move to Task 2 (configure the IKE policy).

Task 2: Configure IKE

The IKE policy specifies a set of parameters that IPSec peers use during IKE Phase 1 negotiations. These parameters include:

- Encryption Algorithm (DES, 3DES, AES 128, AES 192, or AES 256)
- Integrity (hash) Algorithm (SHA-1 or MD5)
- Peer Authentication Method (pre-shared keys, RSA signatures, or DSA signatures)

- Diffie-Hellman Key Exchange Group (group 1 [768-bit], group 2 [1024-bit], group 5 [1536-bit], or group 7 [163 bits Elliptic Curve Diffie-Hellman])

- SA Lifetime (any number of seconds)

The following table lists the individual steps involved in the IKE configuration task and provides corresponding IOS commands.

Steps	Description	ASA Command Example
Step 1—Enable or disable IKE.	Enable or disable IKE.	`fw(config)# isakmp enable outside` `fw(config)# no isakmp enable outside`

Step 2—Create IKE policies.	Create IKE policies.	`fw(config)# isakmp policy 10 encryption aes-256`
		`fw(config)# isakmp policy 10 hash sha`
		`fw(config)# isakmp policy 10 authentication pre-share`
		`fw(config)# isakmp policy 10 group 5`
		`fw(config)# isakmp policy 10 lifetime 86400`

Step 3— Configure a tunnel group.	Create a tunnel group and specify remote access or LAN-to-LAN type.	`fw(config)# tunnel-group mytunnel type ipsec-ra`
Step 4— Configure tunnel group attributes.	Configure pre-shared keys for the tunnel group.	`fw(config)# tunnel-group mytunnel ipsec-attributes` `fw(config-ipsec)# pre-shared-key mypskey`
Step 5—Verify the IKE configuration.	Verify the IKE configuration.	`fw# show running-config crypto isakmp` `fw# show running-config tunnel-group`

Task 3: Configure IPSec

With an appropriate IKE policy configured, Task 3 defines a suitable IPSec policy. Parameters that are specified as part of an IPSec policy include:

- IPSec Transform Sets that define ESP encryption and hash algorithms.

- Global IPSec SA Lifetimes that specify the time SAs remain valid before they must be renegotiated.

- Crypto ACLs that define traffic that is encrypted.

- Crypto maps that define sets of IPSec parameters that IPSec peers use to set up SAs.

The following table lists the individual steps involved in the IPSec configuration task and provides corresponding IOS commands.

Steps	Description	ASA Command Example
Step 1— Create crypto ACLs.	Use extended IP ACLs to define the traffic that is encrypted (interesting traffic). Symmetric ACLs should be configured on the IPSec peers at each end of the tunnel.	`fw(config)# access-list` `my_crypto_acl permit ip 10.1.1.0` `255.255.255.0 10.1.2.0` `255.255.255.0`
Step 2— Configure NAT 0 access list.	Use **nat 0 access-list** statement to exempt interesting traffic from address translation.	`fw(config)# nat (inside) 0 access-` `list my_crypto_acl`

Step 3— Configure IPSec transform set.	Configure transform set suites used by IPSec peers during SA negotiations. Up to two transforms can be configured in each set.	`fw(config)# crypto ipsec transform-` `set mytransform esp-aes-256 esp-sha-` `hmac`
		
		Possible transforms include:
		
		`esp-3des`
		`esp-aes (128, 192, 256)`
		`esp-des`
		`esp-md5-hmac`
		`esp-none`
		`esp-null`
		`esp-sha-hmac`

Step 4— Create crypto maps.	Create crypto maps that group sets of IPSec parameters, including transform sets, peer addresses, crypto ACLs, PFS, and SA-specific lifetime.	`fw(config)# crypto map my_crypto_map` `10 match address my_crypto_acl`
		`fw(config)# crypto map my_crypto_map` `10 set peer 192.168.2.1`
		`fw(config)# crypto map my_crypto_map` `10 set transform-set mytransform`
		`fw(config)# crypto map my_crypto_map` `10 set security-association lifetime` `seconds 86400`
		`fw(config)# crypto map my_crypto_map` `10 set pfs group5`

Step 5— Apply crypto maps to interfaces.	Apply crypto maps to an interface to activate IPSec on the interface.	`fw(config)# crypto map my_crypto_map` `interface outside`

Task 4: Test and Verify

The last task involves testing and verifying IPSec configuration, as outlined in the following table.

Steps	Description	ASA Command Example
Step 1— Display IKE policies, key, and established SAs.	Use the appropriate **show** commands to display configured IKE policies, key, or active SAs.	`fw# show running-config crypto isakmp` `fw# show crypto isakmp sa`
Step 2— Display transform sets.	Use the **show** command to display configured transform sets.	`fw# show running-config crypto ipsec`
Step 3— Display IPSec SAs.	Use the **show crypto ipsec sa** command to display the current state of IPSec SAs.	`fw# show crypto ipsec sa`
Step 4— Display ACLs.	Verify interesting traffic.	`fw# show access-list`
Step 5— Display crypto maps.	Use the **show** command to view configured crypto maps.	`fw# show running-config crypto map`

Step 6— Enable debug for IPSec.	Use the **debug crypto ipsec** and **debug crypto isakmp** commands to debug IKE and IPSec traffic.	`fw# debug crypto ipsec`
		`fw# debug crypto isakmp`
		`fw# no debug all` (turns off all debugging)

Configuring Security Appliance Remote Access Using Cisco Easy VPN

Cisco Easy VPN is its proprietary VPN based on the Cisco Unified Client Framework. It is established on open standards, such as IKE and IPSec with additional Cisco proprietary protocols and mechanism aimed to simplify the configuration, deployment, and management of remote access VPNs. Cisco Easy VPN consists of two components:

- Cisco Easy VPN Remote
- Cisco Easy VPN Server

It is typically used for remote-access VPNs that use Cisco VPN software client and an Easy VPN Server device, such as VPN 3000 Concentrators, Cisco IOS devices, or Cisco PIX 500 Series and Cisco ASA 5500 Series security appliances. It can also be used to build site-to-site VPNs with simpler configuration and management than traditional IPSec site-to-site VPNs.

Cisco Easy VPN Server

The Cisco Easy VPN Server allows Cisco IOS routers, security appliances, and VPN 3000 Concentrators to function as VPN head-end devices to Cisco Easy VPN Remote devices in site-to-site or remote-access VPNs. Easy VPN Servers can push security policies defined at the central site to Easy VPN Remote devices, which allow centralized management of VPN devices and ensure that up-to-date policies are deployed before a connection is allowed. Cisco Easy VPN Servers can also terminate VPN tunnels started by clients who run the Cisco VPN client software on a variety of supported operating systems.

Easy VPN Server functionality is supported by the following devices (please check Cisco.com for the most up-to-date information as this list is likely to change with evolving Cisco product portfolios):

- Cisco PIX 500 Series security appliance models 535, 525, and 515E
- Cisco ASA 5500 Series security appliances
- Cisco IOS devices including 800, 1700, 1800, 2600, 2800, 3600, 3700, 3800, 7200, 7300, and 7500 Series routers
- Cisco VPN 3000 Concentrators

Easy VPN Servers support the following functionality:

- **Mode Configuration Version 6 support**—Supports IKE Mode Configuration (MC).
- **XAUTH Version 6 support**—Allows the Server to request extended authentication information from the Remote device using ISAKMP.
- **IKE Dead Peer Detection (DPD) support**—Keepalive scheme that allows IPSec peers to determine if the other peer is still "alive." DPD removes orphaned connections from the Server.
- **Split tunneling**—Remote clients can be configured to route Internet-bound traffic directly to the Internet in clear text, which removes the overhead for all traffic pass through the encrypted tunnel.
- **Initial contact**—A remote device can be refused a connection request if an existing connection entry appears for it on the server (because of a sudden disconnection). Initial contact prevents this problem because it implements an initial-contact message that is sent by remote devices during the initial connection attempt.
- **Group-based policy control**—Define policy attributes such as IP addresses, DNS, and split tunneling on a per-group or per-user basis.

In addition, Easy VPN Servers support the following IPSec attributes:

- HMAC-MD5
- HMAC-SHA1
- Pre-Shared Keys
- RSA Signatures
- DSA Signatures
- DH Group 2, 5, and 7
- IKE Encryptions DES and 3DES
- IPSec Encryptions DES, 3DES, AES, and Null
- IPSec Tunnel Mode
- LZS payload compression

The following IPSec attributes are unsupported by Easy VPN Servers:

- DSS Authentication
- DH Group 1
- AH
- IPSec Transport Mode
- PFS
- Manual Key Authentication

Cisco Easy VPN Remote

Cisco Easy VPN Remote devices can establish connections with Easy VPN Servers and receive security policies upon a VPN tunnel connection with the server, therefore it minimizes configuration requirements at the remote location.

Easy VPN Remote devices are also significantly simpler to configure than traditional IPSec VPN devices, which further simplify their deployment and reduce their implementation costs. The following devices provide Easy VPN Remote functionality (please check Cisco.com for the most up-to-date information as this list is likely to change with evolving Cisco product portfolios):

- Cisco VPN Client 3.6 or greater
- Cisco VPN 3002 Hardware Client version 3.6 or greater
- Cisco PIX 501 and 506E security appliances with software version 6.3 or greater
- Easy VPN Remote routers (800, UBR900, 1700, and 1800 Series)

Modes of Operation

Easy VPN Remote devices (excluding VPN Software clients) function in one of two modes:

- **Client mode**—In this mode, the clients behind Easy VPN Remote are not directly accessible from the central site. Instead, the remote device uses port address translation (PAT) and the addresses of the individual hosts behind it remain hidden. This mode requires a single private IP address allocated to the remote device. Client mode causes VPN connections to start from traffic on the Easy VPN Remote side so that resources are only used on demand.

- **Network extension mode**—In network extension mode, the clients behind the Easy VPN Remote device are accessible from the central site. The IP addresses of the clients are not translated in this mode. Consequently, an appropriate number of IP addresses must be allocated when network extension mode is used. Note that only single subnet can be accessed behind the Easy VPN Remote Client (that is, you cannot place a router behind a 3002 Hardware Client to route multiple subnets through the tunnel).

Overview of Cisco Easy VPN Operation

The following steps outline the Easy VPN Remote connection process:

Step 1 **Intiate IKE Phase 1**—Peers use pre-shared keys or certificates to authenticate each other.

Step 2 **Establish the IKE SA**—SA parameters are negotiated to determine a common set.

Step 3 **Accept the SA**—Peers agree on an SA proposal and the Easy VPN Server authenticates the device.

Step 4 **Username and password challenge is processed**—The server prompts the user for a username and password and authenticates the user by checking the information against an AAA server using protocols, such as RADIUS or TACACS+, or the local user database of the security appliance.

Step 5 **Mode configuration**—IKE MC starts, and configuration parameters are downloaded to the Remote client.

Step 6 **The RRI process is initiated**—Reverse Route Injection process adds a static entry to the server router's route table for the connected remote client.

Step 7 **Connection is completed with IKE Quick mode**—IKE Quick mode starts to complete IPSec SA negotiations and establishment.

Users and Groups Configuration

Easy VPN uses users and groups to authenticate each user or Easy VPN Remote device. Security appliances use three categories:

- **Default Group**—A template group used to specify a baseline configuration. Each new group created inherits these settings by default.

- **Groups**—Used to separate groups of users and assign customized settings. Groups inherit the settings from the default group, although can then be customized as necessary.

- **Users**—Can be used to apply per-user customized settings as required.

Easy VPN Server Configuration

The following table outlines the general steps required for configuration of Easy VPN Server with extended authentication (XAUTH).

Step	Description	ASA Command Example

Step 1—Create remote VPN access IKE policy.	Create the ISAKMP policy for use on the Easy VPN Server.	`fw(config)# isakmp policy 10 encryption 3des`
		`fw(config)# isakmp policy 10 hash sha`
		`fw(config)# isakmp policy 10 authentication pre-share`
		`fw(config)# isakmp policy 10 group 2`
		`fw(config)# isakmp policy 10 lifetime 86400`

Step	Description	ASA Command Example
Step 2—Create IP Address pool.	Create a pool of IP addresses for Easy VPN clients to use.	`fw(config)#` **`ip local pool mypool`** **`10.1.1.64-10.1.1.127`**
Step 3—Define a tunnel group.	Create a tunnel group and configure attributes.	`fw#` **`tunnel-group mytunnel type ipsec-ra`** `fw(config)#` **`tunnel-group mytunnel`** **`ipsec-attributes`** `fw(config-ipsec)#` **`pre-shared-key mykey`** `fw(config-ipsec)#` **`tunnel-group mytunnel`** **`general-attributes`** `fw(config-general)#` **`address-pool mypool`**
Step 4—Create group policy.	Configure group policy for mode configuration push (DNS, WINS, default domain, idle-timeout).	`fw(config)#` **`group-policy mygrppol`** **`internal`** `fw(config)#` **`group-policy mygrppol`** **`attributes`** `fw(config-group-policy)#` **`dns-server`** **`value 10.1.1.11`** `fw(config-group-policy)#` **`wins-server`** **`value 10.1.1.12`** `fw(config-group-policy)#` **`default-`** **`domain value cisco.com`** `fw(config-group-policy)#` **`vpn-idle-`** **`timeout 900`**
Step 5—Create transform set.	Create the transform set.	`fw(config)#` **`crypto ipsec transform-set`** **`mytransform esp-3des esp-sha-hmac`**
Step 6—Create dynamic crypto map.	Create a dynamic crypto map for remote access VPNs.	`fw(config)#` **`crypto dynamic-map`** **`mydynamap 10 set transform-set`** **`mytransform`**
Step 7—Assign dynamic crypto map to static crypto map.	Link the dynamic crypto map from Step 7 with a static crypto map.	`fw(config)#` **`crypto map ezvpn-map 10`** **`ipsec-isakmp dynamic mydynamap`**
Step 8—Apply crypto map to interface.	Enable the crypto map on an interface.	`fw(config)#` **`crypto map ezvpn-map`** **`interface outside`**
Step 9—Configure XAUTH.	Enable authentication for tunnel access.	`fw(config)#` **`aaa-server ez-aaa protocol`** **`tacacs+`** `fw(config-aaa-server-group)#` **`aaa-`** **`server ez-aaa (inside) host 10.1.1.14`** **`myencp-ky timeout 10`** `fw(config-aaa-server-host)#` **`tunnel-`** **`group mytunnel general-attributes`** `fw(config-general)#` **`authentication-`** **`server-group ez-aaa`**

continues

Step	Description	ASA Command Example
Step 10—Configure NAT 0.	Define traffic to be encrypted and exempt from address translation.	`fw(config)# access-list ezvpn-acl permit ip 10.0.0.0 255.255.255.0 10.1.1.0 255.255.255.0` `fw(config)# nat (inside) 0 access-list ezvpn-acl`
Step 11—Enable IKE DPD.	Enable dead peer detection.	`fw(config)# tunnel-group mytunnel ipsec-attributes` `fw(config-ipsec)# isakmp keepalive threshold 30 retry 5`

WebVPN Configuration

WebVPN provides remote users secure encrypted access to resources that use browser-based Secure Socket Layer and Transport Layer Security (SSL/TLS) encryption, therefore, it eliminates the need to install IPSec client software on the remote workstation. WebVPN is only available with the ASA 5500 Series security appliances.

WebVPN features include the following:

- Secure browser-based access to internal resources.

- Secure access to files on pre-configured file servers or file browsing on the network when you use Windows File Access feature.

- Legacy application support when you use port forwarding.

- Secure email with POP3, IMAP4, and SMTP with POP3S, IMAP4S, and SMTPS SSL email proxies.

- MAPI proxy support for Microsoft Exchange client access.

- Support for web-based email systems, including Microsoft Outlook Web Access (OWA) and Lotus iNotes.

The following table compares WebVPN and traditional IPSec remote access VPN.

WebVPN	IPSec Remote Access VPN
Uses a standard web browser to provide secure access to users.	Uses client software to provide access to internal resources.
Uses SSL/TLS encryption.	Uses IPSec encryption algorithms (3DES, AES).
Access is provided through a portal using proxies.	Client becomes "part of" internal network and has seamless access to applications.
Does not support all applications.	All applications are typically accessible with IPSec remote access VPNs.
Is ideal for unmanaged desktops or times when installation of IPSec client software is undesirable.	Not suitable for occasional users who are not likely to install software.

WebVPN	IPSec Remote Access VPN
Easier to keep up-to-date with little or no end-user software installation.	More difficult to maintain remote user software up-to-date.
Less likely to interfere with other software on remote client systems.	More likely to interfere with other software on remote client systems because of the nature of IPSec remote access VPN software.

General WebVPN Configuration

The following table provides an overview of WebVPN configuration commands.

WebVPN Command Example	Description
General Settings	
fw(config)# `http server enable`	Enables the internal HTTP server, which is required for WebVPN functionality.
fw(config)# `webvpn` fw(config-webvpn)#	Globally enables WebVPN and enters the WebVPN subcommand mode. The global WebVPN settings are configured here.
fw(config-webvpn)# `enable outside`	Enables WebVPN on a specific interface.
WebVPN Group Policy	
fw(config)# `group-policy mywebvpn internal` fw(config)# `group-policy mywebvpn attributes` fw(config-group-policy)# `vpn-tunnel-protocol webvpn`	Configure a group policy for WebVPN and set its VPN protocol type to WebVPN.
fw(config-group-policy)# `webvpn`	Enter the **webvpn** command to set WebVPN-related settings on the group policy.
WebVPN Servers and URLs	
fw(config-group-webvpn)# `functions url-entry file-access file-entry file-browsing`	Enable URL entry, file access, file entry, and file browsing.
fw(config)# `url-list my-urls "homeserver" http://10.1.1.11` fw(config)# `url-list my-urls "MS Share" cifs://10.1.1.12/ms-share`	Create a URL list for use with **url-list** command.
fw(config-group-webvpn)# `url-list value my-urls`	Specify a configured URL list.
WebVPN Port Forwarding	
fw(config-group-webvpn)# `functions port-forward`	Enable port forwarding.

continues

WebVPN Command Example	Description
`fw(config)# port-forward myports 23 10.1.1.11 23`	Define a port forwarding map to use with WebVPN configuration.
`fw(config-group-webvpn)# port-forward value myports`	Uses the configured port-forwarding list to enable WebVPN port forwarding.
Email Proxy	
`fw(config-group-webvpn)# functions mapi`	Enables Microsoft Exchange and Outlook port forwarding at the group level.
`fw(config)# POP3s` `fw(config)# imap4s` `fw(config)# smtps`	Enables POP3, IMAP, or SMTP proxy support.
`fw(config-pop3s)# server 10.1.1.11` `fw(config-pop3s)# authentication-server-group webvpn-auth`	Specify server for email and the authentication server to use for email-proxy. Same settings might be configured for IMAP4 or SMTP. The authentication server group must be previously defined using the **aaa-server** command.
`fw(config-pop3s)# authentication piggyback`	Specify the authentication method. Options include: **aaa**—Use aaa server. **certificate**—Use certificates. **mailhost**—Use remote mail server to authenticate (available only with SMTPS). **piggyback**—Use established HTTPS WebVPN session information.

The following table lists the global WebVPN configuration command attributes used at Web-VPN global configuration subcommand mode (fw(config-webvpn)#).

Command	Function
`accounting-server-group`	Specifies the previously configured accounting servers to use with WebVPN.
`authentication`	Specifies the authentication method for WebVPN users.
`authentication-server-group`	Specifies the previously configured authentication servers to use with WebVPN.
`authorization-server-group`	Specifies the previously configured authorization servers to use with WebVPN.
`authorization-required`	Requires users to authorize successfully to connect.
`authorization-dn-attributes`	Identifies the DN of the peer certificate to use as a username for authorization.
`default-group-policy`	Specifies the name of the group policy to use.

Command	Function
`default-idle-timeout`	Specifies the default idle timeout in seconds.
`enable` *interface*	Enables WebVPN on the specified interface.
`http-proxy`	Specifies the proxy server for HTTP requests.
`https-proxy`	Specifies the proxy server for HTTPS requests.
`login-message`	Configures the HTML text prompt displayed when a user logs in.
`logo`	Configures the logo image that displays on the WebVPN login and home pages.
`logout-message`	Configures the HTML text the security appliance presents to a user logging out.
`nbns-server`	Identifies the NetBIOS name service server for CIFS name resolution.
`username-prompt`	Configures the prompt for a username at initial login to WebVPN.
`password-prompt`	Configures the prompt for the password at initial login to WebVPN.
`title`	Configures the HTML title string that is in the WebVPN browser title and on the title bar.
`title-color`	Configures the color of the title bars on the login, home, and file access pages.
`text-color`	Configures the color of the text bars on the login, home, and file access pages.
`secondary-color`	Configures the color of the secondary title bars on the login, home, and file access pages.
`secondary-text-color`	Configures the color of the secondary text bars on the login, home, and file access pages.

Transparent Firewall

Transparent firewall is a new feature available in Security Appliance 7.0 software. With this option, the firewall is no longer a routed hop. Routed firewall mode is based on IP addresses (OSI layer 3), while the transparent firewall mode is based on MAC addresses (OSI layer 2).

Transparent firewall mode notables include:

- Only two interfaces are supported (inside and outside).

- Single and multiple security contexts are supported.

- The firewall performs MAC lookups instead of routing table lookups.

- Packets are not routed between interfaces; they are instead bridged between the VLANs present on either side of the transparent firewall.

The main benefit of transparent firewall mode is that it requires minimal network reconfiguration because separate networks are not required on each side of the firewall. IP routing issues and associated troubleshooting are also much easier because the firewall can be ruled out as a source of the problem.

However, there are a few missing features with transparent firewall mode:

- NAT is not supported and must be performed on the edge router if required.

- RIP and OSPF are not supported (dynamic routing protocols can, however, be allowed through the security appliance with an appropriate ACL).

- There is no support for IPv6.

- DHCP relay function is disabled; however, the security appliance can function as a DHCP server (DHCP traffic can also be allowed through the security appliance with an appropriate ACL).

- QoS is a layer 3 function and is therefore not supported.

- IP Multicast is not supported directly on the firewall (multicast traffic can, however, traverse the firewall with an appropriate ACL).

- Transparent firewall cannot terminate VPN tunnels on its interfaces, except for management traffic to the security appliance itself (VPN traffic can, however, be allowed through the security appliance with an appropriate ACL).

Transparent Firewall Configuration

To enable transparent firewall mode, use the command:

```
fw(config)# firewall transparent
```

Because the firewall operates at Layer 2, there is no need to configure interface IP addresses. You must, however, configure a management interface IP address for management access to the security appliance and communications with management servers, such as syslog or SNMP servers. Management IP address is configured using the **ip address** command in the global configuration mode (unlike the interface configuration subcommand mode required for routed firewall IP address configuration):

```
fw(config)# ip address 10.1.1.1 255.255.255.0
```

Transparent firewall mode provides the familiar IP extended ACLs for control of IP traffic through the firewall and a new EtherType ACL for non-IP traffic control.

EtherType ACLs are distinguished by the use of **ethertype** option keyword. Predefined EtherTypes exist for the following protocols:

- IPX

- BDPU

- MPLS (unicast and multicast)

Other Ethernet V2/DIX-encapsulated frames can be allowed based on their 2-byte EtherType. Presently, 802.3 encapsulated frames cannot pass through transparent firewall.

```
fw(config)# access-list my-ether ethertype permit mpls-unicast
```

Cisco security appliances operating in transparent firewall mode can be configured to perform ARP inspection for added security. With ARP inspection enabled, the security appliance compares MAC addresses, IP addresses, and the source interface of packets against static entries in its ARP table. When a mismatch is found, packets are dropped. New entries can be forwarded to all interfaces (and added to the ARP table) or dropped, depending on the ARP inspection configuration.

To configure ARP inspection, use the **arp-inspection** command on a per-interface basis:

```
fw(config)# arp-inspection outside enable
```

ARP table maintenance commands allow addition of static ARP entries (**mac-address-table static** command) and can enable or disable automatic MAC addresses that learn on an interface (**mac-learn enable | disable** command).

Security Contexts

Security contexts are new to Security Appliance 7.0 software. They allow virtualization and partitioning of a single physical firewall into multiple logical firewalls.

The number of security contexts that are available on a particular security appliance depends on its hardware capabilities and its specific security context license. Refer to the earlier section "Cisco PIX and ASA Security Appliance Families" to find out which platforms support multiple contexts and the number of supported security contexts.

Typical applications of security context can include:

- Service providers partitioning a single firewall into many logical firewalls dedicated to different customers (highly customized, yet cost effective)

- Enterprises requiring different and separate security policies (logical firewall provide separation at lower costs)

Context Types

Security appliances operating in multi-context mode include three types of contexts:

- **System execution space**—Shared space where new user contexts are created and physical resources for other contexts are allocated. System execution space is not a regular firewall context and cannot process or secure user traffic (not network interfaces or network settings).

- **Administrative context**—A firewall context created for administrative access to the firewall. Unlike the system execution space, the administrative context does function as a true firewall context, although it is typically used only for administrative tasks.

- **Normal context**—The regular firewall contexts that function as virtual firewalls to handle and secure actual user traffic.

Unsupported Features

Security appliances that run in multi-context mode provide similar functionality to single-mode with the following restrictions:

- Dynamic routing protocols (RIP and OSPF) are not supported. Static routes must be used.

- VPN capabilities are not available in multi-context mode.

- Multicast capabilities are not available in multi-context mode.

- Transparent or routed firewall modes are both supported, but all contexts must run in the same mode (that is, you cannot run some contexts in transparent mode and others in routed mode).

Configuration of Multiple Contexts

On a supported platform with appropriate licensing, you can enable multiple security contexts using the **mode multiple** command.

```
fw(config)# mode multiple
WARNING: This command will change the behavior of the device
WARNING: This command will initiate a Reboot
Proceed with change mode? [confirm] Y
Convert the system configuration? [confirm] Y
!
The old running configuration file will be written to flash
The admin context configuration will be written to flash
The new running configuration file was written to flash
Security context mode: multiple
```

When this command is issued, the firewall prompts the user with warnings as shown in the example. After confirming, the security appliance proceeds with creation of several contexts to allow operation and administration of the security appliance in multi-context mode:

- **System context**—System execution space where new user contexts are created and physical resources for other contexts are allocated.

- **Null context**—A system resource context used internally by the system (not directly accessible).

- **Admin context**—A fully functional firewall context created for administrative access to the firewall.

This process creates two new configuration files:

- **old_running.cfg**—This file contains the configuration of security appliance before the upgrade to multiple context mode and is used to restore the configuration in case you need to revert back to single-context mode.

- **admin.cfg**—This file contains a new configuration for the automatically created Admin context.

The Admin security context:

- Provides policies and interfaces to system execution space (which has no traffic-passing interfaces of its own).

- Is used to obtain configurations for other security contexts and syslog messages.

The current security appliance mode can be displayed if you use the **show mode** command. To display the current configured contexts, use the **show context** command. To switch between different context terminal sessions, use the **changeto** command. To change to system configuration, you use the following command:

```
fw(config)# changeto system
```

To change to a different named context, use the following command:

```
fw(config)# changeto context context_name
```

To create a new context while in system configuration (use the **changeto system** command first if you are not in system configuration), use the **context** command:

```
fw(config)# context my-context
```

To delete a context, use the **no context** command.

You can use the **allocate-interface** command to allocate an interface (physical or logical) to a specific security context. Logical interfaces must be defined in system configuration before they are available for allocation to any other context.

```
fw(config-ctx)# allocate-interface ethernet0
```

When the system creates the admin context, its configuration file is automatically stored in the admin.cfg file in Flash memory of the security appliance. When new security contexts are manually created, you must specify the location where the configuration for the context are stored. The **config-url** command is used to specify this information in system configuration (not from the terminal session of the named context):

```
fw(config-ctx)# config-url flash:/my-context.cfg
```

In addition to Flash memory, you can specify FTP, TFTP, HTTP, or HTTPS URLs when you specify the startup configuration file.

Failover

Cisco security appliances feature active/standby and active/active (active/active with Security Appliance 7.0 software) failover functionality for high availability applications.

Failover Types

Security appliances support two main types of failover (PIX 501 and 506E do not support any form of failover):

- Hardware Failover
  - Provides hardware-level redundancy.
  - If the active unit fails, the standby unit becomes active.
  - Connections are dropped and must be reestablished.
- Stateful Failover
  - Provides hardware-level redundancy.
  - Also maintains state session information on standby unit.
  - If the active unit fails, standby unit becomes active.
  - Connections and session information are maintained during failover.

In addition, failover can be enabled in an active/active configuration or an active/standby configuration. Appropriate licensing for each type of failover is required before it can be enabled.

- Active/active
  - Both appliances in the failover pair actively process traffic.
  - Both appliances in the failover pair serve as a standby unit for the other device.
- Active/standby
  - One appliance is the primary unit, is active, and processes traffic.
  - The other appliance is secondary unit, is in standby mode, and does not process traffic unless the primary unit fails or is administratively failed.

The failover pair must be connected to each other to exchange failover hellos. This failover link can be one of the following:

- **A dedicate serial failover cable**—This option is easy to implement for basic failover (not available with ASA 5500 Series).

- **An Ethernet or Gigabit Ethernet interface on the security appliance**—This option provides the capability to place the failover units farther apart from each other (without the restrictions of the serial failover cable).

In addition, with stateful failover, an Ethernet interface is required for synchronization of state session information between the primary and secondary units. This interface must be dedicated to failover traffic and cannot be combined with a regular network-connectivity interface (it can, however, also function as the LAN-based failover link). This link must be a Fast Ethernet or Gigabit Ethernet interface. The serial failover link cannot be used for this purpose.

If stateful failover is configured for any Gigabit Ethernet interfaces, the failover link must also be a Gigabit Ethernet interface. Otherwise, session information might be lost and stateful failover is not possible.

Failover Requirements

Failover is possible with PIX 515E, 525, 535 and ASA 5510, 5520, and 5540 models with the following requirements:

- Failover can function only on two identical models.

- The failover units in a failover pair should have the same hardware specifications, such as RAM, Flash memory, the number of interfaces, the types of interfaces, and any other hardware component.

- With pre-7.0 security appliance software, the units in a failover pair must have exactly the same version of the software installed. With security appliance software 7.0, the unit must have the same major revision (first number) and minor revision (second number). Different software versions are supported during the upgrade process (assuming they are greater than 7.0 version).

- The units in a failover pair should have the same type of activation key installed. For example, both units should have the Triple Data Encryption Standard/Advanced Encryption Standard (3DES/AES) activation key, or they should both have the DES activation key.

- The units in a failover pair must be in the same operating mode (routed or transparent, single or multiple context).

- If you intend to use stateful failover, you need an Ethernet interface (or Gigabit Ethernet if other Gigabit interfaces are installed and active) for that purpose.

- If you intend to use LAN-based failover, you need an Ethernet interface for that purpose (this can be combined with stateful failover interface).

- Appropriate unrestricted and active/active or active/standby failover licenses are required (you can also use two appliances with unrestricted licenses as a failover pair).

Failover Tests

The following are the four different tests used to assess failover status:

- **Link up/down**—This is a test of the NIC itself. If an interface card is not plugged into an operational network, it is considered failed. For example, the hub or switch has failed, the hub or switch has a failed port, or a cable is unplugged. If this test does not find anything, the network activity test begins.

- **Network activity**—This test is a received network activity test. The security appliance counts all received packets for up to five seconds. If packets are received at any time during this interval, the interface is considered operational and testing stops. If no traffic is received, the ARP test begins.

- **ARP**—The ARP test consists of reading the security appliance's ARP cache for the ten most recently acquired entries. ARP requests are sent one at a time to these machines. After each request, the security appliance counts all received traffic for up to five seconds. If traffic is received, the interface is considered operational. If no traffic is received, an ARP request is sent to the next machine. If at the end of the list no traffic has been received, the ping test begins.

- **Broadcast ping**—The ping test sends out a broadcast ping request. The security appliance then counts all received packets for up to five seconds. If packets are received at any time during this interval, the interface is considered operational and testing stops. If no traffic is received, the testing starts over again with the ARP test.

Serial Cable Failover Configuration

Serial cable failover is only available with the PIX 500 Series appliances and includes the following steps:

- Power off the secondary unit.

- Connect each pair of the corresponding interfaces of the primary and secondary units to the same switch or VLAN as required (for example e0 from both units to the external switch, e1 interface from both units to the internal switch, and so on).

- If you implement stateful failover, connect the stateful failover interfaces on the two units to each other (you can use a crossover cable for this purpose).

- Connect the serial failover cable to the primary unit (use the end marked as Primary).
- To configure the interfaces on the primary unit, use the **ip address** command, and use the **standby** option to specify the address for the standby unit.
- For stateful failover, use the **failover link** and **failover interface ip** commands to configure the interface used for session state information.
- Use the global **failover** command to enable failover.
- Use the **clock set** command to configure the clock on the primary unit.
- For faster failover, use the **failover poll** command to change the failover poll frequency to less than the default value of 15 seconds.
- Use the **write memory** command to save the configuration.
- Power on the secondary unit.
- Configuration from the primary unit is then synchronized to the secondary unit.
- To force a failover event, use the **failover active** command on the standby unit or the **no failover active** command on the active unit.

Active/Standby LAN-Based Failover Configuration

Configuration of LAN-based active/standby includes the following steps:

Step 1   Select an Ethernet interface as the failover link on the two units that are connected to the same VLAN on a switch (enable portfast and disable channeling if enabled for these ports).

Use of a crossover cable is not recommended as the LAN/based failover link.

Leave the secondary unit's failover link disconnected at this point.

Step 2   Configure the primary security appliance for failover :

- Use the **ip address** command with **standby** option to configure the standby IP addresses.
- Use the **failover lan interface** command to designate the interface for failover.
- Use the **failover interface ip** command to assign IP addresses to the failover interface.
- Use the **failover lan enable** command to enable LAN-based failover.
- Use the **failover lan unit primary** command to designate the unit as primary.
- Optionally use the **failover key** command to specify key for encrypted and authentication failover traffic.
- Use the **failover** command to enable failover.

Step 3   Use the **write memory** command to save the primary security appliance's configuration.

Step 4   Configure the secondary security appliance for failover. Note that configuration is identical to the primary with the exception of the **failover lan unit** command. The IP addresses used should be the same as the primary unit.

```
fw(config)# failover lan unit secondary
```

Step 5   Connect the secondary security appliance's LAN-based failover interface to the switch.

Stateful Failover Configuration

With stateful failover, state information is sent to the standby unit over a dedicated Ethernet or Gigabit Ethernet failover link. A crossover cable can be used to connect the stateful failover link between the failover nodes.

The following state information is sent to the standby unit:

- NAT table
- TCP connection states
- UDP connection states
- ARP table
- MAC table (transparent firewall mode)
- IKE and IPSec SA table
- HTTP connection states (when HTTP replication is enabled)
- GTP PDP connection database

To enable HTTP replication, use the **failover replication http** command.

Active/Active LAN-Based Failover Configuration

Active/active failover requires multi-context operation mode on the security appliance failover pair. Configuration of LAN-based active/active includes the following steps:

Step 1   Use the **mode multiple** command to enable multi-context mode.

Step 2   From the system execution space, configure the primary security appliance for failover:

- Use the **failover lan unit primary** command to designate the unit as primary.
- Use the **ip address** command with **standby** option to configure the standby IP addresses.
- Use the **failover lan interface** command to designate the interface for LAN-based failover.
- Use the **failover interface ip** command to assign IP addresses to the failover interface.
- Optionally use the **failover key** command to specify key for encrypted and authentication failover traffic.

- Use the **failover lan enable** command to enable LAN-based failover.

- Use the **failover link** command to designate the interface for stateful failover.

- Use the **failover interface ip** command to assign IP addresses to the stateful failover interface.

Step 3 Define the failover groups using the **failover group** command:

- Use the **primary** or **secondary** commands from the **failover group** subcommand menu to designate primary or secondary status for groups 1 and 2.

- Use the **replication http** command from the **failover group** subcommand menu to optionally specify HTTP session replication for the failover group.

- Use the **preempt** command from the **failover group** subcommand menu to allow preemption of the lower priority active unit.

Step 4 Use the **failover** command to enable failover on the primary unit.

Step 5 Configure the secondary security appliance for failover and use identical configuration to the primary with the exception of the **failover lan unit secondary** command. The IP addresses used should be the same as the primary unit.

```
fw(config)# failover lan unit secondary
```

Step 6 Use the **failover** command to enable failover on the secondary unit. Remaining steps are only required on the primary unit.

Step 7 From the system execution space on the primary unit, use the **interface** command to configure physical and logical (VLAN) interfaces.

Step 8 From the system execution space on the primary unit, use the **context** *context_name* command to enter the configuration subcommand mode for each context:

- Use the **allocate-interface** command to configure and allocate interfaces to appropriate contexts.

- Use the **join-failover-group [1|2]** command to assign specific contexts to each failover group.

Step 9 Use the **changeto context** command to switch to the terminal session of each context:

- Use the **ip address** command with **standby** option to configure the interface and standby IP addresses in each context.

Failover can occur on a group level (contexts in the failover group) or on the unit level (in case of failure of one of the units). When active/active failover is enabled, the **failover active group [1|2]** command can be used to activate a specific group. The **failover active** command can still be used to activate a standby unit.

With active/active or active/passive failover, the **show failover** command displays extensive information about failover configuration and status on each unit or group.

Cisco Adaptive Security Device Manager

Cisco Adaptive Security Device Manager (ASDM) is a browser-based configuration and monitoring tool designed for management of PIX and ASA security devices. ASDM offers a simple graphical interface and does not require extensive command-line interface (CLI) experience from the administrator.

ASDM Features

ASDM is a Java-based application that can be accessed as a downloadable Java applet or downloaded and locally installed on the management workstation for faster startup.

ASDM 5.0 provides support for PIX 500 Series and ASA 5500 series devices that run Security Appliance 7.0 software. PIX 501 and 506E are not supported with Security Appliance 7.0 software and cannot run ASDM 5.0.

All communications between the ASDM and the security appliance are SSL-encrypted to ensure security.

Five ASDM sessions per security appliance are supported in Single Context mode. In Multiple Context mode, five ASDM sessions per context are supported up to a maximum of 32 sessions per physical security appliance.

ASDM Requirements

ASDM 5.0 operation requires the following:

- DES or 3DES activation key to support SSL encryption
- Java plug-in 1.4.2 or 1.5.0 (Microsoft JVM is not supported)
- JavaScript and Java must be enabled on the browser
- SSL support on the browser must be enabled
- Security Appliance 7.0 software version
- ASA 5500 Series or PIX 500 Series security appliance (PIX 501 and 506E excluded)

If you run PIX Security Appliance software version 6.3 or earlier, you can use the appropriate version of the PIX Device Manager (PDM):

- Software version 6.0 or 6.1 — Use PDM 1.0 or 1.1
- Software version 6.2 — Use PDM 2.0 or 2.1
- Software version 6.3 — Use PDM 3.0

ASDM 5.0 supports the Windows, Sun Solaris, and Linux platforms with the following requirements:

- Minimum Windows requirements:
  - Windows 2000 (Service Pack 3) or Windows XP operating systems
  - Internet Explorer 6.0 with Java plug-in 1.4.2 or 1.5.0, or Netscape Communicator 7.1 or 7.2, with Java plug-in 1.4.2 or 1.5.0

— Pentium or Pentium-compatible processor running at 450 MHz or higher

— Minimum 256 MB of RAM

— 1024 x 768 pixel display with at least 256 colors

— Windows 3.1, 95, 98, ME, or NT4 are not supported

- SUN Solaris requirements:

  — Sun Solaris 2.8 or 2.9 running CDE Window Manager

  — SPARC microprocessor

  — Mozilla 1.7.3 with Java plug-in 1.4.2 or 1.5.0

  — Minimum 256 MB of RAM

  — 1024 x 768 pixel display with at least 256 colors

- Linux requirements:

  — Red Hat Linux 9.0 or Red Hat Linux WS, version 3 running GNOME or KDE

  — Mozilla 1.7.3 with Java plug-in 1.4.2 or 1.5.0

  — Minimum 256 MB of RAM

  — 1024 x 768 pixel display with at least 256 colors

Configuring the Security Appliance to Use ASDM

Before ASDM can be used to manage the security appliance, you must configure the following:

- Time (**clock set** command)

- Hostname (**hostname** command)

- Domain name (**domain-name** command)

- Inside interface IP address (**ip address** command) of the security appliance

You also need to enable the internal HTTP server and allow HTTP access to the security appliance from your workstation or subnet:

```
fw(config)# http 10.1.1.11 255.255.255.255 inside
fw(config)# http server enable
```

Accessing ASDM

After initial configuration is completed on the security appliance, you can access ASDM using the URL https://asa_ip_address on a supported browser. For example:

```
https://10.1.1.1
```

After ASDM is launched, the home screen is displayed. The following sections are included in the ASDM home screen:

- **Menu bar**—Provides access to File, Options, Tools, Wizards, and Help menu items.

- **Main toolbar**—Provides access to Home, Configuration, and Monitoring windows, and search, context-sensitive help, and save functions. If the security appliance is operating in multi-context mode, context-specific toolbar items are added including the Context button (provides access to user contexts), context drop-down menu (which allow selection of individual named contexts), and the System button (selects the system execution space).

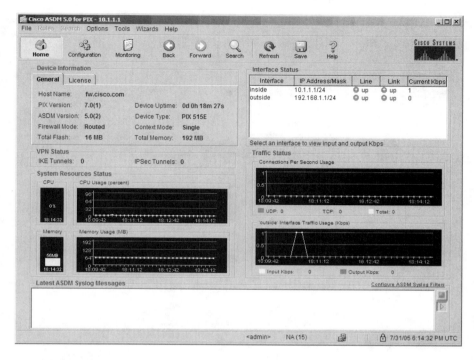

- **Device Information box**—Uses General and License tabs to display security appliance information. The General tab displays information about the security appliance hardware and software in use. The License tab displays encryption level and licensed features on the security appliance.
- **VPN Status box**—Displays the number of IKE and IPSec tunnels established on the security device.
- **System Resources Status box**—Displays CPU and memory usage graphs.
- **Interface Status box**—Displays interface-specific information including IP address and mask, line and link status, and current kbps.
- **Traffic Status box**—Displays TCP and UDP connections graphs.
- **Latest ASDM Syslog Messages box**—Displays the most recent ten system messages generated by the security appliance.

ASDM Configuration

The ASDM provides several wizards to greatly simplify configuration tasks on the security appliance. Wizards available include:

- Startup Wizard
- VPN Wizards
  - Site-to-site VPNs
  - Remote-access VPNs

Standard configurations are performed if you access the main configuration page.

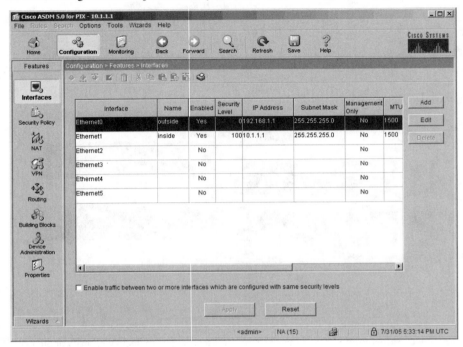

Features that can be configured on this page include:

- Interfaces—Configure logical and physical interfaces (**Configuration > Features > Interfaces**)

- Security Policy (**Configuration > Features > Security Policy**)

  — Access Rules
  — AAA Rules
  — Filter Rules
  — Service Policy Rules
  — Ethertype Rules (transparent firewall mode)

- NAT (**Configuration > Features > NAT**)

  — Translation Rules
  — Translation Exemption Rules

- VPN (**Configuration > Features > VPN**)

  — General VPN Options
    VPN System Options
    Client Update
    Tunnel Group

Group Policy

Default Tunnel Gateway

— IKE

Global Parameters

Policies

Certificate Group Matching (Policy and Rule)

— IPSec

IPSec Rules

Tunnel Policy

Transform Sets

Pre-Fragmentation

— IP Address Management

Assignment

IP Pools

— Load Balancing (ASA 5500)

— WebVPN (ASA 5500)

WebVPN Access

Servers and URLs

Port Forwarding

Homepage

Proxies

WebVPN AAA

NetBIOS Servers

ACLs

— E-Mail Proxy (ASA 5500)

• IPS (**Configuration > Features > IPS**)

— Sensor Setup

Network

Allowed Hosts

SSH

Certificates

Time

Users

— Interface Configuration

Interfaces

Interface Pairs

Bypass

Traffic Flow Notifications

Virtual Link

Filtering

Redistribution

Summary Address

— Multicast

IGMP (Protocol, Access Group, Join Group, and Static Group)

PIM (Protocol, Rendezvous Points, Route Tree, and Request Filter)

MRoute

- Building Blocks (**Configuration > Features > Building Blocks**)

  — Hosts/Networks

  — Inspect Maps (FTP, GTP, HTTP, MGCP, SNMP)

  — TCP Maps

  — Time Ranges

- Device Administration (**Configuration > Features > Device Administration**)

  — Device

  — Password

  — AAA Access

  — User Accounts

  — Banner

  — Console

  — ASDM/HTTPS

  — Telnet

  — Secure Copy

  — Secure Shell

  — Management Access

  — SMTP

  — SNMP

  — ICMP Rules

  — TFTP Server

  — Clock

  — NTP

  — Boot Image/Configuration

  — FTP Mode

  — Certificate

  — Key Pair

  — Trustpoint

  Configuration

  Import

  Export

— Authentication

— Enrollment

— Import Certificate

— Manage Certificates

• Properties (**Configuration > Features > Properties**)

— AAA Setup

AAA Server Group

AAA Servers

Auth. Prompt

— Advanced

Anti-Spoofing

Connection Settings

Fragment

TCP Options

Timeouts

— ARP Inspection (transparent firewall mode)

— ARP Static Table

— Bridging (transparent firewall mode)

MAC Address Table

MAC Learning

— Auto Update

— DHCP Services

DHCP Server

DHCP Relay

— DNS Client

— Failover—Single Mode

— Failover— Multiple Mode, Routed

— Failover— Multiple Mode, Transparent

— History/Metrics

— HTTP/HTTPS

— IP Audit

IP Audit Policy

IP Audit Signature

— Logging

Logging Setup

Event Lists

Logging Filters

Syslog Setup

Syslog Servers

E-Mail Setup

— Priority Queue

— Management IP

— SSL

— SUNRPC Server

— URL Filtering

ASDM Monitoring

ASDM monitoring functions are accessed if you click on the Monitoring button on the Main toolbar.

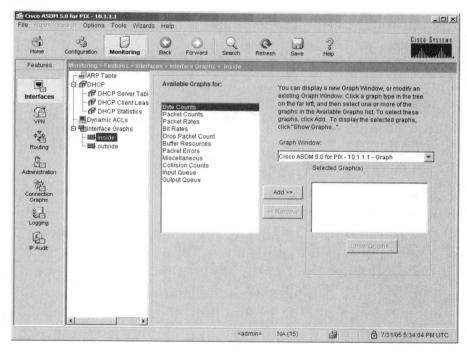

Specific monitoring features accessible from this page include:

- Interfaces
    - ARP Tables
    - DHCP
        DHCP Server Table
        DHCP Client Lease Information
        DHCP Statistics

- — Dynamic ACLs
- — Interface Graphs
- VPN
  - — VPN Statistics
    Sessions
    Encryption Statistics
    Protocol Statistics
    Global IKE/IPSec Statistics
    Crypto Statistics
  - — VPN Connections Graphs
    IPSec Tunnels
- Routing
  - — Routes
  - — OSPF LSAs (Type 1, 2, 3, 4, 5, 7)
  - — OSPF Neighbors
- Administration
  - — ASDM/HTTPS Sessions
  - — Telnet Sessions
  - — AAA Local Locked Out
  - — Secure Shell Sessions
  - — Authenticated Users
  - — AAA Servers
  - — CRL
  - — DNS Cache
  - — System Graphs (Blocks, CPU, and Memory)
  - — Failover (Status and Graphs)
- Connection Graphs
  - — Xlates
  - — Perfmon
- Logging
  - — Live Log
  - — Log Buffer
- IP Audit

Advanced Inspection and Prevention Security Services Module

ASA 5500 Series security appliance capabilities can be expanded if you use an included Security Service Module (SSM) expansion slot. Currently, two Advanced Inspection and Prevention SSM modules (AIP-SSM) are available:

- AIP-SSM-10

- AIP-SSM-20

Both modules provide advanced intrusion detection and prevention capabilities to the ASA security appliances.

The following table lists the technical specifications for each model:

Feature	SSM-AIP-10	SSM-AIP-20
Concurrent Threat Mitigation Throughput (Firewall + Anti-x Services)	150 Mbps with ASA 5510 225 Mbps with ASA 5520	375 Mbps with ASA 5520 450 Mbps with ASA 5540
Memory	1 GB	2 GB
Flash	256 MB	256 MB

Each AIP-SSM module includes a 10/100/1000 Ethernet port, primarily used for management access to the module.

Operation Modes

The AIP-SSM modules can be configured to in one of the following two IPS operation modes:

- **In-line mode**—As the name implies, the AIP-SSM module is inserted in the traffic flow in this mode of operation, and packets must traverse its interface before they reach their destination. Because the module is directly in the data path for all traffic, it can instantly drop packets that are deemed malicious or against the active security policy.

  However, because traffic flows through the AIP-SSM module, it can become a single point of failure and can also result in somewhat degraded performance.

  In-line mode is more typically used with IPS devices.

- **Promiscuous mode**—In this mode, the AIP-SSM is not directly inserted in the path of traffic. Instead, it "eavesdrops" on ongoing activity because it examines a copy of the traffic flowing through the ASA security appliance. In this mode, the AIP-SSM module cannot immediately stop malicious activity because it must rely on other in-line devices to take corrective action.

  Promiscuous mode, however, is less likely to impact performance of the network and is not a single point of failure.

  Promiscuous mode is more typically used with IDS devices.

Another important operation mode variable is the failure mode. AIP-SSM modules can be configured with fail-open or fail-closed options. When configured for fail-closed, all traffic is disallowed if the module fails for any reason. When configured for fail-open, traffic is allowed if there is a failure in the module. If fail-closed is selected while operating in in-line mode, any failure of the module halts all traffic.

Intrusion Prevention Configuration

AIP-SSM modules must be initialized before they can be used to inspect the traffic. The initialization process includes the following steps:

Step 1   Install a software image on the AIP-SSM using TFTP.

Step 2   Initialize the AIP-SSM module.

Step 3   Configure IPS policies on the ASA security appliance.

Installing Software Image

Before you install software on the module, you can use the **show module detail** command and specify the number of the module.

```
fw# show module 1 detail
```

This command displays information about the module including model, hardware, firmware, software versions, and module status.

The **hw-module module recover** command defines the parameters for a software image download to the module (module slot number, TFTP URL for the recovery image, IP address and VLAN of the SSM management interface, and gateway address). The **hw-module module recover boot** command is then used to begin the TFTP download of the image to the SSM.

AIP-SSM Initialization

After the software is loaded and the boot process of the AIP-SSM is completed, you can telnet to the module using the session 1 command from the ASA security appliance. Initial login uses:

```
Username: cisco
Password: cisco
```

After a password change is completed, you can use the **setup** command to initialize the sensor and specify hostname, management IP address, and IP address of hosts or networks with management access to the SSM.

Configuring IPS Policies

After the AIP-SSM module is online and initialized, IPS policies can be configured to enable inspection of traffic using the module. Use CLI or ASDM methods to configure IPS policies. When the AIP-SSM module is installed, ASDM Configuration page includes an IPS option to allow configuration of IPS settings.

As outlined earlier, to enable an inspection policy, you must:

- Define a class-map to identify the traffic flow for inspection.
- Define a policy map to specify the inspection action for the class map.
- Enable the policy map using a service policy.

You can also define promiscuous or in-line operational modes.

Security Appliance Management

Cisco security appliances provide various modes of management access and provide robust AAA features to properly control management access to the devices. They also provide software, license, and configuration file management capabilities.

Management Access to Security Appliance

There are several options for management access to the security appliance:

- Console
- Telnet
- SSH
- HTTPS (ASDM)

Console access is enabled by default and requires physical access to the security appliance via the console port.

To configure telnet access, use the **telnet** command:

```
fw(config)# telnet 10.1.1.0 255.255.255.0 inside
```

To configure a telnet password, use the **passwd** command:

```
fw(config)# passwd mypass
```

The **telnet timeout** command can also be used to terminate inactive sessions after the timeout period is elapsed.

SSH uses RSA public key cryptography to encrypt transmissions between the security appliance and the administrator workstation. SSH access is more secure than telnet and should be used in place of telnet in most scenarios. To enable SSH, use the **ssh** command:

```
fw(config)# ssh 10.1.1.0 255.255.255.0 inside
```

It also requires you to use the **crypto key generate rsa** command to generate RSA keys on the security appliance. You must also use the **hostname** and **domain-name** commands to configure the security appliance host and domain names to generate the RSA keys. If existing RSA keys are present, use **crypto key zeroize rsa** command to delete them before generating new RSA keys.

To enable HTTP access, use the **http server enable** command. The **http** command is then used to specify permitted hosts or subnets:

```
fw(config)# http 10.1.1.0 255.255.255.0 inside
```

Managing User Level Access

To control administrative access to the security appliance, use:

- Enable-level command authorization (privilege levels 0 through 15)
- Local database command authorization
- ACS-based command authorization

Enable-level command authorization involves the creation of enable passwords with different privilege levels between 0 and 15. You can then assign specific commands to a privilege level. Users logging in have access to commands at or below their privilege level. For example, a user logging in with a level 12 password has access to all commands with privilege levels 0 to 12, although not 13, 14, or 15. For example, a user logging in with the enable password of "pass12" has access to the **show crypto** commands, although not the configuration mode **crypto** commands with the following configuration:

```
fw(config)# enable password pass12 level 12
fw(config)# privilege show level 12 command crypto
fw(config)# privilege configure level 14 command crypto
```

With local database command authorization, the **username** command is used to create user accounts in the security appliance's local database (LOCAL). Instead of assigning privilege levels to the enable passwords, they are assigned to the user account in the local database. You still use the **privilege** command to assign different privilege levels to different commands. Local database command authorization is then enabled when you use the **aaa authentication** and **aaa authorization** commands (you cannot have authorization without authentication).

```
fw(config)# username user12 password pass12 level 12
fw(config)# privilege show level 12 command crypto
fw(config)# privilege configure level 14 command crypto
fw(config)# aaa authentication enable console LOCAL
fw(config)# aaa authorization command LOCAL
```

ACS-based command authorization uses the ACS server database for user accounts and list of commands they are permitted to use. You can then enable command authorization as follows:

```
fw(config)# aaa-server myacs protocol tacacs+
fw(config-aaa-server-group)# aaa-server myacs (inside) host 10.1.1.11 mykey
 timeout 10
fw(config-aaa-server-group)# aaa authentication enable console myacs
fw(config)# aaa authorization command myacs
```

Password Recovery

If a security appliance becomes inaccessible because of an incorrect AAA configuration or a lost or forgotten administrative password, password recovery may be the only option to restore access.

PIX 500 Series and ASA 5500 Series security appliances provide a password recovery options for these situations.

To recover the password on a PIX 500 Series security appliance, you must download an appropriate password lockout utility from Cisco.com. The required file depends on the platform and software version in use:

Security Appliance Software Version	Password Lockout Utility File
7.0	np70.bin
6.3	np63.bin
6.2	np62.bin
6.1	np61.bin

Security Appliance Software Version	Password Lockout Utility File
6.0	np60.bin
5.3	np53.bin
5.2	np52.bin
5.1	np51.bin

After the file is downloaded, you can regain access to the PIX security appliance using the following steps:

Step 1   Make a console connection to the appliance.

Step 2   Power off the appliance and turn back on to reboot.

Step 3   Press the Escape key to interrupt the normal flash boot process. This puts you in the Monitor mode.

Step 4   Use the Monitor mode commands to download (via TFTP) the password lockout utility to the security appliance.

Step 5   When prompted, answer **yes** to erase the password.

Step 6   You can now access the appliance if you use the default login password "cisco," the blank enable password, and if you reset the passwords as necessary.

Note that if the **no service password-recovery** command was part of the PIX security appliance configuration, you can regain access to the appliance only after all flash files are erased.

Password recovery on ASA 5500 Series security appliances does not use the password lockout utility. Instead, you must hit the Escape key during the normal flash boot process and modify the configuration registers (similar to IOS routers) to enter the Monitor mode. If the **no service password-recovery** command was part of the configuration, again, you can regain access to the security appliance only if you erase all flash files.

File Management

You can use several file management commands to work with the files stored on the flash memory of the security appliance.

- Use the **dir** command to display the current files.

- Use the **copy** command to copy a file from one location to another, such as from a TFTP server to flash memory.

- Use the **more** command to display the contents of a file.

- Use the **mkdir** command to create a directory on the flash memory to better manage multiple configuration files or system images.

- Use the **copy [tftp|ftp|http|https] flash:/** command to copy a new image to the security appliance.

- Use the **copy [tftp|ftp|http|https] flash:**/*asd_image_name* command to copy a new ASDM image to the security appliance.

- Use the **asdm image flash:**/*asd_image_name* command to specify the ASDM image that the security appliance should use.

Activation Keys

A new activation key can be required for certain image updates or to enable new licensed features on the security appliance. To install a new activation key, use the **activation-key** command along with the appropriate four-element or five-element hexadecimal string Cisco provides you.

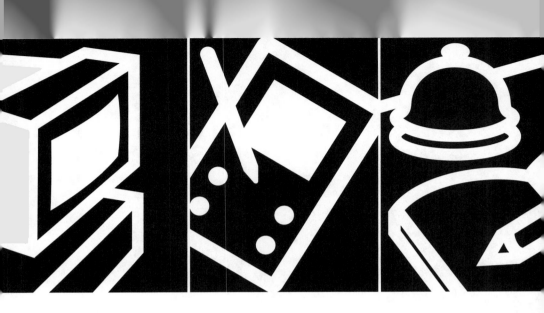

Part IV

CCSP: Implementing Cisco Intrusion Prevention Systems (IPS) Flash Cards

The flash cards in this part of the book focus on preparing you for the Implementing Cisco Intrusion Prevention Systems (IPS) exam (642-532) toward achieving your CCSP certification. Over 150 more questions for this section of the book can be found on the CD-ROM accompanying this book. The flash cards address specific topic areas for this exam and are organized as follows:

- **Section 1: Network Security Overview**—Tests your knowledge of security concepts including policy, attacks, and threats.

- **Section 2: IPS Overview**—Tests your knowledge of IPS and IDS concepts.

- **Section 3: Sensor CLI Activities**—Tests your knowledge of command-line interaction with sensors.

- **Section 4: IPS Device Manager (IDM)**—Tests your knowledge of GUI-based interaction with Cisco sensors.

- **Section 5: IPS Signature Concepts**—Tests your knowledge of IPS signatures and signature engines.

- **Section 6: Sensor Tuning**—Tests your knowledge of signature tuning for optimal performance and information.

- **Section 7: Sensor Blocking**—Tests your knowledge of how to protect network resources from attackers by using blocking as a signature response action.

Section 1
Network Security Overview

Question 1

Describe a closed network.

Question 2

Name two reasons why attacking systems has become easier over the years.

Question 3

What one thing defines the tactical steps for improved security?

Question 7 Answer

A closed network is one that is not connected to other networks, such as the Internet or a business partner's network.

Question 8 Answer

Two reasons why attacking systems has become easier over the years are:

- Widely available software development tools and easy-to-use operating systems.
- The Internet serves as place for attackers to share information and as a spring board for the attacks themselves.

Question 9 Answer

A security policy

Question 4

Name four of the reasons why a security policy is necessary.

Question 5

What is the Cisco Security Wheel?

Question 6

Describe an unstructured threat.

Question 10 Answer

The following are reasons why a security policy is necessary:

- Provides an audit benchmark
- Articulates a security framework
- Articulates organizational security consensus
- Defines permissible and nonpermissible activities
- Defines security incident handling
- Defines detailed implementation procedures
- Demonstrates organizational "due care"

Question 11 Answer

The Cisco Security Wheel is a four-step process to promote and maintain network security.

Question 12 Answer

An unstructured threat comes primarily from inexperienced individuals who use hacking tools available on the Internet (script kiddies).

Question 7

What type of attack is an attempt to map systems and services?

Question 8

Name two reconnaissance activities.

Question 9

What is meant by a port redirection attack?

Question 13 Answer

A reconnaissance attack

Question 14 Answer

The following are reconnaissance activities:

- Ping scans
- Port scans
- Research on targets from public sources

Question 15 Answer

It is an attack that uses an intermediate host that the target trusts as a launching point for an attack.

Question 10

What is IP spoofing?

Question 11

What is a blind spoof?

Question 12

What is a bidirectional spoof?

Question 16 Answer

IP spoofing occurs when an attacker alters his host IP address to mask his real IP address.

Question 17 Answer

In a blind spoof, the attacker does not need or want replies from the target and sends crafted packets with a false address.

Question 18 Answer

In a bidirectional spoof, the attacker wants replies from the target, although she wants to mask her real address. Therefore, she must control the routing table of an intermediate router to forward forged packets back to her real IP address.

Question 13

Which RFC describes network filtering that allows only source packets to be sent to your ISP with network ranges you control and receive packets from your ISP with destination network ranges you control?

Question 14

What does the acronym TLS stand for?

Question 19 Answer

RFC 2827

Question 20 Answer

Transport Layer Security

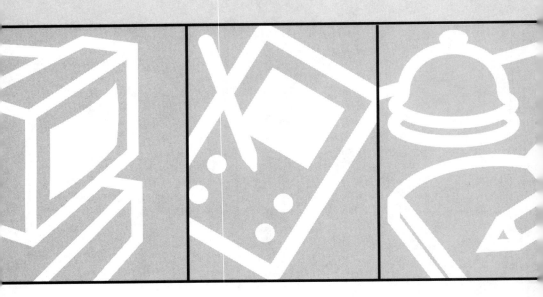

Section 2
IPS Overview

Question 1

What does the acronym IPS stand for?

Question 2

What does the acronym IDS stand for?

Question 3

Name the two high-level objectives of IPS and IDS.

Question 1 Answer

Intrusion prevention system

Question 2 Answer

Intrusion detection system

Question 3 Answer

Two high-level objectives of IPS and IDS are:

- Malicious and unauthorized activity detection
- Definable actions in response to inappropriate network use

Question 4

Which detection mode can stop a trigger packet?

Question 5

Describe profile-based detection.

Question 6

What is meant by signature fidelity?

Question 4 Answer

IPS can stop a trigger packet. A trigger packet is the first packet in an attack flow. Because it is an inline detection technology, the first and subsequent packets can be stopped. With IDS, the first packet cannot be because IDS is outside of the packet stream. Subsequent packets can be stopped with blocking.

Question 5 Answer

Profile-based detection uses statistical analysis to determine if traffic patterns are outside of normal bounds.

Question 6 Answer

Signature fidelity is a confidence rating of signature accuracy and the likelihood that it will not produce a false positive.

Question 7

List two reasons to use IPS bypass mode.

Question 8

Which IPS sensor appliances are diskless?

Question 9

Which IPS unit can monitor for unauthorized activity inside of an IPSec tunnel?

Question 7 Answer

Reasons to use IPS bypass mode include:

- System troubleshooting
- Enables live sensor software upgrades

Question 8 Answer

All current generation appliances are diskless design, including the 4215, 4240, and 4255.

Question 9 Answer

No current IPS unit can decrypt and analyze the encrypted data traffic within an IPSec tunnel. The NM-CIDS can monitor IPSec traffic that is terminated and decrypted at the router, although this is different from monitoring an encrypted stream.

Question 10

Which IPS unit does not have a physical command and control interface?

Question 11

How does the IPS feature set differ if you compare the IDSM-2 for the Catalyst 6500 to the 4255 appliance?

Question 12

Which IPS unit allows monitoring via the command and control port?

Question 10 Answer

The IDSM-2 for the catalyst 6500 chassis does not have a physical management interface.

Question 11 Answer

They do not differ.

Question 12 Answer

None. The command and control port is dedicated to sensor management.

Question 13

Which sensor interface has an IP address?

Question 14

What is the Cisco HIPS solution?

Question 15

Where is CSA installed?

Question 13 Answer

The command and control interface

Question 14 Answer

The CSA or Cisco Security Agent

Question 15 Answer

CSA is installed as an agent on a host or server that requires a safeguard.

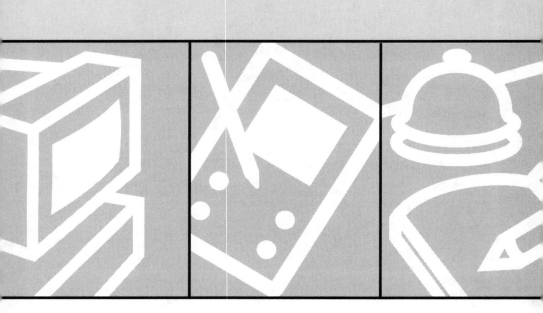

Section 3
Sensor CLI Activities

Question 1

Which monitoring interfaces can be used for sensor management?

Question 2

Which sensor interfaces can you use to reach the command-line interface (CLI)?

Question 3

List the three most important tasks you must perform via a serial console CLI session before you use the IDM for GUI-based sensor management?

Question 1 Answer

None. Monitoring interfaces do not have IP addresses assigned to them and are strictly used for detection.

Question 2 Answer

The command and control network interface and the serial console interface.

Question 3 Answer

The three most important tasks you must perform via a serial console CLI session before you use the IDM for GUI-based sensor management are:

- Assign the sensor's command and control interface an IP address and subnet mask, so that it is accessible
- Assign a default gateway
- Specify trusted hosts permitted to interact with the sensor.

Question 4

Which CLI command is used to install a newer version of sensor software?

Question 5

Which CLI command is used to initially configure a sensor?

Question 6

Which CLI command displays the network path to a remote host?

Question 4 Answer

The **upgrade** command

Question 5 Answer

The **setup** command

Question 6 Answer

The **trace** command

Question 7

You use the CLI and want to know the sensor's software version. Which command can you use to find the version?

Question 7 Answer

The **show version** command

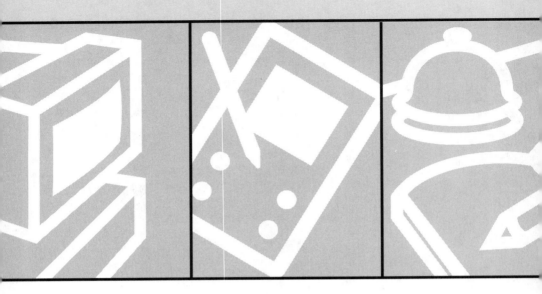

Section 4
IPS Device Manager (IDM)

Question 1

What does the acronym IDM stand for?

Question 2

What is the IDM?

Question 3

What browser plug-in is critical for the operation of the IDM on a client computer?

Question 1 Answer

Intrusion Prevention System Device Manager

Question 2 Answer

The IDM is a web-based Java GUI application used to configure and manage a sensor via the network command and control interface.

Question 3 Answer

Java

Question 4

Which security transport does the IDM use by default?

Question 5

What network protocol is used to get sensor alarms to an IDM?

Question 6

When monitoring data travels from the sensor to the IDM client, does the sensor push the data or does the client pull the data?

Question 4 Answer

Transport Layer Security (TLS)

Question 5 Answer

Security Device Event Exchange (SDEE)

Question 6 Answer

The IDM queries a sensor's Event Store on an ad-hoc basis or continually for real-time monitoring. The client station always pulls data from the sensor, as opposed to the sensor pushing the data to the IDM.

Question 7

Which certificate authority signs the digital certificate generated by a sensor?

Question 8

What are the four types of user account roles?

Question 9

How many users accounts can be assigned to the service role?

Question 7 Answer

The sensor itself signs the certificate, therefore it is a self-signed certificate.

Question 8 Answer

The four types of user account roles are:

- Administrator
- Operator
- Viewer
- Service

Question 9 Answer

One

Question 10

Which account role cannot log into the IDM?

Question 11

Which two account roles can tune signatures?

Question 12

Which account role can create and edit the Service account role?

Question 10 Answer

The service role

Question 11 Answer

Administrator and operator

Question 12 Answer

The administrator role

Question 13

Where are signature alerts stored?

Question 14

How does the IDM learn of a new alert stored in the Event Store?

Question 13 Answer

In the sensor's Event Store

Question 14 Answer

The IDM actively queries the sensor and pulls the alerts from the Event Store.

Section 5
IPS Signature Concepts

Question 1

What is a tuned signature?

Question 2

What is a custom signature?

Question 3

Which types of signatures can be deleted from the sensor?

Question 1 Answer

If one or more built-in signature parameters are modified, it is considered a tuned signature.

Question 2 Answer

If a new signature is built from scratch or is one based upon a copy of a built-in signature, it is considered a custom signature.

Question 3 Answer

Signatures cannot be deleted, although they can be retired or disabled.

Question 4

When a signature is retired, how does it affect the sensor?

Question 5

What is the NSDB?

Question 6

Describe sensor simple pattern matching.

Question 4 Answer

It saves sensor memory resources.

Question 5 Answer

The NSDB is the Network Security Database (NSDB), a complete description of signatures, exploits, vulnerabilities, and benign triggers.

Question 6 Answer

Simple pattern matching occurs when a sensor seeks a particular string of characters in a single packet.

Question 7

Describe sensor stateful pattern matching.

Question 8

Describe sensor heuristic analysis.

Question 9

Describe sensor protocol anomaly.

Question 7 Answer

Stateful pattern matching occurs when a sensor seeks a particular string of characters across multiple packets.

Question 8 Answer

Heuristic analysis occurs when a sensor uses statistical analysis to determine if combinations of observed communications amount to an attack.

Question 9 Answer

Sensor protocol anomaly analysis occurs when a sensor looks for deviations from standard RFC protocol use.

Question 10

What is a response action?

Question 11

What is alert summarization?

Question 12

Describe a fidelity rating.

Question 10 Answer

It defines what the sensor does if the signature fires.

Question 11 Answer

It lumps multiple alerts into a single alert to help avoid information overload.

Question 12 Answer

It is a rating of how accurate this signature tends to be based on how often it tends to produce false positives.

Question 13

To what extent is IPv6 supported on a Cisco 5.0 sensor?

Question 14

What is the difference between Deny connection inline and Deny attacker inline.

Question 15

Which alarm throttling setting creates an Event Store entry for every occurrence of a signature fire?

Question 13 Answer

It enables analysis of IPv4 packets within IPv6 packets.

Question 14 Answer

Deny connection inline drops all TCP packets from an attacker related to a single session, whereas **deny attacker inline** drops all packets, regardless of the type from a single attacker for a specified time period.

Question 15 Answer

FireAll

Question 16

Which alarm throttling setting waits until the end of the ThrottleInterval before it creates a single Event Store entry for all occurrences of a signature fire during the ThrottleInterval?

Question 17

What is the difference between GlobalSummarize and Summarize?

Question 18

What are the four parts to the EventCount key?

Question 16 Answer

FireOnce

Question 17 Answer

GlobalSummarize behaves like the Summarize setting, however, it consolidates identical alarms for all IP address and layer 4 port combinations, and not just unique combinations.

Question 18 Answer

AaBb is defined as: A = source IP, a = source port, B = destination IP, b = destination port

Question 19

What is an IPS engine?

Question 20

What type of tunable parameters are shared across multiple engines?

Question 21

What type of tunable parameter is specific to an engine?

Question 19 Answer

Sensor signature engines are the internal software processes designed to examine the many types of flows that can occur on a network for the purpose of spotting unauthorized activity.

Question 20 Answer

Master parameters

Question 21 Answer

Local parameter

Question 22

What are the two major components of an engine?

Question 23

What is the purpose of the Atomic engine?

Question 24

What is the purpose of the Meta engine?

Question 22 Answer

The parser and the inspector

Question 23 Answer

Inspects individual packets for abnormality

Question 24 Answer

Provides the "intelligence" for event correlation as alerts are noted by one or more engines within a finite time interval

Section 6
Sensor Tuning

Question 1

Why are sensors tuned?

Question 2

Name three things an administrator should know before he tunes a sensor.

Question 3

What is reassembly?

Question 1 Answer

To mold their operation to the unique requirements of the environment and to get the best possible monitoring data and protection

Question 2 Answer

Three things an administrator should know before he tunes a sensor are:

- Organizational security policy
- System boundaries and topology
- General security stance
- An idea of "normal" traffic flow
- Types of applications running
- Operating systems

Question 3 Answer

Reassembly occurs when the sensor reassembles fragmented IP packets or segmented TCP streams.

Question 4

What is IP logging?

Question 5

Describe the concept of an event action override.

Question 6

What is the purpose of an event action filter?

Question 4 Answer

IP logging is a sensor response action to a signature firing. It can log the IP packets of the attacker, the victim, or both. Logging can be set to happen in terms of minutes, number of packets, or bytes.

Question 5 Answer

An event action override is a globally assigned action that is carried out if an event occurs and the assigned risk rating is at a particular level.

Question 6 Answer

Filters are methods to reduce the amount of alert noise that shows up on the monitoring console.

Question 7

Name the three types of filters.

Question 7 Answer

The three types of filters are:

- Event summarization
- Simple signature aggregation
- Timed-interval

Section 7
Sensor Blocking

Question 1

What is blocking?

Question 2

What are the two types of blocks?

Question 3

What is a managed device?

Question 1 Answer

Blocking is an IPS signature response action that prevents an attacker who has triggered a signature from further access to his target.

Question 2 Answer

Block connection and Block host

Question 3 Answer

A Cisco device that modifies its ACLs to block or unblock

Question 4

What is a blocking sensor?

Question 5

What is a managed interface?

Question 6

To create a block, what command does a sensor issue to a PIX?

Question 4 Answer

A Cisco sensor that instructs a managed device to place or remove a block

Question 5 Answer

The interface on a managed device where the blocking entry is applied

Question 6 Answer

The **shun** command

Question 7

What is the default blocking interval time period?

Question 8

What is a pre-block ACL?

Question 9

What is a post-block ACL?

Question 7 Answer

30 minutes

Question 8 Answer

ACL entries that always appear at the top before dynamic blocking entries and are used to consistently permit or deny traffic.

Question 9 Answer

ACL entries that always appear at the bottom after dynamic blocking entries and enable additional traffic permits or denies

Question 10

What is a master blocking sensor?

Question 11

What is a block forwarding sensor?

Question 12

What is the number of master-blocking sensors to which block forwarding sensors can forward alerts?

Question 10 Answer

A master blocking sensor maintains connectivity to the perimeter devices and issues blocking commands on behalf of all block-forwarding sensors.

Question 11 Answer

A sensor that forwards all blocking requests to a master-blocking sensor

Question 12 Answer

Block-forwarding sensors can forward block requests to a maximum of ten master-blocking sensors.

CCSP: Implementing Cisco Intrusion Prevention Systems (IPS) Quick Reference Sheets

Network Security Overview

This section broadly describes fundamental technology security concepts, including security policies, the Cisco Security Wheel, why policies are created, security threats, and sample network attacks.

Please note that there is some overlap of content in the Cisco CCSP certification courses and corresponding exams. We chose to make each section of this book stand on its own, and we covered the material for each exam independently, so that you can focus on each exam without the need to reference a common topic from a different exam's section. Becuase of this, you might notice redundant coverage of topics in certain sections of this book.

The Need for Network Security

Networked systems must be designed and implemented with security in mind because most contemporary systems are interlinked or "open" in contrast to a previous time when systems were "closed" islands. This interlinking, often demanded by business processes and information exchange, increases the risk that system vulnerabilities are attacked and exploited by threats. Comprehensive network security safeguards are needed because attacking systems has become easier for two reasons:

- Software development tools and easy-to-use operating systems provided attackers with a basis to develop attack tools.

- The Internet allows attackers to distribute attack tools and related attack techniques, as well as gain the necessary connectivity required for the attack.

The trend is toward more sophisticated attack tools that require less technical aptitudes to operate. This creates more opportunities for attacks.

Security within a system is important for the following reasons:

- Digital data exchange among businesses is crucial to an economy, and these avenues must be protected from interruption, because the potential for economic risk is great.
- Private data often travels via insecure networks, and precautions must be taken to prevent it from corruption or change.
- Government regulations often dictate standards for information assurance compliance, especially in publicly held organizations.

Network Security Policy

An overall security policy should be the strategic vision that drives the tactical steps used for its implementation. To be effective, network security must be a continuous process, and it must always be built around a security policy. The policy is defined first, and the processes and procedures to support that policy are design around it. RFC 2196, *Site Security Handbook,* describes a security policy as, "...a formal statement of the rules by which people who are given access to an organization's technology and information assets must abide."

Why is a security policy necessary?

- When implemented, provides a benchmark against which you can audit
- Articulates an overall framework for security
- Articulates an organizational consensus for security
- Defines permissible and nonpermissible activities
- Defines how security incidents are handled
- Defines detailed procedures (as required) to implement the overall strategy
- Demonstrates organizational "due care"

A continuous security process is most effective because it promotes re-testing and reapplying updated security measures on a continuous basis. The Cisco Security Wheel provides a four-step process to promote and maintain network security:

Step 1 **Secure**—Implement security safeguards, such as firewalls, identification and authentication systems, and encryption with the intent to prevent unauthorized access to network systems.

Step 2 **Monitor**—Continuously monitor the network for security policy violations.

Step 3 **Test**—Perform tests to evaluate the effectiveness of the in-place security safeguards, such as periodic system vulnerability analysis and application and operating system hardening review.

Step 4 **Improve**—Collect and analyze information from the monitoring and testing phases to improve overall security. This allows you to make judgments on ways to improve your security's effectiveness.

Security policies can be as simple as one document, or they might consist of many documents that describe every aspect of security. The organization's needs and any regulations that the organization must adhere to drive the level of detail. A comprehensive security policy describes some of the following concepts in writing:

- A statement of authority and scope that defines the policy's sponsor and its bounds.
- A definition of organizational information and physical assets, along with their relative values.
- Risk to those assets based upon threats, and the likelihood the threats occur.
- How to implement safeguards to mitigate the effect of threats to assets (Cisco Security Wheel Step 1).
- Acceptable use policies for users when they interact with the organization's technology systems.
- How to monitor safeguards for effectiveness, periodical testing, and systematic improvements (Cisco Security Wheel Steps 2, 3, and 4 respectively).

Primary Types of Threats

Threats to network security can be categorized in four ways:

- **Unstructured threats**—Threats primarily from inexperienced individuals who use hacking tools available on the Internet (script kiddies).
- **Structured threats**—Threats from hackers who are more motivated and technically competent. They usually understand network system designs and vulnerabilities and can create hacking scripts to penetrate network systems.
- **External threats**—Threats from individuals or organizations working outside your company who do not have authorized access to your computer systems or network. They work their way into a network mainly from the Internet or dialup access servers.
- **Internal threats**—Threats from individuals with authorized access to the network with an account on a server or physical access to the wire (typically disgruntled current or former employees or contractors).

Attack Types

The following sections list expected attacks to networks and related mitigation techniques:

Reconnaissance Attacks

Reconnaissance is an attempt to discover and map systems, services, vulnerabilities, and publicly available information about target systems, often as a prelude to more sophisticated attacks.

Reconnaissance methods include:

- **Internet information queries**—Data collection about the organization from public sources, such as newspapers, business registries, public web servers, DNS records, and ARIN and RIPE records.

- **Port scans and ping sweeps**—Used to identify online hosts, their services, their operating systems, and some of their vulnerabilities. To mitigate this, control the available services seen from untrusted networks.
- **Packet sniffers**—After compromised, hosts can become packet sniffers for further reconnaissance when rogue software forces their network cards to promiscuous mode. The sniffing host can collect network data, such as passwords and data on the wire, and then an attacker can retrieve it for use in other attacks. Mitigation techniques include:
  - Use of strong authentication and one-time passwords
  - Switched infrastructures to prevent sniffing
  - Use of host IPS (HIPS) to detect disallowed host activities
  - Cryptography for data privacy

Access Attacks

Access attacks attempt to exploit weaknesses in applications so that an intruder can gain unauthorized access. They include:

- **Password attacks**—An attempt to gain account access by obtaining its password using the following techniques:
  - Online and offline brute force through repeated logon attempts. Mitigated with strong passwords, one-time password (OTP) systems, automatic account disabling after "X" number of failed attempts, limit password reuse, and periodic password testing to ensure policy compliance.
  - Packet sniffing collection of passwords off the medium. Mitigated with encryption, switching, and HIPS.
  - IP and MAC spoofing to appear as a trusted system so that users unknowingly send their passwords to attackers. Mitigated by device authentication.
  - Trojan horse software that collects password information and then sends this information to attackers. Mitigated by use of host and network IPS.
- **Trust exploitation**—An attacker takes advantage of the fact that one host (that has been compromised) is trusted by other hosts who potentially allow unauthorized access. Mitigation techniques include:
  - Creating a restrictive trust model and disallowing Internet hosts complete access to internal hosts via the firewall
  - Use of HIPS
  - Use of private VLANs within broadcast networks to lock down host-to-host communication to only that which is required for the systems to operate
  - Use of access control or firewalling among internal network segments
- **Port redirection**—A trust exploitation attack whereby an attacker, who does not have direct access to an end target, uses an intermediate host (that the end target trusts) as a launching point. The attacker compromises the intermediate host and from this point attacks the end target. Mitigation techniques include:
  - Use of HIPS to detect suspicious events
  - Implementation of a more restrictive trust model with more granular firewall filtering

- **Man-in-the-middle**—An attack whereby an attacker sits in between two-way client and server communications to intercept it. Use of effective cryptography to encrypt communications mitigates this exposure. The following are man-in-the-middle examples:
  - Stealing or analyzing the information contained in packet payloads
  - Altering or introducing new packet data as it flows between the legitimate hosts
  - Hijacking the client's session so that the attacker can pose as the client and gain trusted access
  - Interrupting packet flow to deny service
- **Unauthorized access**—Internal or external attacks by people who attempt access into systems or applications to which no access is granted for the following purposes:
  - **Unauthorized system access**—An intruder gains access to a host that he is not allowed access. Mitigated by one-time password systems, advance authentication, and reduction of attack vectors by using stringent firewall filters to reduce attack opportunity. Warning banners serve to put unauthorized persons on alert that their activities are prohibited and can be logged.
  - **Unauthorized data manipulation by an authorized user**—Reading, writing, copying, or moving files that are not intended to be accessible to the user performing the action. Mitigated by stringent OS trust model controls to control privilege escalation and HIPS.
  - **Unauthorized privilege escalation**—Legitimate users with a lower level of access privileges, or intruders who have gained lower privileged access, get information or run procedures that are not authorized at their current level of access. Mitigated by stringent OS trust model controls to control privilege escalation and HIPS.

IP Spoofing Attacks

IP spoofing occurs when an attacker attempts to impersonate a trusted IP address so that the target accepts communications from the attacker. Spoof attacks are of two types:

- **Blind**—Attackers do not need or want replies from the target, so they craft packets with a false address and send them. Target replies go to the forged address that likely throws them away but the single (atomic) packet can do damage anyway.
- **Bidirectional**—Attackers want replies from the target, although they want to mask their real address. Therefore, they must control the routing table of an intermediate router to forward forged packets back to their real IP address.

IP spoofing mitigation techniques include:

- Use of RFC 2827 filtering on routers and firewalls as follows:
  - Traffic that enters your network should be destined for only IP addresses you control.
  - Traffic that leaves your network should be sourced only with IP addresses you control.
  - Traffic that leaves your ISP's network destined for your network should be destined for only IP addresses you control. Your ISP must implement these filters because they own this equipment.
- Use of RFC 1918 filtering to prevent nonroutable "bogon" addresses from entering or leaving your network.

Denial of Service (DoS) Attacks

DoS is the act of barraging a network or host with more connection requests or data than the network can handle, to permanently or temporarily deny access to systems, services, or applications. DoS and Distributed DoS (DDoS) overwhelm IT services with requests from one or many distributed attackers to disable or drastically slow them down. DoS attacks most often target services that the firewall already allows, such as HTTP, SMTP, and FTP. DoS can consume all available bandwidth to shut down a network

DoS mitigation techniques include:

- Use of RFC 1918 and RFC 2827 filtering.
- Use of QoS rate limiting to control data flow.
- Use of anti-DoS features on firewalls and routers to limit half open TCP connections.
- Advanced authentication to prevent invalid host-to-host trusts.

Worms, Viruses, Trojan Horses, Phishing, and Spam Attacks

Malicious code is most often targeted at workstations and servers and is meant to subvert their operation. Malicious code types include:

- **Worms**—Malicious code that uses an available exploit vector to install a payload onto a host and attempts to replicate to other hosts through some propagation mechanism. After the payload is installed, privilege escalation often occurs.
- **Virus**—Malicious code attached to another program (such as email) that attempts some undesirable function on the host (such as reformatting the hard drive) after the user has run the rogue program.
- **Trojans**—Malicious code that appears to be legitimate and benign, however, is in fact a vector for some kind of internal or external attack.
- **Phishing**—An attempt to deceive users into revealing private information to an attacker.
- **Spam**—Multiple unwanted emailed offers that flood inboxes.

The effects of malicious code are mitigated through:

- Containment with defense in-depth techniques at major network junctions
- Testing and applying relevant OS and application program patches (software fixes)
- Inoculating systems with up-to-date, antivirus updates and antispyware programs
- Quarantining infected machines
- Treating infected machines with appropriate configure fixes
- HIPS software
- Personal firewalls

Application Layer Attacks

Application-layer attacks are the exploitation of flaws in applications and host services, such as FTP, HTTP, SMTP, and DNS. Stateful firewalls generally do not stop these attacks because these devices are not designed to perform deep packet inspection. Proxy firewall functions, such as PIX application inspection (formerly "fixups"), Cisco Intrusion Prevention Systems (IPS), and Cisco Adaptive Security Appliances (ASA) are designed for deeper application inspection and control.

Mitigation techniques:

* Implement application inspection within the firewall device.
* Implement HIPS to monitor OS and specific applications for illegal or suspicious calls.
* Implement network IPS to monitor network communications for known attacks and activity outside of normal baseline.
* Keep the host OS and applications patched.
* Log events, parse events, and perform analysis.

Management Protocols and Functions

The following table describes the major protocols commonly used to manage network-connected devices. Regardless of the management protocols in use, it is recommended that network accessible devices use Access Control Lists (ACLs) whenever possible to selectively filter which remote devices are allowed to connect.

Protocol Name	Secure?	Used For	Standard Port & protocol	Description	Notes
SSH (secure shell)	Yes	Command-line configuration management.	22/tcp	Authenticated and encrypted remote access to devices.	Used as a secure substitute to Telnet.
TLS (transport layer security)	Yes	A method to encrypt higher layer applications, such as a GUI.	443/tcp	Authenticated and encrypted remote access to devices.	Used as a secure substitute to HTTP. Closely related to SSL.
IPSec	Yes	Device to device encrypted communication.	500/udp, protocol 50 & 51	Authenticated and encrypted communication between devices.	Can be more difficult to setup than other secure mechanisms. Can be used to tunnel insecure applications like Telnet.
HTTP	No	GUI-based configuration management.	80/tcp	Cleartext web protocol.	Passwords and data can be intercepted with a network sniffer.
Telnet	No	Command-line configuration management.	23/tcp	Cleartext remote access to devices.	Passwords and data can be intercepted with a network sniffer.

Protocol Name	Secure?	Used For	Standard Port & protocol	Description	Notes
Syslog	No	Logging	514/udp	Cleartext log streams to log collection hosts.	When possible, send syslog data to collection hosts via encrypted tunnels (such as SSH) to mitigate an attacker's interception.
TFTP (Trivial File Transfer Protocol)	No	Data transfer	69/udp and >1023/udp	Cleartext data transfer.	TFTP is insecure because it lacks authentication, encryption, and is UDP-based.
FTP	No	Data transfer	20/tcp, 21/tcp, >1023/tcp	Cleartext data transfer.	FTP is insecure because neither credentials nor data is encrypted.
SCP (Secure Copy)	Yes	Data transfer	22/tcp	Encrypted data transfer.	SCP uses an SSH tunnel to transfer data securely.
SNMP version 1 and version 2c (Simple Network Management Protocol)	No	Device management	161/udp, 162/udp	Read-only and read-write device access and management.	Use complex, nondefault community strings.
SNMP version 3	Yes	Device management	161/udp, 162/udp	Read-only and read-write device access and management with added security.	helps prevent exposure to interception by using encryption.
NTP (Network Time Protocol)	No	Time updates	123/udp	Used to synchronize clocks on devices which is necessary for accurate log timestamps and digital certificate infrastructure functions.	Use NTP version 3 for cryptographic authentication of NTP peers.

IPS Overview

The following sections describe Intrusion Prevention System concepts and definitions and Cisco hardware and software.

IPS Overarching Concepts

Both Intrusion Detection System (IDS) and Intrusion Prevention System (IPS) network sensors have the following qualities:

- Malicious and unauthorized activity detection

- Definable actions in response to inappropriate network use

The main differences between Cisco network IDS and IPS are as follows:

IPS	IDS
An inline-mode security control. IPS devices can be deployed in IDS mode if needed.	A promiscuous-mode security control.
Positioned directly in the packet-forwarding path as a Layer 2 repeater. Analyzes data as it travels between two interfaces.	Positioned outside of the packet stream, but receives a copy of each packet from the switch for analysis *and* detection.
Dropping them inline, resetting TCP connections, and blocking can *prevent* the first and subsequent attack packets from reaching their target.	Resetting TCP connections and blocking can prevent *some* attack packets from reaching their target. Because IDS is outside of the forwarding path, one or more attack packets might reach the target before the response action can be activated to prevent the subsequent packets.

Cisco IDS and IPS detection technologies are described as follows:

- Profile-based detection (also known as anomaly detection) uses a statistical baseline definition of activity types and levels considered normal for your network and fires alerts as events cause conditions to go outside of these bounds.

- Signature-based detection (also known as misuse detection and pattern matching) requires the creation of a "signature" that contains bit patterns that describe an attack. When the patterns are observed on the wire, the signature fires.

- Protocol analysis detection takes signature detection a step further because it audits the way particular protocols are *supposed* to behave according to RFC standards, and it compares them to how they *actually* operate on the wire and fires an alert if they behave in a nonstandard way.

In contrast to IDS analysis, which is passive and external to data flow, IPS analysis must be accurate or sessions can be disrupted if the frames are incorrectly dropped rather than it forwarded by the hardware. Several features are designed into Cisco IPS mode monitoring to provide greater reliability and to avoid a condition of self-inflicted DoS. These features are:

- Risk rating of attacks comprised of three weighted measures that determine the importance of an event and what should be done about it:

  — Target asset value—No value, low, medium, high, and mission critical

  — Attack severity rating—Provides a weight to the successful exploitation of a vulnerability

  — Signature fidelity—Rates the confidence of signature accuracy

- Bypass mode enables the hardware to continue forwarding frames as long as the hardware is still powered, while it bypasses the internal IPS functions for the following purposes:
  - System troubleshooting.
  - Enabling live sensor software upgrades.
- IPS uses detailed HTTP and FTP application inspection to make improved decisions about which traffic should be dropped.
- IPS uses its Meta Event Generator (MEG) to correlate and coordinate alarms that multiple signature engines generate to spot exploitation that exhibits qualities specific to multiple engines.

Sensor Hardware

Cisco IPS devices, all of which are based on Linux and share a common code base, come in several form factors, including:

- "NM" modules for Cisco routers
- Modules for the Catalyst 6500 / 7600 switch chassis lines
- Advanced inspection and prevention security services module (AIP-SSM) for the ASA lines
- Dedicated IPS hardware appliances

The following table details IPS hardware.

NOTE Specifications are subject to change. Check Cisco.com for updates.

Sensor Hardware	Modules			Appliances
Product	NM-CIDS	AIP-SSM	IDSM-2	IPS 4215/4240/ 4255
Platform	Select Cisco routers	ASA	6500/7600 chassis	Dedicated standalone appliance
Throughput Performance (Mbps)	45	150 to 450, which depends on ASA chassis	500 per module	80/250/600
Command & control (management) interface	1 physical	1 physical	1 logical via switch interface	1 physical

continues

Sensor Hardware	Modules			Appliances
Monitoring Method	1 backplane attached interface	Context-based monitoring for most ASA models. Supports multiple VLANs for most ASA models.	Passive mode uses VACLs, SPAN, or RSPAN to capture data for inspection; Inline mode supports one VLAN per module.	Maximum physical interfaces 5/8/8
Inline prevention?	No	Yes	Yes	Yes
Promiscuous detection?	Yes	Yes	Yes	Yes
Diskless design?	No	Yes	No	Yes
Common code base?	Yes	Yes	Yes	Yes
Notes	Allows for inspection of decrypted IPSec traffic before exiting router. One module supported per router.	Each ASA appliance can be partitioned into multiple virtual devices (security contexts). Each context is an independent device and has its own security policy, interfaces, and administrators. One module per ASA chassis.	Switch integrated to passively monitor 1+ VLANs or one VLAN inline. 1 to 8 modules supported per chassis. Four logical ports (TCP RST, C&C, inline port pair).	2+ monitoring interfaces required for IPS function.

IPS hardware notes:

- Current IPS 5.0-capable devices can function as either IPS or IDS Security controls, or as both simultaneously if the sensor has enough available monitoring interfaces. Therefore, simultaneous monitoring of multiple IP subnets is possible.
- IDS mode requires a single monitoring interface for a maximum of eight possible monitored networks on high-end sensors with optional Ethernet monitoring ports installed.
- IPS mode requires that you use pairs of monitoring interfaces for a maximum of four possible monitored networks on high-end sensors.
- All monitoring interfaces (IPS and IDS) use the same overall virtual sensor (vs0) configuration policy.

NOTE In the future, it will be possible to have multiple virtual sensor configuration profiles and assign physical interfaces to those profiles.

- Command and control interfaces are designed for management of a sensor and cannot be used for monitoring.
- Command and control interfaces have IP addresses, whereas monitoring interfaces do not have IP addresses.

- Promiscuous (IDS) mode (as opposed to IPS in-line mode) is the default monitoring mode for all sensors.
- Never assign more than one promiscuous mode interface or one pair of inline mode interfaces to monitor the same network or the sensor generates duplicate alerts and other errors.
- IPS monitoring interfaces can be connected to 802.1q switch and router trunks to monitor several segments with one physical interface.

Notes related to the NM-CIDS:

- Runs the same code as IPS appliances to provide full intrusion protection, in comparison to IOS IPS that offers only a subset of signatures.
- Designed for branch offices that require detection capability.
- In certain cases, eliminates the need for a router *and* an IPS appliance.
- Offloads IPS function to a dedicated processor and subsystem on the network module.
- Analyzes copies forwarded within the CEF path to promiscuously monitor all packets from all router interfaces. IPS mode is not available at this writing. IOS IPS functions more like an IDS because it analyzes packets outside of the packet stream.
- As with all sensor systems, packets that pass through the router in a VPN tunnel must be decrypted before the IPS can evaluate them. When a router with an NM-CIDS (or IOS IPS) is a VPN endpoint, after the VPN packets are decrypted internally, the IPS function can evaluate them.
- Packets going through a NAT process are analyzed when they have the inside address.
- Setting up an NM-CIDS requires the following:
  — Enabling CEF switching
  — Creating a loopback and assigning an IP address to it
  — Specifying the IPS to use the loopback
  — Setting the sensor's clock
  — Configuring and tuning the sensor

Sensor Deployment

IPS implies that all frames are forwarded inline through a pair of in-line interfaces on a sensor, whereas IDS implies that a monitoring interface is passively analyzing packets using its connection to a switch port configured as a SPAN port or a VACL capture port.

Appropriate sensor model selection is based upon:

- The required media (10/100/1000/copper/fiber) types for the network.
- The monitoring performance required. For example, do not deploy an 80-Mbps sensor on a segment capable of 1000 Mbps.
- The required response actions. For example, if inline drops are a required response action, you must use a sensor that supports IPS.
- Whether the network runs within a chassis, allowing for direct monitoring within the chassis as opposed to an appliance.

Times when you should add sensors:

- A new segment is added and requires monitoring.
- The IPS Device Manager log shows that the sensor is missing packets and can no longer effectively monitor all the segment's traffic because the data rates are consistently above the sensor's rated analysis capacity.

Network IPS and IDS should be considered for the following types of segments:

- Dedicated server segments connecting high-value, critical hosts.
- Segments that receive remote VPN connections after they have been decrypted.
- Segments that serve as an Extranet boundaries between business partners or major organizational divisions.
- Key internal segments.
- Segments between the perimeter gateway and the Internet for analysis of traffic that the firewall correctly allows, although it might still contain malicious code. Note that placing IPS on the untrusted side of a firewall might generate more alarms than is useful.

The HIPS and Network IPS Relationship

Defense in-depth refers to the concept of monitoring by using both network IPS on critical network segments and host-based IPS on all hosts (servers and desktops) to form a multilayer security architecture. These technologies are complementary, overlap to some degree, and provide a greater degree of overall protection when used in combination. Cisco Security Agent (CSA) is its' HIPS product, which is an agent software resident on each host responsible for monitoring internal processes. The major CSA functions are described as follows:

- Behavior-based engine to detect and prevent malicious activity, such as buffer overflows.
- A firewall-based engine to enforce firewall-type functionality.
- Application behavior protection to ensure that an application does not perform behavior outside the scope of the application.

Additional IPS Terms

False positive—Nonmalicious traffic causes an alarm.

False negative—Malicious traffic does not generate an alarm. Either the signature is not configured correctly or the system does not have the facility to detect and alert on the situation.

True positive—Malicious traffic generates an alarm. The system is working properly.

True negative—Nonmalicious traffic does not cause an alarm. The system is working properly.

NOTE As a memory aid for these concepts, think of all positives as events that generate alerts and all negatives as events that do not generate alerts. False is an incorrect event; true is a correct event. Therefore, a true positive is an event that correctly made an alert. Only events of note, such as malicious traffic, should make an alert.

Attack Evasion

Attack evasion activities are attempts to go unnoticed by a sensor and IT staff. Evasion techniques include:

- **Flooding**—Sending large numbers of packets with "fake" attacks in the middle of which are the "real" attacks. An attempt to distract administrators.

- **Fragmentation**—Splitting IP packets into fragments to force a sensor to reassemble them and then perform analysis.

- **Obfuscation**—The use of control characters, hexadecimal code, and Unicode as a symbolic substitute for ASCII to force the sensor to translate from one character set to another and then perform analysis.

- **Encryption**—The use of encryption (IPSec, SSL, SSH) from an attacker to a host can prevent the IPS from understanding what is inside the packet because the key is unknown. This strongly implies that the attacker already might have a foothold within the target host.

Sensor CLI Activities

The following sections describe ways to interact with a sensor via the CLI.

CLI Access Methods and Modes

Use the following methods to assess the sensor CLI:

- Via the command and control network interface using:
  - SSH
  - Telnet (disabled by default)
- Serial console cable
- Directly connected keyboard and monitor (if supported on the sensor platform)

Initial CLI configuration of a sensor via a console cable is necessary (and required) before you use SSH or a GUI interface for more advanced, detailed configuration. Regardless of the way you access it, the sensor CLI can be used for the following activities:

- Initialization
  - IP addressing
  - Trusted host access lists
  - User account creation

- Configuration
    - Engine tuning
    - Event actions
- Administration
    - Backing up and restoring a configuration.
    - Re-imaging a sensor
- Troubleshooting
    - Pinging
    - Statistics query

NOTE The CLI is generally used only for initial sensor setup. More extensive configuration activities tend to use the IPS Device Manager (IDM) web GUI. You can also accomplish all CLI functions within the IDM.

The CLI supports the following configuration modes:

- **Privileged EXEC mode**—The base level after authenticating to initialize, reboot, and display settings.
- **Global configuration mode**—Allows configuration settings for user accounts, SSH settings, upgrade/downgrade, and re-imaging. Enter via privileged EXEC mode.
- **Service mode**—Allows configuration settings for individual sensor services. Enter via global configuration mode.
- **Multi-instance service mode**—Allows configuration settings for signature definitions and event actions.

Sensor Upgrades and Initialization

An initialization is the process to define sensor operational parameters. The CLI **setup** command is a script that lets you define the following:

Step 1 Assign a hostname.

Step 2 Assign IP and subnet mask of command and control interface.

Step 3 Assign the sensor's default gateway.

Step 4 Enable Telnet server (default disabled), if desired (not recommended).

Step 5 Assign web server port (default 443/tcp).

Step 6 Specify trusted hosts permitted to interact with the sensor.

Step 7 Set the time and date and NTP settings.

Step 8 Assign unused interfaces as either single promiscuous or inline monitoring pairs to modify the virtual sensor configuration (vs0).

NOTE You can alter all the preceding settings at a later time if you use the IDM GUI.

Other CLI Functions

Diagnostic commands available from the CLI include:

Command	Explanation
ping	Pings a host
trace	Traces a route to a host
banner login	Defines a login banner
ftp-timeout	Defines retry timeout when you use FTP
show version	Shows sensor version and memory usage and signature version
more current-config	Echoes current configuration to screen
show settings	Shows system settings assigned during setup
show events	Shows events that have occurred
default	Resets select services to factory defaults
copy	Copies configurations to internal or external destinations

The following table lists CLI commands that can be used for sensor monitoring and trouble-shooting.

Command	Explanation
show statistics	Shows the state of a sensor's services
show interfaces	Shows a sensor's interface statistics
packet display	Displays live captured packets as they come in an interface to the screen
show tech-support	Captures all relevant operational data about interfaces and network statistics, as well as log files, software versions, configuration files, and other information to be used to troubleshoot the system

IPS Device Manager (IDM)

The following sections describe some of the key features of the IDM, a web-based Java GUI application used to configure and manage sensors via the network command and control interface. Note that this text does not attempt to replicate the many screen shots found in Cisco.com documentation; however, it provides the core essence and description of the IDM's capabilities.

IDM Description, Requirements, and Security

Each sensor has an embedded web server daemon to which authorized administrators can connect to configure and maintain the system. A sensor must have been previously configured with an IP address via the CLI, and the workstation where you launch IDM must be part of the sensor's trusted host list. Then the administrator can communicate with the sensor from one of the following known-working web browser/OS combinations. Note that by default, HTTPS is required, although it can be turned off later.

OS	Browser
Windows 2000 and XP	IE 6.0, Java Plug-in 1.5
	Netscape 7.1, Java Plug-in 1.5
Sun Solaris 2.8 and 2.9	Mozilla 1.7
Red Hat Linux 9.0 and Red Hat Enterprise Linux WS, Ver 3	Mozilla 1.7

High-level IDM features include:

- Task-based web GUI

- General sensor configuration and management

- Signature configuration, customization, and creation

- Using the adjunct program IPS Event Viewer (IEV) to sensor event monitoring

- Access to the Network Security Database (NSDB), a complete description of signatures, exploits, vulnerabilities, and benign triggers

- Online help

- Sensor reboot and power down

When sensor and client communicate, the following security-centric concepts are engineered into the transactions:

- Transport Layer Security (TLS) is used with digital certificates to encrypt communications, as well as provide peer authentication and data integrity.

- Trusted hosts, as defined within the CLI or IDM, are only permitted to interact with the sensor.

- IPS configuration control commands and sensor alarms use Remote Data Exchange Protocol version 2 (RDEP2) or the more advanced device independent and the Security Device Event Exchange (SDEE) application-layer protocols within the HTTPS stream.

- Using SDEE, the IDM queries a sensor's Event Store for alerts on an ad hoc basis or continually for "real-time" monitoring. The client station always pulls data from the sensor, as opposed to the sensor pushing the data to the IDM.

Self-signed X.509 digital certificates are used for the client-to-sensor TLS communication. CLI and IDM allow for the generation of new public/private certificates if desired. Note that the IP address of the sensor is part of the certificate and if it is changed, a new certificate must be generated. The MD5 and SHA1 certificate fingerprints can be accessed via CLI and IDM for manual comparison every time you access the sensor. This serves as a check to the authenticity of the sensor.

SSH is the preferred method for secure CLI access to a sensor. The IDM provides SSH management facilities as follows:

- Importation of trusted host RSA public keys for password-less access
- Importation of trusted blocking device RSA public keys for password-less access
- Generation of sensor key pairs

IDM Events

The IDM interface can be used to view the detailed log files that the sensor produces and stores. The IDM can periodically pull available events from the sensor using SDEE.

The Monitoring panel in the IDM allows for the following interactions with the event store:

- Filter by signature alert event level:
  - Informational
  - Low
  - Medium
  - High
- Filter by sensor error event level:
  - Warning
  - Error
  - Fatal
- Toggle network access controller (sensor Ethernet events) and sensor status events.
- Filter results by the time passed or time within a specific range.

IDM User Accounts

Users can be created within the IDM and assigned to a predefined user account role to control their overall access authorization. User account roles are detailed in the following table. With the exception of the Service role, multiple users can be assigned to a given role.

Privilege	User Account Role			
	Administrator	**Operator**	**Viewer**	***Service**
Can log into the IDM interface	x	x	x	
Can log into the CLI interface	x	x	x	
Provides bash shell root access via a CLI interface				x
Low-level OS access for Cisco TAC use only				x
Can su to root user				x
One account can have this role				x
Can create and edit Service account role	x			
Adds and deletes users. Password administration	x			
Assigns Ethernet interfaces to a virtual sensor	x			
Enables and disabling Ethernet interfaces	x			
Generate SSH keys and digital certs	x			
Modifies sensor address	x			
Defines permitted hosts	x			
Tunes signatures	x	x		
Manages blocking devices	x	x		
View events	x	x	x	
Changes own password	x	x	x	x

*The Service account role, which can be held by only one user at a time, has broad system privileges and allows "su" to the Linux "root" user. It should be used only for troubleshooting at the direction of the Cisco TAC.

IPS Signature Concepts

The following sections describe signature concepts.

Signature Overview

Sensors ship with more than 1000 built-in signatures that are designed to describe network misuse. Cisco periodically produces new signatures as new attacks are isolated and identified. Sensor signature engines, the internal software processes used to examine all types of flows, use various techniques to identify when misuse occurs. Each signature is assigned to an engine that is optimized to examine a particular type of communication. When a signature "fires," there is a match between observed network activity and some definition of misuse found within a signature. Signatures can be configured for multiple response actions when they fire.

Signature facts:

- One or more built-in signature parameters being modified is considered a tuned signature.

- If a new signature is built from scratch or is based on a copy of a built-in signature, it is considered a custom signature.

- A signature can have subsignatures to describe variations of an exploit. Subsignatures are individually tunable.

- Active signatures can be enabled or disabled. If a signature is not currently enabled, the misuse it describes cannot be identified because the sensor does not watch for it.

- Signatures can be retired (disabled) to save sensor memory resources, although they cannot be deleted or renamed. Previously retired signatures can be activated again (brought out of retirement).

- Information about each signature can be obtained from Cisco NSDB. Entries include information like:

  — Signature name, description, ID, and severity
  — Exploit consequences
  — Countermeasures (for example, which patches fix it)
  — Benign triggers (conditions that can cause a false positive) and recommended filters
  — Related signatures
  — Affected operating systems
  — Related vendor advisory links

NOTE The Cisco Intrusion Prevention Alert Center at cisco.com displays the latest security news, has up-to-date IPS support information, and enables you to sign up for IPS Active Update Notifications.

The following table relates analysis techniques to the broad detection technologies described in the "IPS Overarching Concepts" section and describes what the sensor does to achieve effective monitoring for each of them.

	Analysis Techniques	**What the Sensor Is Doing...**
Signature Detection	Simple Pattern Matching	Looks for a particular string of characters in a single packet.
	Stateful Pattern Matching	Looks for a particular string of characters across multiple packets.
	Heuristic Analysis	Uses statistical analysis to determine if combinations of observed communications amount to an attack. For example, slow steady port probes from a remote host, none of which matches a particular signature, but represent suspect behavior.

continues

	Analysis Techniques	What the Sensor Is Doing...
Protocol Analysis Detection	Protocol Decode Analysis	Interprets a protocol (or service), such as a host would, and analyzes for abnormal use of it or exploitation of known vulnerabilities. For example, signature 6056 (DNS NXT Buffer Overflow) watches for DNS server responses that have a long NXT resource where the length of the resource data is > 2069 bytes.
	Protocol Anomaly	Looks for deviations from standard RFC protocol use. For example, a TCP packet with the SYN and FIN bit flags are set simultaneously.
Profile Detection	Statistical Anomaly Analysis	Attempts packet flood detection by noting large increases in traffic flow above what it considered normal.

Tunable Signature Parameters

Individual signatures have configurable tuning parameters described in the following features table:

Feature	Description
Response actions	Defines what the sensor does if the signature fires.
Alert Summarization	Lumps multiple alerts into a single alert to help avoid information overload.
Threshold configuration	Allows setting various network parameters for optimal operation.
Anti-evasive techniques	Allows the signature sensor to recognize attack evasion.
Fidelity rating	A rating of the signature's accuracy is based on how often it produces false positives.
Application firewall analysis	Deep layer 4 through 7 inspection of HTTP and FTP.
SNMP support	Enables sending of traps that signify alerts and errors.
Regular expression matching	Enables processor efficient pattern matching for custom signature creation.
IPv6 support	Enables analysis of IPv4 packets within IPv6 packets.

Signature Response Actions

Cisco IPS sensors are able to produce one or more actions when a condition is met, such as a signature fire. Definable actions when you tune signatures are detailed in the following table.

Definable Actions	Description
Produce Alert	Stores the alert in the Event Store database.
Produce Verbose Alert	Stores the alert in the Event Store database and includes that packet's contents in an encoded dump.
Log Attacker Packets	Stores an alert in the Event Store database and begins logging all IP packets from the attacker. Logging IP packets can be used for subsequent forensic analysis.

Definable Actions	Description
Log Victim Packets	Stores an alert in the Event Store database and begins logging all IP packets from the victim. Logging IP packets can be used for subsequent forensic analysis.
Log Pair Packets	Stores an alert in the Event Store database and begins logging all IP packets from both the attacker and the victim. Logging IP packets can be used for subsequent forensic analysis.
Request Block Connection	Modifies ACLs on blocking devices to block a source IP (the attacker) from communicating with a destination IP (the target) for a specified time period.
Request Block Host	Modifies ACLs on blocking devices to prevent a source IP (the attacker) from communicating with all destination IPs for a specified time period.
Reset TCP Connection	Sends a TCP RST packet to the attacker and target to tear down the connection. This works only with TCP traffic.
Request SNMP Trap	Stores the alert in the Event Store database and sends alarm alerts via SNMP traps to an NMS.
The following applies to IPS-capable devices in IPS mode and requires 2+ monitoring interfaces.	
Deny Attacker Inline	Drops all packets from an attacker for a specified time period.
Deny Connection Inline	Drops all TCP packets from an attacker related to a session.
Deny Packet Inline	Drops an offending packet.

The IDM interface enables you to configure general settings for all related signature actions as follows:

- Deny attacker duration in seconds
- Maximum denied attackers (simultaneous)
- Block action duration in minutes

Signature Alerts

The following describe alert facts:

- Alerts (alarms) are turned on by default for all enabled signatures.
- Signature alerts are assigned to one of the following severity categories:
  - Informational
  - Low
  - Medium
  - High
- You can configure a signature's severity category.
- All alerts are stored in the sensor's Event Store database.
- The IDM uses Security Device Event Exchange (SDEE) to query a sensor's Event Store for alerts on an ad hoc basis or continually for "real-time" monitoring. The client station always pulls data from the sensor, as opposed to the sensor pushing the data to the IDM.

Alarm throttling settings specify whether multiple alarms related to a single, unique, signature over a specified time period are stored individually or summarized in the Event Store. Summarizing alarms reduces the processing load on a sensor and the number of entries an administrator sees on the IDM's monitoring console. The Alarm Throttle master parameter can have one of the following values:

- **FireOnce**—Triggers one alarm for each identical signature received during a time period called the ThrottleInterval. When this time period expires, the alarm is written to the Event Store.

- **FireAll**—Each alarm for each identical signature is stored individually in the Event Store as they occur.

- **Summarize**—Tracks the number of occurrences of identical alarms for a set of IP addresses and Layer 4 ports during the Throttle Interval, and it records one alarm event with the number of times it happened after the time period expires.

- **GlobalSummarize**—Behaves similar to the Summarize setting, but it consolidates identical alarms for all IP address and Layer 4 port combinations, and not just unique combinations.

The Event Count Key and Summary Key parameters use a four-character designation within a signature to set the granularity of the IP address/Layer 4 port combinations mentioned in the previous bullets. An increase in the specificity of the combinations influences the likelihood that signature fires are unique. These keys take the form of AaBa. The legend follows:

- A = source IP address

- a = source port

- B = destination IP address

- b = destination port

- x = wildcard

For example, if a signature specifies an Event Count Key of xxBb, each time an attacker on any source port sends a packet to a unique IP address represented by "B" destined for a unique port "b" within the Throttle Interval, the event count increments by one.

Alarm throttles configured for FireAll and Summarize use a concept called Choke Threshold to automatically reduce the number of individual identical alarms logged during a spike in attack activity. It is a setting defining the number of identical alarms, if received during the Throttle Interval, it causes the sensor to switch the Alarm Throttle parameter to the next higher level. If the number of identical alarms received during the Throttle Interval is >= two times the Choke Threshold, the sensor switches the Alarm Throttle parameter to yet again the next higher level. This reduces redundant alarms during a time interval to reduce stress on the sensor and its administrator. Alarm Throttles set initially to FireAll switch to Summarize and then, if needed, to Global Summarize. Likewise, Alarm Throttles set initially to Summarize switch to Global Summarize.

IPS Engines

Sensor signature engines are the internal software processes designed to examine the many types of flows that can occur on a network for the purpose of spotting unauthorized activity. Each engine is optimized to examine a particular type of communication and each signature is assigned to a particular engine. Therefore, each engine supports a general category of signatures meant to inspect communications in a particular way.

Engines have master and local tunable parameters. Master parameters are more global in nature and a modified setting flows across all engines. Local parameters are those specific to an engine. Some parameters are protected, which means they cannot be changed for a built-in signature. However, they can be changed if you create a copy of the built-in signature, which creates a new, custom signature. Required parameters are necessary for all signatures.

Engines are comprised of:

- A parser to break up the packet before inspection

- An inspector to perform the inspection of packet contents

IPS 5.0 uses the following signature engines. Note that several engines have sub-engines (in the form of enginename.subenginename) that are not necessarily listed here:

- **AIC**—Provides deep analysis of web and FTP traffic to prevent abuse of embedded protocols within HTTP and to watch for illegal use of FTP commands.

- **ATOMIC**—Inspects individual packets for abnormality.

  - **ATOMIC.IP**—Combines Layer 3 and Layer 4 functions to inspect fields, flags, and payloads at any of these points within the packet using Regex.

  - **ATOMIC.ARP**—Inspects the Layer-2 ARP protocol for abnormalities and misuse.

- **FLOOD**—Detects ICMP and UDP floods directed toward individual hosts and networks.

- **META**—Provides the "intelligence" for event correlation as alerts are noted by one or more engines within a finite time interval.

- **NORMALIZER**—Handles communications that are fragmented at the IP layer or segmented at the TCP layer to detect attacks that are spread across packets.

- **SERVICE**—Inspects specific network service protocols that operate at Layers 5, 6, and 7:

  - **DNS**—Inspects DNS (TCP and UDP) traffic.
  - **FTP**—Inspects FTP traffic.
  - **GENERIC**—Inspects custom services and their payloads.
  - **H225**—Inspects VoIP call signaling setup and termination traffic for standards compliance.
  - **HTTP**—Inspects HTTP traffic.
  - **IDENT**—Inspects IDENT (client and server) traffic.
  - **MSRPC**—Inspects Microsoft RPC traffic used extensively in Microsoft networks for inter-host communication.
  - **MSSQL**—Inspects Microsoft SQL traffic.

— **NTP**—Inspects NTP traffic.

— **RPC**—Inspects RPC traffic.

— **SMB**—Inspects Microsoft SMB traffic.

— **SNMP**—Inspects SNMP traffic.

— **SSH**—Inspects SSH traffic.

- **STATE**—Tracks the state machines of SMTP, LPR, and Cisco device logins. Verifies proper transitions through states and alarms when a state transition is violated.

- **STRING**—Searches on regular expression (Regex) strings based on ICMP, TCP, or UDP protocol.

- **SWEEP**—Detects single or multi-protocol ICMP, TCP, and UDP reconnaissance activity, such as Nessus scans.

- **TRAFFIC.ICMP**—Analyzes nonstandard protocols and attack traffic that use ICMP as their vector (TFN2K, LOKI, and DDoS variants).

- **TROJAN**—Inspects for non ICMP, nonstandard protocol variants of BO2K and TFN2K.

Signature Configuration

Signatures can be enabled, disabled, retired, activated, tuned, or created to reflect the unique nature of your environment. For example:

- If you have no *nix-based hosts, you might consider retiring *nix-related signatures to save sensor resources.

- If traffic floods threaten your environment, you might consider tuning (by increasing) the severity level of DoS-related attacks and define more drastic protection mechanisms for these, such as TCP resets and blocking.

- If you have a custom application and you would like to monitor for a certain string of data in the payload, you can create a custom signature. The IDM's custom signature wizard can help with the creation of these signatures.

- If you use a network management system in your environment, its normal periodic probes can be mistaken as an attack; therefore, the sensor can be tuned to ignore its activity.

The IDM interface can organize and sort signatures into logical groupings for easier parameter modification as follows:

- Attack Types

- L2/L3/L4 Protocols

- OS Type

- Signature Release Version

- Service Type (DNS, MS-RPC, SSH, and others)

- Signature ID

- Signature Name

- Action Type

- Engine

The following steps briefly illustrate the requirements to create a custom signature:

Step 1   Select an appropriate signature engine. For example:

- Atomic IP

- Service RPC

- String TCP

- Sweep

- And others...

Step 2   Assign the signature identifiers:

- Signature ID

- SubSignature ID

- Signature Name

- Alert Notes (optional)

- User Comments (optional)

Step 3   Assign the engine-specific parameters.

Step 4   Assign the alert response:

- Signature Fidelity Rating

- Severity of the alert

Step 5   Assign the alert behavior:

- Keep the default or

- Assign an advanced behavior

Sensor Tuning

Sensors and signatures are tuned to get the best quality monitoring data (and ultimately security!) from the monitored networks. There is no such thing as a one-size-fits-all IPS because there are many different types of systems at various security levels that use many types of communication protocols. Furthermore, attackers use varying techniques to subvert systems for different reasons. Administrators who tune their sensors should know their systems well, including:

- Organizational security policy

- System boundaries and topology

- General security stance

- An idea of "normal" traffic flow

- Types of applications running

- Operating systems

These sections explore types of tuning.

Phases of Tuning

The following are the phases of tuning:

Step 1   **Deployment**—The time for initial sensor setup. The sensor generally runs in a default configuration with conservative settings.

Step 2   **Tuning**—A time to examine events that have occurred and study which are considered normal for this network. Filters are implemented. Signatures are modified accordingly.

Step 3   **Maintenance**—The time after initial tuning when the sensor is only periodically updated and audited for operational soundness.

Tuning methods include:

- Enabling and disabling signatures

- Setting alarm severity levels

- Changing signature parameters

- Specifying event actions based on risk rating by using event action overrides

- Removing certain events that are known to happen in the environment using event action filters

- Creating alarm channel event filters

- Specifying the alarms you want to see in the monitoring portion of the IDM by severity level

Global sensor tuning should include tuning of IP logging and reassembly (IP fragment and TCP stream). The following list describes their uses:

- **IP logging**—A sensor response action to a signature firing can be to log the IP packets of the attacker, the victim, or both. Logging can be set to happen in terms of minutes, number of packets, or bytes. Care should be taken when specifying IP logging because there are limits on the amount of storage space available, and it does impact sensor performance.

- **Reassembly**—You can specify IP fragment reassembly to enable the sensor to reassemble fragmented IP packets and then inspect them. Similarly, TCP reassembly reassembles TCP streams.

Event action rules can be tuned to increase the likelihood that your sensor provides you with the protection you desire because it ensures the alerts you do receive are actual threats and the responses taken are appropriate. To reduce false positives and inappropriate response actions, use event actions rules as follows:

- **Calculating a risk rating using these inputs:**

    — Target asset value—No value, low, medium, high, and mission critical

    — Attack severity rating—Provides a weight to the successful exploitation of a vulnerability

    — Signature fidelity—Rates the confidence of signature accuracy

- **Defining event action overrides**—Globally assigned actions that are carried out if an event occurs and the assigned risk rating is at a particular level.

- **Defining event action filters**—These are methods to reduce the amount of alert noise that shows up on the monitoring console using these methods:

    — Summarization places multiple events into one alert to provide basic event aggregation.

    — Simple aggregation mode configures a threshold number of hits for a signature before the alert is sent.

    — Timed-interval counting mode tracks the number of hits per seconds and only sends alerts when that threshold is met. Complete filtering of an event from the IDM interface.

Sensor Blocking

These sections present sensor blocking (also known as "shunning") when used as a signature response action.

Blocking Overview

Sensor blocking is an IPS signature response action that prevents an attacker who has triggered a signature from further access to the target. This is accomplished with dynamic modification of access control lists on perimeter devices that separate the attacker from the target. When a signature fires and the configured response action is to block, the sensor automatically instructs one or more blocking devices to modify their ACLs to include entries that specify X (the attacker) cannot communicate with Y (the target). Blocking can be configured for a specific period of time; when the time period expires, the ACLs are again modified to unblock the X to Y connection. Blocking-related signature response actions are:

- **Request block connection**—Modifies ACLs on blocking devices to block a source IP (the attacker) from communicating with a destination IP (the target) for a specified time period

- **Request block host**—Modifies ACLs on blocking devices to block a source IP (the attacker) from communicating with all destination IPs for a specified time period

Blocking terminology:

- **Managed device**—A Cisco device that modifies its ACLs to block or unblock

- **Blocking sensor**—A sensor that instructs a managed device place a block or unblock

- **Network Access Controller (NAC)**—The software function within the sensor that controls blocking

- **Managed interface / managed VLAN**—The interface on a managed device where the blocking entry is applied

- **Active ACL / Active VACL**—The ACL doing the blocking

Cisco Blocking Devices

The following can be a managed device:

- Routers, IOS 11.2 or later

- PIX Firewall code 6.0 or later on 501, 506E, 515/E, 525, 535 platforms

- Firewall Service Module (FWSM)

- Adaptive Security Appliance (ASA) version 7.0 or later

- Switches

  — Cat 5000 with RSM/RSFC with IOS 11.2(9)P or later
  — Cat 6000 with native IOS 12.1(13)E or later
  — Cat 6000 hybrid mode with 7.5(1) or later

Block methods include ACL, VACL, and shun (which is specific to the PIX platform).

Sensors use Telnet or SSH to communicate with blocking devices via their management interfaces. However, SSH is the recommended method.

Blocking Guidelines

Blocking can start either automatically as a signature response or manually through the IDM when you know you wish to perpetually block a single IP address or range of addresses. Blocking is a protection mechanism that should be used with care to prevent blocking legitimate communications. The following guidelines suggest proper implementation goals:

- Always implement perimeter anti-spoof filtering mechanisms (RFC1918 and RFC2827) to prevent a blocking response on a spoofed address.

- Identify all network entry points and design blocking consistently throughout.

- Ensure that a single sensor controls each managed device. Understand which managed device interface and associate ACL perform the blocking. Organize managed device login credentials and program them into the sensor's configuration properly.

- Identify whether critical hosts should be exempt from any kind of blocking function to prevent mission critical communications from being disabled.

- Identify and configure only the most critical signatures with blocking response actions. Determine an appropriate blocking duration. The default is 30 minutes.

During configuration, the managed interface that will do the blocking must be chosen. An external interface that blocks inbound traffic with an inbound ACL is the best approach because communication is denied before it reaches the internal network and the internals of the router. Optionally, blocking can be performed on an inside interface with an outbound ACL as traffic leaves the router going toward the internal network. Though the latter approach certainly works, an attack can degrade router performance because the communication is allowed to traverse the router's internals before it's blocked.

Blocking Implementation

Step 1   Choose and tune appropriate signatures to have a blocking response.

Step 2   Configure the sensor's global blocking properties:

- Maximum blocking entries

- Define if the sensor's IP can be blocked

- Specify addresses never to be blocked

Step 3   Specify blocking device settings:

- Device type and IP address

- Username and password

- Communication method (SSH or Telnet)

Step 4   Configure a managed device's managed interface:

- Choose the physical or VLAN interface to do the blocking

- Specify the direction inbound or outbound

- Specify Pre-block and Post-block extended ACL/VACL

Step 5   Optionally define a master blocking sensor.

The filtering ACL applied to the managed interface consists of three parts (1 + 2 + 3) as stated in the list below and depicted in the following diagram:

Pre-block ACLs—Defined upfront in the blocking device's configuration. Used to consistently permit or deny traffic. Overrides any dynamic entries because these are processed first.

Dynamically created portion—Created on the fly in response to an attack.

Post-block ACLs—Defined up front in the blocking device's configuration. Enables additional traffic permits or denies.

NOTE   If blocking is not configured, the resulting managed interface's ACL is a combination of the pre-block entries followed by the post-block entries.

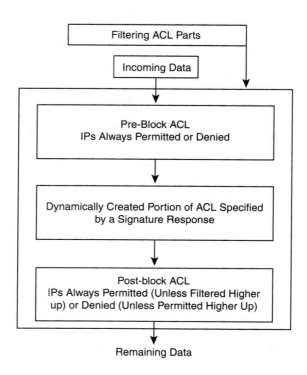

Remaining Data

Master Blocking Sensors

For networks with multiple external connection points, master blocking is a way to distribute blocking commands from a central sensor to all blocking devices (routers and PIX) in response to attacks detected by other sensors. The concept is that most of your sensors can perform the duties of sensing and forward notifications of attacks to a master blocking sensor. A master blocking sensor maintains connectivity to the perimeter devices and issues blocking commands on behalf of all block forwarding sensors. These commands specify modification of ACLs at all untrusted network boundaries to prevent communication from the attacker for the specified time period.

For example, an organization with three Internet connections—block forwarding sensors *London, Chicago,* and *Kyoto*—each monitor their respective Internet perimeters. Master blocking sensor *core-sensor* resides in the central data center and maintains SSH connectivity via the internal WAN to *PIX1, PIX2,* and *PIX3* located at the perimeters. An attack is detected by *Kyoto* from 1.1.1.5 with a signature configured to block the offending host for 30 minutes. *Kyoto,* a block forwarding sensor (similar to *Chicago* and *London*), informs *core-sensor* of the attack. *Core-sensor* instructs each PIX unit to shun (block) 1.1.1.5 for 30 minutes. Therefore, each perimeter blocks 1.1.1.5 for 30 minutes.

Additional master blocking facts:

- Block forwarding sensors can forward blocking requests to a maximum of ten master blocking sensors.

- Multiple block forwarding sensors can forward to a single master.

- Masters can forward block requests to other masters.

- Inter-sensor communications use RDEP and can be encrypted or not encrypted.

Part V

Cisco Secure Virtual Private Networks (CSVPN) Flash Cards

The flash cards in this part of the book focus to prepare you for the Cisco Secure Virtual Private Networks (CSVPN) exam (642-511) toward achieving your CCSP certification. Over 150 more questions for this section of the book can be found on the CD-ROM accompanying this book. The flash cards address specific topic areas for this exam and are organized as follows:

- **Section 1: Network Security Overview**—Tests your familiarity with general network security concepts including policies, attacks, and threats.

- **Section 2: Overview of VPN and IPSec Technologies**—Tests your knowledge of general VPN technology topics including IKE, IPSec, and authentication and encryption algorithms.

- **Section 3: Cisco VPN 3000 Concentrator Series Hardware**—Tests your knowledge of the Cisco VPN 3000 Concentrator Series models and their specific capabilities and features.

- **Section 4: Routing on the VPN Concentrator**—Tests your knowledge of the routing features of the Cisco VPN 3000 Concentrators, which provide static and dynamic routing support.

- **Section 5: Remote Access VPNs Using Pre-shared Keys**—Tests your familiarity with commands and procedures to use pre-shared keys on the Cisco VPN 3000 Concentrator for configuration of remote access VPNs.

- **Section 6: Remote Access VPNs Using Digital Certificates**—Tests your familiarity with digital certificate formats, commands, and procedures to use digital certificates on the Cisco VPN 3000 Concentrator for configuration of remote access VPNs.

- **Section 7: Configuring the Cisco 3002 Hardware Client for User and Unit Authentication**—Tests your knowledge of procedures for configuration of the Cisco 3002 Hardware Client with User and Unit Authentication.

- **Section 8: Backup Servers, Load Balancing, and Reverse Route Injection**—Tests your familiarity with Cisco VPN 3000 Concentrator's high-availability capabilities including configuration of backup servers and load balancing. Reverse Route Injection concepts and configuration requirements are also covered.

- **Section 9: Transparent Tunneling**—Tests your knowledge of transparent tunneling concepts, benefits, and configuration requirements.

- **Section 10: Configuring LAN-to-LAN VPNs on Cisco 3000 VPN Concentrators**—Tests your familiarity with commands and procedures for configuration of LAN-to-LAN VPNs on the Cisco VPN 3000 Concentrator.

- **Section 11: Monitoring and Administration**—Tests your knowledge of the Cisco VPN 3000 Concentrator's monitoring and administrative features designed for effective management of these devices.

- **Section 12: Bandwidth Management**—Tests your knowledge of the Cisco VPN 3000 Concentrators bandwidth management capabilities and features. Bandwidth management configuration procedures and requirements are also covered.

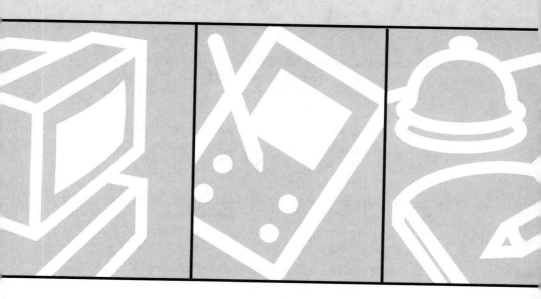

Section 1
Network Security Overview

Question 1

Name the four primary types of threat to network security.

Question 2

What kind of threat usually involves script kiddies?

Question 3

What type of an attack involves an intruder who attempts to discover and map the systems, services, and vulnerabilities in your network?

Question 13 Answer

The four primary types of threat to network security are:

- Unstructured threats
- Structured threats
- External threats
- Internal threats

Question 14 Answer

Unstructured threats are usually carried out by less experienced hackers, sometimes referred to as "script kiddies."

Question 15 Answer

Reconnaissance attacks

Section 2
Overview of VPN and IPSec Technologies

Question 1

What are the two primary types of VPNs?

Question 2

What benefits do VPNs provide?

Question 3

What is the IP protocol number for ESP?

Question 1 Answer

Remote-access VPNs and site-to-site VPNs

Question 2 Answer

The benefits that VPNs provide are:

- Cost savings
- Improved communications
- Security
- Scalability

Question 3 Answer

ESP's IP protocol number is 50.

Question 4

What is the IP protocol number for AH?

Question 5

What port does IKE use?

Question 6

Which IPSec mode of operation creates a new IP header?

Question 4 Answer

AH's IP protocol number is 51.

Question 5 Answer

IKE operates on UDP port 500.

Question 6 Answer

Tunnel mode creates a new IP header. When tunnel mode is used with ESP, the entire IP packet (including the original header) is encrypted and a new IP header is added. When tunnel mode is used with AH, a new IP header is added to the original IP packet (including the original header). This whole new packet is then authenticated.

Question 7

Name the two modes in which IKE Phase 1 can operate.

Question 8

Name an asymmetrical encryption algorithm.

Question 9

What is a transform set?

Question 7 Answer

IKE Phase 1 can operate in Main mode or Aggressive mode.

Question 8 Answer

RSA is an example of an asymmetrical encryption algorithm (encryption and decryption are performed with different keys, private and public in this case).

Question 9 Answer

A transform set is a specific combination of message authentication and encryption algorithms that the concentrator uses.

Question 10

What does interesting traffic mean, as it relates to VPN configurations?

Question 11

What key length does DH Group 5 use?

Question 12

What protocol uses bidirectional SAs?

Question 10 Answer

Interesting traffic is defined as the traffic that IPSec protects.

Question 11 Answer

DH group 5 uses a 1536-bit key.

Question 12 Answer

IKE SAs are bidirectional.

Section 3
Cisco VPN 3000 Concentrator Series Hardware Overview

Question 1

Which models of the VPN 3000 Concentrator are not upgradeable?

Question 2

If you have 350 remote-access users on a model 3020, what is the maximum number of site-to-site sessions that can be supported?

Question 3

How many simultaneous WebVPN users are supported on a 3020 Concentrator?

Question 1 Answer

Models 3005, 3020, and 3080 are not upgradeable (3080 has all the possible upgrades already installed).

Question 2 Answer

You can support 400 site-to-site sessions with 350 remote-access sessions on a 3020 Concentrator. Keep in mind that, the total number of sessions, including site-to-site sessions, cannot exceed the overall simultaneous sessions (750 for a model 3020).

Question 3 Answer

You can support up to 200 WebVPN users simultaneously on a model 3020.

Question 4

What do you need to configure redundancy between SEP modules on a 3080 Concentrator?

Question 5

In what order do SEP modules fail over to another available module?

Question 6

What firewall policy provides centralized policy management on the software clients?

Question 4 Answer

Redundancy between SEP (or SEP-E) modules is enabled automatically. No configuration is necessary.

Question 5 Answer

SEP modules (and SEP-E modules) fail over from top to bottom within a column first, and then across a column, if available and necessary.

Question 6 Answer

Central Policy Protection (CPP) mode is commonly used for implementations that require centralized policy management and enforcement.

Question 7

Which mode of operation should you choose for the hardware client if you want to access the individual hosts behind the hardware client?

Question 8

Which mode of hardware client operation uses PAT?

Question 9

What protocol is used to transfer the image to the hardware client with auto update?

Question 7 Answer

Network extension mode—In network extension mode, the clients behind the hardware client are accessible from the central site. The IP addresses of the clients are not translated in this mode.

Question 8 Answer

Client mode. In this mode, the clients behind the hardware client are not directly accessible from the central site. Instead, the hardware client uses port address translation (PAT) and the addresses of the individual hosts behind it remain hidden.

Question 9 Answer

Auto update uses TFTP to download images onto the hardware client.

Question 10

What are the four primary placement configurations for the VPN concentrator?

Question 11

What is a disadvantage to placing the concentrator in front of the firewall?

Question 12

Which VPN concentrator placement configuration does the Cisco SAFE white papers recommended?

Question 10 Answer

The most common placement configurations for VPN concentrators are as follows:

- In front of or without a firewall
- Behind a firewall
- Parallel with a firewall
- On a DMZ

Question 11 Answer

Because the concentrator is inline (all Internet-bound traffic must pass through it), there is unnecessary overhead and the concentrator becomes a potential point of failure for more than just VPN connections.

Question 12 Answer

The recommended configuration is to place the concentrator in parallel with the firewall.

Section 4
**Routing on the VPN 3000
Concentrator**

Question 1

What are the two main types of routing that the concentrator supports?

Question 2

How many default gateways can you configure on the concentrator?

Question 3

Which dynamic routing protocols are supported on the concentrator?

Question 1 Answer

The concentrator supports static and dynamic routing.

Question 2 Answer

You can have only a single default gateway configured on each concentrator. You can, however, also specify a tunnel default gateway, which applies only to tunneled traffic (such as remote users accessing the VPN).

Question 3 Answer

The concentrator supports RIPv1, RIPv2, and OSPF dynamic routing protocols.

Question 4

How many static routes can configure on the 3005 Concentrator?

Question 5

What is the function of the Tunnel Default Gateway option?

Question 4 Answer

The 3005 Concentrator can support a maximum of 200 static routes.

Question 5 Answer

The tunnel default gateway is the gateway assigned to tunneled traffic, including remote access users, site-to-site tunnels, and hardware clients.

Section 5
**Remote Access Using
Pre-Shared Keys**

Question 1

Which screen on the web-based management interface is used to configure group settings?

Question 2

Name two of the seven tabs used to configure group settings.

Question 3

What are the three split-tunneling policies that you can configure on the concentrator?

Question 1 Answer

Group settings are configured via **User Management > Groups** from the web-based interface.

Question 2 Answer

Group settings are configured with the following seven tabs:

- Identity tab
- General tab
- IPSec tab
- Client Config tab
- Client FW tab
- HW Client tab
- PPTP/L2TP tab

Question 3 Answer

Tunnel everything—This option sends all traffic through the IPSec tunnel.

Allow the networks in list to bypass the tunnel—With this option you specify a list of networks that are bypassed from the tunnel.

Only tunnel network in the list—With this option, traffic destined for specified networks are only sent through the IPSec tunnel.

Question 4

On which tab of the software client do you configure IPSec over TCP settings?

Question 5

Which file is used to enable or disable silent installation and specify automatic reboot after installation in a software client distribution?

Question 6

You use pre-shared keys to make a remote access connection. Which option do you use on the Authentication tab of the Cisco VPN software client?

Question 4 Answer

Transparent tunneling options are accessed via the Transport tab on the Cisco VPN software client.

Question 5 Answer

vpnclient.ini is edited to enable or disable silent installation and specify automatic reboot after installation in a software client distribution.

Question 6 Answer

You must specify the Group Authentication settings.

Question 7

What IKE proposals are best to use with 3.x and 4.x software clients?

Question 8

What default MTU size does the software client use?

Question 9

What is a disadvantage of full tunneling?

Question 7 Answer

IKE proposal with names that begin with CiscoVPNClient are appropriate for use with 3.x and 4.x software clients.

Question 8 Answer

The Cisco VPN software clients set the MTU at 1300 bytes by default.

Question 9 Answer

Increased overhead and bandwidth utilization at the central site

Section 6

**Remote Access Using
Digital Certificates**

Question 1

What is a CA?

Question 2

In which PKI model do subordinate CAs exist?

Question 3

What is a CRL and what function does it serve?

Question 1 Answer

Certificate Authorities (CA) are trusted entities that issue, administer, and revoke when necessary, digital certificates that are used for authentication of peers in IPSec.

Question 2 Answer

Subordinate CAs are found in the Hierarchical PKI model.

Question 3 Answer

Certificate revocation list (CRL) is the mechanism CAs use to revoke active certificates before their time-based expiration.

Question 4

What are the two methods of enrollment with a CA?

Question 5

For what is a PKCS#10 file used?

Question 6

How do you install an identity certificate you obtained if you use SCEP?

Question 4 Answer

Two methods of enrollment with a CA are available:

- Use PKCS#10 certificate requests manually.
- Use the Cisco Simple Certificate Enrollment Protocol (SCEP) automated process.

Question 5 Answer

PKCS#10 certificate requests are used for manual enrollment with a CA on the concentrator and on hardware and software clients.

Question 6 Answer

SCEP is an automated process and installs the identity certificate automatically. You must manually install the identity certificate if you used the manual process with a PKCS#10 certificate request file.

Question 7

How many identity certificates does the 3005 Concentrator support?

Question 8

How many identity certificates does the 3060 Concentrator support?

Question 9

How many CA certificates can you install on the 3005 Concentrator?

Question 7 Answer

Model 3005 can support a total of two active identity certificates.

Question 8 Answer

Model 3060 and all other models with the exception of 3005 support up to 20 identity certificates.

Question 9 Answer

Model 3005 supports up to six CA certificates. All other models support up to 20 CA certificates.

Question 10

What is the standard format used for identity certificates?

Question 11

What three steps are required to configure the concentrator for digital certificate authentication?

Question 12

Which screen on the VPN concentrator displays configured CAs, identity certificates, SSL certificates, and enrollment status?

Question 10 Answer

Standard X.509 identity certificates

Question 11 Answer

Configured CAs, identity certificates, SSL certificates, and enrollment status are viewed at **Certificates Administration > Certificate Management.**

Question 12 Answer

Step 1   Check the active IKE proposal list and if necessary, activate an RSA-based proposal.

Step 2   Check the IKE proposal to make sure the settings are acceptable (authentication, encryption, DH groups, and lifetime).

Step 3   Modify or add an SA that uses the RSA-based IKE proposal.

Section 7
**Configuring the Cisco 3002
Hardware Client
for User and Unit Authentication**

Question 1

Name the three authentication modes available on the hardware client?

Question 2

Which hardware client authentication mode provides the most secure setting?

Question 3

On which screen of the web-based management interface do you configure the authentication settings of a hardware client?

Question 1 Answer

Unit authentication (default)—The hardware client stores and forwards its username and password to the concentrator.

Interactive unit authentication—The hardware client does not store its username and password. Instead, a user must provide the username and password in an interactive process when he initiates the tunnel.

Individual user authentication—The third option provides the most secure setting, because it requires each new user that attempts to access the tunnel to authenticate.

Question 2 Answer

Individual User Authentication provides the most secure setting, because it requires each new user that attempts to access the tunnel to authenticate.

Question 3 Answer

Authentication options for the hardware client are configured on the concentrator from **Configuration > User Management > Groups > HW Client**.

Section 8
Backup Servers, Load Balancing, and Reverse Route Injection

Question 1

How many servers can you specify in the list of backup servers on the concentrator?

Question 2

Which concentrator backup server option clears the list of backup servers configured on VPN clients and disables the function?

Question 3

On which screen of the hardware client's web-based management interface are backup servers configured?

Question 1 Answer

You can specify up to ten backup servers.

Question 2 Answer

Disable and Clear Configured List—This option disables the backup server feature and instructs the clients to clear their list of backup servers.

Question 3 Answer

Backup servers on the VPN 3002 Hardware Client are configured in **Configuration > System > Tunneling Protocols > IPSec.**

Question 4

What is the minimum version of software required on the software and hardware clients to support load balancing?

Question 5

What is a cluster of concentrators?

Question 6

What is the function of a virtual IP address as it relates to a cluster of concentrators?

Question 4 Answer

To support load balancing, the clients must meet the following requirements:

- VPN Software Client version 3.5 or higher
- VPN Hardware Client version 3.5 or higher

Question 5 Answer

To enable load balancing, two or more VPN concentrators can form a cluster.

Question 6 Answer

A virtual IP address is assigned to the cluster for each interface (public and private), and the clients connect to virtual addresses. This allows any member of the cluster, which has a different physical IP address, to service the virtual IP address of the cluster.

Question 7

Who determines the load on each member of the concentrator cluster and redirects new connections to cluster members?

Question 8

What additional service runs on the concentrator when it is a member of a load-balancing cluster?

Question 9

What functions does the VCA provide to the concentrator?

Question 7 Answer

Each cluster has a designated virtual cluster master concentrator, which determines the load information on secondary concentrators and directs clients to concentrators with the least load.

Question 8 Answer

The load-balancing feature uses the services of the Virtual Cluster Agent (VCA), which is a process that operates on each of the concentrators in the virtual cluster.

Question 9 Answer

The VCA provides the following functions:

- Manages joining and exiting from the virtual cluster
- Establishes IPSec connections between virtual cluster members
- Determines the load on each member by periodically polling each member
- Discovers virtual cluster master failures and participates a new virtual cluster master election

Question 10

Why is RRI significant when load balancing is enabled?

Question 11

What is the priority value of a VPN Concentrator 3060 for cluster master elections?

Question 12

On which screen of the concentrator's web-based management interface is RRI configured?

Question 10 Answer

Reverse route injection (RRI) allows the central site to connect to a client regardless of which physical concentrator in a load-balancing cluster the client is connected to.

Question 11 Answer

The Concentrator 3060 has a priority value of 7. Values for other models are as follows:

- 3005:1
- 3015:3
- 3030:5
- 3080:9

Question 12 Answer

RRI settings are configured from **Configuration > System > IP Routing > Reverse Route Injection**.

Section 9
Transparent Tunneling

Question 1

Which transparent tunneling is an industry standard?

Question 2

Which transparent tunneling option encapsulates IPSec packets from the start of tunnel setup?

Question 3

What default port is used with IPSec over TCP?

Question 1 Answer

NAT-Traversal (NAT-T) is a standards-based solution that functions similarly to the Cisco proprietary IPSec over UDP solution. NAT-T uses port 4500 to encapsulate IPSec in UDP.

Question 2 Answer

IPSec over TCP uses a user-specified TCP port number (10000 by default) to encapsulate IPSec packets from the start of tunnel setup.

Question 3 Answer

By default, port 10000 is used for IPSec over TCP on the VPN concentrator.

Question 4

What is the default port NAT-T uses?

Question 5

Which protocol uses NAT-D payloads?

Question 6

On which screen of the concentrator's web-based management interface is transparent tunneling configured?

Question 4 Answer

NAT-T uses port 4500 to encapsulate IPSec in UDP.

Question 5 Answer

NAT-T uses NAT-Discovery (NAT-D) payloads to discover NAT devices that might be present along the transmission path.

Question 6 Answer

Transparent tunneling options are configured using the Client Config tab from **Configuration > User Management > Groups** on the Concentrator and the Transport tab on the Cisco VPN Software Client application.

Section 10
Configuring LAN-to-LAN VPNs on Cisco 3000 VPN Concentrators

Question 1

You run hardware client in network extension mode and are connected to the central concentrator. This is an example of a LAN-to-LAN VPN; true or false?

Question 2

What routing protocol is required for NAD to function?

Question 3

What routing protocol is not supported by NAD?

Question 1 Answer

False. Although this setup provides many of the same capabilities and benefits of a LAN-to-LAN connection, all hardware client connections are considered remote-access.

Question 2 Answer

For proper operation of NAD inbound, RIP must be enabled on the private interface of both concentrators to terminate the ends of a LAN-to-LAN connection.

Question 3 Answer

NAD does not support the OSPF routing protocol.

Question 4

What is the disadvantage of using HMAC-SHA1 for a LAN-to-LAN configuration?

Question 5

On which screen of the concentrator's web-based management interface are LAN-to-LAN connection entries configured?

Question 6

What ESP authentication options are supported for LAN-to-LAN connections?

Question 4 Answer

The larger key size that SHA1 uses increases the processing overhead on the concentrator.

Question 5 Answer

Configuration of LAN-to-LAN connection entries is performed via **Configuration > Tunneling and Security > IPSec > LAN-to-LAN.**

Question 6 Answer

Supported ESP authentication options include:

- None
- HMAC-MD5 (128-bit hash)
- HMAC-SHA1 (160-bit hash)

Question 7

How is NAD configured in a LAN-to-LAN connection entry?

Question 8

How do you configure a LAN-to-LAN VPN with digital certificates?

Question 9

What is the advantage of configuring LAN-to-LAN VPNs with digital certificates?

Question 7 Answer

To enable NAD, you must select Network Autodiscovery from the Routing drop-down menu on the connection entry configuration page for LAN-to-LAN connections, and leave the Local Networks and Remote Networks fields blank.

Question 8 Answer

To use digital certificates, select an installed identity certificate from the Digital Certificate drop-down menu when you configure the LAN-to-LAN connection entry. The Preshared Key field is left blank.

Question 9 Answer

Digital certificates provide better security and are more scalable (you don't have to have a different pre-shared key for every peer).

Section 11
Monitoring and Administration

Question 1

On which screen of the concentrator's web-based management interface can you check the current routing table?

Question 2

On which screen of the concentrator's web-based management interface can you check the current status of the concentrator?

Question 3

On which screen of the concentrator's web-based management interface can you check the concentrator's detailed memory status?

Question 1 Answer

The current routing table can be inspected from **Monitoring > Routing Table** on the concentrator's web-based management interface.

Question 2 Answer

Concentrator status may be inspected from **Monitoring > System Status** on the concentrator's web-based management interface.

Question 3 Answer

The concentrator's detailed memory status can be inspected at **Detailed Monitoring > System Status > Memory Status** on the concentrator's web-based management interface.

Section 12
Bandwidth Management

Question 1

What version of the VPN concentrator software is required for bandwidth management functionality?

Question 2

What are the two main bandwidth management options?

Question 3

What does the concentrator do if it cannot provide the required bandwidth reservation to a new connection request?

Question 1 Answer

Bandwidth management is supported on VPN concentrator software version 4.0 or higher.

Question 2 Answer

You can configure the following bandwidth policies:

- **Bandwidth policing**—This policy sets a maximum transfer rate.
- **Bandwidth reservation**—This policy instructs the concentrator to reserve a minimum amount of bandwidth per connection.

Question 3 Answer

If the minimum bandwidth specified in the bandwidth reservation policy is not available, the connection is refused.

CCSP: Cisco Secure Virtual Private Networks (CSVPN) Quick Reference Sheets

Network Security Overview

This section provides an overview of general network security concepts and Cisco-specific architectures and practices that you may be tested on. Please note that there is some overlap of content in the Cisco CCSP certification courses and corresponding exams. We chose to make each section of this book stand on its own, and we covered the material for each exam independently, so that you can focus on each exam without the need to reference a common topic from a different exam's section. Becuase of this, you might notice redundant coverage of topics in certain sections of this book.

Primary Types of Threats

There are four primary types of threats to network security:

- **Unstructured threats**—Threats primarily from inexperienced individuals using hacking tools available on the Internet (script kiddies).

- **Structured threats**—Threats from hackers who are more motivated and technically competent. Hackers usually understand network system designs and vulnerabilities and can create hacking scripts to penetrate network systems.

- **External threats**—Threats from individuals or organizations working outside your company who do not have authorized access to your computer systems or network. Hackers work their way into a network mainly from the Internet or dialup access servers.

- **Internal threats**—Threats from individuals with authorized access to the network with an account on a server or physical access to the wire (typically disgruntled employees, former employees, or contractors).

Network Attacks

Network attacks can generally be categorized into the following three main types:

- **Reconnaissance attacks**—An intruder attempts to discover and map systems, services, and vulnerabilities.

- **Access attacks**—An intruder attacks networks or systems to retrieve data, gain access, or escalate their access privilege. Access attacks are categorized as follows:

  - **Unauthorized data retrieval**—Reading, writing, copying, or moving files that are not intended to be accessible to the intruder.

  - **Unauthorized system access**—An intruder gains access to a machine, which she is not allowed access to (for example, the intruder does not have an account or password).

  - **Unauthorized privilege escalation**—When legitimate users with a lower level of access privileges, or intruders who have gained lower privileged access, get information or execute procedures that are not authorized at their current level of access.

- **Denial of service (DoS) attacks**—An intruder attacks your network in such a way that damages or corrupts your computer system or denies you and others access to your networks, systems, or services.

Cisco Security Wheel

Network security should be a continuous process built around a security policy. A continuous security policy is most effective because it promotes retesting and reapplying updated security measures on a continuous basis. The Cisco Security Wheel provides a four-step process to promote and maintain network security:

Step 1   **Secure**—This step involves implementing security devices, such as firewalls, identification authentication systems, and encryption with the intent to prevent unauthorized access to network systems.

Step 2   **Monitor**—You monitor the network for violations and attacks against the corporate security policy using a real-time intrusion detection system, such as the Cisco Secure Intrusion Prevention System (IPS). These systems can also maintain detailed logs of network activity, which can be used to identify unsuccessful attacks against the network or assist forensics if a successful attack occurs.

Step 3   **Test**—Test the effectiveness of the security safeguards in place by performing penetration tests using appropriate scanner software.

Step 4   **Improve**—Overall security is improved by collecting and analyzing information from the monitoring and testing phases to make security improvements.

Cisco Security Wheel

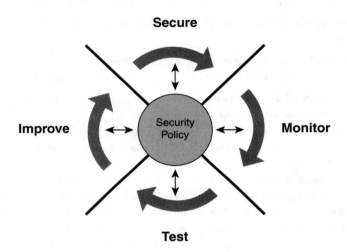

Cisco AVVID and SAFE

Together, the Cisco Architecture for Voice, Video, and Integrated Data (AVVID) framework and SAFE blueprint present a Cisco vision in which new technologies and services are combined to enable a secure and robust infrastructure to serve enterprise businesses.

Cisco AVVID Framework

Cisco AVVID framework describes networks optimized for the support of Internet business solutions and provides best practices for network implementation. It includes the following parts:

- **Clients**—The wide variety of devices that can be used to access the Internet business solutions through the network, such as PCs, personal digital assistants (PDA), and other wired and wireless access devices.

- **Network platforms**—Network platforms are the LAN switches, routers, gateways, and other equipment that interconnect users and servers.

- **Intelligent network services**—Using software that operates on network platforms, intelligent network services are a major benefit of an end-to-end architecture to deploy Internet business solutions.

- **Internet middleware layer**—This component, including service control and communication services, provides the tools for integrators and customers to tailor their network infrastructure and customize intelligent network services to meet application needs. These layers manage access, call setup and teardown, perimeter security, prioritization and bandwidth allocation, and user privileges.

- **Internet business integrators**—As part of the open ecosystem, it is imperative to enable integrators, strategic partners, and customers to deliver complete Internet business.

- **Internet business solutions**—The applications associated with Internet business solutions are enabled, accelerated, and delivered through Cisco AVVID.

Cisco SAFE Blueprint

The Cisco SAFE is a comprehensive modular blueprint that secures today's enterprise network from the ground up. Specific SAFE blueprints are available for networks of various sizes and types. Each blueprint is described in a separate white paper available on Cisco.com.

SAFE blueprints specify the following axioms:

- Routers are targets
- Switches are targets
- Hosts are targets
- Networks are targets
- Applications are targets
- Secure Management and reporting

Overview of VPN and IPSec Technologies

This section provides a general overview of VPN concepts and terminology, and it reviews the IPSec protocol and its operation.

VPN Overview

A virtual private network (VPN) offers secure, reliable, encrypted connectivity over a shared, public network infrastructure, such as the Internet. Because the infrastructure is shared, connectivity can be provided at a lower cost than an existing, dedicated private network.

VPNs can be constructed in one of the following two implementation scenarios:

- Remote-access VPNs
- Site-to-site VPNs

Remote-Access VPNs

Remote-access VPNs connect remote dialup users to their home gateways through an Internet Service Provider (ISP) (sometimes called a Virtual Private Dial Network or VPDN). Remote users need to first connect to the VPN using DSL, Cable, or standard dialup connections. Cisco

VPN software client is then used to establish an encrypted tunnel to the VPN concentrator at the central site.

Remote-Access VPN

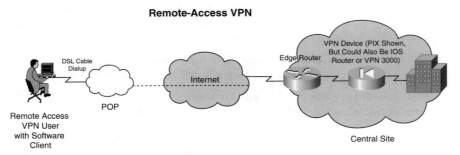

Site-to-Site VPNs

Site-to-site VPNs are used to connect corporate sites over the Internet, replacing costlier wide area network (WAN) options, such as leased lines and frame relay. Hardware devices at each end of the tunnel implement site-to-site VPNs. This type of VPN can also be used to connect networks between business partners to create an Extranet.

Site-to-Site VPN

Intranets

VPN Device (PIX Shown, But Could Also Be IOS Router or VPN 3000) Edge Router

Edge Router VPN Device (PIX Shown, But Could Also Be IOS Router or VPN 3000)

Branch Office

Internet

Central Site

Extranets

VPN Device (PIX Shown, But Could Also Be IOS Router or VPN 3000) Edge Router

Business Partner Nework

Benefits of VPN

VPNs provide the following benefits:

- **Cost savings**—Using the public network (Internet), VPNs provide cost effective connectivity solutions and can eliminate more expensive traditional WAN implementations.

- **Improved communications**—VPNs provide greater access to telecommuters at home and on the road using broadband connections, such as DSL, cable, and standard dialup.

- **Security**—VPNs use advanced encryption and authentication protocols to protect data from unauthorized access.

- **Scalability**—VPNs allow customers to add capacity with less infrastructure overhead by tapping the Internet's infrastructure and its provisioning benefits.

- **Wireless network security**—VPNs provide one of the best methods to secure wireless networks.

IPSec

IPSec acts at the network layer to protect and authenticate IP packets between IPSec devices (peers), such as PIX Firewalls, Cisco routers, the Cisco VPN client, and other IPSec-compliant products. IPSec is a framework of open standards and is not bound to a specific encryption or authentication protocol. Therefore, IPSec can work multiple encryption schemes and can easily be extended when newer and better algorithms become available.

IPSec uses the underlying encryption and authentication algorithms to provide the following functions:

- **Data confidentiality**—Packets are encrypted before transmission across network.

- **Data integrity**—IPSec receiver authenticates IPSec peers and packets sent by the IPSec sender to ensure that the data has not been altered during transmission.

- **Data origin authentication**—IPSec receiver authenticates the source of the IPSec packets sent. This service depends on the data integrity service.

- **Anti-replay**—IPSec receiver can detect and reject replayed packets, helping prevent spoofing and man-in-the-middle attacks.

IPSec Security Protocols

IPSec uses the following security protocols:

- **Authentication Header (AH)**—A security protocol that provides authentication and optional replay-detection services. AH was assigned IP Protocol number 51.

- **Encapsulating Security Payload (ESP)**—A security protocol that provides data confidentiality and protection with optional authentication and replay-detection services. ESP was assigned IP protocol number 50.

IPSec Modes of Operation

IPSec, and more specifically ESP and AH, are configured to operate in two different modes:

- **Tunnel mode**—Tunnel mode for ESP encrypts the entire IP packet, including the original header, and tacks on a new unencrypted IP header. For AH, Tunnel mode adds a new IP header to the entire original IP packet (including the original header). This entire new packet is authenticated.

Tunnel Mode

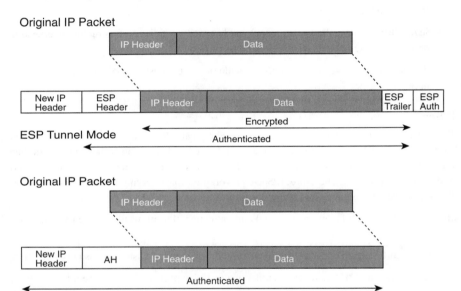

- **Transport mode**—Transport mode leaves the original IP header intact and inserts a new ESP or AH header after the IP header. When you use ESP, only the original IP payload is encrypted. With AH, the entire new packet is authenticated. Because a new IP header is not added, there is less overhead with Transport mode.

Transport Mode

Original IP Packet

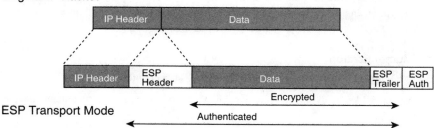

ESP Transport Mode

Original IP Packet

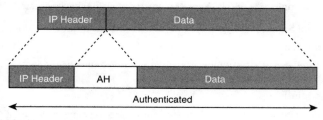

AH Tunnel Mode

IPSec-Supported Algorithms

IPSec relies on the following algorithms to implement encryption, authentication, and key exchange:

- **Data Encryption Standard (DES)**—56-bit encryption algorithm used by ESP to encrypt and decrypt data.

- **Triple-DES (3DES)**—168-bit encryption algorithm used by ESP to encrypt and decrypt data.

- **Advanced Encryption Standard (AES)**—New cipher algorithm with 128-, 192-, or 256-bit encryption used by ESP to encrypt and decrypt data. AES was adopted by the National Institute of Standards and Technology to replace DES and 3DES encryption algorithms.

- **Hash-based Message Authentication Code (HMAC) variant Message Digest 5 (MD5)**—Provides message authentication using a 128-bit shared key secret.

- **HMAC-variant Secure Hash Algorithm 1 (SHA-1)**—Provides message authentication using a 160-bit shared key secret. SHA-1 provides stronger authentication relative to MD5, but with additional processing overhead.

- **Diffie-Hellman (DH)**—DH is a public-key cryptography protocol that enables two parties to establish a shared secret key over an insecure communications channel.

- **RSA (Rivest, Shamir, and Adelman)**—Asymmetrical encryption algorithm used for encryption and decryption. Because asymmetrical encryption algorithms are processor-intensive, RSA is typically used for peer authentication only.

Peer Authentication

Cisco VPN 3000 Concentrator uses several methods for peer authentication:

- **Pre-shared keys**—A shared secret key known to both peers is used to authenticate the peers.

- **RSA signatures**—With RSA signatures, digital certificates issued by a Certificate Authority (CA) are used to authenticate IPSec peers. This method requires more resources to implement, but it's more secure and scalable than preshared keys.

- **DSA (Digital Signature Algorithm)**—DSA is a U.S. government-endorsed public key algorithm for digital signatures. DSA is primarily used for peer authentication.

Each method listed can also be combined with user-based authentication via XAUTH.

Security Association

To successfully establish an IPSec tunnel, peers must agree on a matching set of IPSec-related algorithms and variables. The following terms are important during this negotiation:

- **ISAKMP policies**—ISAKMP policies are specific combinations of algorithms and variables using Internet Key Exchange (IKE) to establish common policies between IPSec peers (ISAKMP policies are referred to as IKE Proposals on the VPN 3000 Concentrator). ISAKMP policies define variables, such as:

  - Encryption algorithm (DES, 3DES, and AES)
  - Hash algorithm (MD5 and SHA-1)
  - Authentication method (preshared keys, RSA signatures, DSA signatures, and XAUTH variations)
  - Key Exchange (Diffie-Hellman group 1, 2, 5, or 7)
  - Security Association lifetime (in seconds or bytes)
  - Protocol used (ESP or AH)
  - Operation mode (Tunnel or Transport)

Parameter	ISAKMP Policy 1	ISAKMP Policy 2
Encryption Algorithm	3DES	3DES
Hash Algorithm	SHA-1	SHA-1
Authentication Method	Pre-share	Pre-Share
Key Exchange	1024-Bit D-H	1024-Bit D-H
IKE SA Lifetime	86,400 Seconds	86,400 Seconds

- **Transform sets**—A transform set is a specific combination of message authentication and encryption algorithms that are used by the concentrator. You can configure multiple transform sets on the concentrator.

- **Crypto maps**—Crypto maps define the combination of variables IPSec peers use during IPSec security association (SA) negotiations (crypto maps are configured as LAN-to-LAN connections on the VPN 3000 Concentrator). Specifically, crypto maps define:
  - Interesting traffic (traffic that is protected by IPSec) using crypto ACLs
  - Peer identification
  - Transform sets to use
  - IPSec SA lifetime (optional)
  - Perfect forward secrecy (optional)

- **Security Association (SA)**—An SA is a unidirectional or bidirectional association established between IPSec peers and is uniquely identified by the IPSec protocol in use, the remote peer's address, and a 32-bit random number called the security parameter index (SPI).
  - IPSec SAs are unidirectional. Therefore, two unidirectional SAs must be established between peers.
  - IKE SAs are bidirectional and only a single SA is required between two peers.
  - SAs are protocol-specific. Therefore, separate SAs are required for ESP and AH, if both protocols are being used.
  - Each SA is valid for the duration of its lifetime, which is established during the negotiation process. The lifetime might be specified by time or the amount of traffic traversing the tunnel. The SA must be reestablished after the SA lifetime expires.

During SA negotiations and setup, the IPSec peers must exchange and authenticate keys to establish the identity of the other peer and setup the appropriate SA. This mechanism relies on the following protocols:

- Internet Key Exchange (IKE)
- Internet Security Association and Key Management Protocol (ISAKMP)

ISAKMP uses the IKE protocol for key exchange, but the two protocols are synonymous in Cisco VPN configurations.

Key Management

IKE relies on two mechanisms for secure key exchange and management:

- **Diffie-Hellman (DH)**—DH is a public-key cryptography algorithm used by IKE that allows two peers to establish a secret key over an insecure communications channel.
- **Certificate Authority (CA)**—CA is a trusted entity that issues digital certificates.

How IPSec Works

IPSec operates in the following manner:

- **IKE Phase 1**—During this phase, an initial secure communications channel is established (IKE bidirectional SA). This channel is used by IPSec peers for IKE Phase 2 negotiations, not to transmit user data. IKE Phase 1 can occur in the following modes:
  - **Main mode**—This mode includes three two-way exchanges between peers:

    First exchange—IKE algorithms and hashes are negotiated. ISAKMP policies are used to improve performance because they avoid the large number of possible combinations of individual variables.

    Second exchange—DH protocol is used to generate a shared secret key, which is then used to generate encryption keys for the secure communications channel.

    Third exchange—In this exchange, identity of the peer is authenticated and the secure communications channel is established for subsequent IKE transmissions.
  - **Aggressive mode**—This mode reduces the number of exchanges as it generates the DH pair on the first exchange, although without identity protection.
- **IKE Phase 2**—Matching unidirectional IPSec SAs are negotiated and established during IKE Phase 2 negotiations. The tunnel is now ready for user traffic. IKE Phase 2 performs the following:
  - Negotiates IPSec transform sets and security parameters
  - Establishes matching unidirectional IPSec SAs
  - Renegotiates the SAs when their lifetime expires
  - Optionally performs additional DH exchange (perfect forward secrecy)
- **Data transfer**—IPSec peers transmit data defined as interesting according to the parameters defined by the crypto ACLs and negotiated in IPSec SAs.
- **Tunnel termination**—SAs are terminated if their lifetime expires or they are deleted.

Cisco VPN 3000 Concentrator Series Hardware Overview

The Cisco VPN 3000 Concentrator Series consists of several different models to meet a variety of requirements and budgets. This section provides an overview of each model and its specifications.

Cisco VPN 3000 Concentrator Series Models

The Cisco VPN 3000 Concentrator Series includes the models detailed in the following table:

Feature	3005	3015	3020	3030	3060	3080
Height	1 U	2 U	2 U	2 U	2 U	2 U
Performance (Mbps)	4	4	50	50	100	100
Simultaneous IPSec Users	200	200	750	1500	5000	10,000
Simultaneous WebVPN Users	50	75	200	500	500	500
Max Site-to-Site Sessions	100	100	500	500	1000	1000
Network Interfaces	2	3	3	3	3	3
Encryption Method	SW	SW	HW	HW	HW	HW
Memory (MB)	32	64	128	128	256	256
Dual Power Supplies	No	Option	Option	Option	Option	Included
SEP Modules	0	0	1	1	2	4
Redundant SEP	—	—	Option	Option	Option	Included
Upgradeable?	No	Yes	No	Yes	Yes	No

Except for VPN 3005 Concentrator, all other models in the series use the same 2U chassis and are differentiated by the installed hardware encryption modules, power supplies, and expandability. Unlimited client licenses are included with all models.

Models 3020 and higher support the use of a hardware Scalable Encryption Processor (SEP) for improved throughput. Consider the following about SEP:

- The original SEP module supports DES and 3DES encryption.

- To enable AES encryption in hardware, an enhanced version of the SEP module called SEP-E is required.

- SEP modules can support up to 100 Mbps of encrypted throughput.

- Multiple SEP modules can be installed for redundancy in models 3030 and higher.

- SEP modules are installed in a two-by-two grid on the back of the concentrator. Redundancy between modules is top to bottom in each column first (SEP modules 1 and 3 on the figure), and across to a second column, if both SEPs in the first column fail.

- Failover within the column preserves active sessions, but sessions are lost if failover occurs across two columns.

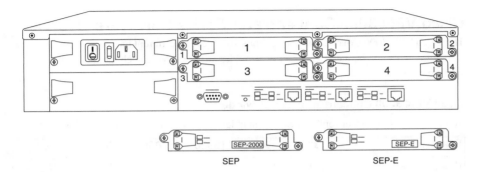

Software Clients

Version 4.x is the latest version of the Cisco software VPN client and provides the following major features:

- Virtual adapter provides better compatibility with PPPoE stacks and fewer conflicts with other VPN clients, such as the Microsoft L2TP/IPSec client
- Support for Microsoft Windows 95/98/ME/2000/XP, Linux, Solaris, and Macintosh
- AES support
- Common GUI for Windows and Macintosh clients
- Personal firewall support
- Split tunneling and split DNS
- Load balancing and backup server support
- Intelligent peer availability detection (DPD)
- Simple Certificate Enrollment Protocol (SCEP)
- Data compression (LZS)
- Auto initiation
- Startup before logon
- Application launcher

Firewall Features

Cisco VPN Client for Windows provides a built-in stateful firewall feature to enhance the security of the host system. The feature can be enabled in one of three ways:

- **Stateful firewall (always on)**—This mode is enabled or disabled by the end user and is effective with or without an established VPN tunnel.
- **Central Policy Protection (CPP)**—This mode is commonly used for implementations that require centralized policy management and enforcement.
- **Are You There (AYT)**—When AYT is configured by an administrator, the concentrator polls the client during initial logon and periodically thereafter. If client firewall is not detected, the concentrator can be configured to refuse or drop the connection.

Auto Initiation

Auto Initiation provides the ability to automatically start a VPN connection based on the network that the client is connected to. This option is typically used to secure clients on wireless LANs (WLANs), which have some inherent security weaknesses.

To expose the Auto Initiation options, you must edit the vpnclient.ini and add:

- The following entry under the [Main] section to enable Auto Initiation:

  AutoInitiationEnable=1

- The following entry under the [Main] section to specify the retry interval by adding:

  AutoInitiationRetryInterval=3 (or any other number you wish)

- The following entry under the [Main] section to specify the connections that will be auto-initiated:

  AutoInitiationList=WLAN1,WLAN2 (example names shown)

You then define the Auto Initiation profiles (for example WLAN1 and WLAN2 in the preceding bullet) in the vpnclient.ini to specify the network and subnet mask what will auto-initiate a connection and specify the connection profile that must be used with that connection.

Hardware Clients

Cisco VPN 3002 Hardware Client is an Easy VPN client and essentially performs the same functions as the software VPN client. The hardware client is a good choice when connecting multiple users from a remote location and provides the following additional capabilities:

- The VPN tunnel is established on the hardware and there is no need to load and run the software client on each host.

- Auto Update features.

Cisco supports Easy VPN Remote functionality on several other hardware platforms, in addition to the VPN 3002 Hardware Client, including (consult Cisco.com for the most up-to-date list of devices that support Easy VPN Remote functionality):

- Cisco PIX 501 and 506E security appliances with software version 6.3 or greater

- Easy VPN remote routers (800, UBR900, 1700, and 1800 Series IOS routers)

Operation Modes

The Cisco VPN 3002 Hardware Client is typically used in small office/home office (SOHO) environments or small branch offices that require access to centralized resources. The hardware client operates in one of two modes to provide the most appropriate type of service:

- **Client mode**—In this mode, the hosts behind the hardware client are not directly accessible from the central site. Instead, the hardware client uses port address translation (PAT) and the addresses of the individual hosts behind it remain hidden. This mode requires a single private IP address allocated to the hardware client.

- **Network Extension mode**—In this mode, the hosts behind the hardware client are accessible from the central site. The IP addresses of the clients are not translated in this mode. Consequently, an appropriate number of IP addresses must be allocated when network extension mode is used. Note that only a single subnet can be accessed behind the 3002 Hardware Client (for instance, you cannot place a router behind the 3002 Hardware Client to route multiple subnets through the tunnel).

The hardware client, particularly when it operates in network extension mode, provides many of the same benefits as a LAN-to-LAN VPN connection, although it is still considered a remote-access client on the concentrator at the central site. Therefore, configuration of the hardware client is similar to Cisco VPN Software Clients and can use preshared keys (group names and passwords) or digital certificates for authentication.

Auto-Update Feature

The auto update feature of the VPN 3002 Hardware Client allows for management of images from the central concentrator, streamlining maintenance operations for hardware clients.

This feature is disabled by default on the concentrator and must be enabled manually. After it is enabled, it can be applied globally or by specific groups of devices.

Settings are configured from **Configuration > System > Client Update** and include:

- **Client type**—The **vpn3002** setting is used for all hardware client updates.
- **URL**—This is the TFTP path for the upgrade image file.
- **Revisions**—This is a case-sensitive name for the image.

After they are configured, hardware clients with older images automatically download and install the new image from the URL specified.

Hardware Client Models

The hardware client is available in two models:

- **3002**—Provides a single private interface and one public interface. To connect additional hosts you must use a separate switch.
- **3002-8E**—This model includes a built-in, eight-port switch and one public port. You can use the built-in switch to connect up to eight hosts or add your own switch for additional hosts.

Both models include auto MDIX ports, which eliminate the need for crossover cables.

VPN Concentrator Configuration

Cisco VPN 3000 Concentrator can be configured using the command-line interface (CLI) or a web-based GUI.

Console settings are as follows:

- Data bits: 8
- Parity: None
- Stop bits: 1
- Speed: 9600 bps

The web-based interface is accessible through a compatible browser and can use HTTP with SSL for increased security. The browser must be JavaScript compatible and cookies must be enabled.

VPN Concentrator Placement

The VPN concentrator can be placed into the network in several different configurations. The most common placement configurations are as follows:

- In front of or without a firewall
- Behind a firewall
- Parallel with a firewall
- On a DMZ

VPN Placement in Front of or Without a Firewall

The VPN concentrator has some firewall capabilities and can apply filters to its interfaces. If you place the VPN concentrator in front of the firewall, you can firewall the traffic after it has been decrypted by the concentrator and add a measure of security. If there is no other firewall in place, the filtering capabilities of the concentrator add to overall security.

In Front of or Without a Firewall

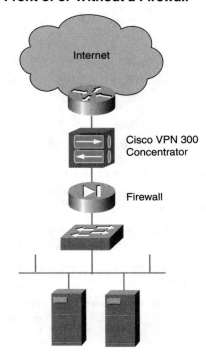

VPN Concentrator Behind a Firewall

In this scenario, the firewall is the first line of defense. You must therefore configure the firewall to allow IPSec traffic (IKE and ESP/AH) through for successful establishment of tunnels. In this layout, VPN traffic traversing the firewall is encrypted and therefore cannot be firewalled.

Parallel with Firewall

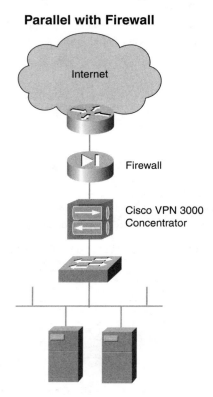

VPN Concentrator in Parallel with a Firewall

This design has several advantages and is the recommended configuration in Cisco SAFE whitepapers. The advantages include:

- The concentrator is directly accessible by remote-access clients and IPSec peers from the outside, which eliminates the need to specifically allow IPSec traffic through the firewall.

- Internet-bound traffic from inside does not have to traverse the concentrator, eliminating the concentrator as a possible point of failure.

- Inbound traffic from the concentrator can still be inspected by the firewall after decryption, which allows you to apply the access rules on the firewall.

Parallel with Firewall

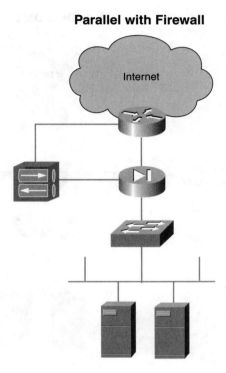

VPN Concentrator on a DMZ

The VPN concentrator can also be placed on a DMZ. This placement has the following considerations:

- This configuration removes the concentrator out of the data path and eliminates it as a possible point of failure for other Internet traffic.

- You must configure the firewall to allow IPSec-related protocols (IKE and ESP/AH) through for successful operation.

- This layout does not allow the firewall to inspect traffic after decryption.

On a DMZ

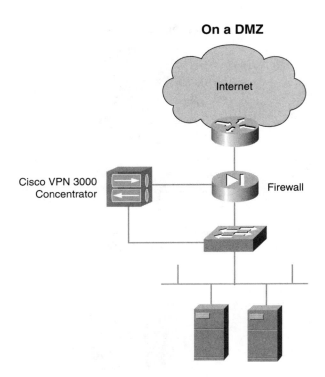

Network Management Solutions

Several management solutions are available to manage the Cisco VPN 3000 platform. These solutions include:

- **Cisco Info Center (CIC)**—Provides proactive management of network events with service level monitoring and diagnostic tools.

- **CiscoWorks**—CiscoWorks is a general management platform that accommodates many different specialized applications designed to manage specific Cisco devices. The Cisco-Works components that relate to the VPN 3000 platform include:

  - **Cisco View**—Provides real time display and monitoring.
  - **Cisco Resource Management Essentials**—The web-based application provides inventory and reporting functions and can distribute software to concentrators.
  - **Cisco VPN Monitor**—The web-based management and monitoring tool for IPSec devices.

- **Cisco IP Solution Center Security Management (IPSCSM)**—Management and provisioning tool primarily aimed at service providers and larger enterprises.

Routing on the VPN 3000 Concentrator

Although the VPN 3000 Concentrator is not a router, it must be able to successfully route packets to destination networks for proper operation. The concentrator supports static and dynamic routing to enable this functionality.

Static Routing

Static routing is the simplest method for adding a few routes to the concentrator. However, as the number of destination subnets increase in larger networks, it becomes more difficult to maintain the routing table.

There are also model-specific limitations on the number of supported static routes. The maximum number of supported static routes for each model is as follows:

- **3002**: 50 routes
- **3005:** 200 routes
- **3015:** 10240 routes
- **3020:** 10240 routes
- **3020:** 10240 routes
- **3060:** 10240 routes
- **3080:** 10240 routes

Regardless of the number of static routes supported, you can only have a single default route (gateway of last resort) configured on each device.

Configuring Static Routes

Static routes are configured from the GUI interface (**Configuration > System > IP Routing > Static Routes**) with the following information:

- **Network address**—Destination network address
- **Subnet mask**—Destination network subnet mask
- **Metric**—Cost for the route with a value between 1 and 16
- **Destination router address**—IP address of the next hop to reach the destination network
- **Destination interface**—Interface that should be used to reach the destination network

You use either the destination router address or the destination interface, but not both, to define the static route.

Configuring a Default Route

The default route is configured from the GUI interface (**Configuration > System > IP Routing > Default Gateway**) with the following information:

- **Default gateway**—IP address of the default gateway device (typically a router).

- **Metric**—Cost for the route with a value between 1 and 16.

- **Tunnel default gateway**—Not to be confused with the standard default gateway, the tunnel default gateway is the gateway assigned to tunneled traffic, including remote-access users, site-to-site tunnels, and hardware clients.

- **Override default gateway**—This option allows default gateways learned from Routing Information Protocol (RIP) or Open Shortest Path First (OSPF) to override the statically configured default gateway.

Dynamic Routing

As the number of routes increase, maintaining a growing routing table with static routes becomes difficult. Cisco VPN 3000 Concentrator supports RIP and OSPF dynamic routing protocols to dynamically update and maintain its routing table.

RIP

RIP is a distance vector protocol and relies on hop count to determine the best route to a destination. VPN 3000 Concentrator supports RIPv1 and RIPv2 for broader compatibility (RIPv2 authentication is not, however, supported on the concentrator).

RIP is enabled on a per-interface basis on the VPN concentrator from the web-based management interface (**Configuration > Interfaces**). You can enable RIPv1, RIPv2, or both on the interface. You can also enable RIP for inbound or outbound direction separately. For example, if you want only to learn routes via RIP, but not advertise them, you enable inbound RIP only.

OSPF

OSPF is a link-state routing protocol that provides better scalability and faster convergence times than RIP. OSPF configuration involves global and interface-specific settings.

Global settings define the following variable for the device:

- **Enabled**—Globally enables or disables OSPF on the VPN concentrator.

- **Router ID**—Assigns the router ID that uniquely identifies the VPN concentrator to its OSPF neighbors.

- **Autonomous system**—When checked, the VPN concentrator functions as Autonomous System Boundary Router (ASBR).

In addition to the preceding variables, you must also configure the following options on a global level:

- **Area ID**—OSPF areas are defined here. Keep in mind that area IDs must be entered as dotted decimals. For example, if area 1 is used on an IOS router, it must be entered as 0.0.0.1 on the concentrator.

- **Area summary**—When checked, the VPN concentrator generates summary link state advertisements (LSA).

- **External LSA Import**—The possible settings are:
  - **External**—The VPN concentrator imports the external LSAs.
  - **No External**—External LSAs are not imported.

After the global settings are configured, interface-specific settings can be configured from the interface configuration screen. Interface-specific settings are as follows:

- **OSPF Enabled**—Enables or disables OSPF on the interfaces.

- **OSPF Area ID**—OSPF areas are defined here as dotted decimals. Entries also appear on the global area list.

- **OSPF Priority**—A number between 0 and 255 used in designated router elections. A value of 0 means the concentrator is ineligible.

- **OSPF Metric**—Cost for OSPF routes on this interface (value between 1 and 65535).

- **OSPF Retransmit Interval**—Interval between transmission of LSAs in seconds (0 to 3600). Default of 5 seconds.

- **OSPF Hello Interval**—Interval between hello packets in seconds (1 to 65535). Default of 10 seconds.

- **OSPF Dead Interval**—Interval before a neighbor is considered out-of-service in seconds (0 to 65535). Default of 10 seconds.

- **OSPF Transit Delay**—Estimated delay in transmitting LSAs on the interface in seconds (0 to 3600). Default of 1 second.

- **OSPF Authentication**—Configures authentication settings:
  - **None**—No OSPF authentication.
  - **Simple Password**—OSPF authentication that uses clear-text passwords.
  - **MD5**—Enables OSPF authentication and uses MD5 hashing to generate an encrypted message digest for authentication.
- **OSPF Password**—Configures the password used with simple password or MD5 options.

Remote Access Using Pre-shared Keys

Preshared keys or digital certificates configure remote-access VPNs. The Cisco VPN software client must be loaded on the systems accessing the VPN remotely. The Software client provides the following major services:

- Negotiates IPSec parameters to establish the tunnel

- Performs user authentication with user and group names and passwords or digital certificates

- Manages security keys for encryption and decryption

- Enforces centralized policies regarding access rights and firewall settings

- Authenticates, encrypts, and decrypts data

Initial Configuration for Remote Access

To configure the Cisco VPN 3000 Concentrator for remote access, the following configuration steps are required (assuming the concentrator has only factory settings):

Step 1 **IP Interfaces**—Each interface is configured with the following parameters:

- **Disabled**—Select to disable the interface.

- **DHCP Client**—Select to obtain the IP address, subnet mask, and default gateway from DHCP.

- **Static IP Address**—Configure the static IP address and subnet mask.

- **Public Interface check box**—Check to make a public interface.

- **MAC Address**—This is the physical address and displayed only. You cannot change this value.

- **Filter**—Select a default or custom filter.

- **Speed**—Set the speed (10, 100, or 10/100 auto).

- **Duplex**—Set duplex (Half, Full, or Auto).

- **MTU**—Specify the maximum transmission unit in bytes, between 68 and 1500. The default is 1500 bytes.

- **Public Interface IPSec Fragmentation Policy**—This setting determines how the concentrator handles fragmentation of packets exceeding the MTU when it uses this interface.

Step 2 **System Information**—Basic information such as device name, contact name, time, DNS servers, domain name, and the default gateway are configured.

Step 3 **Protocols**—Enable desired tunneling protocols (IPSec, PPTP, or L2TP).

Step 4 **Address Assignment**—Specify the method of assigning addresses to a client from one of the following four options:

- **Use Client Address**—Uses the IP address supplied by the client.

- **Use Address from Authentication Server**—Uses an IP address from an authentication server such as CSACS.

- **Use DHCP**—Uses DHCP to obtain an IP address for the client.

- **Use Address Pools**—Uses internal address pools configured on the VPN concentrator.

Step 5 **Authentication**—Select the authentication method using the following variables:

- **Server Type**—Choose RADIUS, NT Domain, SDI (SecurID server), Kerberos, Active Directory, or Internal Server.

- **Additional Settings**—Depending on the type of server chosen in the preceding step, you may have to specify the address of the authentication server and other server type-dependent information.

Step 6   IPSec Group—To use remote-access VPNs with pre-shared keys, you must specify the group name and password.

Step 7   Admin Password—Specify the administrative password for the device.

IKE Proposals

Appropriate IKE proposals must be configured on the Cisco VPN 3000 Concentrator for proper operation of remote-access VPNs. IKE proposal are nothing more than a specific combination of IKE variables including:

- Authentication mode
- Authentication Algorithm
- Encryption Algorithm
- Diffie-Hellman group
- Lifetime (data or time based)

When a client attempts to connect to the VPN concentrator, it sends an IKE proposal to the concentrator. The concentrator looks for a matching IKE proposal on its list to make the connection.

Keep in mind that the order in which the IKE proposals are configured on the concentrator is important. If remote access-specific proposals (names beginning with CiscoVPNClient) are not at the top of the list, Unity clients may not be able to successfully connect.

Group Configuration

Group settings are configured via **User Management > Groups** from the web-based interface. You can configure the settings for the Base Group or specific groups that are created. The Base Group sets the default group settings that is initially applied to any newly created group. Each group's settings can then be further modified with the following seven tabs:

- Identity tab
- General tab
- IPSec tab
- Client Config tab
- Client FW tab
- HW Client tab
- PPTP/L2TP tab

Major settings configured on these tabs include such items as:

- Group name and password
- Number of simultaneous logins allowed
- DNS and WINS settings delivered to clients

- IPSec SA

- Tunnel type

- Authentication method

- IPComp settings

- Mode configuration

- Banner

- NAT-T and IPSec over UDP/TCP settings

- Backup server lists

- Split tunneling and split DNS settings

- Firewall requirement settings

- PPTP and L2TP settings

Split Tunneling

Split tunneling is one of the significant options during remote-access VPN configuration, and it's worth a brief review. When you configure remote-access VPNs, you can configure the concentrator to:

- **Tunnel everything**—This option sends all traffic through the IPSec tunnel. This option is typically considered to be most secure, although it's costly in terms of bandwidth and processing overhead imposed on the central site.

Tunnel Everything

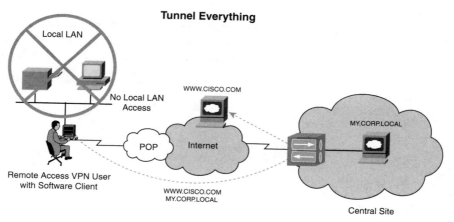

- **Allow the networks in list to bypass the tunnel**—With this option you specify a list of networks that are bypassed from the tunnel. All other traffic is sent through the IPSec tunnel. You must define the list of networks that are to be bypassed elsewhere in the web interface and select them from a drop-down menu here. A built-in network, defined as "VPN Client Local LAN (Default)" allows local LAN access while tunneling all other traffic.

**Allow Networks in List
to Bypass the Tunnel**

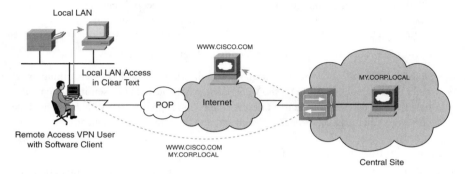

- **Only tunnel networks in the list**—With this option, traffic destined only for specified networks are sent through the IPSec tunnel. All other traffic (typically internet browsing traffic) is sent in clear text. This option lowers the impact on the central site's bandwidth and CPU utilization.

Only Tunnel Networks in the List

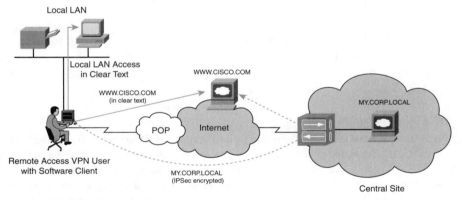

Cisco VPN Software Client for Windows

The VPN Software Client terminates the VPN tunnel on the remote client PC. The software provides the capability to create multiple profiles or connection entries, which allow the remote host to connect to different concentrators and VPN headends, as necessary. However, one connection might only be active at any time. To connect using an alternate profile, you must disconnect from the current active connection first.

Connection entries are created using the following primary configuration tabs:

- **Authentication**—Group name and password or digital certificate information is configured in this tab.

- **Transport**—Transparent tunneling (IPSec over UDP or TCP) settings and local LAN access options are configured here.

768 CCSP: Cisco Secure Virtual Private Networks (CSVPN) Quick Reference Sheets

Keep in mind that settings configured here must also be configured and permitted on the concentrator to have any effect. In other words, if the VPN 3000 Concentrator is configured to disallow local LAN access, enabling the local LAN access option on the VPN Software Client does not override the settings on the concentrator, and local LAN access is not possible.

- **Backup servers**—Backup servers are configured here for redundancy.

- **Dial-up**—This tab allows you to specify a default Microsoft Dial-Up Networking or other third-party connection for the VPN Software Client. With this setting configured, if the client is started and no active Internet connection is present, the VPN client uses the configured dialup entries to make a connection to the Internet automatically.

Preconfiguration of the Client for Distribution

To facilitate the distribution of the VPN Software Client in the enterprise, several options are available to preconfigure certain settings for installation and initial configuration of the client.

- Oem.ini is used to enable or disable silent installation and specify automatic reboot after installation.

- Vpnclient.ini is used to configure startup settings, such as:
  - Default connection entry
  - Log settings
  - Simple Mode or Advanced Mode operation
  - Stateful firewall settings

- Profile (.pcf) files define authentication, transport, backup servers, and dialup settings for each profile.

SetMTU Application

One of the issues that software clients may have to deal with is IP fragmentation and the MTU size. When IP packets are tunneled using other protocols, such as IPSec or GRE, the additional headers and trailers that other protocols may add can increase the packet size to more than the typical MTU of 1500 bytes. The VPN concentrator must then fragment the packets to reduce the size and comply with the MTU settings. Certain protocols used with remote-access connections, such as PPPoE used with DSL and Cable services, also impact packet size and have an effect on fragmentation.

One method to reduce fragmentation and its impact on applications that are affected is to configure a smaller MTU setting for traffic that traverses the IPSec tunnel. The Cisco VPN Software Client automatically sets an MTU setting of 1300 bytes. This setting allows approximately an additional 200 bytes for various protocols to use (PPPoE, ESP, AH, and others).

If additional changes are necessary, the SetMTU utility can be used to set the MTU size to an appropriate value. Remember, if you set the MTU value too low, it can impact the network performance negatively.

Remote Access Using Digital Certificates

Remote-access VPNs with digital certificates provide an alternative authentication method to preshared keys. Unlike preshared keys, authentication relies on digital certificates and not on a shared secret for the group. This approach provides better security and scalability, but requires more upfront resources and is more difficult to initially implement.

CA Overview

For digital certificates to be valuable, one must trust the institutions that issue and back the authenticity of the certificates. Certificate Authorities (CA) are trusted entities that issue, administer, and revoke digital certificates that are used for authentication of peers in IPSec.

Cisco VPN 3000 Concentrator supports the following CAs:

- Entrust
- RSA Security
- PGP
- Baltimore
- Microsoft
- Verisign

Public Key Infrastructure

Digital certificates rely on asymmetrical encryption algorithms and require public and private keys to function. A Public Key Infrastructure (PKI) is the end-to-end system (hardware, software, policies, procedures, and people) that allows a CA to manage the distribution, maintenance, and revocation of digital certificates in a secure manner.

Two PKI models exist:

- **Central**—In this model, a single root CA signs all certificates. This is typically appropriate for use in smaller networks and domains.

- **Hierarchical**—A hierarchy of root and subordinate CAs are used in this model. The root CA signs the certificates for the subordinate CAs, which then sign the certificates for individuals, devices, and possibly additional lower-level CAs within their own locations. This model provides a better option for large, geographically dispersed companies.

Certificate-Based Authentication

Certificate-based authentication proceeds as follows:

Step 1   Users generate public and private keys and submit a request to register with the CA.

Step 2   The CA verifies the authenticity of the request and the identity of the users and issues certificates signed with its private key.

Step 3   Users send certificates to other parties that want to authenticate their identity.

Step 4   The other party authenticates the digital certificate using the CA's public key.

Step 5   The other party sends its digital certificate back.

Step 6   The other party's digital certificate is verified using the CA's public key.

Step 7   Both sides are authenticated and ready for further transactions.

Certificate Generation

To generate certificates, the following three steps are required:

Step 1   A private and public key pair is generated and submitted to the CA as a Public Key Cryptography Standards (PKCS) #10 certificate request.

Step 2   The CA creates a digital certificate and returns root and identity certificates to the requester.

Step 3   The root certificate is installed on the VPN 3000 Concentrator. The concentrator validates the authenticity of the certificate by using the public key of the CA.

Configuring the Cisco VPN 3000 Concentrator for CA Support

Digital certificate support on the VPN 3000 Concentrator requires the following four general tasks:

- Enroll with a CA on the concentrator.
- Install a CA certificate on the concentrator.
- Enroll and install identity certificate on the concentrator.
- Enroll and install identity certificates on clients.

To use digital certificate-based authentication, the concentrator must have at least one CA certificate and one identity certificate configured. However, additional CA root and identity certificates can be configured on the concentrator. The maximum number of CA certificates and identity certificates supported are:

- **Model 3005**—6 CA certificates, 2 identity certificates
- **All other models**—20 CA certificates, 20 identity certificates

Configuring Digital Certificates

To enroll with a CA and use digital certificates, you must obtain a concentrator certificate first. Two methods are available:

- Enroll using PKCS#10 certificate requests manually.
- Use Cisco Simple Certificate Enrollment Protocol (SCEP) automated process.

Certificate management tasked are accessed from **Administration > Certificate Management** section on the web-based management interface of the concentrator.

Manual Enrollment

PKCS#10 certificate requests used for manual enrollment include the following information:

- Common Name (CN)
- Organizational Unit (OU)

- Organization (O)

- Locality (L)

- State/Province (SP)

- Country

- Subject Alternative Name (FQDN)

- Subject Alternative Name (Email Address)

- Key Size (choice of RSA 512 bits, RSA 768 bits, RSA 1024 bits)

After a request is generated, it is submitted to a CA. The CA validates the request and sends back the appropriate root and identity certificates for installation on the concentrator.

The installation screen is accessed via **Administration > Certificate Management > Installation on the Concentrator**.

SCEP Enrollment

SCEP provides an automated method of enrollment with a CA and involves direct conversation between the CA and the enrolling party. The actual information that is provided as part of the request is the same as the manual process, but most of the steps, including installation of root and identity certificates, are automated. SCEP can be used if the CA supports that method of enrollment.

Certificate Revocation Lists

An important aspect of certificate management is the ability to invalidate, or revoke, a certificate before its time-based expiration. This is required for security reasons, for example, if an employee leaves a company, the certificate should no longer be valid.

Certificate revocation list (CRL) is the mechanism CAs use to revoke active certificates before their time-based expiration.

Configuring the Concentrator for Remote-Access VPN with Digital Certificates

After the concentrator has been enrolled with a CA, remote-access authentication via digital certificates is possible. However, such authentication also requires proper configuration of IKE proposals and SAs:

- Configure and enable an IKE proposal, which uses RSA Digital Certificates as its authentication mode.

- Check the IKE proposal to make sure that authentication, encryption, DH, and lifetime requirements are satisfactory.

- Configure and enable an SA that uses the IKE proposal with RSA Digital Certificate as the authentication mode.

Cisco Software VPN Client Certificate Support

The VPN clients require a similar enrollment process to the concentrator. The same two options are available here as well:

- Manual enrollment using PKCS#10 certificate requests

- Automated enrollment using SCEP

In version 4.0 and higher of the Cisco VPN Software Client, certificate management is performed via the Certificates tab of the application. Prior versions included a separate application for certificate management.

After a successful manual or automated request process, the CA issues root and identity certificates to the client in the form of X.509 digital certificates.

With SCEP, the root and identity certificates are automatically installed on the client. If you use the manual enrollment process, the X.509 certificates must be installed on the client.

Connecting a Remote-Access VPN Using Certificates

With the concentrator and the VPN client configured with digital certificates, authentication using certificates is now possible. To enable certificate-based authentication on the client:

- Change the authentication type to Certificate Authentication on the Authentication tab of the Cisco VPN Software Client.

- Select the appropriate certificate from the drop-down menu.

- Provide the password for the certificate.

Configuring the Cisco 3002 Hardware Client for User and Unit Authentication

The Cisco 3002 Hardware Client provides a means of entry into the private network at the central site for individual users on the network behind it. This alleviates the need to load and run the Cisco VPN Software Client on individual PCs. However, this also eliminates the individual user authentication that would occur if each user used the software client. The hardware client provides a user and unit authentication mechanism to compensate for that loss of functionality.

Three authentication options exist:

- **Unit Authentication (the default)**—The hardware client stores and forwards its username and password to the concentrator. The hardware client is only authenticated and all users behind it have access through the tunnel. This is an appropriate option if only there are no concerns about unauthorized users having physical access to the hardware client.

- **Interactive Unit Authentication**—The hardware client does not store its username and password. Instead, a user must provide the username and password in an interactive process when initiating the tunnel. Keep in mind that only the unit is authenticated with this option. After the tunnel is established, anyone behind the hardware client has access to the tunnel without further authentication.

- **User Authentication**—The third option provides the most secure setting, as it requires each new user that attempts to access the tunnel to authenticate.

Authentication options for the hardware client are configured on the concentrator from **Configuration > User Management > Groups > HW Client**.

Backup Servers, Load Balancing, and Reverse Route Injection

Cisco VPN 3000 Concentrators include redundancy and load balancing capabilities designed for high availability applications. These features and the reverse route injection function of the concentrator are presented in this section.

Cisco VPN Client Backup Servers

Backup servers provide redundancy by specifying additional concentrators that clients can connect to if their primary concentrator is not available.

The list of backup servers may be configured on the concentrator, the hardware client, or the software client. Depending on the configuration settings on the concentrator, the list of backup servers configured on clients may or may not be used. Up to 10 servers may be configured in order of highest to lowest priority.

Backup Server Configuration on Concentrator

Backup servers on the concentrator are configured on the Client Config tab in Group setup. Three options are available:

- **Use Client Configured List**—This option allows the client to use its own list of backup servers.

- **Disable and Clear Configured List**—This option disables the backup server feature and instructs the clients to clear their list of backup servers.

- **Use List Below**—This option instructs the clients to use the list of backup servers configured on the concentrator and replaces any list that might already be configured on the clients.

Backup Server Configuration on Clients

You may also configure lists of backup servers on the hardware client and the software client. If the setting on the concentrator is Use Client Configured List, the local list configured on the client is used to locate backup servers.

Backup servers on the VPN 3002 Hardware Client are configured in **Configuration > System > Tunneling Protocols > IPSec**.

Backup servers on the VPN Software Client are configured via the Backup Servers tab of the application.

Cisco VPN Client Load Balancing

Load balancing provides the capability of distributing sessions across multiple concentrators to improve performance. The clients must meet the following requirements for load balancing:

- VPN Software Client version 3.5 or higher

- VPN Hardware Client version 3.5 or higher

To enable load balancing, a group of concentrators form a cluster. A virtual IP address is assigned to the cluster for each interface (public and private), and the clients connect to virtual addresses. The actual physical addresses of the concentrators are only relevant to the cluster.

Load Balancing

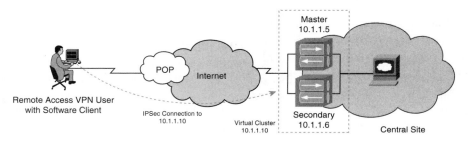

Each cluster has a designated virtual cluster master concentrator, which determines the load information on secondary concentrators and directs clients to concentrators with the least load. The cluster master is selected by an election process and preference is given to higher models.

The load-balancing feature uses the services of the Virtual Cluster Agent (VCA), which is a process that operates on each of the concentrators in the virtual cluster.

The VCA provides the following functions:

- It manages the joining and exiting concentrators from the virtual cluster.

- It establishes IPSec connections between virtual cluster members.

- It determines the load on each member by periodically polling each member.

- It discovers virtual cluster master failures and participates in a new virtual cluster master election.

To enable load balancing:

- Add VCA capability to each of the interfaces of concentrators (**Configuration > Policy Management > Traffic Management > Filters**).

- Configure each concentrator for load balancing (**Configuration > System > Load Balancing**) and assign the virtual cluster IP addresses.

- Configure the clients to use the virtual IP addresses to connect to the concentrator.

Reverse Route Injection

Reverse route injection (RRI) allows the central site to connect to a client regardless of which physical concentrator in a load balancing cluster the client may be connected to.

Client RRI works with software clients and hardware clients in client mode. Network Extension RRI works with hardware clients in network extension mode. RRI is enabled by default and the settings may be changed from **Configuration > System > IP Routing > Reverse Route Injection**. Note that if you do not enable a dynamic routing protocol (OSPF or RIP) on the inside interface of the concentrator, you cannot enable RRI on this menu.

Transparent Tunneling

Chances are good that clients start VPN connections to the concentrator from behind a NAT or PAT device. In fact, in today's environments, clients that are not behind a NAT or a PAT device are exceptions to the rule, not the norm. This presents a problem because NAT and PAT can interfere with some of IPSec protocols' normal operations.

Cisco VPN 3000 Concentrator provides three methods to encapsulate IPSec packets and enable operation over NAT and PAT devices:

- **IPSec over UDP, Cisco proprietary**—This method wraps IPSec in UDP using a user-specified port number or the default UDP port 10000. IPSec operation over UDP is negotiated by the two peers during tunnel setup. Cisco developed this proprietary solution before a standards-based solution was available.

- **NAT-Traversal (NAT-T), standards-based IPSec over UDP**—This is a standards-based solution that functions similarly to Cisco proprietary IPSec over UDP solution. NAT-T encapsulates IPSec in UDP using port 4500 and performs two tasks:

  — Automatically detects if devices at both ends of the tunnel support NAT-T

  — Detects any intermediate NAT devices in the transmission path

- **IPSec over TCP, Cisco proprietary**—This method is another Cisco proprietary option for transparent tunneling and wraps IPSec in TCP using a single or multiple user-specified port numbers or the default TCP port 10000. Settings must be configured on the concentrator and on hardware and software clients using the same TCP port. If all transparent tunneling options are configured, IPSec over TCP takes precedence over NAT-T and IPSec over UDP.

Transparent tunneling options are configured using the **Client Config** tab from **Configuration > User Management > Groups** on the concentrator and the **Transport** tab on the Cisco VPN Software Client application.

Transparent tunneling options are summarized in the following table:

Transparent Tunneling Option	Port Used	Precedence
IPSec over TCP (Cisco proprietary)	TCP 10000 (default) or up to 10 user-configured TCP ports	1
NAT-T (industry standard)	UDP 500 (IKE) and UDP 4500	2
IPSec over UDP (Cisco proprietary)	UDP 500 (IKE) and UDP 10000 (default) or another user-configured UDP port	3

Configuring LAN-to-LAN VPNs on Cisco 3000 VPN Concentrators

Configuration of LAN-to-LAN VPNs is different from remote-access VPNs, but relies on the same general concepts, such as transform sets, IKE proposals, SAs, and authentication methods.

As was the case with remote-access VPNs, you can configure LAN-to-LAN VPNs with:

- Pre-shared key authentication
- Digital certificate authentication

Configuring LAN-to-LAN VPNs with Pre-Shared Keys

To configure LAN-to-LAN VPNs, you must create appropriate connection entries. Connection entries define the various variables required to establish a VPN connection to a peer, such as:

- IP address of the peer
- Interface used to terminate the connection on
- Connection type (bidirection, answer-only, or originate-only)
- Authentication type (preshared key or digital certificates)
- IKE proposal
- ESP authentication and encryption options (similar to transform sets)
- Filters that may be applied
- Transparent tunneling options
- Routing
- Bandwidth policies
- Local and remote networks (defining the interesting traffic)

Configuration of LAN-to-LAN connection entries is performed via **Configuration > Tunneling and Security > IPSec > LAN-to-LAN**.

To configure the LAN-to-LAN VPN with pre-shared keys, enter a pre-shared key in that field and configure the other peer with the same key. The VPN tunnel is established using the pre-shared key for authentication.

After a connection entry is configured, the concentrator automatically creates the necessary LAN-to-LAN group, security associations, and filter rules for the connection.

Network Auto Discovery

When creating the connection entry for LAN-to-LAN VPNs, you can specify the local and remote networks associated with the connection. These settings define the interesting traffic for the tunnel. Traffic from the networks configured as local (in the connection entry) and destined for networks configured as remote are sent through the tunnel.

If the Network Auto Discovery option is selected in the routing field, the Local Network and Remote Network field entries are ignored, and the concentrator can dynamically discover and continuously update the list of networks on each end of the tunnel using Network Auto Discover (NAD). For NAD operation, inbound RIP must be enabled on the interface. NAD does not currently work with OSPF.

Configuring LAN-to-LAN VPNs with Digital Certificates

The procedure to create LAN-to-LAN VPNs with digital certificates is almost exactly the same as with pre-shared keys. The only difference is that when creating the connection entry, the Preshared Key field is left blank and the Digital Certificate drop-down menu is used instead to specify a previously configured identity certificate on the concentrator.

Monitoring and Administration

The VPN 3000 Concentrator provides options for monitoring and administering the device, including the following tasks:

- Checking the current routing table
- Viewing dynamic filters
- Viewing and filtering the event log
- Viewing the system status
- Viewing active sessions
- Viewing general statistics

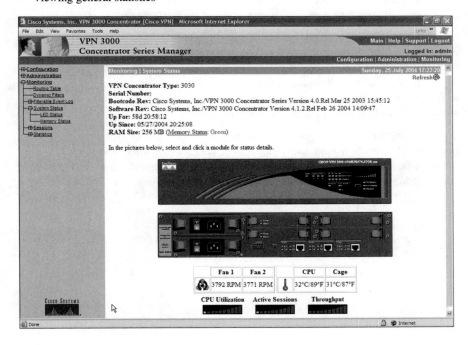

You can also administer the following:

- Sessions
- Software updates
- System reboot
- Reboot status
- Ping (check connectivity)
- Access rights
- File management

Bandwidth Management

Starting with version 4.0, the Cisco VPN 3000 Concentrator added bandwidth management capabilities to the system. Bandwidth management provides administrators the ability to control the amount of bandwidth consumed by specific LAN-to-LAN or remote-access connections. Without bandwidth management, a single connection can consume a disproportionate amount of bandwidth, which reduces the performance of the system for other users.

The following bandwidth policies can be configured:

- **Bandwidth Policing**—This policy sets a maximum transfer rate.
- **Bandwidth Reservation**—This policy instructs the concentrator to reserve a minimum amount of bandwidth per connection. Additional connections are refused if the minimum rate set by bandwidth reservation cannot be met.

After you configure bandwidth policies, you can apply them to an interface or a group, or both. If you apply a policy to an interface only, it applies to each user on the interface. If you apply a policy to a group, it applies only to the users in that group. If you apply one policy to an interface and a different policy to a group, users who are members of that group use the group policy, and all other users use the interface policy.

When you apply a bandwidth policy to a group, you can also specify the bandwidth aggregation value. Bandwidth aggregation is similar to bandwidth reservation, which was discussed earlier. Bandwidth reservation reserves minimum bandwidth for each connection or user, whereas bandwidth aggregation reserves bandwidth for the entire group.